America's National Historic Trails

By Kathleen Ann Cordes

PHOTOGRAPHS BY JANE LAMMERS

UNIVERSITY OF OKLAHOMA PRESS : NORMAN

ALSO BY KATHLEEN ANN CORDES

(with Hilmi Ibrahim) *Outdoor Recreation* (Dubuque, 1993)

(with Hilmi Ibrahim) *Applications in Recreation and Leisure* (St. Louis, 1996)

To Hilmi Ibrahim, my colleague, mentor and friend.

And to all the volunteers who have made the National Historic Trails a reality.

Text design by Martha Farlow.

LIBRARY OF CONGRESS CATALOGING-IN-PUBLICATION DATA

Cordes, Kathleen A.
    America's national historic trails / by Kathleen Ann Cordes ;
photographs by Jane Lammers.
        p.   cm.
    Includes bibliographical references and index.
    ISBN 0-8061-3103-9 (paper : alk. paper)
        1. United States — Guidebooks. 2. Trails—United States—
Guidebooks. 3. Historic sites—United States—Guidebooks.
    4. United States—Description and travel. I. Title.
    E158.C825   1999
    917.304'929—dc21   98–45075
                                                          CIP

Contents

Illustrations

Maps

Acknowledgments

Many people wanted this book to happen. They wanted more people to know about our national trails—and were willing to smooth the way whenever and wherever possible. Director/editor-in-chief of the University of Oklahoma Press John Drayton, with a clear vision of the book, offered strong support throughout. Associate editor Jo Ann Reece patiently and skillfully transformed the manuscript into a book. Copy editor Ursula Smith diligently shaped the manuscript's style and provided me with encouragement at just the right time. Researcher John Strey always found the answers to the difficult questions, and the experts at each of the national trails never failed to provide the best reference materials, including their valuable trail comprehensive plans. Portions of these plans are included in the book, and credit is due to the many public servants who contributed to these works. I am most appreciative of the advice from readers Mark Morgan, of Kansas State University, and Larry Mutter, from Georgia Southern University, and am grateful to Steve Elkinton, program leader, National Trails System Programming, Washington, D.C.; David M. Gaines, superintendent of the National Park Service Long Distance Trails Group Office—Santa Fe; Meredith Kaplan, National Park Service Long Distance Trails administrator in San Francisco; Jere L. Krakow, superintendent of the National Park Service Long Distance Trails Office in Salt Lake City; Keith Thurlkill, Nez Perce National Historic Trail administrator with the USDA Forest Service in Missoula; Richard N. Williams, National Park Service manager of the Lewis and Clark National Historic Trail Office in Madison, Wisconsin; Rich Sussman, National Park Service Overmountain Victory National Historic Trail in Atlanta; and Mike Zaidlicz, Iditarod National Historic Trail coordinator with the Bureau of Land Management in Anchorage.

People like Marc Magliori in Chicago and Sandy LaRouche in Missouri extended their support over and over to two foot-weary travelers who had crisscrossed the country researching and photographing the trails. Sometimes it felt as if I were carrying a sort of national trails Olympic torch and all of you along the way were cheering me on. You kept me going. Thank you for your constant encouragement and support, especially Marc Magliori and Dominick Albano of Amtrak; Nona Reid of Trails West in South Pass, Wyoming; Steve Losi and Joe DeLaura of Canon; Lucette Brehm of the Delta Queen Steamboat Company; Jean Jackson, who housed Martin Luther King during the Selma events and shared her experiences; Louise Mitchell of the Brown Chapel AME Church; Jamie Wallace, reporter during the Selma protests, and Louri Cothran, both of the chamber of commerce in Selma; Joann Bland of the National Voting Rights Museum in Selma and Amy Simpson of Alabama Tourism; Lori Egge of Sky Trekking Alaska and Richard Bendeville of Nome Adventures in Alaska; Larry of Lassen Mineral Lodge in Mineral, California; Jay Mennenga of Back O'Beyond in Pocatello and Georgia Smith of the Idaho Visitors Bureau; the Blankenships at the Walnut Street Inn of Springfield, Gary Chilcote of Patee House Museum in St. Joseph, Jacqueline Lewin of the St. Joseph Museum, Joey Austin of St. Joseph Chamber of Commerce, and Sandy LaRouche of Missouri Tourism; Mike Pitel and Gary Romero of New Mexico Tourism; Lori Shahan of the Lovill House Inn and Curtis Smalling of *Horn in the West* Outdoor Drama in Boone, Betsy Maxey at Ol' Smokey Log Cabins in Cherokee, Connie Smart at Merry Heart Cabin in Nebo, Dick Hemmes of Albemarle Inn in Ashville, and Christine Mackey and Karen Crocker of North Carolina Tourism; Kelly Hurrell of Tahlequah Visitors Center in Oklahoma; Diane Allen of the Ashland Chamber of Commerce, Michelle and B. A. Hanten at Morrison's Rogue River Lodge, Pat McMill of Klamath Falls, Warner's Slough House of Baker City, Michael Lomax and Brandy Hilgren of America West Steamboat Company, and Susan Soleri of Portland Convention and Visitors Bureau in Oregon; Stephanie Andersen of TW Services at Yellowstone National Park and Christie Levitt of Wyoming Tourism; Michael Brooks of Rocky Shoes and Boots; Rob Fennimore of Kaufman Footwear; Frank Fetterer of Redfeather Snowshoes; Nancy Lammers of Alexandria, Virginia; Pentax Binoculars and Smartwool Socks; and Jamie Tipton of North Face.

I would like to thank photographer Jane Lammers for capturing the spirit of each trail while joining me on horseback and in wagon; on snowshoes and cross-country skis; in kayaks, canoes, and steamboats; on dogsled and bicycles; in bush planes, trains, and automobiles; and, of course, on foot. Thanks to my parents who too often said goodbye during these years on the trail. My thanks especially to all of the national trail volunteers throughout America who have been willing to work hard to make a difference for generations to come. Finally, I would like to thank the National Park Service, the USDA Forest Service, and the Bureau of Land Management employees who have worked so diligently to develop and administer our country's national trails and all state, county, and city park personnel, private landowners, museum personnel, and others who have supported the trail concept. By joining as partners, these committed people have contributed in a significant way to the preservation of our country's expansive trail corridors, which hold tangible reminders of our nation's history.

Abbreviations

The following abbreviations are used frequently in the text, especially in the Points of Interest sections.

CNHT	California National Historic Trail	**National**
INHT	Iditarod National Historic Trail	
JBANHT	Juan Bautista de Anza National Historic Trail	**Historic**
LCNHT	Lewis and Clark National Historic Trail	**Trails**
MPNHT	Mormon Pioneer National Historic Trail	
NPNHT	Nez Perce National Historic Trails	
ONHT	Oregon National Historic Trail	
OVNHT	Overmountain National Historic Trail	
PENHT	Pony Express National Historic Trail	
SFNHT	Santa Fe National Historic Trail	
SMNHT	Selma to Montgomery National Historic Trail	
TTNHT	Trail of Tears National Historic Trail	

ANST	Appalachian National Scenic Trail	**Other**
BLM	Bureau of Land Management	
CDNST	Continental Divide National Scenic Trail	**Trails,**
DAR	Daughters of the American Revolution	
FNST	Florida National Scenic Trail	**Agencies,**
IANST	Ice Age National Scenic Trail	**and Sites**
NB	National Battlefield	
NCNST	North Country National Scenic Trail	
NF	National Forest	
NHL	National Historic Landmark	
NHS	National Historic Site	
NHT	National Historic Trail	
NM	National Monument	

NMP	National Military Park
NP	National Park
NPS	National Park Service
NRHP	National Register of Historic Places
NRNL	National Register of Natural Landmarks
NSA	National Scenic Area
NTNST	Natchez Trace National Scenic Trail
NWR	National Wildlife Refuge
PCNST	Pacific Crest National Scenic Trail
PCT	Pacific Crest Trail
PHNST	Potomac Heritage National Scenic Trail
RA	Recreation Area
SHP	State Historic Park
SHS	State Historic Site
SM	State Monument
SP	State Park
TVA	Tennessee Valley Authority
USFS	United States Forest Service
USFWS	United States Fish and Wildlife Service
WLR	Wildlife Refuge

America's National Historic Trails

The author approaches Santa Fe's Cross of the Martyrs, a point which offers a picturesque view of the southern terminus of the Santa Fe Trail.

Introduction

Few will have the greatness to bend history itself, but each of us can work to change a portion of events. . . . It is from numberless acts of courage and belief that human history is shaped.

ROBERT KENNEDY

With the passage of the National Trails System Act in 1968, our nation embarked on one of the most significant recreational endeavors of our time. This legislation spurred the development—to date—of twelve national historic trails, eight national scenic trails, and over eight hundred national recreation trails. An ambitious undertaking, the act was fueled by the efforts of thousands of dedicated volunteers and public and private partnerships at the local, state, and federal levels. Today no other country in the world has a trail system with as much diversity as that found in the United States.

National Historic Trails (NHT), the focus of this book, recognize past routes of exploration and migration and of freedom-seeking and military actions. They preserve stories of our country's past that have been told for centuries and are part of the fabric of the American spirit. Not necessarily continuous, the National Historic Trails identify historic routes, remains, and artifacts that together tell the story of past adventures and conflicts. Some segments of the trails are so reminiscent of the past that they invite today's adventurer back into time and into an environment that was familiar to and experienced by earlier inhabitants, explorers, pioneers, and entrepreneurs. Along the trail, people can still learn about America's past through hands-on trail experience. The stories of the Oregon, California, and Mormon Pioneer Trails; the Santa Fe Trail; the Lewis and Clark and the Juan Bautista de Anza expeditions; the overmountain campaign; the Pony Express; the Trail of Tears; the flight of the Nez Perce; the Iditarod race for gold and the Selma-to-Montgomery voting rights march have all captured the national spirit and have kept alive our rich—and, at time, tragic—national heritage.

Embarking on the historic trails, the traveler can retrace paths of American Indians, mountain men, explorers, pioneers, entrepreneurs, Revolutionary soldiers, and civil rights advocates. With wagon ruts still in clear view, the era of migration comes alive, and vistas of our nation's historic corridors await the adventurer. Popular means of travel include wagons, steamboats, canoes, kayaks, rafts, horses and llamas, snowshoes, cross-country skis, dogsleds, snowmobiles, bicycles, bush planes, trains — and one's own two feet. Many of the National Historic Trails have established motor routes marked with distinctive signs and interpretive centers along the way. The anticipation and preparation for a vacation along one of these routes provides an exciting focus on a particular period in our country's history. The imagination of schoolchildren comes alive when they relive our country's history as they follow a trail. The tired business traveler who seeks out a section of the trail after a conference or meeting is rewarded with an enriching experience — and with ideas for a later family vacation.

National Scenic Trails (NST) are (or will be) continuous, extended routes of outdoor recreation within protected corridors. Winding past some of the nation's most striking natural beauty, these trails take recreationists to the rhododendron gardens of Roan Mountain on the Appalachian Trail, past moraines and kettle lakes on the Ice Age Trail, and around volcanoes on the Pacific Crest Trail. Vistas from the Continental Divide, waterfalls in the North Country, and sunken paths of the Natchez Trace stimulate one's sense of beauty and foster an appreciation for the most precious aspects of life. Seeing the nation's Capitol from the Potomac Heritage Trail or bird-watching among graceful cypress trees along the Florida Trail are examples of the diversity of experiences available. These long-distance trails are footpaths to nature and reveal the nation's beauty. They will be described in detail in the coming volume, *America's National Scenic Trails,* to be published by the University of Oklahoma Press.

The other two trail categories of the national trails system comprise the national recreation trails and the side and connecting trails, which receive their designations from the secretary of the interior or the secretary of agriculture upon application. *National recreation trails* are located in every state, the District of Columbia, and Puerto Rico. More than eight hundred recreation trails total more the nine thousand miles, and most are found on federal lands. They are managed by public and private agencies at the local, state, and national levels and include nature trails, river routes, and historic tours. These trails include a wide variety of trail types, uses, lengths, topography, and physical challenges. Although only two have been designated thus far, *side and connecting trails* are intended to encourage travel between major trails and from trails to towns and cities; they will also link parks, forests, and historic sites.

National scenic and historic trails can only be designated by Congress. Fifteen of the twenty established national trails in our country are administered by the National Park Service, four by the U.S. Forest Service, and one by the Bureau of Land Management. Land along each trail corridor, however, comes under the full range of public or private ownership. Sites and segments of a trail on nonfederal land are certified by the trail's federal administrator. Certified trail sites and segments must meet the preservation, interpretation, and recreational purposes of the National Trails System Act. Not all points of interest shown in this book are certified sites, although they might one day become certified. Likewise, certified components could lose their status if they fail to continue to meet the act's criteria. For sites on private property, the trail visitor should be especially aware of trespassing laws, and permission to visit these sites should be obtained. The process for arranging visits to certified sites and segments on private property is generally clear. Certified sites and segments, and trail components on federally owned lands, are clearly marked with a trail logo. These trail logos also appear widely on auto routes, connector trails, and bicycle routes. Auto routes allow reasonably simple and direct travel on or parallel to the historic route, while connector trails are used to maintain continuity when the trail deviates from the historic route. A bicycle route sign denotes a bikeway on the historic trail. Logos may also appear on other directional signs, for instance, on signs denoting trail crossings or ruts.

Trail associations, state agencies, local communities, historical societies, and other organizations play a critical role in establishing and maintaining these trails. For example, the American Hiking Society provides important stewardship as advocate for the national trails system; it is the organization that founded and coordinates National Trails Day, America's largest celebration of the outdoors. And without the support of thousands of volunteers organized by hundreds of trail associations, the trails would not have become a reality. As a means to coordinate their work with Congress and the federal agencies, the Partnership for the National Trails System was formed in 1991. The nation is indebted to its many talented member-volunteers for their invaluable support and hard work.

Come join in for an adventure of a lifetime. Visit a segment of a national trail in your community or while on vacation with family and friends. A visit for a week, a day, or even a few hours to locations along a historic trail can stimulate the imagination and curiosity in mysterious and powerful ways. It may even entice you to later follow a trail in its entirety. Either way, memories of the visit will enrich your sense of history and your understanding of America. The rush for gold and the race of the Iditarod dog mushers to Nome to deliver serum, the legendary journey of Lewis and Clark, the flight of the Nez Perce to freedom, and the expeditions of Juan Bautista de Anza come alive in a way that was not possible before the National Historic Trails were designated. With wagon ruts clearly visible under your feet, time does not seem so distant since the pioneers emigrated over the Oregon, California, and Mormon Trails. The forced exodus of the Cherokees from their ancestral homelands, the five-day voting rights march from Selma to Montgomery, and the route of the Revolutionary War patriots along the Overmountain Victory Trail are tangible reminders of American strife and hardships. Stories of the entrepreneurs along the Santa Fe Trail who profited from the burgeoning Mexican trade and of the speed and daring of the Pony Express riders remind the adventurer of our country's ingenuity and resourcefulness. The National Historic Trails tell stories of America's bold men and women, stories that bring history

to reality like no textbook ever can.

The purpose of this book is to celebrate and share the wealth of our country's historic trails with all people, regardless of whether they live in the United States or are visiting from abroad. Each of the following chapters introduces a trail. Each chapter provides background data about the trail, gives the history of the trail, highlights a person or event of special interest in the trail's history, describes the trail's setting today, and details points of interest. The points of interest are marked on an accompanying map and specify certified segments of the trail and peripheral sites. Photographs by my fellow adventurer, Jane Lammers, will tease you into a visit.

It is our hope that whenever you plan a trip you'll take a look at this book and see if there isn't a trail nearby. A national trail can be a planned destination, or a visit to a trail can be a secondary activity. For example, visit the Nez Perce Trail when taking the family to Yellowstone, the Lewis and Clark Trail after a conference in St. Louis, or the Mile 0 marker of the Iditarod Trail when your cruise ship makes port in Seward.

Just a warning, once you start you'll never want to stop.

NOTE

The trails system is ever-growing and ever-changing. The purpose of this book is to serve as an overall guide. Because only general maps are included, it may be necessary to consult highway maps or topographical maps or to make local inquiry to find some sites. Appendixes A and B can help the serious traveler get more information on routes and safety precautions. Some sites are not developed, are in the development phase, or have no public access. Please respect the rights of private property owners. Always make certain that someone else knows where and when you are going. Happy trails!

The national trail system has depended upon the cooperative efforts of thousands of dedicated volunteers, and more volunteers are always needed. Readers who may be particularly interested in working with associations committed to national trail growth may contact the associations and offices listed at the beginning of each chapter. Choosing to work at a trail close to home can be an especially rewarding volunteer experience.

Table 1 provides a listing of the twenty national trails.

TABLE 1

Trail Name	Category	Mileage	Administered by	States
Appalachian	Scenic	2,144	NPS	Conn., Ga., Maine, N.H., Vt., Mass., Md., N.C., N.J., N.Y., Pa., Tenn., Va., W.Va.
California	Historic	5,665	NPS	Calif., Colo., Iowa, Idaho, Kans., Mo., Nebr., Nev., Ore., Utah,Wyo.
Continental Divide	Scenic	3,200	USFS	Colo., Idaho, Mont., N.Mex., Wyo.
Florida	Scenic	1,300	USFS	Fla.
Ice Age	Scenic	1,000	NPS	Wisc.
Iditarod	Historic	2,450	BLM	Alaska
Juan Bautista de Anza	Historic	1,200	NPS	Ariz., Calif.
Lewis and Clark	Historic	3,700	NPS	Iowa, Idaho, Ill., Kans., Mo., Mont., N.D., Nebr., Ore., S.D., Wash.
Mormon Pioneer	Historic	1,300	NPS	Iowa, Ill., Nebr., Utah, Wyo.
Natchez Trace	Scenic	110	NPS	Ala., Miss., Tenn.
Nez Perce (Nee-Me-Poo)	Historic	1,170	USFS	Idaho, Ore., Mont., Wyo.
North Country	Scenic	3,200	NPS	Mich., Minn., N.D., N.Y., Ohio, Penn., Wisc.
Oregon	Historic	2,170	NPS	Idaho, Kans., Mo., Nebr., Ore., Wash.
Overmountain Victory	Historic	300	NPS	N.C., S.C., Tenn., Va.
Pacific Crest	Scenic	2,638	USFS	Calif., Ore., Wash.
Pony Express	Historic	1,966	NPS	Calif., Colo., Kans., Mo., Nebr., Nev., Utah, Wyo.
Potomac	Scenic	704	NPS	Md., Pa., Va., D.C.
Santa Fe	Historic	1,203	NPS	Colo., Kans., Mo., N.Mex., Okla.
Selma to Montgomery	Historic	53	NPS	Ala.
Trail of Tears	Historic	2,052	NPS	Ala., Ark., Ga., Ill., Ky., Mo., N.C., Okla., Tenn.

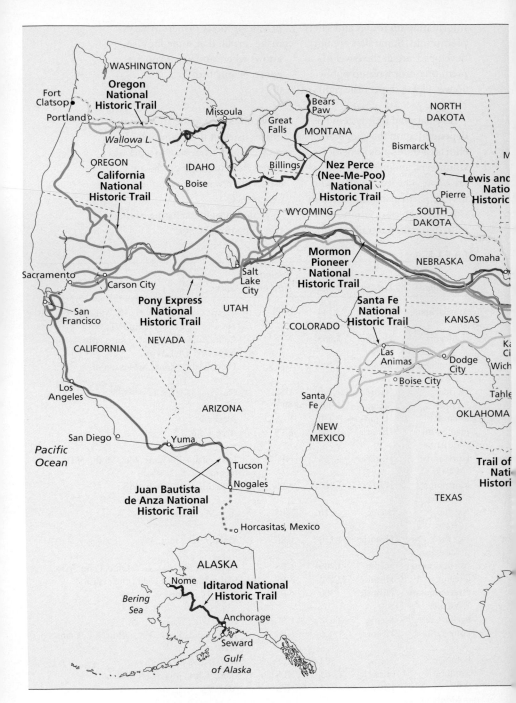

WASHINGTON

Fort Clatsop
Portland

Oregon National Historic Trail

Missoula

Wallowa L.

OREGON

California National Historic Trail

IDAHO
Boise

Great Falls

Bears Paw

MONTANA

Billings

Nez Perce (Nee-Me-Poo) National Historic Trail

NORTH DAKOTA

Bismarck

Lewis and Natio Historic

Pierre

SOUTH DAKOTA

WYOMING

Sacramento

Carson City

Pony Express National Historic Trail

San Francisco

CALIFORNIA

NEVADA

Salt Lake City

UTAH

COLORADO

Mormon Pioneer National Historic Trail

NEBRASKA Omaha

Santa Fe National Historic Trail

KANSAS

K; Ci

Las Animas

Dodge City

Wich

Boise City

Tahl

Los Angeles

ARIZONA

Santa Fe

NEW MEXICO

OKLAHOMA

San Diego

Pacific Ocean

Yuma

Juan Bautista de Anza National Historic Trail

Tucson

Nogales

TEXAS

Trail of Nati Histori

Horcasitas, Mexico

ALASKA

Nome **Iditarod National Historic Trail**

Bering Sea

Anchorage

Seward

Gulf of Alaska

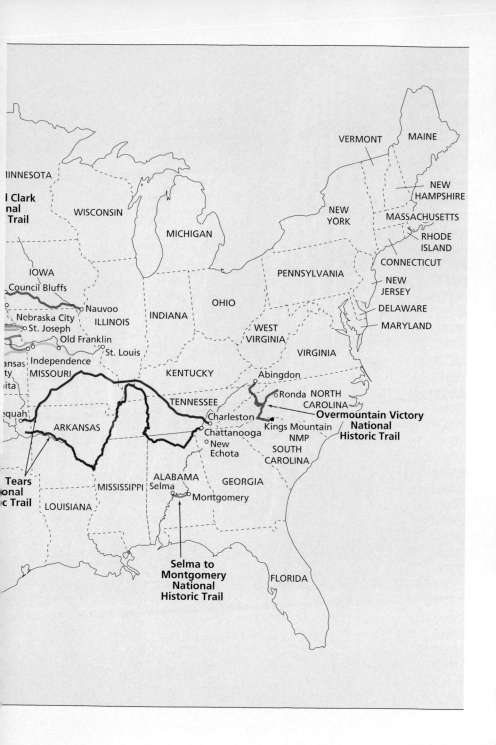

VERMONT   MAINE

MINNESOTA

l Clark
nal
Trail

WISCONSIN

MICHIGAN

NEW
YORK

NEW
HAMPSHIRE

MASSACHUSETTS

RHODE
ISLAND

CONNECTICUT

IOWA

Council Bluffs

Nauvoo

Nebraska City   ILLINOIS
○ St. Joseph

Old Franklin

○ St. Louis

ansas Independence
ty   MISSOURI
ita

equah'

ARKANSAS

Tears
onal
c Trail

MISSISSIPPI

LOUISIANA

INDIANA

OHIO

WEST
VIRGINIA

PENNSYLVANIA

NEW
JERSEY

DELAWARE

MARYLAND

VIRGINIA

KENTUCKY

TENNESSEE

Charleston

Chattanooga
○ New
Echota

ALABAMA
Selma

Montgomery

Abingdon

○ Ronda NORTH
CAROLINA

Kings Mountain
NMP

SOUTH
CAROLINA

GEORGIA

Overmountain Victory
National
Historic Trail

Selma to
Montgomery
National
Historic Trail

FLORIDA

**GIANT
SAGUARO**

Hikers are
dwarfed by
the giant
saguaro in
Saguaro
National
Monument
outside
Tucson,
Arizona.
Some may
reach a
height of
fifty feet
and an age
of two
hundred
years. In
May and
early June,
creamy-
white
blossoms
appear in
clusters on
the ends
of the
branches,
and later
its fruit
provides
food for
numerous
desert
creatures.

Juan Bautista de Anza National Historic Trail

The port of San Francisco . . . is a marvel of nature, and might well be called the harbor of harbors. . . . Indeed, although in my travels I saw very good sites and beautiful country, I saw none which pleased me so much as this. And I think that if it could be well settled like Europe there would not be anything more beautiful in all the world.

FATHER PEDRO FONT, MARCH 28, 1776

The Juan Bautista de Anza National Historic Trail (JBANHT) commemorates the route taken by Anza in 1775–76 when he led a group of colonists from what is now Horcasitas, Sonora, Mexico, to found a presidio and mission for New Spain on San Francisco Bay. He returned to Monterey, and eventually to Mexico after exploring the east side of San Francisco Bay. Before leading that historic expedition, Anza had embarked a year earlier on an expedition into the desert of present-day southern California to determine the route and feasibility of moving 198 emigrants and almost a thousand head of livestock northward. Watering spots and pasturage, so important to a desert crossing, were carefully charted and contacts were established with the American Indians along the route. A unique combination of political, economic, religious, and military circumstances prompted the Anza expeditions.

ADMINISTRATING AGENCY
National Park Service
Pacific Great Basin Systems Support Office
600 Harrison Street, Suite 600
San Francisco, CA 94107-1372
415-744-3968
http://www.nps.gov

FURTHER INFORMATION
Heritage Trails Fund
Amigos de Anza
1350 Castle Rock Road
Walnut Creek, CA 94598
510-926-1081

Anza Trail Coalition of Arizona
P.O. Box 396
Tumacacori, AZ 85640-0396
520-398-2150

ESTABLISHED
1990

APPROXIMATE MILEAGE
1,200 miles (1,930 kilometers)

STATES
Arizona, California

The History of the Trail

In the mid-eighteenth century, rulers of the Spanish empire in the New World had consolidated their power around Mexico and Central America.* In 1773, when Anza was planning his expedition, Spain had already claimed an immense territory, stretching as far north as present-day Alaska and including what is today the western United States, Florida, and the Philippine Islands. Colonies had been established in New Mexico for nearly 175 years, and Spanish influence extended as far north as the Gila and Colorado Rivers in present-day Arizona. Also, Baja (Lower) California was being settled, and the need for strategically placed harbors and outposts in Alta (Upper) California was foremost.

As the mines of Mexico and Central America were depleted, the riches of the Philippines became critical to the health of the Spanish empire. Yet the galleons from Manila suffered greatly from pirate attacks and their crews from scurvy. It became clear that ports along the western coast of California, from Cabo San Lucas to Monterey, were needed to protect Spanish interests. By the 1760s, Russian ships, searching for seal and otter pelts, were being reported as far south as Oregon. Russian plans to settle northern California were quite

*Material in this section is taken from the National Park Service's *Juan Bautista de Anza National Historic Trail Draft Comprehensive Management and Use Plan and Environmental Impact Statement.*

clear. In the meantime, English and French freebooters were becoming more of a problem in the Pacific and constantly threatened the slow-sailing Spanish treasure galleons. Additionally, the crowns of both England and France were supporting voyages of discovery. The discovery of the elusive Northwest Passage would provide Spain's enemies with a quick and easy passage between the Atlantic and Pacific Oceans. Spain needed an overland route to California, and needed it quickly.

Other political factors were changing the course of events in Spanish America. In 1767, Carlos III of Spain, reacting to the growing influence of the Society of Jesus throughout his empire, expelled the Jesuits from all his realms, and transferred their established missions in the New World to the Franciscan order. Long desiring a foothold in the New World, the Franciscans were eager to seize the opportunity to expand their mission frontier into Alta California. This desire was supported by the wishes of the newly appointed minister of the Indies, José de Gálvez. With his 1768 appointment came the strong push to return the empire to the old days of wealth and glory. Like the Franciscans, Gálvez cast his eyes northward. Plans were made for a major expedition from Lower California to the north.

The July 1769 Portolá expedition began as a combination of exploration and settlement, both by land and by sea. The land ex-

AMERICA'S NATIONAL HISTORIC TRAILS

pedition was divided into two groups under Don Gaspár de Portolá and Capt. Fernando Rivera y Moncada. Rivera led the advance detachment and Portolá followed with the energetic Franciscan, Fray Junípero Serra (who would soon establish the California mission chain). The expedition reached San Diego Bay, which had been discovered in 1542 when Juan Rodríguez Cabrillo, sailing under the Spanish flag, led the first European exploring expedition along the California coast. There on the bay, Portolá and Serra established California's first fortress and mission, San Diego de Alcalá. By October, the expedition had reached Monterey, and in November a scouting party stumbled upon San Francisco Bay, which had eluded seaborne explorers for more than a century. A presidio and the second mission, San Carlos Borromeo de Carmelo, were established in 1770. Three additional missions followed: San Antonio de Padúa in 1771, San Gabriel Arcángel in 1771, and San Luís Obispo de Tolosa in 1772.

A small force composed of sixty-one soldiers and eleven Franciscan friars manned the missions and presidios, rendering the frail new California settlements completely dependent for survival during their early years. Yet the prevailing winds and currents along the California coast made shipping provisions for the struggling settlements hazardous. Supply ships attempting to beat their way northward from Baja California to Monterey often took five times as long to reach their destination as did those sailing south. Some were blown out to sea to disappear forever or were driven to destruction along the rocky coastline. Overland travel from Baja California was also long and arduous, and the harsh barren lands of Baja provided little food to spare for export. The settlements and outposts necessary for the protection of the empire's treasure line and for the Franciscans as they pursued missionary activities could be strengthened only if a dependable overland route could be opened between Alta California and the Mexican province of Sonora. Such a route could lure more settlers to California and would allow food to reach the new settlements from the farms of northern Mexico.

The prospect of opening a land route between Sonora and Monterey had a long history, going back to Fray Eusebio Kino at the end of the seventeenth century. The Spanish military and the early missionaries braved the unknown, establishing routes later followed by adventurers like Fray Francisco Garcés, who traveled to the Pimas on the Gila River and who once crossed the Colorado to approach the foot of the San Gabriel Mountains. In the 1730s the first Juan Bautista de Anza urged opening a land route from Sonora to the Pacific after hearing tales of such a route from the American Indians. The final impetus to exploration did not come, however, until 1769. Anza's son, Capt. Juan Bautista de Anza, commander of the small presidio of Tubac (in present-day Arizona), learned through the local Pimas that a tribe to the west of the Yumas had reported white men on the west coast and had drawn outlines of Spanish ships. He speculated that if communications were possible between American Indians on one side of the mountain and those on the ocean side then there must be an overland route that joined the two areas. Although the Spanish could not find a land route to Alta California, Anza* became convinced that there was one across the desert and over the mountains.

His request for permission to lead an overland expedition to California was granted by Antonio María Bucareli y Ursúa in 1773. The viceroy, eager to secure Alta California for Spain, was influenced by the support of Costansó, the engineer with the Portolá expedition, and by Father Serra, who happened to be in Mexico City at the time. Anza left

*Some confusion exists about whether "to *de* or not to *de.*" Anza signed all official documents with his full title of nobility—Juan Bautista de Anza. Less prestigious documents were signed with only his surname—Anza, never "de Anza," and when his contemporaries referred to him by surname, not title, they always called him "Señor Anza," "Capitán Anza," "Gobernador Anza," or just "Anza." Therefore, the National Park Service uses Anza when referring to him by surname.

Tubac on January 8, 1774, with a small band of twenty soldiers, a dozen servants, and a herd of two hundred cattle and pack animals. Father Garcés accompanied the expedition to lend spiritual guidance and desert experience and to seek out the friendly Indian villages he had visited on previous travels. An additional guide was Sebastián Tarabal, a Baja California Indian and a runaway from Mission San Gabriel, who showed up at Tubac just before the expedition started. Reluctantly, he agreed to guide the explorers back over his trail. Juan Bautista Valdéz, one of the soldiers who had accompanied Portolá and Serra on their pioneering trek to San Diego and Monterey in 1769, was assigned to guide the party from San Gabriel Mission to Monterey.

The expedition went by way of Caborca in the Altar Valley to replace horses that had been stolen in an Apache raid at Tubac. This route put Anza on the classic short road to the Colorado, later known as El Camino del Diablo, which, with its sparse water holes and rock tanks, was passable only by small units. The route, commonly used by patrols from Altar, was not suitable for a large colonizing expedition because of its lack of forage and water. For this reason, Anza explored the Gila drainage basin on his return to determine the feasibility of this route for a larger contingent of settlers. Reaching the Yuma Indian villages at the junction of the Colorado and Gila Rivers without difficulty, Anza courted the favor of the Yuma (Quechan) chief, Olleyquotequiebe, whom Anza named Salvador Palma. The friendship ensured a safe passage at this crucial point in the journey. After several false starts and despite tensions arising from thirst and starvation, the expedition succeeded in finding a mountain pass leading toward coastal California. On March 22, 1774, Anza and his small party finally arrived at Mission San Gabriel. Since San Gabriel was already linked by known trails to the growing chain of missions between San Diego and Monterey, the beginning of the famous El Camino Reál, the overland route to California, was now open.

Because the padres had little food, four men were sent from San Gabriel to the San Diego mission for supplies. After a short rest, Anza sent all but six of his soldiers back to Tubac and continued north to Monterey. Clearly, the overland route to California was practical and safe for settlers. Returning to Tubac on May 26—five months after he had left the frontier presidio— Anza traveled on to Mexico City to report the success of his trip. Now Spanish authorities could lay the cornerstone in a grand scheme of protection and settlement of Alta California—an outpost on the recently discovered San Francisco Bay. This harbor could be defended against all enemies and could provide a perfect northern anchor for Spanish defenses.

If San Francisco was to be settled and developed as soon as possible, Anza was considered the only person to lead such an effort. Quickly, he was promoted to lieutenant colonel, given appropriate recruiting authority, and commanded to lead an expedition of settlers to the port of San Francisco. There a presidio, mission, and village were to be established. Anza selected as his second in command José Joaquín Moraga, second lieutenant of the company at the Royal Presidio of Fronteras. Moraga's father had met death in the American Indian frontier wars just as Anza's father had. Eventu-

DON GARATE AS ANZA

Park Ranger Don Garate bears a striking resemblance to Juan Bautista de Anza. Sporting this period costume, he reenacts the role of Anza during special occasions at Tumacácori National Historical Park near Tubac, Arizona.

CASA GRANDE

Campers and stargazers enjoy the evening skies once scrutinized by the Hohokam Indians who moved into the Gila Valley around 300 B.C. This perplexing four-story structure, thought to be an astronomical observatory, was named by Father Eusebio Kino in 1694. The Hohokam ruins can be visited at the Casa Grande Ruins National Monument.

ally, Lieutenant Moraga would lead the colonists in founding the Presidio of San Francisco in the name of Spain.

Anza began his recruitment in Culiacán and Sinaloa which, after two hundred years of settlement, had a population among whom he might find many willing to risk a forbidding journey for opportunities in a new settlement. The volunteers gathered at the Presidio of San Miguel de Horcasitas, Sonora's provincial capital, located about 175 miles south of today's international border. On September 29, 1775, 177 persons left for Tubac. At Tubac, Apache raids caused delays and depleted the company's stock. Finally on October 23, the expedition set out as the first immigrants to march the overland route from New Spain to Alta California. With Anza were 3 officers, 18 veteran soldiers from the presidios of Sonora and Tubac, 20 soldier-recruits, 29 women (wives of the soldiers), 4 volunteer families, 128 children, 20 muleteers, 3 vaqueros, 3 servants, 3 Indian interpreters, 695 horses and mules, and 355 cattle. Friar Pedro Font, a Franciscan missionary, was selected as expedition chaplain because of his ability to read latitudes. Both Anza and Font kept detailed diaries of the entire journey. Father Garcés also set out with the expedition, as did Father Thomas Eixarch of Tumacácori.

Garcés kept an expedition diary as far as the Colorado, where he and Eixarch left the expedition to answer Chief Palma's request for missionaries.

The expedition had barely moved north from Tubac when a death occurred—María Manuela Piñuelas died from complications after childbirth. The baby survived to live in California, and the mother was buried at Mission San Xavier del Bac, a mission to the Pima Indians. Despite the hardships endured, the expedition recorded no other deaths. But trouble of another kind came when two of the expedition's muleteers deserted. When the Pima Indians found and returned them, they were punished with strokes of a whip. There was another short pause to celebrate three marriages, all conducted by Font and all probably involving girls who had come of age and who had already been living with their grooms. Leaving San Xavier del Bac on October 26 was momentous for the colonists for they were leaving the last outpost of Spanish civilization in Sonora. Realistically, they could not expect to see another Spaniard until they reached San Gabriel in Alta California.

From San Xavier del Bac the expedition moved northward up the Santa Cruz River valley, past present-day Tucson. A rest near the Gila River enabled Anza and Father Font to visit the ancient Casa Grande ruins. The party then followed the Gila west toward the Colorado River. Delays were numerous because of sicknesses and another birth, but the expedition reached the Colorado on November 28, whereupon Chief Palma and the friendly Yuma Indians helped the colonists cross the river without any serious mishaps. (Although two men were swept downstream, they were rescued by soldiers stationed by Anza for that purpose.) The Yuma, surrounded by hostile desert (but also by fertile soil and endless water), were able to cultivate beans, maize, wheat, calabashes, watermelons, and other food crops. After an exchange of complimentary speeches by the two parties, Anza dispersed gifts and received food, including nearly three thousand watermelons that had been preserved in the desert sand by the Yuma Indians.

Leaving Fathers Eixarch and Garcés behind, the expedition set out to follow the Colorado west on December 4, 1775. Now they had to conquer their most formidable obstacle, the shifting sands of desert wastelands. The way was difficult, the toll on the animals was great, water was scarce, and the winter was bitterly cold. They were headed for a known water source at San Sebastián Marsh, named the year before by Anza for the Indian who had guided him on the first expedition. Anza divided his train into three groups, traveling a day apart so the water holes could refill before a new party arrived. By December 17, the entire party had reached the haven of San Sebastián (now called Harper's Well near Anza-Borrego Desert State Park in California). At the oasis, they were met with snow. The Mexican farmers, who had never seen snow, struggled through it. Several persons nearly froze to death. To save the life of one farmer, it was necessary to bundle him up for two hours between four fires. Several pack animals and cattle were lost.

Despite the cold weather, the colonists set forth on the next day, December 18, to resume their march across the desert, camping on a dry flat at the entrance to the Borrego Valley, which Anza called Los Puertecitos (Little Pass). Next they came to a site in the San Felipe Wash that he named San Gregorio — later to be known as Borrego Spring. The warming sunshine did not last long, and soon the animals were dying from cold and hunger. Dry camps alternated with wet. At one dry camp, thirst-plagued cattle (meant to provide meat for California) stampeded and only a few were recovered. The water conditions gradually improved as the expedition made the ascent of the foothills, but forage grew scarcer. On Christmas Eve night a baby was born at Fig Tree Spring. In celebration, Anza issued a ration of strong liquor and a dance was held. When Font accused Anza of causing drunkenness among the expedition members, Anza answered that the king had given him the liquor with instructions to issue it to the people at appropriate times for the purpose of

celebration. Font described the event in his diary: "It was somewhat discordant, and a very bold widow who came with the expedition sang some verses which were not at all nice, applauded and cheered by all the crowd."

On December 26 Anza led his party out of Coyote Canyon. The colonists reached the summit, descending through San Carlos Pass. They were now only fifty miles from San Gabriel and had at last reached fertile land. Their arrival at the Santa Ana River on December 31, and Mission San Gabriel Arcángel on January 4, 1776, more than doubled the European population of Alta California. Though composed of crude buildings, the new site of the mission was surrounded by cultivated fields. Cattle, sheep, and hogs thrived. Food, water, and rest revived the colonists' spirits.

The stay at San Gabriel was much longer than expected. First, Anza decided to help Fernando Rivera y Moncada, the commandante of California, suppress hostilities between the Spanish and Kumeyaay peoples in San Diego, which had arisen when the mission was attacked and Father Jayme and two Spanish workmen were killed. Anza also hoped to find additional supplies for the journey to Monterey, since the colonists were straining the resources of San Gabriel. Further delays occurred at San Gabriel when several soldiers deserted with precious food. Eventually, on February 21, the expedition set forth toward Monterey, while Lieutenant Moraga stayed behind to chase the deserters. Following known trails, the colonists were pleased with the seacoast around Santa Barbara, and they were graciously received at Mission San Luís Obispo and Mission San Antonio. Moraga, who had captured the deserters, rejoined the expedition.

On March 10, after a journey of 130 days and nearly two thousand miles from Horcasitas, the colonists reached Monterey. The presidio there, now six years old, boasted a chapel, a barracks, some small houses, and a stockade. The mission itself had earlier been moved by Father Serra to Carmel Valley, a short distance away, where the land was more suitable for farming. The colonists settled down once again while Anza set out on March 23 to explore the San Francisco Bay area and to pick a site for settlement. His party of twenty people consisted of Father Font, Lieutenant Moraga, eight soldiers from Tubac, muleteers, and some local guides. They moved northward up the bay shore and westward toward what is now Lake Merced. After a stop at Mountain Lake, they climbed the headlands to look down on the magnificent bay, an obvious setting for a presidio and settlement. A suitable site for a mission was also chosen, near an arroyo, and was named Arroyo de los Dolores, after the day of its discovery, "Friday of Sorrows" (Good Friday). Although Father Serra christened

ANZA SAND AND PRICKLY PEAR

Even when rainfall is scarce, prickly pear lightens the trail with May and June blooms. Wildflower displays in California's Anza-Borrego Desert State Park in Borrego Springs vary each year according to the amount of rainfall, sunlight, and warmth they receive. Their season begins in February and peaks from mid-March to early April.

the mission San Francisco de Asís, the name Mission Dolores is still commonly used.

Following orders to explore the extent of the bay, the party moved southward to the southern end of the bay, then to the northeast, traversing the low foothills to the Carquinez Strait, before heading south again, arriving back in Monterey on April 8. The colonists themselves were destined to wait for several more months before they had their first view of the Bay of San Francisco. Rivera, the commandante of California, had made his own exploration of the bay area in 1774 and had decided that it was not suit-

able for settlement. Despite an enthusiastic report sent from Anza to Rivera at San Diego, the colonists would not be given permission to leave Monterey for another two months.

Tired of waiting and with the major part of his task now completed, Anza himself set off on April 14 for the return trip to Sonora and Mexico City, where he was promoted to governor of New Mexico. Father Font, the ten soldiers from Tubac, some servants, and one couple who had decided not to stay in California went with him, reaching Horcasitas on June 1, after an absence of eight months. In the meantime, after considerable delays, Commandante Rivera finally relented, and the colonists left Monterey for their new home on June 17. Under the command of Lieutenant Moraga, they reached the site of Mission Dolores and began the tasks of building the mission, the presidio, and their new homes.

These early settlers were a multicultural group of Spanish, Native American, and African heritage who had almost all been born on this continent. With them they brought their languages, customs, traditions, and general expressions of Hispanic culture as it existed in the New World. These influences had a significant impact on the development of California as well as on the cultures of the indigenous peoples encountered along the way, including the Seris, Mayos, Yaquis, Opatas, Pintos, Opas,

LA PURÍSIMA

On the proposed auto route, La Purísima Mission State Historic Park interprets California's Spanish colonial history. The mission was founded in 1787 and was moved east of Lompoc after it was destroyed in an earthquake in 1812.

Lobaipuri, Papago, Pimas, Quechan, Mojave, Cahuilla, Gabrieleños, Chumash, Salinan, Rumsen, Esselen, and Ohlone, all of whom had their own distinct culture and language. Diaries from the two Anza expeditions reveal some of the details of these cultures, of the daily lives of the indigenous peoples, and of the landscapes encountered. In turn, the natives affected the expedition, from the friendly Yumas to the feared Apaches. From the moment Anza's party left the Yaqui River in Sonora until they reached the Colorado River, everything done by the expedition depended on what they perceived the dangerous Apaches to be doing.

Anza's vision for an overland route for emigration and supplies to Alta California had been accomplished, and that vision became an integral part of Spanish foreign and colonial policy in the New World. His vision allowed Spain to contain England, France, and Russia while extending her hold to new territory. He confirmed that San Francisco Bay was a great harbor. And his remarkable leadership abilities brought the expedition safely over a little-known route through a hostile environment with only one death—and three births. (Five more babies were born during the portion of the journey that preceded the group's departure from Tubac.) In establishing the route, Anza noted locations of water, forage, and fuel, which opened the route between Sonora

THE PRESIDIO

Converted from active military use in 1994, the Presidio in San Francisco is now managed by the National Park Service. In California, Florida, and Louisiana, presidios were used as points of defense against European rivals. Others, built from Arizona to Texas, and Sonora to Coachella, were primarily bastions against Apaches and other mounted foes.

and Alta California and made the resulting pioneer settlement possible. Only after an uprising of the Yuma Indians in 1781, caused by increasing demands on Yuma hospitality and pasturage, was the overland route largely abandoned. But by then the trail had already allowed the passage of enough cattle, settlers, and soldiers to ensure the survival of the pueblos of San José and Los Angeles and other existing settlements. Sections of Anza's trail were used well into the nineteenth century by missionaries, settlers, forty-niners, soldiers, stagecoach lines, and the first Americans to make their homes in southern California.

A HELMET OR A BROAD-BRIMMED HAT?: THE UNIFORM OF THE EXPEDITION SOLDIER

A number of modern representations of Anza's expeditions show the lieutenant colonel's men bedecked with steel breastplates, morion helmets, and matchlock muskets. Yet the Anza expeditions took place during the period of the American Revolution, not during Cortés's conquest of Mexico. Ironically, Anza would have been no more familiar with this equipment than with the flight suit of a modern-day astronaut. Abundant documents and contemporary pictorial evidence do offer an authentic view of the appearance of the men who followed Anza on his long trek to San Francisco. The leather-jacketed soldiers (*soldados de cuera*) used a dramatic and colorful military costume. When loaded down with weapons and armor, they were formidable opponents.

The Anza expeditions occurred at an important turning point in the military history of northern New Spain. Up until 1772, the arms and equipment of the *soldados de cuera* were covered by the regulation of 1729 that specified that troops wear a uniform designed by their commanding officer. As a result, the soldiers stationed in the presidios of northern New Spain wore a con-

Source: Material used here was taken in part from *Noticias de Anza* (June 1994) by Jack S. Williams.

fusing array of red, green, and blue. And because of the unwillingness of the captains, or their officers' lack of funds, the great majority of the troops made do with no uniform at all.

In spite of this regulation, the outfits worn by Anza's troops impressed the Marqués de Rubí so much that he noted with pleasure the excellent appearance of the soldiers he inspected in Tubac in 1766. These men, he wrote, were equipped with blood-red coats with blue cuffs, lapels, and collars. They also wore blue pants, leather sword belts (bandoliers), black broad-brimmed felt hats, woolen socks, and shoes. The pants and coat were equipped with brass buttons, and each soldier wore a massive blue cape lined with red felt. Apparently, the Marqués de Rubí liked the outfits so much that he used them as a model for developing a set of recommendations for new uniforms. Carlos III approved these recommendations, making some minor modifications. Battlefield victories of Frederick the Great had created a style craze in Europe for Prussian military designs. As a result, the king changed the color of the coats from red to blue. The new regulation of 1772 specified that the entire army in northern New Spain wear a blue coat with red lapels, collars, and cuffs; blue trousers; a shoulder bandolier with the name of the presidio; a black tie; a pair of shoes; and a black hat.

Inspections and instructions, dating from the 1772–80 period, indicate that the new coats were cut shorter than those used a decade before. Underneath the coat was a white shirt, while ribbons adorned the hat and hair. Officers wore tricorn hats while on garrison duty. Both the enlisted men and the officers were ordered to wear flat, broad-brimmed hats when on campaign. About 1780, the men were ordered to wear a linen or leather vest. A button was added to the hat so that the brim could be folded up on the right side to enable the soldiers to aim and fire their carbines and muskets. All the hatbands were a standard red color—the traditional national military color of Spain. The shoulder belt for the sword was dropped, and a blue serape was officially adopted as regulation equipment. Many of these changes were probably based on the innovations of frontier commanders such as Anza.

The dress version of the soldier's outfit was essentially the same as the campaign version, although the leather jacket, because of its excessive weight and heat, was not normally worn in the presidios. During formal inspection, the men were expected to arrive fully equipped with their weapons, uniforms, and mounts. Throughout the eighteenth century, the soldiers on campaign wore knee-high, wraparound leather leggings called *botas*. These devices were cheap and effective alternatives to regular military boots.

According to custom, Anza's outfit would have differed from that of his soldiers in quality of materials as well as overall design. In 1780, the dress uniform of presidio officers consisted of a blue dress coat with red collar and lapels and decorated with gold braid and gold buttons, a pair of blue trousers with gold buttons, a tricorn hat with gold braid, and a blue vest with gold buttons. When on campaign, the officers wore a shorter blue jacket with red collars and cuffs. This garment was more suitably worn with the leather jacket. Other campaign gear included a vest of linen, leather, or wool, with gold braid; a black or white brimmed hat with gold trim; and a pair of leggings. Officers were also allowed to wear a blue serape with gold trim. The commanders wore their hair in a long ponytail and were allowed to use hairnets known as *reducillas*.

Because the new regulation was gradually implemented in Sonora between 1772 and 1775, the men of the first Anza expedition of 1774 may have still worn their red coats. But during the second expedition, Anza's soldiers definitely wore the new uniforms. The figure below shows how two soldiers of Anza's second expedition might have appeared. The soldier to the left is wearing a field uniform; on the right is a soldier in encampment.

Uniforms and weapons of the second Anza Expedition, 1775–76, field uniform (left); uniform of soldier in encampment (right), from Jack S. Williams, *Noticias de Anza* Vol. 3, no. 2, June 1994 (National Park Service Western Region Office, San Francisco.)

Long before Anza's time, steel helmets and breastplates had disappeared from the frontier army. The body armor worn by presidio soldiers of the time was the *cuera*, which consisted of eight layers of well-dressed white deerskin, varying from midthigh to knee length. Because of its weight, the sleeveless attire was usually only worn when danger was imminent. A leather shield was the other piece of armor used by the Anza expedition members. Two distinct styles were popular: the *adarga*, a heart or figure-eight-shaped shield, and the *rodela*, a round or oval shield. Most were made of two or more thicknesses of bullhide. Officers' shields were usually decorated with the royal crest. They were carried on the left arm, which was thrust through two leather loops sewed on the back of the shield.

During the period of the Anza expedition, frontier troops were armed primarily with lances, swords, and carbines. After 1772, a brace of pistols was issued to each man. Some men also carried large knives called *buldeques*, or *navajas*. The main weapon of the presidio soldier was the lance, which was about nine feet in length. Most surviving lance heads are lozenge-shaped and measure ten to thirteen inches in length. *Soldados de cuera* used swords of various styles, ranging from the crude *espadas anchas* (broad swords) made on the frontier to the more elegant weapons imported from Europe. When mounted, the soldiers generally suspended the sword in a scabbard tucked into the saddle. When on foot, the soldier used a bandolier worn over or under the *cuera*. Most firearms had flintlock mechanisms. The term used for Anza's carbines, *escopetas*, has the same meaning as "shotgun" in modern Spanish. When mounted, soldiers carried handguns and carbines in specially constructed holsters attached to their saddles. When on foot, they could thrust their pistols into their belts.

The 1975–76 reenactment that did so much to promote the trail made every effort to employ the true Anza uniform, which appears on the trail marker.

A 1975–76 re-enactment of the 1775–76 Anza expedition was designated as an approved bicentennial project by the American Revolution Bicentennial Administration and was sponsored by the California and Arizona Bicentennial Commissions.* A committee in Sonora, Mexico, also cooperated in the planning. Ceremonies were initiated in Mexico City, where the issuance of the royal decree mandating the expedition was simulated. Subsequently, the decree was carried by the memorial expedition to San Francisco, being passed from one group to another along the way. Leaving Horcasitas in September, equestrians and others closely followed the schedule and the route of the original party, halting each night as close as possible to the identified location of the campsite. In retracing the steps, the party was indebted to the painstaking work of the late University of California professor Herbert Bolton, who many years prior had translated the detailed diaries of Anza and Chaplain Pedro Font. He had also spent months in the field determining the precise route of the expedition and its relation to modern-day landmarks.

The authentically costumed

*Material in this section is taken from the National Park Service's *Juan Bautista de Anza National Trail Study Environmental Assessment* and the NPS's *Comprehensive Management and Use Plan Final Environmental Impact Statement Juan Bautista de Anza National Historic Trail.*

participants received a great deal of media attention. Additionally, ceremonies held at a number of locations along the route provided opportunities for others to become involved in the event. Years later, some of the participants gave testimony to the re-enactment as a "life-altering experience," and helped to promote the reality of the route as a national historic trail for future generations.

The Anza trail corridor has a long and varied history, making it expecially interesting to visit. Anza was led by American Indians and followed their trails. In turn, other groups such as the Army of the West, the Mormon Battalion, southern immigrants, and the Butterfield Stage used portions of the same route. In parts of California, the Anza route followed what later became El Camino Réal.

The Juan Bautista de Anza National Historic Trail begins on the Arizona border near the city of Nogales. From there, the route continues north along the Santa Cruz River past Tucson where it turns west to join the Gila River near Gila Bend. From there, the route follows the Gila River all the way to Yuma. After crossing the Colorado River near Yuma, the route drops south into Mexico to avoid a large expanse of sand dunes and continues on for several miles before reentering the United States southwest of El Centro. At this point, the route continues north through Anza-Borrego State Park, the San Ber-

The Trail Today

nardino National Forest, and the San Bernardino–Riverside metropolitan areas before reaching the San Gabriel Mission and the Los Angeles metropolitan area.

Moving west and north from the mission, the route passes through the Santa Monica Mountains, descending to the coastline near Oxnard, where it follows the coast through Ventura and Santa Barbara Counties before moving inland toward the northern portion of Vandenberg Air Force Base above Lompoc. The route continues through the Coast Range through San Luis Obispo and Atascadero before following the Salinas River en route to Monterey. Traveling north and inland from Monterey, the route passes San Juan Bautista, Gilroy, and San Jose, then moves along the San Francisco Peninsula through the low uplands facing the bay before turning inland at San Bruno, where it continues to the vicinity of the Presidio.

In its reconnaissance expedition to the East Bay, the expedition retraced their steps from San Francisco to the south end of the bay. There, they followed the inland course of the bay and the Carquinez Strait north and east to the Sacramento–San Joaquin delta, where exploration was terminated and the party headed south through the hills to rejoin their northbound route in the vicinity of Gilroy.

Over half of this historic route is now paved roadway. Other parts of it are affected by rail de-velopment: Amtrak's Coast Starlight and Sunset Limited routes generally follow the Anza Trail from Riverside in southern California to San Francisco, offering some beautiful scenic views. Some areas of the trail are protected, including several miles in Arizona, particularly between Tucson and Yuma, across the deserts of southern California, and along the California coast from Gaviota to Guadalupe. Traversing some of the most rural and some of the most urbanized areas in the United States, the route passes through over one hundred cities and towns. Because the trail's corridor passes by so many urbanized areas, it is a part of the daily lives of large numbers of people. For example, in Tucson, the Santa Cruz River Park follows the historic route, and citizens of Santa Cruz County have completed a 4.5-mile segment of the trail from Tumacácori National Historical Park to Tubac Presidio State Historic Park. Henry W. Coe State Park, located southeast of San Francisco Bay, has a trail that parallels the Anza route.

A total of thirty-five historic sites, eight in Arizona and twenty-seven in California, have direct connection with the 1775–76 journey. These sites include missions, presidios, landmarks, river crossings, campsites, water sources, mountain passes, and beaches. The majority are National Register sites or National Historic Landmarks. Twelve of these sites are on federal land, eleven on state land, five on local public agency land, and seven on private land. The private sites are all missions or chapels owned by the Franciscans, except for one owned by the Claretians and one by the Diocese of San Luis Obispo. The local agency sites are county beaches along the Santa Barbara Channel. Three landscape areas on the historic corridor in California are on the National Register. These are Sears Point Archeological District in Yuma County, Yuha Basin Discontiguous District in Imperial County, and the Fages-de Anza Trail–Southern Emigrant Road in San Diego County. San Felipe Creek and the Nipomo Dunes are recognized as National Natural Landmarks, and an additional ninety-nine interpretive sites, thirteen in Arizona and eighty-six in California, have been identified.

Only a small portion of the trail passes through federal land. In Arizona the trail crosses some land under the administration of the Bureau of Land Management: however, most of it passes through lands that are privately owned, including several Indian reservations. In California a small portion crosses National Forest land in Bautista Canyon through the San Bernardino National Forest. A larger segment of the route passes through Bureau of Land Management lands located between the international border and the Salton Sea. Several miles of the historic route pass through Anza-Borrego Desert State Park

on the northeastern edge of San Diego County. This section of trail is shown on park maps. In addition to the Henry W. Coe State Park in eastern Santa Clara County, the route passes through Perris Lake State Recreation Area near Riverside and several beach parks along the Santa Barbara Channel. In all, the trail passes through twenty-one state parks in California.

For the entire length of his expedition, Anza passed through American Indian lands. Today the trail passes through the Tohono O'odham districts of San Xavier and San Lucy, the Gila River Indian Reservation (Akimel O'odham), and the Cahuilla Indian Reservation in California. The Quechan have a land base at the Fort Yuma Indian Reservation and the Chumash have one in Santa Ynez, California. Most mission-influenced Indian cultures of California, from San Gabriel to San Francisco, are interpreted through the missions and other sites. Some areas of the trail pass through sensitive sites, such as Pilot Knob in Imperial County, which is sacred to the Quechan, and Sears Point in Yuma County, which is also important to the Quechan and other groups. Because Anza used Indian guides and generally followed established Indian trails, the historic and recreational routes are apt to be associated with Indian burial sites and sacred objects, which must be respected and left as they are. Additionally, the descendants of the expedition members, many of whom continue to live along the trail route, provide a direct link to the past. Landscape, place and street names, architectural traditions, some land use patterns, and other influences are still evident through much of the twelve-hundred mile trail route.

The Juan Bautista de Anza National Historic Trail passes numerous north-south mountain ranges interspersed with alluvial fan basins in Arizona and a small portion of southern California. The natural beauty of such formations is the result of faulting and uplift. Widely separated short ranges in desert plains are passed in the Sonoran Desert section, while the Salton Trough includes desert alluvial slopes and the Gulf of California's delta plain. The route along the California coast is characterized by parallel ranges and valleys on folded, faulted, and metamorphosed strata; the Los Angeles ranges are characterized by narrow ridges, broad fault blocks, and alluviated lowlands.

The climate still influences travel just as it did in Anza's time. By leaving when he did, Anza hoped to avoid the severe heat of the Sonoran Desert. Extreme summer temperatures limit active midday recreation plans. The winters are generally mild and ideal for all types of outdoor recreation, including hiking, horseback riding, biking, four-wheel driving, and auto touring —all according to restrictions. Amounts of rainfall tend to be low, but the timing differs significantly between eastern and western sections of the desert. In eastern Arizona, most of the rainfall occurs in the summer months as a result of storms originating in the Sea of Cortés, but Pacific storms also bring winter rains. As a result of the dual rainy season, the eastern Arizona desert, which contains a range of plant and related animal life not found elsewhere in the Sonoran Desert, is worth extra attention. Western portions of the desert receive most of their precipitation in the months of December, January, and February. The climate in coastal California is mild in the summer and mostly frost-free in the winter because of the buffering influence of the Pacific Ocean. This makes it an ideal area for year-round outdoor recreation.

As previously mentioned, the plant and animal life in the Sonoran Desert is actually quite varied and interesting. The common denominator throughout the desert is the creosote bush, usually found mixed with other plant life, but occasionally located in pure stands. Other common shrubs are burrobrush, brittlebrush, and crucifixion thorn. An unusual feature of this desert is the large variety of trees, including the smoke tree, desert willow, paloverde, ironwood, elephant tree, and honey and screwbean mesquite. Willows, cottonwoods, and salt cedars are found near water drainages, although the latter was introduced after Anza passed through the area and is actually considered an undesirable species in the ecosystem. California palm is found in some of the locations in the mountains surrounding the Salton Sea. Cacti provide their most magnificent displays in the upland area of Arizona. The massive saguaro—rare west of the Colorado River—dominates the scene, some standing up to fifty feet high. A wide variety of smaller cacti, including the cholla, the buckhorn, the beavertail, and the prickly pear, add to the atmosphere of the area, all flowering in the spring. Ocotillos, yuccas, agaves, and a wide variety of other flowering plants complete the unique floral display of the region.

There are a wide variety of migratory and resident birds found in the desert. Of special interest to most is the roadrunner. The mammal populations are dominated by an assortment of small rodents, but many larger mammals exist. In fact, this desert would not be complete without the coyote, kit fox, gray fox, bobcat, mule deer, desert bighorn sheep, and the endangered Sonoran pronghorn (now limited to a few animals in extreme southwest Arizona). A species unique to the Arizona portion of the Sonoran Desert is the piglike javelina, which has an uneasy disposition. The wide assortment of amphibians and reptiles includes the rare desert tortoise and the poisonous Gila monster. Desert blooms should never be enjoyed without carefully watching for the snakes of the region. They include several varieties of rattlesnakes, such as the western diamondback, the sidewinder, and the coral snake, which is limited to Arizona.

Since the Anza Trail generally follows major river corridors, it is frequently within floodplains and/or skirts wetland areas. Within Arizona, most of the trail is along the Santa Cruz or Gila Rivers, which historically flowed alternately above and under ground, spreading out in large floodplains rather than in defined channels. In California the route follows several river corridors, including the San Felipe Wash, San Jacinto River, Los Angeles River, San Antonio River, and Coyote Creek, and crosses numerous streams and several larger rivers, including the Colorado, Santa Ana, San Gabriel, Rio Hondo, Santa Clara, Santa Ynez, Santa Maria, and Guadalupe. These rivers have been affected by land use and management, although the San Felipe Wash and Coyote Creek are generally natural and protected within state parks and federal areas. The San Jacinto River outlet has been changed, affecting Mystic Lake, a large wetland that Anza named Laguna de Bucareli. The Los Angeles River is largely channelized, although some natural areas remain. The San Antonio River has been dammed to create San Antonio Reservoir, while the Salinas River remains free-flowing.

Many more wetlands existed at

the time of the expedition than exist today. Generally, these areas have been drained and put to agricultural or urban uses. Three wetlands have achieved some measure of protection along the historic route: San Sebastián Marsh at the confluence of Carrizo Wash and San Felipe Wash, a National Natural Landmark administered by the Bureau of Land Management; Mystic Lake, which is adjacent to the San Jacinto Wildlife Area administered by the California Fish and Game Department; and San Francisco Bay, portions of which are protected by private, local, regional, state, and federal agencies.

The future of this trail is exciting. There was a great deal of interest expressed during the planning process by individuals on both sides of the international border to recognize the full length of Anza's colonizing expedition by creating the Juan Bautista de Anza International Historic Trail. An international trail would recognize the six hundred miles of historic trace followed by Anza and his group of colonizers in Mexico, beginning as far south as Culiacán in Sinaloa, Mexico, where his recruitment efforts began. From the Royal Presidio of Horcasitas in Sonora, the expedition followed the Río Zanjon north to the Río Madalena to Nogales Wash on the approximate alignment of today's Mexico Highway 15. In addition, after leaving Yuma, Anza traveled for several miles in what is Baja California, Mexico, today. An in-

ternational trail would complete the Anza story.

Plans are being made to mark and interpret the historic features along the route so that it can be followed from end to end and so that information can be received en route. To accommodate a wide range of users, including hikers, bicyclists, equestrians, four-wheel drivers, and tourists in automobiles, parallel trails may be developed within the historic corridor that will allow for different uses. Allowable uses will vary with the land manager as well as time and place. Some areas may be open year-round, others only during limited periods to minimize resource damage. In some areas, one use (such as hiking) would be suitable, while in other areas multiple uses (such as hiking, biking, and horseback riding) may be accommodated. The National Park Service will encourage development of user facilities such as trail access parking, picnic sites, campsites, horse corrals, water sources, bicycle racks, and storage units, while encouraging public transit to recreational-trail staging areas and historic sites.

Remember that driving can be hazardous. Dust storms can strike without warning. Even though they usually last only a few minutes, they should be avoided whenever possible. If you see one coming, you should not drive into it. Instead, it is recommended that you pull off the roadway as far as possible, then stop and turn on your lights and set the emergency brake. If you are already into the storm before you realize it, do not stop. Rather, try to pull off the roadway or, if that is not possible, drive slowly ahead with your lights on, using the center line as a guide.

ARIZONA

1. NOGALES. Though not available for public visits, the campsite of Las Lagunas lies in an unprotected marsh immediately north of St. Andrew's Church. This is the start of the JBANHT in the United States.* The international boundary separates Nogales, Arizona, from Nogales, Sonora, Mexico. Plans to include six hundred miles of the route that lie within Mexico could make the Anza Trail the first international historic trail in the world. A passport is not required but is recommended for travel to Culiacán, Sinaloa, Mexico, for the beginning of the Anza expedition. *Nearby:* Peña Blanca RA.

2. TUMACÁCORI NATIONAL HISTORIC PARK. Tumacácori was listed (1691) as an outlying *visita* (without resident missionaries) by the famous Jesuit missionary Eusebio Francisco Kino. The village became a *visita* of the mission at Guevavi (1701), and, under the Franciscans, its primitive church was made the head mission of the district (1771) when Guevavi was abandoned. Father Pedro Font spent several days at Tumacácori while Anza

*Some of the material in this section comes from the National Park Service's *Comprehensive Management and Use Plan Final Environmental Impact Study Juan Bautista de Anza National Historic Trail.*

was in Tubac preparing for the trip. Font said mass (October 17, 1775) as the expedition moved toward Tubac. The historic park includes the remains of the mission church San José de Tumacácori and the associated cemetery, a mortuary chapel, the Calabasas and Guevavi sites, a visitor center (NHL), and a museum. Only a portion of the church at Los Santos Angeles de Guevavi still stands, and the San Cayetano de Calabasas Church is located halfway between Nogales and Tumacácori. Special events at the historic park include the Fiesta de Tumacácori (first weekend in December) and a luminaria display (December 24). The first section of the hiking and equestrian portion of the JBANHT in Arizona lies between the NHP and Tubac Presidio SHP.

3. TUBAC PRESIDIO STATE HISTORIC PARK. The Presidio de San Ignacio de Tubac (1752) was founded in response to a Pima revolt; it had been a Pima village before becoming a mission farm. The fifty cavalrymen garrisoned at the remote outpost were to control the Pimas, protect the frontier from the Apaches and Seris, and further explore the Southwest. Juan Bautista de Anza, second commander of the presidio, staged two overland expeditions to Alta California from this place. The ruins of his house can

Points of Interest

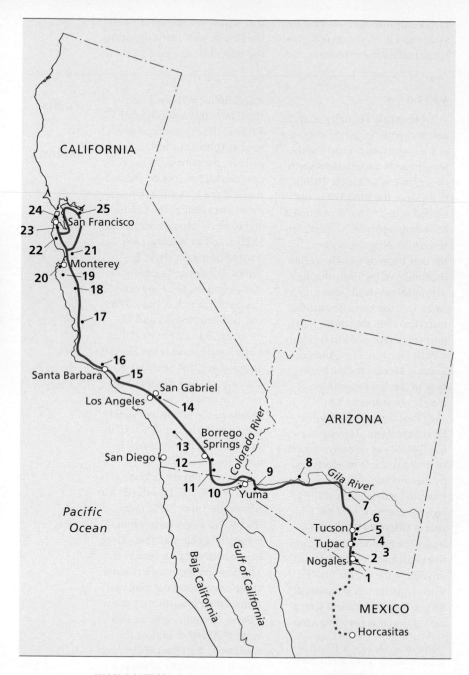

CALIFORNIA

24 — 25
23 — San Francisco
22 — 21
20 — Monterey — 19
— 18

— 17

— 16
Santa Barbara — 15
Los Angeles — San Gabriel
— 14

Borrego Springs
13 — 12
San Diego
11 — 10 — Yuma — 9

Colorado River

ARIZONA

8
Gila River
— 7

6
Tucson — 5
Tubac — 4
Nogales — 2 — 3
— 1

Pacific Ocean

Baja California

Gulf of California

MEXICO

Horcasitas

JUAN BAUTISTA DE ANZA NATIONAL HISTORIC TRAIL

be viewed through an underground archaeological exhibit. *Nearby:* La Canoa, the campsite where the expedition suffered its only loss of life, is interpreted by the Arizona Department of Transportation rest stop on I-19; Coronado NF.

4. MISSION SAN XAVIER DEL BAC. "The White Dove of the Desert" is located along the Santa Cruz River and is part of the O'odham Reservation. The still-active parish is administered by the Franciscans. The mission (NHL) was established by Father Kino (1692) at the site of an existing Piman village. A full-time resident missionary (1732) was eventually needed to attend to it and its *visita*, Tucson. Like all the other missions, San Xavier del Bac was under Franciscan administration when the Anza expedition stopped there (October 25, 1775) to mourn its only death and celebrate three marriages. Construction of the present mission church was started in 1783, south of Tucson.

5. TUCSON. The Spanish developed a substantial complex, Mission San Agustin del Tucson, on the site of a Piman village. Foundation walls and other signs of past occupation remain sufficiently intact, and there are plans to develop a cultural park, which would interpret the many cultures that previously occupied the site. On the eastern side of the Santa Cruz River, now under downtown Tucson, the Presidio San Agustin del Tucson was founded (1775) to replace the Tubac presidio as the main Spanish defense of the region. When Anza's expedition passed through in October, the presidio had been planned but not constructed. Plaques on city streets mark the location of several corners of the old structure, and a citizen's group would like to re-create part of the presidio. The Santa Cruz River Park contains a multiuse trail. *Other attractions:* Arizona State Museum; Tucson Museum of Art; Tucson Botanical Gardens; Sentinel Peak Park; Arizona-Sonora Desert Museum. *Nearby:* Coronado NF; Sabino Canyon RA. To the extreme north end of the Tucson Mountains near the Santa Cruz River are Puerto del Azotado and Los Morteros Archeological Site, once a large Hohokam village named for the bedrock mortars found near its center. The Anza expedition campsite, Puerto del Azotado, was in the vicinity of Los Morteros.

6. SAGUARO NATIONAL MONUMENT. Giant saguaro cacti, unique to the Sonoran Desert, sometimes reach a height of fifty feet in this cactus forest, which covers the valley floor, rising into the Rincon and west Tucson Mountains. *Nearby:* Tucson Mountain Park; Papago Indian Reservation; Kitt Peak National Observatory.

7. CASA GRANDE RUINS NATIONAL MONUMENT. The ruins were visited and named by Fray Kino (1694) when friendly Indians took him to see the already abandoned mysterious complex. Camped approximately five miles

to the northwest, Font and Anza visited the ruins (October 31, 1775) to record measurements. The park near Coolidge offers a site bulletin presenting information on the expedition. *Nearby:* Picacho Peak SP overlooks a campsite area and the Anza route through the Santa Cruz River valley. The Gila River Indian Reservation has campsites where the expedition was well received by the Pima Indians. Fortaleza (NRHP) is an important spiritual site located on top of a volcanic escarpment on the reservation. The site was probably settled about A.D. 1200 by migrants from the Tucson area after it was abandoned by the Hohokam. The village contained three large reinforced adobe ceremonial chambers. To the south is Organ Pipe Cactus NM.

8. PAINTED ROCKS. The Painted Rocks (NRHP) petroglyph site, under BLM management, offers a fine example of early Indian petroglyphs etched on a small mound of black rocks. It can be reached from I-8 west of Gila Bend, exit 102. Camping is available. *Nearby:* Campsites were located in Aqua Caliente and Mohawk. Wellton, further west, was also a campsite, and a prominent geologic feature beside the Gila River contains prehistoric petroglyphs and groundstone quarry sites. Historic cultural resources include Euro-American pictographs, the Butterfield Stage route, and the Antelope Hill Stage Station, Antelope Valley Canal headgates, the Antelope Hill/

Continental Bridge, and the Southern Pacific Railroad trestle bridge. The site is jointly managed by BLM and Bureau of Reclamation.

9. PRISON HILL, YUMA CROSSING NATIONAL HISTORIC LANDMARK. Long before Anza's time, Yuma had become a crossroads where prehistoric trails converged at the junction of the Gila and Colorado Rivers. Anza's strategy was to cross the Gila first and then the Colorado. The Yuma (Quechan) chief, Palma, helped him on both expeditions. By preventing access to this strategic crossing in a revolt (1781), the Yumas closed the Anza trail for the duration of the Spanish colonial period. Anza's crossing was two to three miles upstream of Yuma Crossing. There is an overlook at the state park in Yuma.

ARIZONA / CALIFORNIA

10. YUMA. The Fort Yuma Quechan Museum offers displays about Native American culture and Spanish expeditions. *Other attractions:* Yuma Quartermaster Depot SHP. *Nearby:* Cocopah Indian Reservation; Cibola and Imperial NWRs. To the west in California, about seven miles northwest of Mount Signal and four miles above the boundary with Mexico, the Wells of Santa Rosa (Yuha Well), on the south side of what is now Dunway Road, provided the expedition its first good water. The well, a California Register of Historic Landmarks, was called Santa Rosa de Las Lajas (Flat Rocks) by Anza

and was used (March 8, 1774) by the exploring expedition and by the three divisions of Anza's colonizing expedition (December 11–15, 1775). Above Brawley, the San Sebastián Marsh/San Felipe Creek (NNL) in the vicinity of the junction of State Highways 86 and 78 is the site of prehistoric villages and a stable water source in the desert environment that served as a campsite (1774 and 1775–76). On the 1774 expedition, Anza named it for his Indian guide, Sebastián Tarabal.

CALIFORNIA

11. SAN FELIPE CREEK. This creek was followed by the expedition from San Sebastián Marsh to Borrego Sink. The creek trail is available to the public within Ocotillo Wells SVRA. *Nearby:* Los Puertecitos (Little Pass) is the site where the expedition passed through (December 19, 1775) a gap in the clay hills, after camping along San Felipe Wash; the site is located on State Highway 78, 1.6 miles east of the town of Ocotillo Wells. Ocotillo Badlands, the clay hills, sprawl across the entrance to Little Borrego Valley (California Register of Historic Landmarks). San Gregorio was a campsite for both Anza expeditions; today's Borrego Spring is probably located on San Felipe Wash, where the valley narrows before entering the broad flats of Borrego Valley (also a California Register of Historic Landmarks).

12. ANZA-BORREGO DESERT STATE PARK. The park contains two stretches of the Anza route,

preserving the surrounding lands in an undeveloped state so that they appear much as they would have at the time of the expedition. A short segment of the trail exists in the southeast section of the park and passes near the San Gregorio marker. In the northwest section, a rough jeep and horseback trail parallels Anza's route through Coyote Canyon, marking El Vado, Santa Catarina, and Christmas Eve campsites. These two areas provide a rare opportunity to retrace the precise route. The Fages-de Anza Trail–Southern Immigrant Road (NRHP) is noted on park maps but is not open from June 1 to September 30. *Other attractions:* Middle Willows, the site of a spring and an Indian village, has exceptional historic value to the trail because of its natural integrity.

13. SAN BERNARDINO NATIONAL FOREST. In Riverside County, Turkey Track Grade, from Lower Willows near the mouth of Coyote Canyon to Terwilliger Valley and San Carlos Pass (Cary Ranch) site, closely follows Anza's route on both expeditions. Bautista Canyon Road, a portion of which passes through the national forest, connects the town of Anza with Hemet, roughly following the trail. *Nearby:* Mystic (Burcareli) Lake, adjacent to the San Jacinto Wildlife Area, was described by Anza (1774). At Lake Perris SRA the Bernasconi Pass was used from Burcareli Lake to Alessandro Valley. Santa Ana River Cross-

ing (California Register of Historic Landmarks), the narrows near the Union Pacific bridge, in Martha McLean–Anza Narrows Park in Riverside, is a crossing of both expeditions and the New Year's Eve campsite (1775–76).

14. SAN GABRIEL MISSION. Mission San Gabriel Arcángel (1771), a destination and place of rest for both expeditions, was the fourth in the chain of twenty-one California missions. Anza visited the first San Gabriel Mission site on his first trip and the current site on the colonizing expedition. Construction of the present mission (NRHP) was begun in 1792 and completed in 1805. It is administered by the Claretian fathers. *Nearby:* In El Monte, the Whittier Narrows Nature Center and trailhead is near the site of the original San Gabriel Mission. (A plaque marks the location at San Gabriel Boulevard and Lincoln in Montebello.) In Los Angeles, El Pueblo de Los Angeles Historic Monument includes the Plaza, Olvera Street, Avila Adobe Museum, and other historic buildings. One of the first settlers of El Pueblo de la Reina de Los Angeles was Vicente Féliz, an Anza expedition member whose wife had died in childbirth at La Canoa, the first night out from Tubac; at Elysian Park, a plaque (California Register of Historic Landmarks) interprets the Portolá crossing of the Los Angeles River at the site of the Broadway Bridge, which is believed to have been the crossing point of the Anza party as well; Griffith Park is part of the original land grant of an Anza party member, José Vicente Félix; Sepulveda Basin encompasses about a four-mile segment of the route along the Los Angeles River; and at Exposition Park, the Natural History Museum of Los Angeles County offers exhibits of American Indian culture.

15. SANTA MONICA MOUNTAINS NATIONAL RECREATION AREA (SAMO). A small portion of the historic route and portions of the recreational retracement route are within SAMO. The park also includes the Satwiwa Native American Indian Natural Area, the Native American Culture Center, Rancho Sierra Vista, and a visitor center, with many areas of the park overlooking the historic route (U.S. Highway 101). *Nearby:* Malibu Creek State Park is the site of an annual reenactment of the February 22, 1776, ride and encampment and preserves a landscape similar to that of the time. At Thousand Oaks is the Oakbrook Park Chumash Indian Interpretive Center. Ventura has the Olivas Adobe; the Channel Islands National Park, which interprets the Chumash; and Mission San Buenaventura, the ninth mission (1782). Located on the historic corridor are San Buenaventura State Beach, Emma Wood SP, Hobson and Faria County Parks, and Rincon County Beach Park.

16. SANTA BARBARA MISSION. The "Queen of the Missions" (1765, NRHP) was completed in 1820 and is one of the best-

preserved missions, offering information on the Chumash Indians. *Other attractions:* Santa Barbara Museum of Natural History; Historic Adobes. El Presidio de Santa Barbara SHP encompasses the site of the original presidio (1782, NRHP) and interprets life in California under Spanish rule. Many of the original garrison were members of the Anza expedition. *Nearby:* Chumash Painted Cave; Goleta Beach County Park, the site of one of Chumash villages of Mescalitan; Ocean Beach County Park, where an expedition camp was located at the mouth of the Río de Santa Rosa (now Santa Ynez River). Other state beaches and county parks along the original route include El Capitan, Refugio, Gaviota, and Point Sal State Beach Parks and Arroyo Burro, Goleta, and Ocean County Beach Parks. West of Buellton, La Purisíma Mission (1787, reconstructed 1820) SHP interprets Spanish colonial history.

17. **MISSION SAN LUÍS OBISPO DE TOLOSA.** The original mission (1772) was visited by the expedition (March 2–3, 1776). Anza became godfather to an Indian boy who was christened during the stay. Under Franciscan administration, the mission (NHL, California Register of Historic Landmarks) serves as a parish church. *Other attracitons:* Dallidet Adobe in Cuesta Canyon County Park and Stagecoach Road, a bicycle road along San Luis Creek, which was the probable route of the expedition. *Nearby:*

The Guadalupe–Nipomo Dunes Preserve (NHL) contains the dunes and Oso Flaco Lake, which are referenced in the expedition diaries. The pristine coastal dunes and wetlands in the area contain at least eighteen species of rare, endangered, or sparsely distributed plants, and more than two hundred birds live in or migrate through the preserve. Pismo Beach SP and Pismo Dunes SVRA are also located in the historic corridor.

18. **MISSION SAN ANTONIO.** Mission San Antonio de Padúa (NRHP), established by Father Junípero Serra, became the third California mission (1771). Located in the midst of Fort Hunter Liggett, the setting generally looks much as it did when seen by Anza and his emigrants. It serves as a seminary for the Franciscan order and is open to the public. *Nearby:* Lake San Antonio RA has scenery similar to what was experienced by the expedition. The San Lorenzo County Park Agricultural and Rural Life Museum is in King City, and Mission Nuestra Señora de la Soledad (1791) is in Soledad.

19. **CARMEL MISSION.** Mission San Carlos Borromeo de Carmelo (founded in Monterey in 1770 and moved to Carmel in 1771) was the second mission in the California chain and home to Serra, who went to Monterey to greet Anza and bring him back to the mission (NHL) for a rest. *Nearby:* Point Lobos State Reserve.

20. **MONTEREY STATE HISTORIC PARK.** The seven-acre site

preserves the historical and architectural heritage of old Monterey. The landing site of Sebastián Vizcaíno (1602), and later of Father Serra, is located near the park. The Presidio of Monterey (1770) was the northern outpost of the Spanish empire. Anza left his colonists here while he recovered his health at Carmel Mission and scouted San Francisco Bay. The Royal Presidio Chapel was built in 1794. *Other attractions:* The Monterey Bay Aquarium. *Nearby:* Toro County Park.

21. SAN JUAN BAUTISTA MISSION/SAN JUAN CANYON HISTORIC DISTRICT. The Anza party passed near the site of the mission (1797), which has been in almost continuous use since its dedication. The historic district contains prehistoric sites relevant to study of the way native societies organized themselves and historic sites connected with the mission. *Nearby:* In Gilroy, Uvas Creek Park Preserve encompasses an area passed by the expedition; Chitactac-Adams Heritage County Park, near Uvas Creek, commemorates an Ohlone village. In San Jose, first site of El Pueblo de San José, is a state landmark monument that recognizes Moraga's arrival with fourteen settlers to found California's first civil settlement. Also in San Jose, the Luís María Peralta Adobe; the Plaza de Caesar Chavez; St. Joseph Cathedral; and San Jose Historical Museum. In Santa Clara stands Mission Santa Clara de Asís (1777). Parks found in the trail's corridor include Rancho

San Antonio County Park, De Anza Park, Mountain View Shoreline Park, Sunnyvale Bayland County Park, and Henry W. Coe SP, which has a landscape that can still be recognized from the expedition journals.

22. EL CAMINO RÉAL. Thought to be the historic route of the Anza expedition from Palo Alto to San Bruno Mountain, the full length of the road, from San Diego to San Francisco, is commemorated as the road between the missions and is marked with mission bells. *Nearby:* Parks and scenic areas found within the trail's corridor include Coyote Point County RA, San Mateo Bayside Park, Burlingame Waterfront Park, Lake Merced and Harding Park, Golden Gate Park, and Mountain Lake.

23. MISSION DOLORES. Mission San Francisco de Asís (NRHP)—commonly known as Mission Dolores—was sited by Anza and his scouting party. Construction began on June 27, 1776, and was completed in 1791, making it the oldest intact building in San Francisco. José Joaquín Moraga is buried in a tomb next to the altar.

24. GOLDEN GATE NATIONAL RECREATION AREA/PRESIDIO OF SAN FRANCISCO. This site was the goal of the expedition. Anza came to establish a Spanish presence on San Francisco Bay, and he succeeded. The presidio (NRHP, NHL), founded by Anza's colonists under the command of Lieutenant Moraga (September 16, 1776), became the northern-

most permanent outpost of Spain. The site, containing a portion of the original commandant's quarters and subsurface remains of the Spanish-Mexican period presidio, has been managed by the NPS since the fall of 1994.

25. **JOHN MUIR NATIONAL HISTORICAL SITE.** Located within the grounds of the naturalist's home and gravesite in Martinez is the Vicente Martinez Adobe (1848), home of Moraga's great-granddaughter. The adobe offers the opportunity to interpret the passage of the Anza expedition and the subsequent Spanish and Mexican periods. *Nearby:* San Leandro Memorial Park; Coyote Hills Regional Park offers interpretation of the Ohlone culture. To the south in Oakland, Mills College offers an overlook of the historic route and bay.

FLOWER-ING DOGWOOD

From April through June flowering dogwood trees glitter in the filtered light of the woodlands.

Overmountain Victory National Historic Trail

The Overmountain Victory National Historic Trail (OVNHT) commemorates the fourteen-day march of frontier militias from Virginia, North Carolina, and today's Tennessee to Kings Mountain.* There on October 7, 1780, the patriot army composed of rugged individualists with no formal training and

*Material in this section is taken from the National Park Service's *Overmountain Victory National Trail Comprehensive Management Plan.*

armed with squirrel rifles joined local militias in South Carolina to engage and defeat the British loyalists. News of this decisive victory revived the spirits of the fledgling nation and strengthened the conviction that the war could be won. Considered a turning point in the American Revolutionary War, the battle of Kings Mountain set into motion events that eventually culminated in the surrender of the British at Yorktown just one year later.

ADMINISTERING AGENCY
National Park Service, Southeast Support Office
Atlanta Federal Center
1924 Building
100 Alabama Street SW
Atlanta, GA 30303
770-760-1668

FURTHER INFORMATION
Overmountain Victory Trail Association
c/o Sycamore Shoals State Historic Area
1651 West Elk Avenue
Elizabethton, TN 37643

ESTABLISHED
1980

APPROXIMATE MILEAGE
300 miles (485 km)

STATES
Virginia, Tennessee, North Carolina, South Carolina

After five years of being stalemated in the northern colonies, England turned its military strategy toward conquest of the South.* In May 1780 British Gen. Charles Cornwallis defeated a large American army at Charleston. Convinced that southern Whigs would flock in droves to the loyalist camp if British strength were shown, Cornwallis ordered Maj. Patrick "Bull Dog" Ferguson as inspector of militia in the southern provinces to foray into the Carolinas to recruit followers to the king's cause. That summer, the energetic Ferguson, a renowned marksman and inventor of an improved breech-loading rifle, and his provincial corps of American loyalists began to hunt out and harass "rebels" who continued to resist British authority.

Ranging over the Carolina upcountry, Ferguson's regiment engaged in small military actions against patriot militia regiments and "overmountain" (over-the-mountain) men who hailed from west of the Blue Ridge, from the valleys of the Watauga, Holston, and Nolichucky Rivers in the present states of North Carolina, Tennessee, and Virginia. These small, remote frontier settlements, established only a few years before, were all but independent of the royal authority to

*Though King's Mountain was the spelling first used for the site, the National Park Service has standardized the spelling as Kings Mountain, and that is the form we use here.

which the eastern colonies were subject.

In late summer of 1780 some units of overmountain men who had been resisting the loyalists retired to their homes to rest and regain their strength. By then the British held Georgia and most of South Carolina. Knowing that the Continental army had suffered many important and disappointing defeats, Cornwallis devised a strategy he hoped would sweep the South and carry the war into Virginia, where he planned to crush the American Revolution. In a three-pronged attack through the Carolinas, his right wing on the east would march along the coast to secure supply lines; Cornwallis himself would command the main army in the center and drive through North Carolina to Virginia; and the western wing, commanded by Ferguson, would protect Cornwallis from those feisty overmountain men.

But after taking post in Gilbert Town, a small hamlet near the present-day city of Rutherfordton in North Carolina, Ferguson made a critical mistake. He paroled Sam Phillips and gave him a message to deliver to his fellow overmountain men. Ferguson arrogantly promised the "backwater men," as he called them, that if they did not desist from their opposition to the British arms, he would "march his army over the mountains, hang their leaders, and lay their country waste with fire and sword."

It was a threat that galvanized

the overmountain people. In the rich interior expanses of meadow, forest, and wilderness, they had found land like they had never known. It was their security, their purpose; it lay at the heart of their commitment. It offered them a freedom that most of them had not experienced in the past as indentured servants or as the sons and daughters of indentured servants. Perhaps their determination was partially inherited from their ancestors, the Scotch-Irish, the French Huguenots, and the German Palatines who had suffered circumstances of harsh poverty and had abandoned their hopelessness and made their way to America for personal independence and property. At any rate, when Ferguson made his threat, the overmountain men were ready to settle the matter.

Taking the initiative, hundreds of overmountain men mustered on September 25 at Sycamore Shoals on the Watauga River in the present state of Tennessee. Colonel John Sevier selected 240 men from Washington County, North Carolina (now Tennessee), and Isaac Shelby selected about the same number from Sullivan County. These North Carolinians were joined by four hundred Virginians under the command of Col. William Campbell. Colonel Charles McDowell's 160 North Carolinians from Burke and Rutherford Counties were already underway. On the march across the mountains, these units would rendezvous and join forces

SYCAMORE SHOALS

Reenactors create a fun-filled weekend each June at the annual muster at Sycamore Shoals State Historic Park in Elizabethton, Tennessee. A trail from reconstructed Fort Watauga leads to the historic shoals of the Watauga River, and a visitor center interprets America's first majority-rule system of democratic government.

with other militia units. The rest, under Maj. Charles Robertson, would remain behind to defend the home front.

Before the units broke camp at Sycamore Shoals on September 26, Rev. Samuel Doak recounted for them the saga of Gideon and the Lord, then holding his arms high, he pronounced, "Let that be your battle cry: the Sword of the Lord and of Gideon." Repeating the phrase, the men turned up Gap Creek, marching in a southerly direction. They camped in rain their first night at Shelving Rock and in snow the next night at Yellow (Roan) Mountain. But, traveling over the Blue Ridge Mountains, they moved into the warmer climate of the upper Catawba River valley of the Piedmont. Here, numbers swelled as 350 militia forces from the east under Cols. Joseph Winston and Benjamin Cleveland of Wilkes and Surry Counties joined the march.

The colonels jointly developed a unique system of command. After planning strategies together at night, a different colonel would step into the command during the day. The system of rotation continued until they reached Bedford's Hill, about a mile east of the South Mountains and west of Upper Creek. Expecting now to go into battle soon, they recognized the need to select one commander. Rain provided an excuse to delay travel, so they remained at their campsite on October 2.

McDowell had been commissioned before the others, and they liked him personally but did not support his leadership in battle. Probably not wanting to hurt his reputation, they decided to send a request to Gen. Horatio Gates, commander-in-chief in the South, to name a general officer to take command, one who could "keep a proper discipline without discussing the soldiery." To their inquiry they added, with McDowell's consent, "Colonel McDowell will wait on you with this."

With McDowell off on a four-hundred-mile round-trip, the council found it necessary to select a commander. It was decided that, since Campbell was the only officer from out of state, had tra-

veled the greatest distance, and had the largest detachment, he should take the premier position. At the same time, policy would continue to be set at the regular council meetings.

As the men grew anxious, Colonel Cleveland, "Old Round-About," announced that the enemy was "at hand," to which Shelby added, "You who desire to decline, will march three paces to the rear." When no one moved,

PERIOD COSTUME

Each September 23, visitors in Abingdon, Virginia, find members of the Overmountain Victory Association (and anyone else who would like to participate) clothed in period garb and ready to follow the Overmountain Victory National Historic Trail to Kings Mountain. In October, participants re-create the battle at Kings Mountain National Military Park. In contrast to this formal uniform, many reenactors have a "backwoodsman" appearance.

morale grew, and Shelby explained, "When we encounter the enemy don't wait for the word of command. Let each one of you be your own officer and do the best you can. If in the woods, shelter yourself and give them Indian play. The moment the enemy gives way, be on alert and strictly obey orders."

Advancing down Cane Creek, the patriots arrived at Gilbert Town on October 4, only to find that Ferguson had fled. With other ideas in mind for the overmountain men, Col. James Williams of South Carolina sent word to them there that Ferguson was headed toward a British outpost called Ninety Six. Williams secretly hoped to trick the overmountain men into capturing the outpost for South Carolina, but Col. William Lacey, also of South Carolina, learned of Williams's plan and rode off to provide warning. Finding them camped at Alexander's Ford along the Green River on October 5, Lacey further advised the patriots that Ferguson had requested reinforcements. Regretting now their costly delay at Bedford's Hill they sent in pursuit only their best men mounted on horses. Lacey heightened their spirits by setting a rendezvous point with the South Carolina patriot militia at the ranch that would later become the site of the famous battle at the Cowpens, one of the most important of the American Revolution.

After covering twenty-one miles, the marksmen reached their destination where they were joined by partisan groups in the area, including South Carolina troops under Cols. Lacey and William Hill. The duplicitous Williams, along with another faction, was reluctantly allowed to join. Then on October 5, Colonel Campbell learned that Ferguson was headed eastward toward Charlotte Town (now Charlotte). The patriot force was immediately trimmed from about 1,100 to approximately 910 mounted volunteers.* Behind them were an uncounted number on foot.

Ferguson's force of about 1,000, mostly composed of Southern, New York, and New Jersey militia, took post on Kings Mountain on October 7. The rocky, wooded spur of the Blue Ridge gave Ferguson a seemingly excellent defensive position. His second in command, Capt. Abraham DePeyster, nicknamed "the Bull Dog's Pup," did not like the choice of position but did not enter into dispute with his commander-in-chief. Ferguson, in the meantime, boasted that "All the rebels in Hell and outside" wouldn't be able to drive him off.

Through a night of pouring rain, the troops pushed on to reach the base of Kings Mountain at noon. The overmountain men

*It has been estimated that in addition to Campbell's 200, Shelby's 120, Sevier's 120, Cleveland's 110, McDowell's 90, and Winston's 60, the troops selected for battle included 100 of Lacey's, 60 of Williams's, and 50 of Graham and Hambright's to equal approximately 910 mounted volunteers.

**FERGUSON MONUMENT AND
KINGS MOUNTAIN OBELISK**

After Major Patrick Ferguson threatened to march into the mountains and lay waste the country "with fire and sword," a furious army of overmountain men defeated him at the battle of Kings Mountain, where Ferguson lost his life. A monument (left) at Kings Mountain National Military Park in South Carolina commemorates him, and an obelisk (right) commemorates the patriot participants and their victory. Camping, horseback riding, and water-related sports are available at the adjacent Kings Mountain State Park.

had now traveled over fifty miles from Green River with only a brief stop at the Cowpens where they had butchered some cattle and stripped a cornfield. Arrang-

ing themselves in a horseshoe around the mountain, they began their attack about three o'clock, taking the defenders by surprise.

From the crest, the loyalists rained down a volley of fire, but the densely wooded sides of the mountain provided the attackers with cover as they fought toward the summit. Additionally, the open crest exposed their enemy to the aim of the long rifles, also known as Pennsylvania or Kentucky rifles, carried by the squirrel hunters, Indian fighters, and marksmen of the "backwoods." Three times the overmountain men fell back under bayonet charges, but each time they rallied from below and moved up the craggy slope by taking advantage of each tree, rock, shrub, and log. The cliffs were so steep and the brush so thick that the provincials' normal tactic of firing a volley and following with a bayonet charge had to be abandoned. As a result, they relied on their bayonets throughout the engagement. The bayonet, however, proved to be a disaster for the Tories. Throughout the "sulphurous blaze," Ferguson's shrill whistle of command was heard again and again as he raced back and forth on his horse. An easy target, he was eventually shot and killed. With one foot caught in a stirrup, Ferguson's body was dragged across the battlefield amidst cheers of victory.

An hour after the initial attack, the white flags were raised, but the zealous and angry overmountain men continued to fight. Colonels Campbell and Shelby moved about the battlefield attempting to restrain their men from further bloodshed. Clearly Ferguson and his loyalist troops had been soundly defeated: 225 loyalists lay slain, 163 were wounded, and 716 were taken prisoners. In contrast, the patriots counted 28 of their own slain and 62 wounded.

The next morning, fearing that Cornwallis would send a force in pursuit, the patriots hastily buried dead Tories in piles under old logs and rocks and simply left enemy wounded behind. Some victors returned to their homes, while others marched their prisoners northward to turn them over to the Continental army at Hillsborough, North Carolina. There were reports of brutality

committed during the march; it was said that prisoners were shot or hacked with swords. The message being sent to loyalists was clear, and it would later be amplified by the hasty trial that followed at Biggerstaff's Old Fields.

Just outside of Gilbert Town, where earlier in the year several patriots had been killed, an outdoor trial was held in accordance with North Carolina law. On October 14, thirty-six loyalists were found guilty of "breaking open houses, killing men, turning the women and children out of doors, and burning the houses." Their sentence was death by hanging. After the ninth hanging, a halt was called, and the rest were pardoned. As a warning to other loyalists, the dead were left dangling from the giant oak known thereafter as Gallows Oak. "Would to God every tree in the wilderness bore such fruit as that," said one of the bystanders.

After the pardons, a reprieved Tory confided to Shelby that Ferguson was expecting a relief force the next morning. The patriot camp was instantly aroused and on the march, only to hear belatedly that the Tories were actually retreating after hearing of the news of Kings Mountain. Late that day, the patriots reached Quaker Meadows, where they began to disperse. The prisoners who had not escaped were exchanged for patriot prisoners.

After Kings Mountain, no one would fail to take seriously the fierce, tenacious determination and practical democracy of the people of the western waters. In a brief hour of battle, the "backwater men" had contributed significantly to the birth of a new nation. As news of the victory spread, it gave the patriots confidence that they could win. The loss of his left flank delayed Cornwallis's plan for three months. Additionally, many loyalists, hearing of the brutal fighting and the bloody march afterwards, were reluctant to enlist in the British cause. The delay gave the Continental army precious time to rally and organize a new offensive in the South. In December, Gen. Nathaniel Greene replaced Gen. Horatio Gates as the Continental army's commander of the Southern Department. Greene seized the military initiative in the Carolinas, and Cornwallis, never able to regain it, was forced to surrender at Yorktown, Virginia, a year later. The victory at Kings Mountain was, in the words of Thomas Jefferson, "the turn of the tide to success."

THE WATAUGANS

It was not until England turned her military strategy toward conquest of the South that the overmountain settlers became directly threatened by the war of the American Revolution. Functioning as small farmers, herders, and artisans, these tenacious people were determined to form a practical democracy in the West by pushing back the frontier. Their story begins with the end of the French and Indian War in 1763 when the Treaty of Paris eliminated French authority in North America. As a result, Canada and the eastern half of the Mississippi basin went under British rule, while the western half, along with the town of New Orleans, went under Spain.

For the British, this victory meant they had inherited the problems of governing the native population. King George III's proclamation of 1763 forbade settlement beyond the crest of the Appalachians and also forbade private purchase of land from American Indians. This unpopular law affected those who had already claimed territories to the west and called back any individual who had settled beyond the crest of the mountains. But speculators and hunters had already whetted the appetites of those who had heard the glowing reports of fertile valleys beyond the mountains. The line was crossed, forcing a treaty with the Cherokee in 1768 to legitimize squatters' holdings. This treaty only led to more migrations and additional spillover into lands claimed, but not occupied, by the native peoples. In a natural progression, some of the Virginia settlers penetrated the wilderness southwest along the Watauga River. Others from North Carolina moved west to avoid political pressures such as the Regulator Movement, which was a farmers' revolt against oppressive taxation. Fugitives, speculators, and a few descendants of English nobility soon followed, and many of these residents came to be known as "the Wataugans."

The first permanent settlement of record in the Watauga valley was established by William Bean in 1769. He was followed by James Robertson, who settled in the Sycamore Shoals vicinity. Robertson would eventually found Watauga (Tennessee) and also play an early role in the development of Nashville, for which he is remembered as "the father of Tennessee" and "the father of Middle Tennessee." By 1772, there were approximately seventy-five farms along the banks of the river, and neighbors were settling in adjoining valleys. Jacob Brown founded the nearby Nolichucky settlement, which would unite with Watauga in 1775. Stores were opened by Evan Shelby in the north and by John Carter, who catered to Cherokee hunters and migrants floating down the Holston River to Natchez (NTNST).

As illegal residents, the Wataugans were ordered by the British to leave. It is said that Wataugan Daniel Boone persuaded his fellow overmountain men to stay, saying, "Now's the time to keep the country." In a strategic move, Wataugans asked for and received a delay until their crops were in and used the time to arrange a lease with the Cherokees. Brown followed with a similar lease arrangement for a section of the Nolichucky. Later, to no avail, the Cherokee lodged a complaint that all of their chiefs were not present for the deal. But by this time, the British had already conceded and agreed with the Wataugans that they could stay.

As a direct result, the settlers formed the Watauga Association in May 1772, the first form of government in the overmountain country—and essentially the first free and independent community on the continent. Although their constitution and records of government have since perished, a clue to their nature can be found in the Cumberland Compact, which was signed in Nashville in 1780. Similarities are likely, since it was influenced by James Robertson, who had participated in the early Watauga Association court and was also a leader of the Cumberland migrants.

Under the association, the overmountain residents formed their own militia; conducted negotiations with the Cherokee, British, and royal governments of Virginia and North Carolina; and selected five commissioners to represent their interests. Two quiet years followed, but a continual flow of migration into the valley created tensions with the Cherokee. Robertson was among the two ambassadors who succeeded in preventing a Cherokee attack and in undermining a Cherokee alliance with the Shawnee that was designed to stop advancing migration in the Ohio

Valley. Without the Cherokee, the Shawnee surrendered all claims below the Ohio, opening central Kentucky to settlement. This defeat challenged the Cherokee to sell their land on the Kentucky River in hopes of turning the white migration west.

At the 1775 Treaty of Sycamore Shoals, the largest private purchase of land in American history occurred. The Transylvania Company, in collaboration with Daniel Boone, secured some 20 million acres of land, including the watersheds of the Cumberland River and the southern half of Kentucky. Also purchased was a corridor through the Cumberland Gap, which secured a path between Transylvania and Holston settlements, including Carter's Valley, which was deeded to Boone. In a separate negotiation, the Wataugans bought their leased lands and more, and Jacob Brown purchased lands on the Nolichucky. At Sycamore Shoals, an impassioned speech by the Cherokee chief Dragging Canoe failed to convince the council not to sell their land. Dragging Canoe said that other nations who had yielded to the land hunger of the whites had "melted away like balls of snow before the sun." Nonetheless, the 1775 Treaty of Sycamore Shoals did not change the fact that the Proclamation Line of 1763 made the land purchase illegal. Eventually the Transylvania Company lost the vast holdings acquired in this illegal purchase, but events in the East connected with the Revolutionary War aided the Wataugans in their fight to hold onto their land.

After the first Continental Congress denied the authority of the British Parliament to tax the colonies, a clash took place at Lexington and Concord. This full-scale Revolutionary conflict occurred only one month after the Wataugans had signed their land treaty. Two factors would be significant for the Wataugans in determining their allegiance in the war. First, a war with Britain would mean that the Wataugan border settlements might be attacked by the Cherokee, who were expected to side with the British. Second, a British defeat could legalize their recent land purchase. Considering these factors, the settlers of Watauga and Nolichucky met in the fall of 1775 and declared for the American cause.

As expected, the Cherokee aligned with the British in January 1776. With Dragging Canoe ready to chase the immigrants back over the mountain, the British called for the settlers' voluntary removal. Remembering their previous strategic success with delays, the Wataugans asked for and received additional time. Quickly moving into action, they appealed to the East for help, built Fort Watauga near the Sycamore Shoals, and began construction at Fort Lee on the Nolichucky frontier. In Virginia, Fincastle County responded with supplies of lead and powder, which helped the Wataugans raise a company of men who were stationed between the Cherokee and the community.* Meanwhile, a British invasion of Charleston caused some of the settlers' riflemen to leave and join a regiment in South Carolina.

The Cherokee attack was stopped at Fort Watauga as well as other areas, but it was the subsequent campaign of retaliation by the Virginians, Carolinians, and Georgians that eliminated the Cherokee threat. These overwhelming forces caused the Cherokee to flee into the hills while their homes were razed and their stock and goods seized. The Cherokee never fully recovered from this war, and two generations later, they faced forced evacuation to the west, an event known as the Trail of Tears. (See the chapter on the Trail of Tears National Historic Trail.)

The Cherokee attack caused the Wataugans to recognize the weakness caused by isolation, and they soon turned to North Carolina for annexation. On July 5, the day after the declaration of American independence, the Wataugans approved a petition that put an end to their own independence. The settlers' petition for annexation was approved, with the understanding that the West would remain loyal to the patriot cause and that North Carolina would recognize the land holdings of the Wataugans. The annexed land, comprising most of present-day Tennes-

*Fincastle County of southwestern Virginia no longer exists.

see, was the Washington District for the commander of the American military forces. John Carter was selected chairman of district militia and was sent as a senator to North Carolina's first legislature. James Robertson, named Indian agent to the Cherokees for North Carolina, consequently left Watauga. After resigning in 1778, he led a colony of settlers on the Cumberland River and founded Nashborough. In 1777, the legislature authorized a road survey, which led to the construction of a road across the Roan–Yellow Mountains through Carver's Gap, allowing more settlers to emigrate west, particularly the soldiers who had seen the land during the Cherokee War.

Renegade Indian problems with Dragging Canoe and dissidents from other tribes located on the Chickamauga Creek continued. The "Chickamaugans" were encouraged by the British to burn cabins of border settlers. A settlers' expedition, led by Col. Evan Shelby in 1779, resulted in seizure of the area and of British supplies and pushed the tribes further down the Tennessee River. This was the same year that the British turned their attention to the South, and Watauga became a patriot refuge and a place to sequester loyalist prisoners.

When Ferguson issued his call for the overmountain people to take an oath of loyalty to the king, their answer become history. Upon receiving Ferguson's message, Isaac Shelby, Evan's son, rode to Nolichucky to John Sevier's. The two colonels conferred at Shelby's Fort, deciding that a strong offense was the best defense. They ordered their captains to muster their companies at Sycamore Shoals on September 25, 1780, and the historic battle at Kings Mountain took place two weeks later.

After Kings Mountain, the Wataugans fought both the British and Indians to the war's conclusion. Further Cherokee losses led to continued migration into Kentucky via the Cumberland Gap. In 1784, North Carolina passed an Act of Cession, which offered to turn over its lands west of the Appalachians to the United States. Angry that the transfer was advanced without consent, the Wataugans, led by Sevier, and their neighbors decided to form a separate and distinct state, but Franklin, meaning "Freeland," lasted only four years and was never recognized by Congress or by North Carolina. When

North Carolina repealed the Act of Cession, a dispute over jurisdiction erupted. North Carolina triumphed when Sevier and his followers were defeated in 1788 at the battle of Franklin. Taken prisoner, Sevier was eventually released in 1789 after charges against him were dropped. Franklin was again ceded to the United States in 1790, but a step had been taken toward territorial status and eventual statehood. Later, Sevier became the first governor of Tennessee, where the spirit and tradition of Watauga and Franklin lived on through his influence and that of Robertson. The two men helped draft the Tennessee constitution with a young attorney named Andrew Jackson, who would become Sevier's successor and eventually the nation's president. Isaac Shelby was a leader at the convention to write Kentucky's constitution, and he became that state's first governor.

The Trail Today

Each fall men and women make their way to Kings Mountain in a reenactment of the overmountain victory march.* The reenactments first began in 1975 as a celebration of the bicentennial of the American Revolution. That year, descendants of patriots and loyalists alike carried petitions for the creation of the

*Material in this section is taken from the National Park Service's *Overmountain Victory National Trail Comprehensive Management Plan.*

Overmountain Victory National Historic Trail. Five years later, in 1980, just before the two hundredth anniversary of the October 7 battle, Congress approved the National Historic Trail designation.

Cooperative efforts of the National Park Service, the U.S. Forest Service, the U.S. Army Corps of Engineers, the Overmountain Victory Trail Association (OVTA), state and local governments, citizens' associations, and historical societies have led to the development, protection, and interpretation of the trail that led the way to a major victory in our nation's struggle for independence.

Trail designations include a popular motor route, the route used each year by the OVTA, and the historic route, which is at times inaccessible. The motor route follows much of the historic route, and in many cases, the roads are identical to those used in reenactment marches of the Overmountain Victory Trail Association. The main route is from Abingdon, Virginia, to Kings Mountain National Military Park in South Carolina. The Wilkes-Surry branch from Elkin, North Carolina, leads to the main branch near Morganton, North Carolina.

Because the historical march to Kings Mountain was a one-time event that lasted only fourteen days and took place over two hundred years ago, little authoritative information remains to help establish the exact route of the patriots. Also, the initial force of overmountain men was supplemented by additional volunteers from local mustering sites all along the primary route. As a result, the officially designated Overmountain Victory National Historic Trail focuses on the primary southward route taken through Virginia, Tennessee, and North Carolina to Kings Mountain, South Carolina. This route was generally prescribed by the National Trails System Act: "from

the mustering point near Abingdon, Virginia, to Sycamore Shoals (near Elizabethton, Tennessee); from Sycamore Shoals to Quaker Meadows; from the mustering point in Surry County, North Carolina, to Quaker Meadows; and from Quaker Meadows to Kings Mountain, South Carolina."

To identify the route, a study team relied on the 1881 account of the march by historian Lyman C. Draper in *King's Mountain and Its Heroes.* Draper's work and supporting manuscripts represent the only available source of primary authoritative research. However, Draper only identifies certain points on the trail. Other trail segments are the subject of conjecture. Such segments were plotted by the study team after consulting old maps of the territory and considering suitability of the terrain for passage by an army. Many other people in the study area, including local historians and descendants of battle participants, furnished valuable information about the location of historical roads and trail traces. The detailed route identified is, therefore, considered the most probable route on the basis of authoritative research and terrain conditions.

Beginning in Abingdon, Virginia, at a muster site on Wolf Creek, the trail moves southward through the Great Knobs and into the Watauga and Holston Valleys east of the Tennessee Valley Authority's South Holston Lake. In Tennessee, the route proceeds southward through the Holston Valley and across the South Fork of the Holston River at Bluff City. Veering to the southeast through steep, forested slopes of the Great Knobs and past scattered valley farmlands and houses, the trail continues to Sycamore Shoals State Historic Area in Elizabethton. The course continues south through Roan Mountain State Park and past private farms before crossing a small section of the Cherokee National Forest on the Tennessee–North Carolina line.

The route in North Carolina assumes a general Y shape, with segments extending from the North Carolina state line in Avery County to Morganton and from the Surry County western boundary to Morganton. From Morganton the trail passes briefly into Polk County just before Green River, to Sandy Plains, and then back into Rutherfordton before entering South Carolina. The main western route proceeds from the North Carolina–Tennessee state line in Avery County through a small section of the Pisgah National Forest over Roan Mountain through Yellow Mountain Gap, crossing the Appalachian National Scenic Trail.

The historic route taken by the troops splits at Grassy Creek in Spruce Pine. Campbell's unit crossed Gillespie Gap into Turkey Cove and down the Catawba, joining up with the others at the Linville River. Shelby and Sevier took their men through Heffner Gap to North Cove. After crossing Linville Mountain, they picked up the Linville River below its gorge and followed it to the Catawba River. United again, Campbell, Shelby, and Sevier proceeded along the Catawba to Quaker Meadows. Taking this into account, the motor route crosses the Appalachian Trail, and then it proceeds over private lands and across the Blue Ridge Parkway National Scenic Byway at Gillespie Gap, where the trail splits. The western and eastern routes continue through the Blue Ridge Mountains, with the eastern leg crossing a small section of the Pisgah National Forest over Linville Mountain. The two routes rejoin in the area of Lake James, a hydroelectric and recreational reservoir, and the trail continues eastward from Lake James to Quaker Meadows, a floodplain area on the Catawba River on the west side of Morganton.

The eastern fork of the Overmountain Victory Trail begins at Elkin in Surry County, North Carolina, and continues along the north bank of the Yadkin River through Wilkesboro and North Wilkesboro. The trail passes through the U.S. Army Corps of Engineers' W. Kerr Scott Reservoir, a lake available for public recreation. Proceeding southwest, the trail passes through Lenoir, North Carolina, to Quaker Meadows in Morganton. This seventy-mile branch is mainly rural, with railroads and highways closely following much of the trail. From Quaker Meadows, it proceeds southward through farmlands and small roadside communities into the vicinity of two landmark elevations: Pilot Mountain, which lies on a plain above Cane Creek, and Marlin's Knob, which lies lower down Cane Creek, almost at its confluence with the second Broad Brook. The trail moves southward through Rutherfordton to the North Carolina–South Carolina state line through Chesnee, South Carolina, into Cowpens National Battlefield Site, finally moving eastward through level Piedmont farmlands to Gaffney, then down to Broad Brook and across to Kings Mountain National Military Park.

This overall route of the Overmountain Victory National Historic Trail passes through an area encompassing the eastern Appalachian and western Piedmont regions. Agriculture and the manufacture of textiles, furniture, and lumber products dominate the area. Mining and tourism also play a significant role in the northwest section of the trail. Metropolitan cities of the region include Bristol, Virginia-Tennessee; Kingsport, Tennessee; Asheville, Charlotte, Gastonia, and Statesville, North Carolina; and Greenville and Spartanburg, South Carolina. Principal towns along the route include Abingdon, Virginia; Elizabethton, Tennessee; North Wilkesboro, Wilkesboro, Lenoir, Morganton,

and Rutherfordton, North Carolina; and Gaffney, South Carolina. These towns are linked by major highways.

Portions of the trail cross over federal lands, including Cherokee National Forest in Tennessee; Pisgah National Forest, the Blue Ridge Parkway National Scenic Byway, and W. Kerr Scott Reservoir in North Carolina; and Cowpens National Battlefield and Kings Mountain National Military Park in South Carolina. The historic and reenactment routes also cross rights-of-way associated with the Appalachian National Scenic Trail on the North Carolina and Tennessee border. Nonfederal public lands along the route are found in Tennessee and include Sycamore Shoals State Historic Area, Roan Mountain State Park, and a small riverside city park in Bluff City. On nonfederal lands, the historic route passes through contrasting scenes of urban and agricultural developments, highways, railroads, and forested mountains. Historical remnants relating to the Overmountain Victory Trail include two traces of road ruts extending about seventy-five feet in combined length, numerous area locations, a number of graves, and a few structures. Several other historic sites are within the location of the route, many relating indirectly to the 1780 overmountain march. The National Park Service has certified a number of official sites and trail segments.

Points of Interest

VIRGINIA

1. CRAIG'S (AKA DUNN'S) MEADOWS. This was the muster site for the Washington County, Virginia, militia en route to Kings Mountain. A branch of Wolf Creek flows through this grassy meadow in Abingdon, Virginia, which was founded (1778) at the junction of two Indian trails where Daniel Boone had camped some years before. Known as a handicraft center, the town is also the site of a tobacco market (November) and tobacco festival (September). *Nearby:* In Chilhowie, the gravesite of Col. William Campbell is a Virginia Historic Landmark (NRHP).

TENNESSEE

2. PEMBERTON OAK. The massive oak at this certified NHT site (NRHP) east of Bristol is thought to be over five hundred years old: it was a mustering point for those joining the overmountain patriot forces. A Daughters of the American Revolution (DAR) commemorative plaque is embedded in its trunk. Bristol, located on the Virginia-Tennessee border, evolved as a city after its founder, Evan Shelby, built a stockade there (1776). Daniel Boone and others bartered at the fort and helped plan the campaign that ended at Kings Mountain. *Other attractions:* Bristol International Raceway is home to the NASCAR

Material in this section is taken from the National Park Service's *Overmountain Victory National Trail Comprehensive Management Plan.*

circuit, and Appalachian Music Days take place each year in early June.

3. FORT WOMACK. This fort, sited on private land in Bluff City, was used to protect the overmountain people from Indian attacks.

4. CHOATES FORD. The ford, also in Bluff City, was used by the overmountain men to cross the South Holston River on the old Watauga Road that led from Abingdon to Sycamore Shoals.

5. ROCKY MOUNT. Located at this certified NHT site in Piney flats is the beautifully restored (NRHP) Cobb-Massengill home (1770) with museum, visitor center, interpretive exhibits, and living-history tours. William Cobb is said to have outfitted over nine hundred of the overmountain men who are believed to have camped here (September 24, 1780). The site became the capital of the Southwest Territory (1790–92), and the home was on the old stagecoach road that led from Abingdon. *Nearby:* Tipton-Haynes Historical Site in Johnson City marks the site of the battle of the Lost State of Franklin, a siege by the forces of John Sevier (first and only governor of Franklin) against the farm of Col. John Tipton, a North Carolina militia leader. The battle (1788) led to the demise of Franklin. Each year the second week in September a reenactment of the battle is held. Hot-air balloons take visitors above the trail. Tobacco auction market offers public viewing on weekdays from

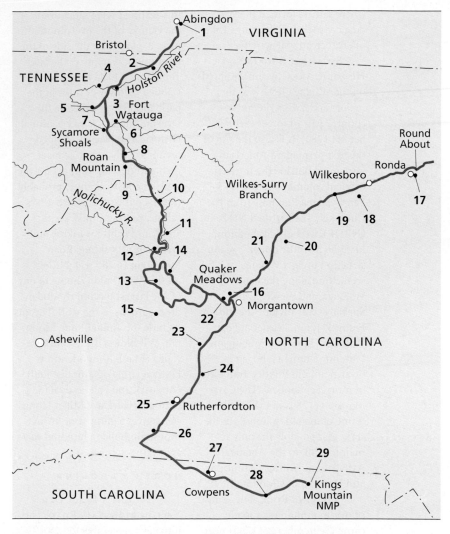

OVERMOUNTAIN VICTORY NATIONAL HISTORIC TRAIL

late November to January. TVA's Boone and Fort Patrick Henry Lakes offer water sports, and Buffalo Mountain and Winged Deer Parks offer miles of hiking. Davy Crockett Birthplace SP is outside Limestone.

6. **FORT WATAUGA HISTORIC MONUMENT.** An outpost against Indian attacks for settlers in the Watauga region, the original historic site west of Elizabethton is commemorated by a DAR stone monument with an interpretive marker on a small, steeply banked hill. *Other attractions:* Elizabethton Courthouse has a bronze slab in front that marks the spot

where settlers formed the Watauga Association; Watauga Lake offers recreational activities.

7. SYCAMORE SHOALS STATE HISTORIC AREA. Sycamore Shoals on the Watauga River was the major rendezvous site for upcountry patriot forces (September 25, 1780). It is also the site of the first permanent American settlement outside the thirteen original colonies and the 1775 Pennsylvania Purchase from the Cherokee. The certified NHT site (NRHP), west of Elizabethton, includes a visitor center, a reconstruction of Fort Watauga, a scenic trail along the banks of the Watauga, and picnic facilities. Special events include the Indian Festival (June), Muster at Fort Watauga (June), the Wataugans Outdoor Drama (July), and Overmountain Victory Trail Celebration (September). The Carter Mansion (1780) in Elizabethton is one of the oldest houses in the state, and possibly the only remaining link to the Watauga Association. *Nearby:* Gatlinburg and Great Smoky Mountain NP.

8. SHELVING ROCK. The army of overmountain men made camp (September 26, 1780) near this rock and used the shelter of its overhanging ledge to store their powder and supplies during the rainy night. A DAR marker commemorates the site but is located on a blind curve and motorists cannot safely stop; Roan Mountain SP (ANST).

9. ROAN MOUNTAIN STATE PARK. A stone monument at the entrance of the visitor center of this certified NHT site honors the victory of the overmountain men. A plaque on the side of the monument recognizes the late Tom Gray, a local man who developed wildflower trails in the park and helped conceive the Overmountain Victory National Historic Trail. He also helped organize early march reenactments to develop support for the trail. The historic route probably traversed the park, which offers cabins, campgrounds, picnic areas, and trails for hiking and cross-country skiing. Roan Mountain (6,285 feet, NRNL) is on the ANST and is home to one of the largest natural rhododendron gardens in the world. Events include the annual Roan Mountain Wildflower Tours and Birdwalks (May), Rhododendron Festival (June), Naturalist Rally (August), and Fall Festival (September). The Dave Miller Homestead gives a glimpse of life in a mountain holler a hundred years ago.

NORTH CAROLINA

10. BRIGHT'S TRACE OLD YELLOW MOUNTAIN ROAD. The journey (September 27–28) followed a local footpath called Bright's Trace across Yellow Mountain and Roan Mountain down Roaring Creek and the North Toe River to the place of a settler named Bright. The men made camp at a spring flowing into Roaring Creek. The Yellow Mountain segment involves a small section of the Cherokee and Pisgah National Forests in North

Carolina and Tennessee and follows a portion of the ANST. Today only two traces of the Yellow Mountain Trail are visible. One set of road ruts extends (about fifty feet) up a moderate slope in a northwesterly direction not far from the edge of U.S. Highway 19E about 4.4 miles northeast of Spruce Pine. *Nearby:* Boone, North Carolina, is named for the legendary Daniel Boone, who had a cabin in the area (1760s). *Horn in the West* outdoor drama (held each summer) brings Daniel Boone's story to life; Hickory Ridge Homestead (on the grounds of the same complex) offers hands-on activities reflecting the Appalachian Mountain culture; the Appalachian Cultural Museum exhibits and interprets the people and crafts; an Appalachian Summer (July) arts festival is held annually at Appalachian State University. Other recreation opportunities in the area include rafting on the Nolichucky, New, and Watauga Rivers and the Upper and Lower Wilson's Creek and hiking the ANST.

11. **Davenport Springs.** The army made its way to Davenport's place, now on private land, where they rested by the spring (September 28). While the exact location of the spring is unknown today, it is said a period sword was found there (1850). John Sevier's brother Robert was buried in the Linville Falls area on October 16 after he died of wounds received at the battle of Kings Mountain. *Nearby:* Linville

Caverns and Grandfather Mountain, a United Nations International Biosphere Reserve that offers hiking and a nature museum.

12. **Grassy Creek (aka Cathey's Plantation and later Cathey's Mill).** The patriots camped here (September 28) on the south bank of the North Toe River. The historic trail splits at Grassy Creek, south of Spruce Pine. *Nearby:* The Blue Ridge Parkway National Scenic Byway passes the area, with a visitor center at the Museum of North Carolina Minerals south of Spruce Pine. Mount Mitchell SP to the southwest near Burnsville contains the highest mountain peak (6,684 feet) east of the Mississippi and has a lookout tower and picnic area. Asheville's many attractions include the Biltmore Estate (NHL), the largest private residence in America. George Vanderbuilt commissioned Frederick Law Olmsted, planner of New York City's Central Park, to design the grounds with gardens that are still exquisite. Gifford Pinchot, first director of the U.S. Forest Service, began his career as a consulting forester here. The Biltmore Village, a historic area and local historic district, has shopping in restored English-style houses. See also the home of the novelist at Thomas Wolfe Memorial SHS; the University Botanical Gardens; and park headquarters for the Blue Ridge Parkway, with its Folk Art Center.

13. **Turkey Cove.** After splitting forces at Gillespie Gap in the

Blue Ridge Mountains, a portion of the army made its way to the place of Henry Gillespie and Col. William Wofford's fort in Turkey Cove, the name of the bottom-land area of Armstrong Creek, a tributary of the North Fork of the Catawba River. Under the command of Col. William Campbell, this contingent sought to gain intelligence from Gillespie. They made camp (September 29, 1780) at the fort.

14. NORTH COVE. From Gillespie Gap in the Blue Ridge Mountains, the overmountain army under Sevier, Shelby, and McDowell followed an easterly route to the confluence of Honeycutt Creek and the North Fork of the Catawba River in the area named North Cove, where they made camp (September 29, 1780).

15. JOSEPH McDOWELL HOUSE (AKA PLEASANT GARDENS). Major Joseph McDowell, cousin of Col. Charles McDowell, served as captain at Kings Mountain, leading troops from the Upper Catawba Valley. He was also renowned as an Indian fighter and statesman. This federal style house (late 1780s), now altered, is located near Marion. *Nearby:* At Nebo on North Carolina Highway 126 between Marion and Morganton is Lake James SP at the base of Linville Gorge; the park offers hiking and scenic vistas of the Black Mountain Range.

16. CHARLES AND JOSEPH McDOWELL HOUSE. The overmountain men reached the estate of Col. Charles McDowell and his brother Maj. Joseph McDowell (cousins of the Joseph McDowell of Pleasant Garden) and made camp (September 30, 1780) in the fields called Quaker Meadows. The Charles McDowell house in Morganton is not the original house, although the one that now stands in the vicinity of the original is also historical (1806, NRHP). Charles McDowell is thought to have lived in it until his death (1815). South of Morganton on North Carolina Highway 18, South Mountian SP offers camping, hiking, and horseback riding.

THE WILKES-SURRY BRANCH OF THE TRAIL

17. ROUND-ABOUT. At Ronda, this was the homesite of Col. Benjamin Cleveland under whom a small militia force moved west to join the main patriot force.

18. TORY OAK. At this certified NHT site patriots hanged five Tories during the Revolutionary War. Tours can be arranged with the Old Wilkes Walking Tour of Historic Wilkesboro. *Other attractions:* The Old Wilkes Jail where the legendary Tom Dula of "The Ballad of Tom Dooley" was imprisoned before going to the gallows (1868) and the North Wilkes Wilkesboro Speedway. *Nearby:* Rendezvous Mountain Education State Forest.

19. W. KERR SCOTT RESERVOIR. The troops under Winston and Cleveland crossed the Yadkin River at the mouth of Warrior Creek (September 28, 1780). The

area is now inundated by the U.S. Army Corps of Engineers' (1,470-acre) dam and reservoir. The park, southwest of Wilkesboro, is a certified NHT site and offers hiking, nature study, and water-sport opportunities, a visitor center, and interpretive exhibits. Roaring Gap and Stone Mountain SPS recreational activities are nearby.

20. FORT DEFIANCE. The homesite (1788) of William Lenoir, who fought at Kings Mountain under Colonel Cleveland and later rose himself to the rank of general, is in Lenoir. Not yet built in 1780, the house took the name of an old Indian fort that was standing then. Now restored, the house, which is a certified NHT site, is open to the public on a limited basis.

21. FORT CRIDER. This was the site of an old Indian lookout fort, which the men under Colonels Cleveland and Winston passed. A DAR marker commemorates the site in Lenoir. *Nearby:* Southwest of Lenoir, the Tuttle Education State Forest offers recreational opportunities.

THE MAIN BRANCH OF THE TRAIL

22. QUAKER MEADOWS. The broad floodplain meadow (NRHP) adjacent to the Catawba on the west side of Morganton is leased as a county fairground and golf course. A state historical marker and DAR monument offer interpretation. Once joined by the troops of Colonels Cleveland and Winston, the army numbered fourteen hundred. The Quaker

Meadows Cemetery contains the graves of Charles McDowell, a leading organizer of the historic march, and his brother Joseph McDowell, who fought at Kings Mountain and assumed his brother's command of militia troops from the Upper Catawba River valley. Dams on the river provide lakes for recreation.

23. BEDFORD'S HILL. This small, round hill (1,200 feet) in Dysartsville in McDowell County was a strategic military site because it commanded Cowan's Ford (aka the Upper Crossing) on Cane Creek. McDowell's troops had earlier met loyalist forces at Bedford's Hill (September 12, 1780) and an indecisive skirmish took place. British Maj. James Dunlap, one of Ferguson's officers, was wounded. News of the fight spread through the overmountain communities and among patriots in Wilkes and Surry Counties, inspiring determination to seek out British Major Ferguson at Kings Mountain.

24. CANE CREEK. The army traveled down Cane Creek (October 3), probably staying at the place of Whig (patriot) sympathizer Samuel Andrews near the base of Marlin's Knob. The next day the army learned that Ferguson had retreated from Gilbert Town to evade them. Marlin's Knob, 1,100 feet above the valley (it eventually reaches an elevation of 2,138 feet) is a prominent landmark. *Nearby:* In Rutherfordton, the New Britain Church Cemetery (the original church

was dated 1768, the present church 1852) contains a number of DAR-marked graves of patriot soldiers who fought at Kings Mountain.

25. **GILBERT TOWN.** Loyalist troops camped here several times, and patriots camped here on October 4 and again on October 11 after their victory. *Nearby:* East of Rutherfordton is Biggerstaff's Old Fields (aka Bickerstaff), where, at Shelby's insistence, a court was assembled on October 14 under North Carolina state statutes. Hastily, twelve qualified North Carolina jurors were selected, including Shelby and Cleveland. Holding court, they found thirty-six Tory prisoners guilty of criminal offenses and sentenced them to death. Nine of the prisoners were hanged on Gallows Oak before Shelby recommended that the others be pardoned. The tree is no longer standing. Chimney Rock Park offers trails, stairs, and an elevator to the summit; Hickory Nut Falls is one of the highest falls in the eastern United States. At Flat Rock, to the west, is the Carl Sandburg NHS. Farther west, near Brevard, is the Cradle of Forestry in America NHS, which consists of two interpretive trails detailing the history of U.S. forests and one of the first schools of forestry.

26. **GREEN RIVER.** Reaching Alexander's Ford on the Green River in present-day Polk County (October 5, 1780), the patriots selected seven hundred of their best men to continue. Early the next morning Colonel Lacey of South Carolina informed them of Ferguson's position and set a rendezvous point with the South Carolina patriot militia at the Cowpens.

SOUTH CAROLINA

27. **COWPENS NATIONAL BATTLEFIELD.** The army marched twenty-one miles to rendezvous with the troops at the Cowpens (October 6, 1780, raising the full complement of forces to nearly 1,100). Approximately 900 of the best armed and best mounted were selected to push on to Kings Mountain. They were followed by approximately 85 foot soldiers. The park, administered by the NPS, also commemorates a later Revolutionary War battle (1781), which helped drive British forces from the South. The certified NHT site, west of Gaffney, includes a visitor center, interpretive exhibits, and trails. *Nearby:* Spartanburg is one of the world's largest peach-shipping centers in the state's largest peach-producing county. It is also one of the South's leading manufacturing centers. A statue honoring Gen. Daniel Morgan, hero of the battle of Cowpens, stands in Morgan Square. The Walnut Grove Plantation has a nature trail and garden.

28. **CHEROKEE FORD.** Cherokee Ford was used to cross the Broad River in the early morning of October 7, 1780. It is located eighteen miles from Cowpens and is east of Gaffney. A DAR marker labels the gravesite of

Colonel Williams (located on the corner of Limestone Street and Baker Boulevard).

29. KINGS MOUNTAIN NATIONAL MILITARY PARK. Administered by the NPS, and located near I-85 on the North Carolina–South Carolina border, this is one of the largest military parks in the United States. The park commemorates the overmountain men's victory (October 7, 1780) over Ferguson. Features at this certified NHT site include a monument to battle participants, a visitor center, and self-guided interpretive trails. Horseback riding, camping, and water sports are some of the recreational activities offered at the adjacent Kings Mountain SP, east of Gaffney. *Other attractions:* Schele Museum of Natural History and Planetarium to the northeast, in Gastonia, North Carolina; Crowder's Mountain SP, which offers camping, hiking, horseback riding and mountain climbing; Ninety Six NHS, in Ninety Six, South Carolina, which was the scene of repeated confrontations between patriots and loyalists during the American Revolution.

FORT CLATSOP

Reaching the Pacific Ocean, the Lewis and Clark expedition wintered on the Oregon coast after they had built Fort Clatsop. Rangers in frontier costume at Fort Clatsop National Memorial Park interpret the Lewis and Clark experience at the reconstructed site near Astoria, Oregon.

Lewis and Clark National Historic Trail

Ocian in view! O! the joy.

WILLIAM CLARK, NOVEMBER 7, 1805

The Lewis and Clark National Historic Trail (LCNHT) commemorates the route of the Corps of Discovery's expedition from the Mississippi River to the Pacific Ocean at the mouth of the Columbia River. A deeply significant episode in the history of the United States, the eight-thousand-mile journey fired the imagination of the American people and drew their attention to the trans-Mississippi section of the country. Extending over a period of two years, four months, and nine days, the epic feat not only offered geographers excellent new materials for maps, it brought to science knowledge of many previously unknown animals and birds, including the antelope, mountain sheep, grizzly bear, mule deer, blacktail deer, prairie dog, sage grouse, Clark's crow, and Louisiana tanager. Its influence upon subsequent political acts of the United States affecting the Oregon country and international boundary lines was undoubtedly great, and it unquestionably strengthened the young country's national conviction.

ADMINISTERING AGENCY

National Park Service
Lewis and Clark National Historic Trail
700 Rayovac Drive, Suite 100
Madison, WI 53711
608-264-5610

FURTHER INFORMATION

Lewis and Clark Trail Heritage Foundation
P.O. Box 3434
Great Falls, MT 59403

ESTABLISHED

1978

APPROXIMATE MILEAGE

3,700 (5,960 kilometers)

STATES

Illinois, Missouri, Kansas, Nebraska, Iowa, South Dakota, North Dakota, Montana, Idaho, Washington, Oregon

Thomas Jefferson first proposed the exploration of
lands west of the Mississippi in
1783. Once he became president
in 1801, the opportunity to finally
translate his dream into reality
presented itself. As a scientist,
Jefferson had a curiosity about
the flora and fauna of the unknown land and the native inhabitants of the region, but beyond
that, as president, he wanted to
obtain more information about
the water routes through the area.
It seemed probable that a more
direct passage than the lengthy
and dangerous one around the
Cape Horn at the tip of South
America could be found. In 1803,
even though the territory of Louisiana was owned by the French,
Congress secretly appropriated
$2,500 for the expedition. Pass-
ports for the would-be explorers
were sought from Spain, France,
and Britain.

Jefferson selected his private
secretary, Capt. Meriwether
Lewis, First Infantry, to head the
expedition. Lewis had previously
been selected to go up the Missouri with French botanist Andre
Michaux in 1801, but he had to
forego that opportunity when the
French government directed the
botanist to withdraw. Like Jefferson, twenty-nine-year-old Lewis
felt a passion for exploring the
uncharted wilderness, mountains,
and desert that lay west of St.
Louis, the nation's farthest outpost. At last the opportunity
came. This time, he was able to
select his own partner. He chose
William Clark, younger brother

of the famed Revolutionary War
general, George Rogers Clark, as
his co-leader. Four years his
senior, Clark had served as
Lewis's commanding officer at
the battle of Fallen Timbers but
had since resigned his commission. Because the expedition
was organized as a military detachment under orders of the
secretary of war, Clark was re-
instated in the army but only as
a second lieutenant in the less
prestigious Corps of Artillery.
This gave senior rank to Lewis,
despite his objections. The for-
malities were soon forgotten,
however, with Clark even signing
his journals as "Captain."

The partnership offered com-
plementary strengths throughout
the journey. By its end, Lewis was
the accomplished analytical scientist. His preparation in Philadelphia before the expedition had
included the study of science and
medicine, and in the course of
the journey he recorded thousands of detailed descriptions of
flora and fauna in his scientific
journal and, out of necessity,
practiced medicine for the benefit
of his crew and of other peoples
along the way. At the same time,
Clark, the talented geographer,
prepared amazingly accurate
maps that he continued to update
even after the expedition. Their
friendship can readily be seen in
Clark's acceptance of his associate's proposal: "This is an immense undertaking fraited with
numerous difficulties," he wrote
Lewis in July of 1803, "but my
friend I can assure you that no

man lives with whom I would prefur to undertake and share the Difficulties of such a trip than yourself."

Days before Lewis left Washington, D.C., that July, official news reached the capital city that Napoleon Bonaparte had deeded all of Louisiana Territory to the United States for a sum of $15 million. As it turned out, the United States's attempt to purchase New Orleans came at a time when war threatened Europe and just after France had suffered a loss in its attempt to take possession of Haiti and Santa Domingo. France needed the money, and Napoleon renounced Louisiana and sold it before he could change his mind. On December 20, 1803, the United States formally took possession of the heartland of the North American continent, nearly doubling the size of the country. The vast region, totaling some 828,000 square miles, consisted of the present-day states of Arkansas, Missouri, Iowa, Minnesota west of the Mississippi, North Dakota, South Dakota, Nebraska, Oklahoma, nearly all of Kansas, the portions of Montana, Wyoming, and Colorado east of the Rocky Mountains, and Louisiana west of the Mississippi but including New Orleans.

Exploration of the newly acquired domain was now an additional duty of the Corps of Discovery, as they were called. A primary objective was to find a practical transportation link between the Louisiana Territory

A CLOSER LOOK

Hundreds of species of fish, reptiles, amphibians, mammals, birds, plants, trees, and shrubs, some completely new to the world of science, were described by Lewis and Clark.

and the Oregon country. The Oregon country had been claimed by the United States following the 1792 discovery of the Columbia River by American sea captain Robert Gray, who named the river after his ship. The corps was under orders to follow the Missouri River to its source, searching for a water route to the Pacific; to gather scientific findings about the soils, animals, plants, and minerals; and to learn about the people and geography along the way.

After celebrating the Fourth of July, 1803, in Washington, D.C., Meriwether Lewis departed the capital to begin preparations for his journey and to organize the trek. At the Harpers Ferry and

Schuykill arsenals he gathered supplies of arms and military stores, and in Pittsburgh and Philadelphia he purchased other supplies, including gifts. Eventually, after all the supplies were loaded aboard a specially designed keelboat, Lewis headed for St. Louis. He wrote in his journal that he departed "with a party of 11 hands" down the Ohio River on August 30. At Clarksville, across from Louisville, Kentucky, he joined his co-commander. The men then spent nearly two weeks in the area, where they learned a great deal about the frontier from George Rogers Clark. Their party then traveled down the Ohio and up the Mississippi, recruiting more men along the way. On December 12, they reached the site of their winter quarters.

The expedition established Camp Wood above St. Louis along the Mississippi at Wood River in present-day Illinois, just opposite the mouth of the Missouri. The camp was built there because at that time the Spanish were in control of St. Louis and would not allow the Americans to locate on the west side of the river. Besides the two leaders, the party at Camp Wood included nine Kentucky volunteers, fourteen soldiers, two French rivermen, one hunter, and Clark's black servant, York. (More boatmen and soldiers would be hired before the expedition reached the Mandan Indian villages in North Dakota the next fall.) Lewis's Newfoundland, Seaman, also accompanied the corps on their

journey. Outstanding among the recruits were John Ordway, Patrick Gass, George Drouillard, John Colter, the Field brothers, and George Shannon. While Clark ran the camp, Lewis performed other tasks in St. Louis. Late that December Clark joined Lewis in St. Louis to attend the transfer ceremonies when the upper Louisiana Territory was formally ceded to the United States.

On May 14, 1804, the expedition began its journey up the Missouri River in the fifty-five-

FORT OSAGE

Visited by Lewis and Clark in June 1804, a site near Sibley, Missouri, was noted in expedition journals as a favorable one for a military installation. In 1808, Clark returned to supervise the construction of Fort Osage, now a National Historic Landmark. Living-history interpreters at the reconstructed fort transport visitors back to busy days of frontier activity.

foot keelboat and two smaller, more maneuverable craft called "pirogues." The boats traveled against a swift current, the trip was slow and arduous, and it was often necessary to attach a line to the bow of the larger ship to be pulled by a long line of men along the shore. The expedition proceeded at a rate of approximately ten miles a day, slower than planned. After taking care of last-minute details in St. Louis, Lewis caught up with Clark and the others in St. Charles, the first permanent white settlement on the Missouri River, which had been founded in 1769 as a fur-trading post. Soon after they departed St. Charles, the party almost met disaster. Lewis, who liked to roam freely, slipped while climbing a three-hundred-foot cliff. Taking a twenty-foot fall, he barely managed to save himself.

As they moved farther north, Lewis and Clark wrote about the change of the countryside into the high prairie and recorded new species such as antelope and prairie dogs. The explorers had hoped to find the Oto and Pawnee in the area around today's Nebraska City, but because it was the Indians' hunting season they did not encounter either tribe. Just north of present-day Fort Atkinson State Historic Park in Fort Calhoun, Nebraska, beyond the mouth of the Platte River, the corps finally met with the Oto and held council on August 3, 1804. This was the first tribe to convene with the expedition. To commemorate the occasion, the site was named "Council Bluff."* When council commenced with the Oto, gifts were distributed, including the Jefferson Peace Medal, which displayed a likeness of President Jefferson on one side and two clasped hands on the other. Speeches were exchanged in which Lewis and Clark told of the Great Father in the East.

Near present-day Sioux City, Iowa, on August 20, the expedition experienced the only fatality of the entire journey. Sergeant Charles Floyd, a volunteer engineer, became ill with what experts now believe was acute appendicitis and died. A stream flowing into the Missouri near his grave was named the Floyd River in his honor. Proceeding on, the corps entered present-day South Dakota where they met and held council with the Yankton Sioux at Calumet Bluff near what is today the site of Gavins Point Dam.

At the mouth of the Teton (or

*With a slight change of name, Council Bluffs is now located on the opposite bank of the Missouri, some twenty miles further upriver in Iowa. The Oto had arrived on the Missouri River in the early 1700s, having been pushed there by more powerful tribes in the east. Their history was little more than an account of their struggles to defend themselves against more powerful peoples and of their resultant constant migration. The Oto were agriculturally oriented but supplemented their diet by seasonal hunting of game such as buffalo. By the late 1700s, they had been decimated by smallpox and a war with the Sauk and Fox, but an allied tribe of Missouri Indians had taken up residence with them by the time of the Lewis and Clark expedition.

Bad) River, they made contact with the feared Teton Sioux, holding council on September 25. Hostile actions resulted in confrontation that nearly turned to armed conflict. Clark was forced to draw his sword when several chiefs he had taken to shore insisted on keeping his canoe. Lewis brought about the swivel guns on the keelboat and sent troops ashore. Finally a chief intervened and suggested that instead of keeping the canoe the Sioux would be satisfied if the expedition remained so their women and children could meet the men. Outnumbered ten to one, the expedition was lucky that the conflict never escalated. The captains did lose several nights' sleep when they agreed to accommodate a handful of Sioux who wanted to sleep on the keelboat. The weary captains later gave their visitors some tobacco and left after they learned that this may have been an attempt to delay the group while plans were made to attack. On October 4, the expedition held council with the friendly Arikara Indians near present-day Mobridge. According to Clark, the Arikara were fascinated with York, the first black man they had seen, and examined him from "top to toe."

By October 26, the group had reached the five Villages of the Mandan near the confluence of the Knife and Missouri Rivers, over sixteen hundred miles from the expedition's starting point. Here a productive winter was spent near present-day Wash-

burn, North Dakota, with the friendly Mandan and Hidatsa Indians.*

During the winter of 1804–5, the commanders gained valuable knowledge about the countryside to the west, built three-sided Fort Mandan on the north bank of the river, and met Sacagawea, the pregnant wife of Toussaint Charbonneau. Lewis and Clark reportedly hired her husband as their French-Canadian interpreter, knowing that he would bring along his Shoshone wife, whom they believed would be a valuable member of the expedition. Sacagawea had been stolen as a child by the Hidatsa and was made a slave until she was either bought or won in a gambling game by Charbonneau. Joining the expedition with her husband, the courageous woman was noted in Lewis and Clark's report for her extraordinary service.

On April 7, 1805, a dozen men commanded by Cpl. Richard Warfington were sent back to St. Louis in the keelboat with dispatches for the president, a collection of natural specimens including five live animals, and numerous American Indian artifacts. On the same day, the main expedition of thirty-three persons continued into the un-

*The Mandans, the largest tribe in the West, totaling nearly four thousand at the time of the expedition, were nearly wiped out by a smallpox epidemic in 1837. Their descendents have since consolidated with the Hidatsa and Arikara Indians to form the Three Affiliated Tribes of North Dakota.

known West in their two pirogues and six cottonwood dugouts. This group included the two captains, three sergeants, twenty-three privates, and five civilians. Nonmilitary personnel included Charbonneau, Sacagawea, and their two-month-old child, Jean Baptiste—whose delivery had been assisted by Lewis and whom Clark would later nickname "Pomp"—Clark's black slave, York, and the interpreter and hunter, George Drewyer.

On April 26, the expedition reached the mouth of the Yellowstone River, where the men celebrated the occasion with a dram of whiskey. Lewis recorded that "this soon produced the fiddler and they spent the evening with much hilarity, singing and dancing." On June 2, they reached another large tributary and named it the Marias River after a cousin of Lewis's. There a pirogue was left behind. On June 13, Lewis heard "a roaring to tremendious to be mistaken for any cause short of the great falls of the Missouri." After leaving the other heavy pirogue behind, the group was forced to portage the remaining canoes and equipment around the expansive falls, which caused the expedition much hardship and resulted in nearly a month's delay. Two more dugout canoes were then built. Upon reaching the source of the Missouri, they named the three large forks feeding into it the Jefferson, Madison, and Gallatin Rivers for the president and two of his cabinet members who had been significant in arranging funding and support for the expedition.

Following the Jefferson, the largest of the three rivers, the expedition pressed on, eager to come in contact with the Shoshone Indians, from whom they expected to acquire horses. On August 1, Lewis decided to travel ahead with a smaller group, hoping to show their friendly intentions and desperate to trade for the horses they badly needed for the journey over the mountains. Walking west up Horse Prairie Creek, Lewis came upon the natural spring from which all the great waters of the Missouri flowed. Taking a drink, he expressed his joy: "Judge then of the pleasure I felt in all[a]ying my thirst with this pure and ice-cold water." Soon—on August 12—the group became the first white Americans to stand on the Continental Divide. Now for the first time, Pacific-bound waters would flow at their feet.

After crossing the divide, the party began to descend the western side of the mountains in present-day Idaho. There Lewis met three Shoshone women to whom he gave gifts of beads, moccasins, and pewter mirrors. The women agreed to take him to their village, but Lewis and his men were soon met by sixty armed warriors, including the Shoshone chief, Cameahwait, all "mounted on excellent horses." The small party of explorers put down their weapons, and the women "exulting shewed the presents." Judging them to be peace-

THREE FORKS

Lewis and Clark traced the Missouri to its beginnings outside what is now Three Forks, Montana. Missouri Headwaters State Park offers an excellent interpretive display, camping, picnicking, a trail to the riverbank, fishing, and boating access to the three rivers the explorers named the Jefferson, Madison, and Gallatin.

ful, the warriors bestowed the customary hugs of friendship upon the explorers. It was from these Shoshone that Lewis learned that the ocean could not be reached by way of the Salmon River.

After some prodding, twenty-eight of the Shoshone, including Chief Cameahwait, followed Lewis back to meet the others in the expedition. To everyone's astonishment, Chief Cameahwait was discovered to be Sacagawea's brother. According to journal entries, when Sacagawea recognized Cameahwait, she instantly jumped up and ran to embrace him, throwing her blanket over him and "weeping profusely." This relationship undoubtedly enhanced the expedition's ability to trade for the horses they needed so badly to cross the Bitterroot Mountains. Their camp of August 17–23 was named Camp Fortunate. Although Sacagawea could have stayed with the Shoshone, she continued on with the group, following an old Shoshone guide named Toby over Lost Trail Pass.

On September 9, more horses were purchased from helpful Flathead Indians and the corps camped at Traveler's Rest near the present town of Lolo, Montana. Here Toby informed them that they were to leave the Bitterroot River and turn west up Lolo Creek on the Nez Perce trail, known today as the Lolo Trail. After reaching Lolo Pass on September 14, they began the most difficult portion of their journey.

Lewis noted that "the men are unwell of the disentary, braking outs, or irruptions of the skin." They saw their horses give out or slip and fall down mountainsides, and they had to endure blinding snowstorms and freezing temperatures. On September 16, 1805, Clark wrote, "indeed I was at one time fearfull my feet would freeze in their mockirsons I wore." Compelled to subsist on rations of berries, candles, horses, and unpalatable dried soup, the entire party often went hungry.

After crossing the Bitterroots, the weakened expedition descended into the broad, fertile Weippe Prairie in present-day Idaho. Unknowingly, they had entered the native peoples' root-gathering grounds along the Clearwater. The camas, a member of the lily family, served the locals as an important and protected food staple. Here, another Shoshone woman came to their rescue. She had been adopted by the Nez Perce but, like Sacagawea, had been taken by another tribe when she was a child. She was either sold or traded to a white man in southern Manitoba, Canada. Although she had been treated well, she returned to her beloved Nez Perce after she learned that the white man planned to take her to Scotland. When Wet-khoo-weis (meaning "returned from a far place") learned that the explorers were in danger, she explained to her people that the visitors were like those who had helped her. As a result, the Nez Perce received the expedition graciously, gave them supplies, and told them about the river route to the Pacific. Thus began a friendly relationship between the Nez Perce and the whites that would last nearly sixty years.

Leaving their horses with the Nez Perce, the expedition departed in dugout canoes they had made of ponderosa pine and followed the Clearwater River, which they called the "Kookooskie," to the Snake, which carried them from present-day Idaho into present-day Washington. By October 16, they had reached the Columbia River at the today's Sacajawea State Park. Spirits rose with each passing mile as their mission neared completion. In fact, Clark mistakenly recorded in his journal on November 7 that he had seen the ocean: "Ocean in view! O! the joy." In actuality, he was observing the large estuary of the Columbia and his elation was short-lived. Terrible weather conditions from November 10 to 14 pinned them to the rocky shore at Point Ellice. In mid-November the storm subsided and they finally reached the Pacific Ocean, which Clark had previously noted was the "object of all our labors, the reward of all our anxieties."

After making preliminary campsites on the north shore, or Washington side, of the Columbia, the group voted to move south to a location suitable for winter quarters, where game would prove more plentiful and the land less exposed to the fury

LOCKS ON THE COLUMBIA

Traveling in greater comfort than the Corps of Discovery, passengers on the *Queen of the West* sternwheeler observe the Army Corps of Engineers' locks in the Columbia River Gorge National Scenic Area between Oregon and Washington. The boat stops at various sites along the Lewis and Clark National Historic Trail and provides onboard interpretation.

of winter storms. The names of all members of the party, including York and Sacagawea, were called out to take a vote. On December 8 timber was felled, and amid constant downpours, a stockaded outpost was built. Completed on December 30, it was named after local Indians. Fort Clatsop, nestled in a lush spruce and hemlock forest, reflected the expedition's military origin. The forest became a hive of activity; the men served on wood and guard details, in hunting parties, and in a coastal salt-making camp in the present resort town of Seaside. The leaders organized their data, and Clark prepared many of the maps, which were among the most significant contributions of the

expedition. Because the local Indians had been exposed to Europeans, they were expert at bargaining, and the expedition's gift supplies were quickly depleted. Constant rain spoiled the spirits of the company and the dampness caused in nearly everyone rheumatism, colds, and other illnesses. Lewis vigorously treated those who suffered from disease or injury.

The expedition had hoped to locate a ship that winter in order to purchase badly needed supplies and to send back to Washington news of their accomplishments, along with some of the materials gathered in their travels. Since no vessels appeared during the long, damp winter, Lewis and Clark decided without regret to abandon their outpost in early spring for the eastward journey back to the United States. On March 23, 1806, Clark wrote, "at this place we wintered and remained from 7th Decr. 1805 to this day and have lived as well as we had a right to expect." On the other hand, Patrick Gass, who became sergeant after Floyd's death, noted that there had been only six entirely clear days between November 5 and March 25.

Strengthened by the knowledge that the expedition had surmounted all previous difficulties, the men began their return trek paddling upriver. Just below the Dalles, they traded medical assistance and canoes for horses. Then the overland journey began. At the Clearwater near present-day Kamiah, Idaho, they camped for three weeks, regained their strength, and waited for the snow to melt in the high country. While there, Sacagawea gathered roots, and additional horses were collected from their highly regarded Nez Perce friends. On June 10 some of the party hunted in the area of Weippe Prairie, where the camas plants were in bloom. Then, on June 15, assuming that the snow on the high mountains had melted sufficiently, they made their first attempt to cross the Bitterroot Range. Unsuccessful, they launched a second attempt nine days later. The passage of time had reduced the snowpack by nearly four feet, and with their Nez Perce guides and sixty-six horses they successfully crossed the Bitterroots. At Traveler's Rest in the Bitterroot Valley, the party divided, with Lewis taking nine men toward the northeast and Clark taking the remainder toward the south, retracing the path of the outward-bound expedition. On July 3, 1806, Lewis recorded, "I took leave of my worthy friend and companion Cpt. Clark . . . feeling much concern on this occasion."

The Lewis party crossed the dividing ridge of the Rocky Mountains at the point now called Lewis and Clark Pass on July 7 and four days later reached the Missouri River, where they found vast herds of buffalo. In canoes made of green buffalo hides, they crossed the river to their old camp at White Bear Islands, where a cache left on the westward

SEASIDE

Cycling, skating, and all sorts of beach activities abound at End of the Trail Monument at Oregon's oldest ocean resort, Seaside, near the reconstruction of the expedition's original salt cairn.

journey was opened. Any article not damaged by the invasion of high water was taken out and hidden again. Anticipating that help would be needed with portaging, Lewis left six men to meet a group sent down the Missouri by Clark under Ordway's leadership. At present-day Three Forks, Ordway and his nine men had split from Clark and headed down river in dugout canoes.

While the others waited, Lewis and three of his men explored the Marias River. It was on this side trip that the only serious conflict with American Indians occurred. When a band of Blackfeet Indians attempted to steal the guns and horses of Lewis's party, two were killed, one by Lewis, who escaped with his horses and his men. After a long hard ride, the group met their larger party at the mouth of the Marias the next day. At this point the horses were turned loose, and the group proceeded

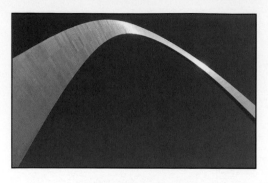

THE ST. LOUIS ARCH

Visitors ascend the 630-foot Gateway Arch which stands over the original St. Louis business district where Lewis conducted preexpedition business and postexpedition duties as governor. Now a riverfront park, the Jefferson National Expansion Memorial honors President Jefferson and the opening of the West. Underground, the Museum of Westward Expansion houses an excellent Lewis and Clark display.

down the river in canoes to rendezvous with Clark at the mouth of the Yellowstone.

On August 11, 1806, while hunting, Lewis was accidentally shot. As he described it, "a ball struck my left thye about an inch below my hip joint, missing the bone it passed through the left thye and cut the thickness of the bullet across the hinder part of my right thye; the stroke was very servere. . . . I was happy to find that it had touched neither bone nor artery." As it turned out, his nearsighted hunting companion, Cruzatte, had mistaken him for an elk! Though the wound caused a considerable amount of pain,

the captain began to heal rapidly.

In the meantime, Clark's party had followed the eastern slopes of the Bitterroots to the Beaverhead, then down that river to the Jefferson, their horses trailing all the while along the banks. From the mouth of the Jefferson, Clark's party proceeded up the Gallatin River and across the Gallatin Range. With the aid of Sacagawea, who shared her knowledge of trails and passes, they entered the valley of Yellowstone. The route down the Yellowstone was by land until the hooves of the horses became worn and tender. While canoes were being constructed, twenty-four of the horses were stolen by Indians. The main party boarded the canoes on July 24 (as it turned out that was one day before the Lewis party would have their encounter with the Blackfeet). Three of the men were detailed to trail the remaining horses along the riverbank, but eventually the Crow succeeded in stealing all the expedition's horses. On July 25, Clark climbed, signed, and named Pompeys Pillar, the now-famous landmark near the present-day town of the same name located east of Billings, Montana.

On August 12, 1806, the Lewis and the Clark parties were reunited, and Clark took command while Lewis recovered from his wound. They pushed on by canoe down the Missouri to Fort Mandan, which was reached on August 14. Spending only three days at their former winter quarters, they traveled on, reduced in number by four. The French interpreter Charbonneau and his family remained behind and so did the trapper John Colter. When the group arrived in St. Louis on September 23, 1806, the townspeople flocked to the banks of the Mississippi to greet them.

The journey was thus brought to a close but it opened a gateway for further exploration and development. Lieutenant Zebulon (Zeb) Pike had already begun his explorations of the upper Mississippi Valley and the Colorado region. In 1807 John Colter returned with an astonishing story of natural wonders; he may well have been describing a part of what is now known as Yellowstone National Park, once called Colter's Hell. By 1808 fur traders based at St. Louis were beginning to invade the Rockies.

Lewis and Clark and their Corps of Discovery were the first Americans to traverse the whole continent of North America. In doing so, they delivered to their country an entire wilderness expanse that was previously only an area of rumor. Along their eight-thousand-mile, two-and-a-half-year journey to the Pacific and back, the Corps of Discovery encountered nature's hazards and beauty. They established peaceful contact with most of the American Indian tribes they met along the way. Their diplomacy in dealing with the native inhabitants was, in fact, so successful that they were known among the American Indians for years after their trip for their fairness and decency. One or the other was often specifically asked for when tribes had to deal with the government—even after both had died. Their journal entries served for years as the leading reference work of what was to become the western United States. They had skillfully mapped the region and meticulously documented the habitat with scientific accuracy, discovering 178 new plants and 122 new animal species. But most of all, they had shaped the course of history by staking our geographical boundaries past the Mississippi River and helping to solidify the American claim to the Oregon country, which became Idaho, Washington, Oregon, and parts of Wyoming and Montana. Finally, their glowing reports of astounding natural resources, great plains, and barrier peaks whetted the American appetite to go west to a land that had previously been shrouded in mystery.

LEWIS AND CLARK

In temperament, Meriwether Lewis and William Clark were

Material in this section is taken from the *Lewis and Clark Trail* by the National Park Service and the Lewis and Clark Heritage Trail Foundation.

opposites. Lewis was introverted, melancholic, and moody; Clark, extroverted, even-tempered, and gregarious. More refined and better educated, Lewis possessed a philosophical, romantic, and speculative mind that dealt easily with abstract ideas. The pragmatic Clark was more practical and a man of action. Each used their talents to supply vital qualities that balanced the partnership.

Born near Charlottesville, Virginia, on August 18, 1774, Meriwether Lewis was a boyhood neighbor of Thomas Jefferson. After his father died, his mother remarried, and at the age of 10 he moved to Georgia where his family had plantations in present-day Oglethorpe County. He became an expert hunter and developed an early interest in science and the flora and fauna of the vicinity. Returning to Virginia at the age of thirteen, he studied under private tutors. His plans to attend William and Mary College came to an end with the death of his stepfather. As the eldest son, he managed his family's Virginia plantation near Charlottesville instead.

When duty called, he joined the militia and, with the rank of ensign, was attached to a sub-legion of Gen. "Mad Anthony" Wayne, to a unit commanded by Lt. William Clark. In sharing the experiences of the northwest campaign against the British and Indians, Lewis and Clark formed the bonds of an enduring friendship. Lewis was later transferred to First Infantry and commissioned a lieutenant. Placed in command of a company at Fort Pickering near Memphis, he learned the customs of the Chickasaw Indians. In 1801 he was stationed at an outpost in Detroit.

When Jefferson was elected president, he offered Lewis the post of private secretary and invited him to live in the executive mansion. Lewis's understanding of the customs of the American Indian, his hunting abilities, and his scientific interests later made him Jefferson's choice to lead an expedition into the Far West.

William Clark, also a native Virginian, was born August 1, 1770. The ninth child, he inherited red hair that, according to family tradition, meant force and vitality. Indeed, his name among the American Indians was "Red Head." With little formal education, he grew up learning to ride and hunt, to survey land, and to accurately draw birds, animals, and maps. Always the frontiersman, he still acquired the etiquette of a gentleman in his southern boyhood home during the Revolutionary War. The daring frontier deeds of his brother, George Rogers Clark, led to the elder Clark's promotion to general to protect the western settlements.

After the close of the war, the family joined General Clark in Kentucky, where William lived until he undertook the expedition to the Pacific. During that time, he joined a militia on a mission against the White River Indian towns near the Wabash and helped guard the western frontier against attack. He was commissioned in 1792 as a lieutenant of infantry and served as an army officer for Gen. Anthony Wayne for four years. In 1793 he was placed in charge of a rifle corps that included several Chickasaw Indians. He continued with Wayne until victory over the allied Indians came at Fallen Timbers, where Meriwether Lewis served in his division. Before resigning his commission, Clark was sent down the Mississippi to Natchez to meet with the Spanish under a flag of truce. There he made friends with the Spanish governor, who provided him with a passport to visit New Orleans. He traveled widely before returning to his home. Then, in 1803, came the letter from Lewis that changed his life dramatically.

In background and capability, Lewis and Clark had much in common. Both were relatively young, intelligent, adventurous, resourceful, and courageous. Born leaders, experienced frontiersmen, and seasoned army officers, they were cool in crises and quick to make decisions. Their relationship ranks high in the realm of notable human associations. During their long journey, there is not a single trace of a serious quarrel or dispute between them. Despite the frequent stress, hardships, and other conditions that could have easily bred jealousy, mistrust, or contempt, they proved to be self-effacing equals in command and leadership. They were able to share responsibilities for the conduct of a dangerous enterprise without losing the respect or loyalty of others.

After the expedition, Lewis was appointed Governor of Louisiana Territory. Clark was promoted to brigadier general of militia for Louisiana (later Missouri) Territory and appointed to the superintendency of Indian affairs at St. Louis, which became his home. At age thirty-five, on October 11, 1809, Lewis died tragically, just three years after completing the expedition. His grave lies within the Natchez Trace Parkway in Tennessee, which is a designated National Scenic Byway and a portion of a National Scenic Trail. Lewis had been on his way to the nation's capital to give an accounting of his governance of the Upper Louisiana after having been accused by a jealous assistant of financial irregularities. He was found shot in the body and head at Grinder's Inn, an old Trace hostelry. Despite the severe wounds, he lingered painfully and begged his servant to end his life. "I am no coward," he said, "but I am so strong, so hard to die."

Though his death remains a mystery, the accounts of those on the scene led President Jefferson to believe that he had committed suicide. Lewis was said to have been deeply depressed and to have suffered an earlier mental breakdown. Only a week before the incident, he had been deprived of gunpowder in order to prevent an attempt on his life. Jefferson, who held lifelong affection for his protege, is credited with the Latin inscription on the Lewis's tombstone which translates, "I died young: but thou, O Good Republic, live out my years for me with better fortune."

William Clark was startled at news of the death of his friend and turned down the opportunity to serve as his successor in the governor's office. He went on to live a long and productive life. He married Julia Hancock for whom he had named the Judith River in Montana, and they eventually had four children. His sons were named Meriwether Lewis Clark and George Rogers Hancock Clark for his friend and his brother. Named governor of the Missouri Territory in 1813, he was called on to protect the frontier from attacks from the American Indians who were allied with the British. After leading an expedition up the Mississippi River to the mouth of the Wisconsin, he built a log fort named Shelby, which hoisted the first American flag to fly over what is now Wisconsin. After the war, he helped negotiate a series of treaties with the American Indians. When his first wife died, he married Harriet Kennerly. They had a son named Jefferson Kennerly Clark. Their home was always open to the American Indians, and Clark made constant pleas to the government for humane treatment and justice for natives. In 1824 he was named surveyor general for Illinois, Missouri, and Arkansas, and in 1828 he laid out the town of Paducah, Kentucky. Clark died peacefully in 1838 at age sixty-eight and was buried in the Clark family plot in Bellefontaine Cemetery in St. Louis.

Meriwether Lewis and William Clark are among the recognized members of that generation of heroes in our nation's early history who bred a nationalistic vision and a patriotic will that would form the spirit and richness of America itself.

SACAGAWEA

Sacagawea, the Shoshone interpreter for the Lewis and Clark expedition, was born a chief's daughter around Lemhi, Idaho, in 1787. She was captured by a Hidatsa war party at the Three Forks of the Missouri in 1800 and taken to the mouth of the Knife River. There, she and another slave were sold to or won in a gambling game by Toussaint Charbonneau, who married them both according to the American Indian custom. At Fort Mandan, Sacagawea gave birth to a son whom she carried on her back throughout the long expedition. Clark later offered to educate the boy as his own.

Soon after the expedition ended, Sacagawea and her husband and son traveled to St. Louis, where Charbonneau tried unsuccessfully to farm. Joining another expedition led by fur trader Manuel Lisa, the couple left Pomp with Clark. After returning to the Knife River, Sacagawea bore a daughter, Lizette. The family then established itself at Fort Manuel on the Missouri, where it is assumed that Sacagawea died in 1812. According to a fort record, the wife of Charbonneau died of fever that year. She was described as "a good and the best Women in the fort." There are other theories. One claims that she returned to her people and lived to be nearly one hundred years old. Her life has evoked a great deal of admiration and tribute. No other American woman has been honored with as many memorials as Sacagawea.

The Trail Today

With much of its pristine beauty yet intact, the Lewis and Clark Trail offers a modern-day pilgrimage that can elevate the sense of discovery still alive in us. Visits to ancient Indian grounds can be a mystical experience, and numerous interpretive signs, exhibits, museums, visitor centers, and living-history displays along the route provide the traveler with an opportunity to take part vicariously in the adventure almost two hundred years after the fact. Unlike the scenic trails, such as the Appalachian Trail, there is no continuous hiking corridor for the Lewis and Clark Trail. Instead, the route consists of rivers and impoundments, short trail segments, and marked highways that follow the outbound and return routes, all of which can be explored on foot, by car, and/or by boat.

Water trail segments are designated sections of Lewis and Clark's route where the expedition traveled by canoe, keelboat, or pirogue on the Missouri, Yellowstone, Snake, and Columbia Rivers and their tributaries. These segments can be retraced today in a boat, although the traveler must cope with a series of dams and im-pounded lakes.

Through a cooperative effort with the National Park Service, the Army Corps of Engineers administers the Missouri National Recreation River. Two protected stretches, one from Ponca State Park in Nebraska to Gavins Point Dam near Yankton, South Dakota, and a second above Lewis and Clark Lake, still exhibit the river's dynamic character, with conditions much like those encountered by Lewis and Clark. Boats can be rented at Gavins Point Dam on the Nebraska side where excellent interpretation is offered at the visitor center on top of Calumet Bluff. Access to the river is also available at Ponca and Niobrara State Parks in Nebraska and Clay County Park and Yankton County Community Park in South Dakota. Gavins Point Dam holds back the Missouri River to create a large reservoir, a popular spot for water sports and camping. A brick path from Yankton leads to Lewis and Clark State Recreation Area, where Far West Riverboat offers historic cruises.

The Bureau of Land Management administers the 149-mile Upper Missouri National Wild and Scenic River in Montana where one finds opportunities to retrace a section of the Lewis and Clark route that has changed very little since their exploration. The Upper Missouri Wild and Scenic River visitor center at Fort Benton offers displays and a slide presentation about the expedition. Outfitters in Fort Benton offer float and boat excursions. A statue of Lewis and Clark and Sacagawea and her son can be seen on the riverboat levee.

Separating Washington and Oregon, the Columbia River Gorge National Scenic Area provides spectacular scenery and one of the most diverse and exciting places in the national forest system. The eighty-mile-long river canyon is the only sea-level route through the Cascade Mountain Range. Leaving Portland, the America West Steamboat Company has a seven-night Lewis and Clark cruise that travels the Columbia and Snake past many of the area's Lewis and Clark points of interest. Dams on the Columbia River have locks while those on the Missouri do not. Canoes can be used to explore Goose Lake or the Forlorn Lakes near Willard, Washington; Trout Lake near Trout, Washington; Lost Lake near Mount Hood, Oregon; or any of the inlets of the Columbia River for a Lewis-and-Clark-style adventure.

Commercial boat trips are popular in Great Falls and at the Gates of the Mountains in Montana, and Salmon, Idaho, is headquarters for some of the best whitewater rafting down the

Salmon River that two hundred years earlier Clark had found unnavigable, thus ending the quest for a water passage to the Pacific.

Land trail segments for travel on foot or horseback already have been developed and others are planned. Developed trails include the Katy Trail in Missouri from St. Charles to Franklin, the Lewis and Clark Discovery Trail in South Dakota, the Lost Trail Pass with hiking trails in the Salmon and Bitterroot National Forests in Idaho and Montana, the Lolo Trail in Idaho, and the trail over Tillamook Head in Ecola State Park in Oregon. The overland route is marked along modern roads that precisely, or very nearly, follow the historic route. It is usually not feasible to establish a footpath for retracement in these areas. *Motor route segments* are marked with rectangular National Historic Trail signs that display the silhouette of Lewis and Clark. A Lewis and Clark audio tour recounts the adventures of the expedition as listeners follow the Lewis and Clark path to Cascade Historical Museum at Giant Springs Visitor Center near Great Falls, Montana.

The trail in its entirety has approximately three hundred public and private recreation and historic sites. These include several National Park Service areas such as the Jefferson National Expansion Memorial in Missouri, the Knife River Indian Villages National Historic Site and the Fort

Union Trading Post National Historic Site in North Dakota, the Nez Perce National Historic Park in Idaho, the Fort Vancouver National Historic Site in Washington, and the Fort Clatsop National Memorial in Oregon. Numerous recreational sites exist along the trail. Following the expedition's land route over the Lemhi Pass into Idaho, for example, leads to several Lewis and Clark sites that offer opportunities to hike near the Lemhi and Salmon Rivers. By cutting back into Montana, the adventurer reaches Lost Trail Pass where the expedition lost their way in the Bitterroot Range. Montana's Lolo Trail, a National Historic Landmark, crosses the Clearwater and Lolo National Forests where the expedition ran out of food and experienced the most difficult portion of their journey. Travelers motoring into remote areas are advised to bring along extra supplies such as water, food, and warm clothing. Weather reports and road conditions should be checked ahead of time when traveling the lonely Lolo Motorway. This primitive dirt road closely parallels the original trail. It calls for four-wheel drive and is generally open from July to September, weather permitting.

Other major points of interpretation along the Lewis and Clark Trail include the Western Historic Trails Center in Council Bluffs, Iowa; the Fort Atkinson State Historical Park near Fort Calhoun, Nebraska; the North Dakota Lewis and Clark Interpretive Center in Washburn, North Dakota; Fort Mandan, operated by the McLean County Historical Society in North Dakota; the Forest Service's Lewis and Clark National Historic Trail Interpretive Center in Great Falls, Montana; the Lewis and Clark Interpretive Center at Fort Canby State Park in Ilwaco, Washington; and the Columbia Gorge Interpretive Center in Stevenson, Washington.

The National Frontier Trails Center in Independence, Missouri, and the new U.S. Forest Service Center in Great Falls, Montana, provide exhibits and opportunities for interpretation and research. Headquartered in Great Falls, Montana, the Lewis and Clark Trail Heritage Foundation rotates its annual meeting among locations in the states crossed by the trail. It also publishes the newsletter *We Proceeded On*. New activities and exhibits are planned as federal agencies, towns, and cities along the trail prepare for the Lewis and Clark Bicentennial of 2004–6. An outgrowth of the foundation, the National Lewis and Clark Bicentennial Council, headquartered in Vancouver, Washington, was formed to help commemorate the journey, rekindle its spirit of discovery, and acclaim the contribution and goodwill of the American Indians by planning educational programs, recreational events, and commemorative observances.

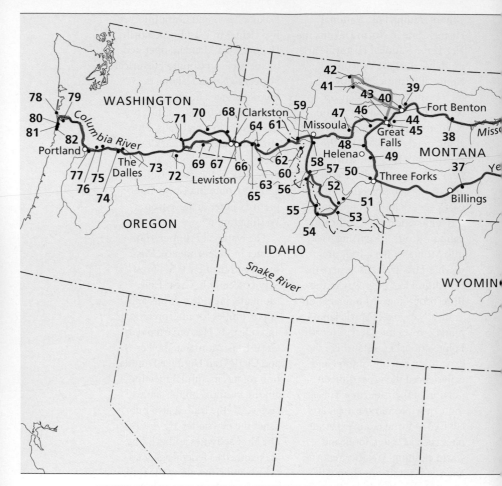

LEWIS AND CLARK NATIONAL HISTORIC TRAIL

Points of Interest

ILLINOIS

1. LEWIS AND CLARK MEMO-RIAL. At Hartford, stone pillars at the certified NHT site mark the expedition's winter quarters at Camp Wood (1803–04) and the point where the expedition started their journey.* The actual

*Water and land routes and selected interpretation and recreation sites are shown on the map. Because it is only a general map, it will be necessary to consult highway maps or make local

site was destroyed by river channel migration. *Nearby:* In Collinsville, Cahokia Mounds SHS, with a visitor center and interpretation, protects one of the largest known mound complexes (A.D. 900–1300) of the Mississippian

inquiry to find some sites. Remember too that some sites have no development and/or no public access. Respect the right of private property owners and always obtain permission before crossing over onto private land.

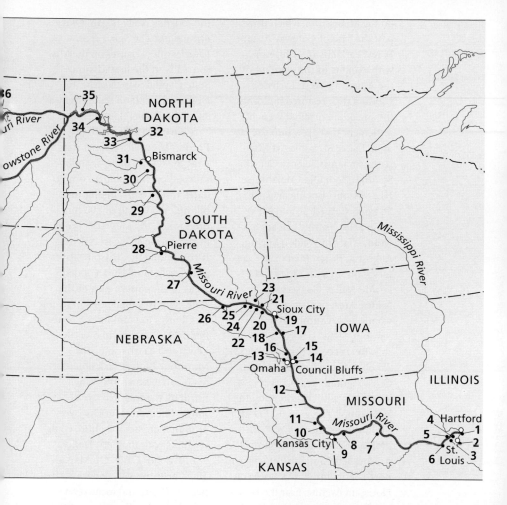

culture. Near Alton, two hundred to four hundred American bald eagles winter annually along the Mississippi River; Dam #26, Melvin Price Lock, and Alton Lake are popular viewing areas, and Piasa Bird re-creates the pictograph discovered here by Pere Marquette in 1673. Clark Bridge is a unique bridge that links Missouri and Illinois.

MISSOURI

2. JEFFERSON NATIONAL EXPANSION MEMORIAL. Established by Franklin D. Roosevelt, the park, on the banks of the Mississippi in St. Louis, honors Thomas Jefferson, the Louisiana Purchase, and those who opened the West, as symbolized in the prize-winning stainless-steel Gateway Arch (630 feet). A tram carries visitors to an observation deck at the top of the arch. The visitor center houses the Museum of Westward Expansion with exhibits and interpretive programs. *Other attractions:* Seasonal cruises

on the Mississippi, which flows past the base of Gateway Arch; Forest Park History Museum, with exhibits of the opening of the American West; Laclede's Landing with restored buildings, the site of the original French settlement that grew into the city of St. Louis; St. Louis Art Museum; St. Louis Science Center; St. Louis Zoo; Old Courthouse NP; Missouri Botanical Garden; St. Louis Cathedral; and Mastodon SHS. *Nearby:* Ulysses S. Grant NHS; in Weldon Spring, August A. Busch Memorial Conservation Area; in Kirkwood, Powder Valley Conservation Nature Area; in Glencoe, Rockwoods Reservation; in Gray Summit, Shaw Arboretum.

3. BELLEFONTAINE CEMETERY. An obelisk and bust of William Clark mark his grave, which is located on a hill overlooking the Mississippi. The grave of Senator Thomas Hart Benton, a champion of westward expansion, is nearby. Bellefontaine Cemetery is north of downtown St. Louis on Florissant Avenue, near the Broadway Avenue entrance to I-70.

4. ST. CHARLES. Near the certified NHT site of Lewis and Clark Center in the historic district is the campsite (May 16–20, 1804) where the party waited for Lewis, who was gathering information and supplies in St. Louis. The expedition also camped here September 21, 1806, on the return trek. The center's museum depicts the expedition's adventures and accomplishments; St. Charles's locals say this is where the journey really began. *Other attractions:* The *Spirit of St. Charles* offers cruises on the Missouri River; the first Missouri State Capital SHS. *Nearby:* In Defiance, south on State Highway 94, is the Daniel Boone Home.

5. THE KATY TRAIL STATE PARK. This multiregional state park makes use of an abandoned railroad corridor and accommodates wheelchairs, hiking, and biking. At a length of 200 hundred miles, the Katy Trail is one of the nation's longest rail-trails. It runs along the Missouri River and passes bluffs and wooded areas in the eastern part of the state. The 165-mile portion from St. Charles to Franklin is a certified NHT site that follows the Lewis and Clark route. The Monitour Bluffs Clark noted in his journal are visible. When finished, the trail will stretch 235 miles. The American Discovery Trail that crosses the entire country links with the Katy Trail.

6. TAVERN CAVE. On May 23, 1804, near this cave, now a certified NHT site and located on private land in the village of St. Albans near Washington, Missouri, Lewis took a fall that could have ended in disaster. The historic area offers walking tours and the J. E. Rennik Riverfront Park. *Nearby:* The party's campsite in Jefferson City is marked on Adam Street. At the Missouri state capitol there is a bronze relief of the signing of the Louisiana Purchase and murals by N. C. Wyeth. Jefferson Landing SHS is located here.

7. ARROW ROCK STATE HIS

TORIC SITE. The bluffs were noted by Clark in his journal on June 9, 1804, as a good site for a fort. This is also where the Santa Fe Trail met the Missouri River. The site includes several historic buildings, including the Old Tavern (1834), and offers guided walking tours. Located in Arrow Rock, the Lyceum Theatre opens during the summer, and the state interpretive center offers helpful information about the area. *Nearby:* Stump Island Park in Glasgow interprets the expedition's campsite of June 10–11, 1804; Boone's Lick SHS; Van Meter SP with a visitor center in Marshall protects a large Indian earthwork.

8. FORT OSAGE. During the expedition Clark noted the advantages of this site northwest of Buckner for a fort and trading post. In 1808, under Clark's supervision as superintendent of Indian Affairs, the fort was constructed to aid trappers and improve American Indian relations. The certified NHT site has a reconstructed fort, a visitor center, museum, and special events offered by the Jackson County Parks and Recreation Department. Authentically attired interpreters engage in activities of the day. Santa Fe Trail ruts run through the southeast corner of the property near the cemetery. *Nearby:* Little Blue Park in Jackson County is a certified NHT site.

MISSOURI/KANSAS

9. NATIONAL FRONTIER TRAILS CENTER. Located in Inde-

pendence, Missouri, this certified NHT interpretive center, with exhibits and a research library, offers interpretation on the Lewis and Clark expedition, fur trade, and western trails. *Other attractions:* Independence, Missouri, was the jumping-off point for the Oregon, California, and Santa Fe Trails. *Nearby:* Lewis and Clark Point, located on a high bluff in Kansas City, offers overlooks of the confluence of the Kansas and Missouri Rivers. It marks an early terminus and outfitting point for the Oregon, California and Santa Fe Trails. *Other attractions:* In the historic Westport district, the Kansas City Museum offers artifacts and exhibits on Kansas City's role in westward expansion; Westport Landing has summer steamboat excursions; Kansas City Art Institute and Nelson-Atkins Museum of Art are both located in the city. There are twenty-five lakes in the vicinity for picnicking and water activities.

10. FORT LEAVENWORTH. Located near Leavenworth, Kansas, the Frontier Army Museum has exhibits on the fur-trade era and the Corps of Discovery. A trail leads through hardwood forests that the expedition itself passed through. Leavenworth Riverside Park offers Lewis and Clark interpretation. This area is also important to the Oregon, Pony Express, and Santa Fe Trails.

KANSAS

11. INDEPENDENCE PARK. The campsite (July 4, 1804) named

Independence Creek in honor of Independence Day is located in Atchison, known for the Atchison, Topeka and Santa Fe Railway. The old Santa Fe depot has a visitor center. *Nearby:* Lewis and Clark SP to the northwest of Atchison offers interpretation and a lake.

NEBRASKA

12. INDIAN CAVE STATE PARK. The expedition met a violent storm near the area (July 14, 1804). The park, near Nemaha on the banks of the Missouri River, offers interpretive exhibits, camping, hiking, and horseback riding as well as cruises on the river in season. *Nearby:* Brown-ville SRA marks another Lewis and Clark campsite (July 15, 1804). The area's centerpiece is the Meriwether Lewis Museum on the dry-docked *Meriwether Lewis,* which operated between 1932 and 1969. The *Spirit of Brownville* offers two-hour paddlewheel cruises. The tourist center offers guided tours of the historic district. *Nearby:* Nebraska City is the oldest town in the state and has many ties to westward expansion. Lewis and Clark camped nearby on July 18–19, 1804, and Riverview Marina RA and Arbor Lodge SHP are located here.

13. N. P. DODGE MEMORIAL PARK. The riverfront park in Omaha, with a marina and camping, is a certified NHT site that interprets the Lewis and Clark camp (July 28, 1804) and the first American Indian encounter. *Other attractions:* In Omaha the

Lewis and Clark National Historic Trail intersects the California and Mormon Pioneer National Historic Trails. Other noteworthy attractions in Omaha include Winter Quarters, the Joslyn Art Museum, the Henry Doorly Zoo, and Boys Town. *Nearby:* Standing Bear and Glenn Cunningham Lakes offer water activities, and the Trailwood Ski Area offers downhill skiing and horseback riding in season. Waubonsie SP, a certified NHT site near Hamburg, Iowa, offers an overlook, with hiking, equestrian trails, and camping.

IOWA

14. WESTERN HISTORIC TRAILS CENTER. The center in Council Bluffs commemorates the Lewis and Clark Trail and other western emigrant trails. *Other attractions:* Long's Landing County Park, a certified NHT site, holds the annual Lewis and Clark White Catfish Camp Reenactment festival on July 4 weekends; Railswest Railroad Museum; Stemple Bird Collection; Wabash Trace Nature Trail. *Nearby:* Lake Manawa SP.

15. LEWIS AND CLARK STATE MONUMENT. This certified NHT site offers interpretation and an outstanding view of the Mississippi and surrounding area of Council Bluffs.

NEBRASKA/IOWA

16. FORT ATKINSON STATE HISTORICAL PARK. The "Councile Bluff" where Lewis and Clark had their first council with

American Indians, the Oto and the Missouri (Aug 3, 1804), is located east of this certified NHT site in Fort Calhoun, Nebraska. Clark recommended the site for a future trading establishment and fortification. President Monroe dispatched a military expedition to establish the fort at this junction of the Yellowstone and Missouri Rivers (1819). Abandoned in 1827, Fort Atkinson was replaced by Fort Leavenworth in Kansas, which was better situated to protect the Santa Fe Trail. The reconstruction has a visitor center and museum open on a seasonal basis. Displays and a slide show interpret the Louisiana Purchase, the Lewis and Clark expedition, the fort's military history, and pioneer trails. *Nearby:* Desoto NWR has a visitor center that interprets the impact of westward expansion on wildlife and habitat. Wilson Island SRA, a certified NHT site, has camping, cabins for the mobility-impaired, hiking, and fishing.

17. **Lewis and Clark State Park.** The expedition camped in the area (August 10, 1804). Keelboat and pirogue replicas, with interpretation, can be seen in this certified NHT site in Onawa, Iowa. The Lewis and Clark Festival is held the second weekend in June; visitors in costume may get a chance to ride the keelboat *Discovery. Nearby:* Loess Hills is a twelve-thousand to fourteen-thousand-year-old land formation such as is found only here and in China. Huff Warner access in Onawa and Little Sioux and

Remington access near Woodbine are certified NHT sites.

18. **Blackbird Hill.** The Omaha chief Blackbird's grave (1800) was visited and decorated by Lewis and Clark and ten others in the party (August 11, 1804). Today the reservation area offers no access to the public, but a certified NHT site at a wayside interpretation facility 2.5 miles north of Decatur on U.S. Highway 75 offers a similar overlook from a vantage point several miles south of the actual site. *Nearby:* Tonwontongathon (1775), twenty miles north, recreates a village that coincided with Chief Blackbird's rise to power. A shelter at the site protects a re-created earth lodge. The annual Omaha powwow is held on the Omaha Indian reservation the weekend nearest the full moon of August, and a Winnebago powwow takes place the last full weekend in July on the Winnebago Indian reservation. Visitors are welcome. Light House Marina, a certified NHT site, has a campground.

19. **Sergeant Floyd Riverboat Museum and Welcome Center.** The one-hundred-foot-tall white stone obelisk south of Sioux City, Iowa, marks the burial place of Sgt. Charles Floyd, the only member of the expedition to die en route (August 20, 1804). He previously had served with Clark's brother, George Rogers Clark. The certified NHT site offers an excellent view of Sioux City and the Missouri River and was the first National Historic

Landmark to be designated in the United States. The Sergeant Floyd Welcome Center and Museum, a certified NHT site on a steamboat in Sioux City, has a special focus on the expedition, with dioramas relating to the history of the Missouri River. *Other attractions:* Sioux City also boasts of the certified NHT Sioux City Riverfront Trail, certified NHT Snyder Bend Park, Sioux City Public Museum with American Indian displays, Loess Ridge Regional Nature Center, Siouxland Historical Railroad Association (SHRA) Railroad Museum, Sioux City Art Center, Sioux City Public Museum with Indian artifacts, and Grandview Park. *Nearby:* Stone SP, eight miles northwest of Sioux City, is a certified NHT site with Elk Point overlook, fishing, camping, hiking, and an equestrian trail.

20. PONCA STATE PARK. North of Ponca, Nebraska, the certified NHT site has a trail to Three State Overlook, which offers a view of the Missouri River Valley, and interpretive sign, cabins, equestrian trail, and access to the river.

NEBRASKA/SOUTH DAKOTA

21. MISSOURI NATIONAL RECREATIONAL RIVER. The conditions encountered from Ponca SP to Gavins Point Dam are still much as they were at the time of the expedition. Fishing and boating are popular activities in the area managed by the U.S. Army Corps of Engineers, Omaha District, through a cooperative

agreement with the NPS.

22. IONIA VOLCANO. Clark noted (August 24, 1804) that the bluffs, now located on private land outside Newcastle, Nebraska, were hot to the touch. Scientists eventually learned the heat was generated by the oxidation of shale. Access can be gained by obtaining permission from the private landowner. There is an interpretive sign in Newcastle City Park.

23. SPIRIT MOUND. This landmark seven miles north of Vermillion, South Dakota, on private land is visible from State Route 19, where an interpretive sign is located. The leaders visited (August 25, 1804) this hill with a conical shape (NHL, NRHP), believed by local American Indians to be the residence of "deavels" armed with arrows. *Nearby:* Clay SRA.

24. CALUMET BLUFF. Lewis and Clark camped on the bottomlands (August 28 to September 1, 1804) and held council with Yankton Sioux here. The site is interpreted at Gavins Point Dam Visitor Center in Nebraska and at the certified NHT site of Lewis and Clark SRA in Yankton, South Dakota.

25. GAVINS POINT DAM VISITOR CENTER. The Corps of Engineers visitor center outside Crofton, Nebraska, offers excellent interpretation, displays, and an audiovisual presentation focusing on Lewis and Clark, the lake, the Gavins Point Dam, the Missouri River Basin, and area history.

26. Niobrara State Park. Located where the Niobrara and Missouri Rivers meet at Lewis and Clark Point, the certified NHT site in Nebraska offers an interpretive shelter, cabins, camping, swimming, trail rides, and rafting on the Missouri River.

SOUTH DAKOTA

27. Chamberlain/Oacoma. I-90 meets the Missouri River at this certified NHT site, which is a popular spot for walleye fishing and hunting. When the expedition was in the area (September 16, 1804), they named their campsite Camp Pleasant. Lewis wrote of abundant deer, elk, and antelope and of immense herds of buffalo. An interpretive sign at the visitor center commemorates the visit. *Other attractions:* At Chamberlain, the Akta Lakota Museum explores the rich culture of the Great Sioux Nation. Hiking is available on the six-mile Lewis and Clark Discovery Trail. *Nearby:* Certified NHT site of Snake Creek RA, south of Chamberlain near Platte; the Crow Creek, Rosebud, and Pine Ridge Indian Reservations; Badlands NP and Buffalo Gap, National Grassland located near Wall; Wounded Knee NHS in Wounded Knee; and near Keystone, Crazy Horse NM, Mount Rushmore NM, Custer SP, Wind Cave NP, Jewel Cave NM, and the Black Hills NF. The Peter Norbeck National Scenic Byway passes by many of these sites.

28. Teton Council Site. In present-day Fort Pierre, a council held with the Teton Sioux (September 25, 1804) at the mouth of the Bad River nearly ended in armed conflict. The site is located at Lily Park; a certified NHT site is located at West Bend RA. A sign interpreting the expedition is located at Verendrye Monument, which commemorates, and is named after, two French Canadian explorers who passed this area in 1743 in search of the Northwest Passage. *Nearby:* The state capital's Cultural Heritage Center in Pierre exhibits the effigy of a Sioux horse and a tipi; eight miles north on State Route 1806 the Oahe Dam and Reservoir has tours and a visitor center. The large Oahe Lake is popular for camping and water sports. The expedition passed an abandoned Arikara village (October 4, 1804) at the certified NHT site of West Whitlock RA, located on Lake Oahe, west of Gettysburg. Another certified NHT site, Farm Island RA, south of Pierre, offers a visitor center and recreation activities such as camping, hiking, canoeing, horseback riding, fishing and other water sports, cross-country skiing, wildlife viewing, and bird-watching. Fort Pierre National Grassland is in this area.

29. Site of Fort Manuel. Probably located near the west shore of present-day Lake Oahe was the Missouri Fur Company post where Sacagawea is said to have died (December 20, 1812). There is no public access, but an interpretive sign is found on a bluff along State Route 1806 south of Kenel. *Nearby:* North of Mobridge, near Pollock, is a certified NHT site Lewis and Clark historical marker. Southwest of Mobridge, near Sitting Bull's possible burial site, is Sacagawea Monument; in Mobridge, the Scherr-Howe Arena houses Oscar Howe Indian Murals, symbolizing the history and ceremonies of the Sioux, and the Klein Museum has Lakota Sioux artifacts. The expedition camped (October 18, 1804) and observed wildlife at today's Fort Rice Historic Site, a certified NHT site across the state line in Fort Rice, North Dakota. *Other attractions:* In the area surrounding Mobridge, Standing Rock Indian Reservation, Swan Creek RA, Grand River National Grassland, Pocasse NWR.

N O R T H   D A K O T A

30. **FORT ABRAHAM LINCOLN STATE PARK.** South of Mandan, this certified NHT site has five reconstructed earth lodges. Lewis and Clark visited this abandoned Mandan village (1650–1750) on October 20, 1804. A museum interprets Lewis and Clark and the Mandan culture and has living-history demonstrations. Sightseeing cruises from Bismarck to Fort Abraham Lincoln are available aboard the *Lewis and Clark.* The expedition hunted (October 19, 1804) at Kimball Bottoms, seven miles southeast of Bismarck on State Route 1804, an area known for its acres of sand dunes and cottonwood trees. It is a certified NHT site and is part of the Oahe Wildlife Area. *Other attractions:* Lt. Col. George Custer rode out from the fort (1872–91) with

the Seventh Calvary against the Sioux at Little Bighorn. Events include the Historical Walking Drama in July, Native American Cultural Celebration in August, and Fur Traders Rendezvous in August. The secluded seventeen-mile-long Roughrider Trail offers opportunities for hiking, horseback riding, and snowmobiling along the Missouri River.

31. **NORTH DAKOTA LEWIS AND CLARK INTERPRETIVE CENTER.** This certified NHT site in Washburn provides interpretive displays of the winter the expedition spent with the Mandan. There are exhibits of Native American culture, and the Bergquist Gallery features artwork of the Upper Missouri by Karl Bodmer. *Nearby:* In Bismarck, a statue honors Sacagawea on the state capitol grounds. The certified NHT site of Double Ditch SHS, north of Bismarck, has deep rings and mounds from the three-hundred-year-old Mandan village, where Lewis and Clark arrived October 22, 1804. South of Bismarck, in Emmons County, is Langeliers Bay RA, a certified NHT site. Granger Park is a certified NHT site in Morton County; and the certified NHT site off I-94 called Mandan Overlook offers interpretation.

32. **FORT MANDAN HISTORIC SITE.** The expedition spent more time here (the winter of 1804–5) than at any other place on the journey. The original fort, located along the Missouri near present-day Washburn, was erased by the Missouri's shifts. The certified

NHT site has a replica of the fort and visitor center that stands downstream a few miles from the original site where the expedition reached the villages of the Mandans, Hidatsa, and Amahamis. The party camped (October 24, 1804) at today's certified NHT site of Painted Woods RA. *Other attractions:* Fahlgren Memorial Park, next to Fort Mandan, preserves one of the last remaining unaltered bottomlands along the river; the McLean County Historical Society has a museum, and Indian Hills RA is a certified NHT site in the same county, as is Lewis and Clark Wildlife Management Area, another certified NHT site. *Nearby:* Cross Ranch SP and Nature Preserve, a certified NHT site, has Mandan archeological sites, a visitor center, recreational activities, and bison.

33. KNIFE RIVER INDIAN VILLAGES NATIONAL HISTORIC SITE. The site, north of Stanton, has remnants of three Hidatsa villages where Lewis and Clark obtained services of Sacagawea and her husband (October 25–26, 1804). The visitor center provides interpretation, exhibits of the area's eight-thousand-year history, and brochures for walks to villages and preserved travois trails. *Nearby:* A certified NHT site, Fort Clark SHS, contains foundations of a Mandan village built in 1822 and later used by the Arikara from 1830 to 1861. This was also the site used by the Fort Clark fur-trading post established in 1830 by James Kipp, an employee of the American Fur

Company. *Other attractions:* Beulah Bay RA in Mercer County, a certified NHT site; Fort Berthold Indian Reservation; Lake Sakakawea SP in Pick City; Riverdale Garrison Dam and Power Station in Riverdale; Fort Stevenson SP, a certified NHT site in Garrison; Audubon NWR near Coleharbor.

34. FOUR BEARS MEMORIAL PARK. The certified NHT site in New Town has a museum that offers interpretation and artifacts of Arikara, Hidatsa, and Mandan Indians. Crow Flies High Butte Historic Monument, where the party camped on their trek west (April 14, 1805) and again on their return (August 12, 1806), is a certified NHT site that offers panoramic views of Lake Sakakawea and the badlands, plus boat rentals. Pouch Point RA in Mountrail County is a certified NHT site. White Earth Bay RA, a certified NHT site, commemorates the expedition's campsite (April 15 and 16, 1805) and has camping and a boat ramp.

35. LEWIS AND CLARK STATE PARK. This park near Williston lies close to the site where Lewis was shot in a hunting accident on the return trip (August 11, 1805). Located on Lake Sakakawea with badlands scenery, the certified NHT site has a trail through native prairies, outdoor activities, wildlife viewing, and the western terminus of the NCNST. *Nearby:* The certified NHT site of Tobacco Garden Bay (April 21, 1805) is a major recreation area on Lake Sakakawea, where Lewis and Clark observed four wooden-

raft ferries and remains of Indian camps; Fort Buford SHS is the certified NHT site where the expedition celebrated reaching the confluence of the Missouri and Yellowstone Rivers (April 25–26, 1805) and marks the place where Chief Sitting Bull surrendered. It contains the guardhouse that held him and that had also held Chief Joseph after the latter's attempt to lead his people to Canada. *Other attractions:* Fort Union Trading Post NHS (April 26, 1805), a reconstructed site with a visitor center, marks the original site of an American Fur Company post (1829). Lewis commented in his journal that a fort should be established here. Theodore Roosevelt NP (north unit) is located in the North Dakota badlands.

M O N T A N A

36. **FORT PECK DAM.** Journal entries from 1806 include extensive descriptions of this area. Interpretive signs are located at the spillway and at overlooks. There is a museum, and powerhouse tours can be enjoyed. *Nearby:* The Pines RA campsite (May 11, 1805); in Glasgow, the Valley County Pioneer Museum with Lewis and Clark exhibits. *Other attractions:* Charles M. Russell NWR, the largest wildlife refuge in the continental United States; Fort Peck Indian Reservation; Fort Belknap Indian Reservation; Chief Joseph Battlefield of the Bear's Paw SM in Chinook.

37. **POMPEYS PILLAR.** This huge sandstone formation near

Billings was named Pompey's Tower by Clark after Sacagawea's son "Pomp." American Indians called it "the place where the mountain lion lies." Clark inscribed his own name and date on it (July 25, 1806); the inscription still exists today and is covered by glass. The NHL with a Bureau of Land Management visitor center also bears names of early trappers, soldiers, and settlers. Several outfitters lead river trips to the site. Buffalo Mirage access at Park City is where Clark's party constructed two canoes to explore the Yellowstone River. *Nearby:* The Western Heritage Center and the Yellowstone Art Center in Billings; Chief Otter Trail follows the edge of the Billings Rimrocks; Lake Elmo SRA; Lake Josephine RA; Pictograph Cave SM; Halfbreed NWR and Hailstone NWR; the Crow Indian Reservation; the Northern Cheyenne Indian Reservation; the Little Bighorn Battlefield NM; the Bighorn Canyon NRA; the Cooney Reservoir RA; and Yellowstone NP in Wyoming.

38. **UPPER MISSOURI NATIONAL WILD AND SCENIC RIVER.** From James Kipp RA to Fort Benton, the 149-mile section provides retracement opportunities with little changed since 1805–6. Commercial boat trips are available. *Nearby:* Cow Island Landing RA; Judith Landing RA; Slaughter River Landing RA; Hole in the Wall Landing RA; Citadel Rock RA; and Coalbanks Landing RA.

39. **MARIAS RIVER.** Lewis named the river for his cousin,

Maria Wood. Lewis spent nine days exploring the river in June 1805. There is an interpretive sign in Loma.

40. **FORT BENTON.** The historic town has a large statue of Lewis and Clark and Sacagawea and her son. Designated a certified NHT site, it is located on the riverfront levee. The Bureau of Land Management's Upper Missouri Visitor Center offers a Lewis and Clark slide presentation and interpretation. The Museum of the Upper Missouri River interprets early trading and river steamers. Outfitters in the area organize river trips. *Nearby:* Lewis and Clark NF offers float, canoe, and motorized pontoon boat trips.

41. **TWO MEDICINE FIGHT SITE.** Two Blackfeet Indians were killed in a skirmish with Lewis and three of his men at this site in Pondera County. The deaths were the only casualties the expedition inflicted on the American Indians. The site is on the Blackfeet Indian Reservation. Access is with four-wheel drive by permission only.

42. **CAMP DISAPPOINTMENT.** In Glacier County, on the Blackfeet Indian Reservation is the northernmost point reached and named by Lewis on Marias River. Overcast weather prevented him from obtaining a good astronomical fix to determine the exact location. Access with four-wheel drive is by permission. There is an interpretive sign on U.S. Highway 2 about twenty-two miles west of Cut Bank. *Nearby:* Browning, the headquarters of the Blackfeet Indian Reservation; Museum of the Plains Indians; Scriver's Museum of Montana Wildlife and Hall of Bronze; gateway to Glacier NP.

43. **GREAT FALLS AND LEWIS AND CLARK NATIONAL HISTORIC TRAIL INTERPRETIVE CENTER.** Montana's second largest city is named after the "grand specticle" Lewis observed. Expecting to find one waterfall, the expedition found a series of five cascades (June 13, 1805). Spanning a ten-mile stretch. The falls may be viewed from overlooks at the Montana Power Company's certified NHT site at Ryan Dam Park and outside of town on River Drive past 25th Street at Black Eagle Falls Overlook. At Broadwater Overlook one can see the broad river valley that once supported thousands of buffalo, elk, and grizzly. West Bank Park, a certified NHT site, is where Lewis had an encounter with a grizzly bear (June 14, 1805). The interpretive center operated by the U.S. Forest Service in Great Falls features the portage around the Great Falls and the expedition's relationship with American Indians of the Northern Plains. The Lewis and Clark Festival and Re-enactment is held in late June, and the Meriwether Lewis Run is held over the Fourth of July. *Other attractions:* Cascade County Historical Museum sponsors a Lewis and Clark auto tour and the chamber of commerce has self-guided tour brochures. Local outfitters provide float trips.

44. **Portage around the Great Falls.** The statue, *Explorers at the Portage,* is a certified NHT site. Clark found the shortest and best portage route was on the south side of the river and nearly eighteen miles long (June 16, 1805). The portage was difficult for the men, who had to contend with prickly pear cacti and deep, dried mud ridges formed by the hoofprints of buffalo herds. The rough portage delayed the expedition for nearly one month. Today most of the land is privately owned and permission is required. A brochure is available from the Portage Route Chapter of the Lewis and Clark Trail Heritage Foundation, P.O. Box 2424, Great Falls, MT 59403.

45. **Giant Springs Heritage State Park.** During the portage (June 18, 1805) past Great Falls, Clark discovered the spring that forms Roe River, the world's shortest river. The multi-use park, a certified NHT site, has a large natural spring, a fish hatchery, and displays. An interpretive center was recently opened. Rainbow Falls Overlook is about one mile east of the Giant Springs area and offers a view of two waterfalls. Of the second falls, Lewis wrote, "again presented by one of the most beautiful objects in nature, a cascade of about fifty feet . . . hissing, flashing, and sparkling." Another overlook can be reached along the Lewis and Clark Overlook Trail, which is then a trailhead for a longer nature walk along the river.

46. **Square Butte.** The explorers named the landmark "Fort Mountain" on the way west. On their return trip, the butte helped guide Lewis to the Great Falls. It is seen just outside of Great Falls. Ulm marks the site where the corps camped (July 10–14, 1805) and built dugout canoes. *Other attractions:* Ulm Pishkun SM preserves a buffalo jump, pictographs, and prairie-dog town.

47. **Lewis and Clark Pass.** An Indian trail followed by the Lewis party as a shortcut on their return trip to the Great Falls in 1806 is accessible by foot trail along Montana State Route 200; directions can be obtained from the Helena NF ranger station.

48. **Gates of the Mountains.** This spectacular Missouri River canyon, north of Helena on I-15, was named by Lewis. The mountains are so close to the river on both sides that the party was forced to travel along the steep mountain walls. The area can only be reached by boat or wilderness trail. Commercial boat and fishing trips in the recreation area are available at Wolf Creek. *Nearby:* Helena, which offers the Montana Historic Society Museum, Library, and Archives with a C. M. Russell collection and Last Chance Gulch train tours; the state capitol with C. M. Russell's painting of Lewis and Clark; River's Edge Trail passes the site where Lewis met a grizzly. Also Helena NF; Gates of the Mountains Wilderness; Prewett Creek, Stickney Creek, Mountain Palace,

Wolf Creek Bridge, Holter Lake, and Beartooth and White Sandy RAs.

49. **CANYON FERRY RECREATION AREAS.** A popular recreation area near York, Canyon Ferry Dam and Village has a visitor center. There are numerous state recreation areas around the lake. Some on the west side of the lake have interpretive signs.

50. **MISSOURI HEADWATERS STATE PARK.** Trail, interpretation, campground, and scenic overlooks are available at this certified NHT site located near Three Forks, where the Jefferson, Madison, and Gallatin Rivers join to form the Missouri River. Headwaters Heritage Museum pays homage to Sacagawea, who had lived in the area until kidnapped by the Hidatsa. The site became an important geological landmark to trappers who arrived in the area later on. *Nearby:* Madison Buffalo Jump SHS; Lewis and Clark Caverns SP; Yellowstone NP; Beaverhead NF; Gallatin NF.

51. **BEAVERHEAD ROCK STATE MONUMENT.** North of Dillon on State Highway 41, this large landmark rock formation resembles the head of a swimming beaver. Recognizing it from her childhood memories, Sacagawea (August 10, 1805) knew that the Shoshone should be in the area. *Nearby:* Nevada City and Virginia City mining towns; Beaverhead NF.

52. **CLARK'S LOOKOUT STATE MONUMENT.** A scenic overlook of Beaverhead Valley, northwest of Dillon, was climbed by Clark

(August 13, 1805). *Other attractions:* Beaverhead County Historical Museum with woodcutting of Sacagawea's reunion with her brother; a motorist's shortcut over the divide; the gateway to the Big Hole Valley; Bannack SP; Beaverhead NF.

53. **CAMP FORTUNATE OVERLOOK.** Southeast of Grant is the site where Lewis and the Shoshones waited for Clark and the main party. It was named for Clark's timely arrival and the discovery that the chief was Sacagawea's brother. *Nearby:* Clark Canyon Reservoir.

IDAHO/MONTANA

54. **LEMHI PASS:** West of Dillon, Montana, on State Highway 324, the expedition crossed the Continental Divide (August 12, 1805) for the first time by following the Shoshone hunting trail. A trip in the summer can generally be made by most vehicles, although high-clearance vehicles are recommended. Crossing in a vehicle pulling a trailer is never recommended. More information can be obtained from the Challis NF headquarters and the BLM in Salmon, Idaho.

55. **CAMEAHWAIT'S SHOSHONE CAMP.** There is no public access to the site of the Shoshone village where horses were obtained to cross the Bitterroot Mountains. *Nearby:* Near Tendoy, Idaho, Sacajawea Birthplace Plaque is posted at mile 12.0 on State Highway 28, and Sacajawea Monument is one-half mile further; Salmon NF.

56. **Lost Trail Pass.** This pass in the Bitterroot NF, south of Medicine Springs, Montana, took Lewis and Clark through the Bitterroot Range. It provides interpretation of the Lewis and Clark expedition, the Nez Perce, and the battle of the Big Hole. *Nearby:* Big Hole NB; Painted Rocks Lake RA.

M O N T A N A

57. **Ross's Hole.** Here, south of Darby, the expedition met the Flathead Indians at a mountain cove and traded for additional horses. The area was named for Alexander Ross, a Hudson's Bay Company trapper who nearly perished here with his wife and child after being caught in a snowstorm. *Nearby:* Bitterroot NF; Sula SF.

58. **Traveler's Rest.** A campsite used in 1805 (September 9–11) and again in 1806 (June 30–July 3) on the return, this NHL site is the point where the parties separated en route home. An interpretive sign is located near the junction of U.S. Highways 93 and 12 south of Missoula at Lolo. *Nearby:* Missoula offers a historical museum at Fort Missoula and the Rocky Mountain Elk Foundation/Wildlife Visitor Center. *Also nearby:* Smokejumpers' Base Aerial Fire Depot; the Ninemile Remount Depot and Ranger Station with hiking trail; Flathead Lake; Glacier NP; Rattlesnake Wilderness NRA; Placid Lake State RA; Frenchtown Pond SP; Moiese Bison Range; Pablo NWR; Council Grove SM;

Lolo NF; Flathead Indian Reservation; Flathead NF.

59. **Lolo Hot Springs.** Here, east of Lolo on U.S. Highway 12, the expedition camped and bathed. The expedition passed the hot springs on their initial trip (September 13, 1805) and en route home (June 29, 1806). Today it is commercially operated, and Lolo NF surrounds the area.

I D A H O / M O N T A N A

60. **Packer Meadows.** This campsite (Sept. 13, 1805) south of Lolo on U.S. Highway 12 has an interpretive sign and offers views of the Bitterroot Mountains much like the expedition would have seen.

61. **Lolo Pass Visitor Center.** The Clearwater NF operates a summer visitor center with Lewis and Clark interpretation. A brochure, "Lewis and Clark across the Lolo Trail," is available.

62. **Lolo Trail.** Used by the expedition in 1805 and 1806, and later by the Nez Perce, to cross the Bitterroot Mountains, the trail is now a NHL. Forest Service Route 500, known as the Lolo Motorway, is a primitive dirt road that closely follows the original route. Vehicles with good clearance are advised. Portions of the actual trail are marked and open for hiking, mountain biking, and horseback riding. At mile 160, east of the Powell ranger station, a local outfitter can meet groups for tours by van, on mountain bike, or on horseback. Interpre-

tive and directional signs mark campsite locations and other historic and cultural features along the way. A map-brochure is available from the Clearwater and Lolo NFs. The trail and roads are open from mid-July to mid-September. Adequate supplies of fuel, water, food, and warm clothing should be carried. Inquire about travel conditions at the Lolo Pass Visitor Center or at Forest Service offices in Powell, Kooskia, Kamiah, and Orofino in Idaho, or Missoula, Montana.

IDAHO

63. LEWIS AND CLARK LONG CAMP (NEZ PERCE NHP). This campsite was used for twenty-seven days while the expedition waited for the snow to melt before crossing the Bitterroot Mountains in eastbound travel. It offers an interpretive sign at the roadside Nez Perce NHP near Kamiah.

64. WEIPPE PRAIRIE (NEZ PERCE NHP). During westbound travel, the starving expedition met the Nez Perce on September 22, 1805, at their root-gathering place on this large prairie near Weippe (Nez Perce NHP). On June 10, 1806, they returned to the area to hunt and prepare for the return trip over the Bitterroot Mountains. Outfitters take visitors on horseback adventures on the trail used by the expedition.

65. CANOE CAMP (NEZ PERCE NHP). Five canoes were made at this campsite using the Nez Perce

technique of burning and then digging out the center of the ponderosa pine logs. These canoes were used for the final leg of the journey down the Clearwater, Snake, and Columbia Rivers. The party arrived in the area September 26 and left October 7, 1805, with two new guides. Old Toby remained behind. West of Orofino, the site is located on the Nez Perce Indian Reservation. *Nearby:* Nez Perce and Clearwater NFs; Dworshak Dam and visitor center (Nez Perce NHP).

66. NEZ PERCE NATIONAL HISTORIC PARK. The park is composed of a collection of thirty-eight scattered historic sites that contain significant cultural resources. A complete tour is about a four-hundred-mile trip. The Lewis and Clark and Nez Perce Trails and Nez Perce culture are interpreted at the visitor center and museum in Spalding, which has one of the few remaining expedition medals. Spalding is named for Rev. Henry H. Spalding, who with his wife traveled with the Whitmans to Oregon (1836). The Spaldings established their mission among the Nez Perce. *Nearby:* Lewiston, at the confluence of the Clearwater and Snake Rivers, is the site where Lewis and Clark camped in 1805 and again in 1806. *Other attractions:* Luna House Museum in Lewiston has displays on the American Indian and pioneer artifacts; the gateway to Hells Canyon has jetboat excursions to North America's deepest canyon.

WASHINGTON

67. CHIEF TIMOTHY STATE PARK. The park, named for a Nez Perce chief, has a full range of recreational activities. The certified NHT site, Alpowai Interpretive Center east of Clarkston, tells the story of Lewis and Clark's meeting with Nez Perce Indians. Six-thousand-year-old petroglyphs are accessible from River Road. *Nearby:* There is a certified NHT site roadside marker near Clarkston and another near Alpowai Summit. Wenatchee and Mount Baker–Snoqualmie NFs offer raft and canoe trips.

68. BOYER PARK. This recreation complex and marina with interpretive sign is located approximately two miles upriver from the expedition's campsite (October 11, 1805). A roadside sign near Pomeroy marks Three Forks Indian Trail, a certified NHT site. Lower Granite Dam is near Almota.

69. LEWIS AND CLARK TRAIL STATE PARK. Located on U.S. Highway 12 west of Dayton on the overland route used on the expedition's return to the Missouri, the certified NHT site preserves a number of plants common along the river in Lewis and Clark's time. Campfire programs celebrate the Lewis and Clark expedition, and the park holds an annual Lewis and Clark Trail Day in May. *Nearby:* Umatilla NF; Whitman Mission NHP in Walla Walla.

70. LYONS FERRY STATE PARK. This certified NHT site at the confluence of the Snake and Palouse Rivers near Riparia on Washington Highway 261 provides an interpretive sign and offers a marina and recreational activities. A Jefferson peace medal given to a chief by Lewis and Clark was found here in July 1964. *Nearby:* Palouse Falls SP.

71. SACAJAWEA STATE PARK. This certified NHT site near Pasco uses the local spelling of the Shoshone woman's name. It lies at the confluence of the Snake and Columbia Rivers, where the expedition camped (October 16–17, 1805). The interpretive center highlights Sacagawea's role in the expedition and exhibits American Indian artifacts. *Other attractions:* Franklin County Historical Museum; Lee Harbor Dam with visitor center; McNary NWR with an evening jetboat cruise on the Columbia. *Nearby:* Juniper Dunes Wilderness.

OREGON/WASHINGTON

72. HAT ROCK STATE PARK. This park in Umatilla, Oregon, just west of the junction of U.S. Highway 730 and Oregon State Route 37, gives evidence of the tectonic forces that pushed this and other basalt flows to the surface around the Columbia River. The landmark was named and climbed by Clark (October 19, 1805) on the westward trek and passed again (April 27, 1806) en route home. *Other attractions:* McNary Dam, the first of four on the Columbia on the Oregon/Washington border. Irrigon Marina Park and Umatilla City

Park are certified NHT sites. *Nearby:* Juniper Dunes Wilderness; Crow Butte SP; Maryhill SP and Maryhill Museum, which has an outstanding display of Indian baskets; John Day Dam at Rufus, Oregon, with visitor centers on the north and south sides, marks the beginning of the best windsurfing in North America.

73. HORSETHIEF LAKE STATE PARK. The expedition encountered the Great Falls of the Columbia (Celilo Falls) and began to portage. As a result of the dams, the falls no longer exist. The park, near present-day Wishram, Washington, has an interpretive sign and is famous for its excellent Indian petroglyphs. Tours are available by reservation. The Spearfish Roadside Marker above the park is a certified NHT site.

74. THE DALLES. Lying on the great bend of the Columbia, The Dalles marks the entrance into the Columbia River Gorge NSA where treacherous falls once caused navigational barriers. Lewis and Clark amazed the locals by riding their canoes through the narrows. An interpretive marker is located at the certified NHT site of the expedition's Rock Fort camp. *Other attractions:* The Dalles Dam with visitor centers on the Washington and Oregon ends; Discovery Center at Crates Point; Fort Dalles Museum; and a certified NHT site roadside marker at Celilo Park. *Nearby:* Hood River, Oregon, the unofficial gorge headquarters, hosts some of the

world's premiere windsurfing competitions; Hood River County Historical Museum; gateway to Mount Hood NF with historic Timberline Lodge; Mount Hood Railroad (1906) to Parkdale provides a good view of Mount Hood. When the expedition saw this magnificent snow-covered cone named by a sea captain thirteen years earlier (in 1792), they knew they were no longer in uncharted territory. At Cascade Locks, the sternwheeler *Columbia Gorge* offers cruises during the summer, with narration of the Lewis and Clark expedition and the Oregon Trail. There is a visitor center at Cascade Locks. The Bridge of the Gods, used by hikers on the Pacific Crest National Scenic Trail, can be taken to each side of the locks. An Indian legend recounts that a natural bridge once spanned the Columbia River near the Cascade Locks, hence its name. There is a Forest Service visitor center on the Washington side and the Pacific Crest National Scenic Trail continues north through Gifford Pinchot NF.

75. BONNEVILLE DAM AND THE COLUMBIA GORGE INTERPRETIVE CENTER. Bonneville Dam offers in-terpretation of the expedition at the oldest of the Columbia River dams (NRHP, NHL), which forms a connecting link between the two states. The Army Corps of Engineers has visitor centers in both states—at Bonneville, Oregon, and at North Bonneville, Washington. *Other attractions:* John B. Yeon SP with Elowah

Falls on McCord Creek Trail at North Bonneville; the Bonneville Dam—Washington Shore Visitor Center; Sternwheeler Cruises offers narrated tours on the Columbia River, departing from the dam visitor center in Stevenson, Washington, and from Cascade Locks in Oregon. *Nearby:* In Oregon, the Multnomah Falls FS Visitor Center on the Columbia River Scenic Highway offers hiking to other famous gorge waterfalls. At Stevenson, Washington, the new Columbia Gorge Interpretive Center features movie and slide programs and exhibits on the expedition, the creation of the gorge, and natural history.

76. BEACON ROCK STATE PARK. The certified NHT site, basalt landmark near Skamania, Washington, was noted and named by Clark. Here the explorers first detected the effects of Pacific Ocean tidewater. The rock can be climbed by convenient steps, offering a view of the Columbia River. The Biddle family, descendants of Nicholas Biddle, the first editor/publisher of the expedition journals, donated the area and landmark to the state. Further west, down the road in Clark County, are two certified NHT roadside markers. One site designates the Lewis and Clark campsite, and the other commemorates the Corps of Discovery at Cree Creek. *Nearby:* Fort Vancouver NHS, Mount St. Helens NM.

77. LEWIS AND CLARK STATE PARK. The expedition stopped here (November 3, 1805) to explore the mouth of the Sandy River and the sandbar at the channel entrance. The name "Quicksand River" was shortened to Sandy River. Near Troutdale, Oregon, the certified NHT site offers a self-guided trail that interprets plants whose botanical discovery is credited to Lewis and Clark. *Nearby:* Portland offers cruises down the Columbia, Willamette, and Snake Rivers on the America West Steamboat Company's *Queen of the West,* which offers onboard interpretation and explores Lewis and Clark and Oregon Trail sites; the Oregon History Center has a research library, exhibits, and a Lewis and Clark mural; Washington Park has two statues—*Coming of the White Man* and *Sacajawea*—dedicated by Susan B. Anthony at the opening of the Lewis and Clark Exposition (1905); the Governor Hotel has murals of the Lewis and Clark expedition; the Captain William Clark Monument, a certified NHT site, is located on the campus of University of Portland; Leach Botanical Garden offers native species; Hoyt Arboretum with loop trails; the World Forestry Center has exhibits on northwestern old-growth forests; the Audubon Society of Portland has a wildlife sanctuary; and there is a Rose Festival in June.

78. FORT CANBY STATE PARK. Here Lewis and Clark achieved their ultimate goal of reaching the Pacific Ocean. The Lewis and Clark Interpretive Center, a certified NHT site near Ilwaco,

Washington, provides a comprehensive overview of the expedition. It is located on Cape Disappointment, named in 1788 by British sea captain John Meares. The park houses the Cape Disappointment Lighthouse. *Nearby:* The Ilwaco Heritage Museum interprets the Chinook Indians. Long Beach, Washington, a popular oyster farming and vacation center, offers deep-sea fishing, a boardwalk on 2,300 feet of beachfront, and the International Kite Festival held each August. Fort Columbia SP in Chinook, Washington, is a certified NHT site; Stevens SP in Hammond, Oregon, marks the beginning of the Columbia River Estuary with a driving tour that starts in Astoria, Oregon.

O R E G O N

79. **FORT CLATSOP NATIONAL MEMORIAL.** After reaching the Pacific Ocean, the explorers developed their winter quarters (1805–6). Southwest of Astoria, the fort is a replica of the expedition's stockade; it offers a visitor center, museum, living-history programs, a canoe launch, and wetland habitat for birdwatching. The renovated Astoria Column on Coxcomb Hill in Astoria has scenes from Lewis and Clark's expedition. *Other attractions:* The Columbia River Maritime Museum in Astoria.

80. **SALT WORKS.** Four bushels of salt were extracted here by the expedition through use of a process of boiling seawater. The salt was needed at Fort Clatsop and for the return journey. *Other attractions:* The End of the Trail Monument can be found at the foot of Broadway in Seaside. The Lewis and Clark Pageant is staged in late July and early August; Seaside Museum and Historical Society offers Clatsop Indian items; Tillamook Head Trail retraces Lewis and Clark to Ecola SP in Cannon Beach.

81. **ECOLA STATE PARK.** This park outside Cannon Beach yields some of the most spectacular views on the Oregon coast, including that of Haystack Rock, one of the world's largest monoliths. Recording his view from Tillamook Head, Clark wrote, "from this point I beheld the grandest and most pleasing prospects which my eyes ever surveyed, in my front a boundless Ocean." The five-mile Tillamook Head Trail takes the traveler to Ecola SP by following the footsteps that Clark, Sacagawea, and others took (January 7–8, 1806) on their way to the site of a beached whale. Indian Beach is the site of an ancient American Indian village.

82. **LES SHIRLEY PARK.** Also in Cannon Beach, this certified NHT site is located near the mouth of the Ecola Creek, where a whale washed ashore and the party purchased about three hundred pounds of blubber from the local Indians. It also offers an interpretive sign and a view of Haystack Rock.

SAN MIGUEL CHAPEL, SANTA FE

Built on the site of a pueblo occupied as early as A.D. 1300, San Miguel Chapel dates to Santa Fe's settlement by the Spanish in 1609.

Santa Fe National Historic Trail

The old Governor's Palace has been turned into a historical museum, and if you look you will find there many beautiful relics of the days that are gone with the wind.

MARION SLOAN RUSSELL, 1845–1936

L ike so many trails in North America, the Santa Fe Trail can be traced to the country's early history. Long before the Spanish arrived, portions of the trail served as a link in ancient Indian trade networks. As settlements spread across the land, networks grew. Passing through many hands, items from the Southwest reached the Mississippi Valley through travel across the Great Plains. In New Mexico, there is solid evidence of Plains artifacts dating to around 1200 B.C. No doubt, direct trade strengthened ties and influenced early cultural characteristics of the residents along the route.

ADMINISTERING AGENCY
National Park Service, Southwest Region
Long Distance Trails Group Office
P.O. Box 728
Santa Fe, NM 87504-0728
505-988-6888

FURTHER INFORMATION
Santa Fe Trail Association
Santa Fe Trail Center
Route 3
Larned, KS 67559

ESTABLISHED
1987

APPROXIMATE MILEAGE
1,203 miles (1,937 kilometers)

STATES
Missouri, Kansas, Oklahoma, Colorado, New Mexico

When the Europeans arrived, subsequent exploration of the continent revealed routes of old trade networks.* Francisco Vásquez de Coronado, in his search for the fabled Seven Cities of Cibola, reached an American Indian settlement near the center of the continent around present-day Lyons, Kansas, in 1541. On his return to New Mexico he traveled a route that closely followed what would become the Santa Fe Trail. Thereafter, the Great Plains were visited by other Spanish explorers from the west and Frenchmen from the east. Their motivation was essentially the same: trade and the search for riches. Almost as soon as the Spanish villa of Santa Fe was established in 1610, rumors reached the French of its riches and mines. Soon the words "Santa Fe" became a lure for those seeking personal fortune.

Sparring for control and influence, the French and Spanish explored the plains, making treaties and alliances with the American Indian nations. Spain, seeing an opportunity for wealth, restricted its trade to its province even though cheaper goods could have been obtained elsewhere. In the 1700s, despite Spanish rules against it, trading began with the French from the Mississippi Valley until higher authorities closed the market. Thereafter, those who ventured into Santa Fe from the

*Material in this section is taken from the National Park Service's *Santa Fe National Historic Trail Comprehensive Management and Use Plan.*

outside were thrown into jail. With the Treaty of San Ildefonso in 1762, the Great Plains, then encompassing the area known as Louisiana, were ceded to Spain by the French. Now the Spanish controlled all legal commerce, with the exception of the most covert smuggling, from St. Louis in the east to Santa Fe in the west.

Realizing their potential for profit, the Spanish sent Pedro Vial from Santa Fe to St. Louis in 1792 to open a route of trade. After traversing the plains to reach St. Louis, Vial returned to Santa Fe. The anticipated trade never developed, however, and in 1800 the Louisiana tract was returned to France. Much to Spain's surprise, France sold the Louisiana Territory to the United States in 1803. (See the previous chapter.) This action prompted several trading expeditions from the St. Louis area to Santa Fe. For the most part the expeditions failed, though some of the traders stayed in New Mexico, and one even sold his goods before returning to the United States. The vast majority, though, were thrown in jail— after their goods had been confiscated.

Ever defensive about real or perceived boundaries, Spain continued to try to stop explorations into its territory. Explorer Zebulon Montgomery Pike was arrested in 1807 and brought to Santa Fe from his camp near the headwaters of the Arkansas River. After being sent to Chihuahua, he was eventually allowed to return to the United States. Publishing his journal of travels in 1810, he excited a frontier with the possibilities of trade with New Mexico.

That same year, rebellion was taking place in Mexico against Spain. Though it failed, rumblings against the Spanish monarchy continued. In the meantime, American expeditions to New Mexico in 1808 and 1812 sent warnings to Spain of its neighbor's ambitions to infiltrate the area. Even though until 1820 members of the expeditions were jailed, American expansion could not be stopped. Fur trade lured more and more entrepreneurs west, and exploration continued. The expedition of Stephen Long traveled quietly through New Mexico Territory by following the Canadian River. By 1821, conditions were ripe for the success of William Becknell. First, a financial panic in 1819 placed many on the Missouri frontier in serious debt. In a desperate move to change their luck, at least three parties made midsummer plans to travel to Santa Fe. Becknell was among those willing to take a chance. Second, the sputtering revolution in Mexico had gathered steam in February 1821. By September, Mexico was an independent nation. Third, the Great Plains were well enough known by this time that directions to Santa Fe could be easily obtained in Franklin, Missouri, the eventual beginning of the Santa Fe Trail.

On September 1, 1821, Becknell and five others headed west with plans to trade, to trap for

CHAMISO GOLD

Chamiso gold, found along the Sante Fe National Historic Trail, reminds the traveler of the golden allure that made the trail famous.

fur, and to catch wild horses along the Arkansas River. The daring group ventured to the Arkansas at the edge of the mountains, traveling south into forbidden Spanish territory. In New Mexico, Gov. Facundo Melgares knew that events in Mexico would probably lead to independence, but he had a more immediate problem to contend with—the Navajos were trying to reclaim land occupied by New Mexican settlers. Several military expeditions were sent against them, including one that left Abiquiu on November 2, 1821, commanded by Capt. Don Pedro Ignacio Gallego. Shortly into their expedition, Gallego was ordered to the east to pursue Plains Indians who had raided the little village of San Miguel on the Pecos River.

By the time Captain Gallego departed San Miguel for the east

American Indians sell their wares in front of the Palace of the Governors in Santa Fe, New Mexico. The town, the nation's oldest state capital, was built of adobe in 1609–10.

and the plains, 445 Pueblo Indians, soldiers, and militiamen had joined the command. On November 13, just south of present-day Las Vegas, New Mexico, Gallego's command encountered the six Americans. To their surprise, the Americans were greeted as guests rather than trespassers. Gallego sent for an interpreter and routed the Becknell party to Santa Fe, where on November 16, they met Governor Melgares, who officially welcomed them and permitted them to trade.

The desperate gamble had paid off. Legend has it that Becknell left Santa Fe with a handsome profit of almost two thousand percent! The story continues that when the traders returned to

Franklin in late January 1822, as they unloaded their goods on the sidewalk, one of the men cut the thongs on a rawhide bag and silver coins spilled out on the cobbled street. This act fired the imagination of Missouri's frontierspeople. After two centuries of isolation, the Santa Fe Trail was born, and a new era of prosperity began.

In May, Becknell headed out for Santa Fe once more. This time, he traveled with over twenty men and three wagons. It was the use of wagons that may have made his second trip even more important than the first. Wagons had not been used on the plains since Juan de Oñate's expedition in 1602, and Becknell's wagons were the first ever used on the Santa Fe Trail. En route, Becknell crossed the Arkansas River, heading southwest toward the Cimarron River, where he pioneered a desert passage that later came to be known as the Cimarron Route.

This became the only wagon trail to New Mexico until the 1840s when the Mountain Route was opened. Arriving in Santa Fe in July, the expedition found the New Mexicans starved for goods and eager to purchase the cheaper American merchandise which was, in most cases, of better quality than the Mexican goods shipped from the interior of the country. Silver coins, furs, and mules completed the exchange. For his efforts, Becknell has been called "the father of the Santa Fe Trail."

Although the trail was attractive to adventurers and mountain men, its typical travelers were businessmen who financed hundreds of caravans of freight wagons hauled by thousands of mules and oxen. Traveling at the rate of twelve to fifteen miles a day, the wagons carried a vast supply of manufactured goods from Missouri, including cotton cloth, silks and velvets, French wines and champagne, pianos, pins and needles, canned oysters, and strawberry jam. They risked accidents, disease, starvation, Indian attacks, drought, storms, and floods for profit and adventure.

For the New Mexicans, the trail not only brought an ever-increasing supply of less expensive goods from the eastern United States, it also brought new people with a new language, new skills, and new customs. But seeing that profits could also be made from local goods at distant coastal markets, many New Mexicans joined the

trade, sending caravans east. Both governments responded to the trade potential. In 1825 the U.S. government conducted a survey of the route, starting from Fort Osage, and made treaties with American Indian tribes near the eastern end of the trail. Beginning in 1829, military protection was occasionally offered to trading parties, and the New Mexican troops and Pueblo soldiers also helped protect the traders in 1829 and again in 1843.

The highway of commerce first stretched more than nine hundred miles. From Missouri, the

DINOSAUR FOOTPRINTS-CLAYTON

Tracks of those who came before are found off the Cimarron Route in Oklahoma and New Mexico. This print appears at one of the most extensive dinosaur trackways in North America at Clayton Lake State Park Dam near Clayton, New Mexico.

After following the same route from Independence, Missouri, the Santa Fe and Oregon Trails separated at this fork in the road near Gardner, Kansas.

trail cut diagonally through Kansas to southeast Colorado and into the tip of the Oklahoma panhandle, eventually reaching Santa Fe, the capital of New Mexico. It was a two-way trail, with eastern and western trailheads. It began in Santa Fe as much as it began in Missouri, and it ended in Missouri as much as it ended in Santa Fe. However, it progressively shortened as the American frontier crept westward. Commodities were shipped up the Missouri River from St. Louis before being transferred to wagons for the trip to Santa Fe. The earliest wagon trains left from Franklin, Missouri, and later from other river towns such as Arrow Rock and Lexington. By the early 1830s most traffic began at Independence, Missouri, which remained the major outfitting point until the 1840s when West-

port and Fort Leavenworth, Kansas, became major points of departure. Near Council Grove, Kansas, was a major point of rendezvous for caravans organizing for the trip westward.

During the trail's early years, the first settlement in New Mexico reached by westbound traders was San Miguel del Vado, which served for a time as a port of entry. San Miguel was eventually replaced in that regard by Las Vegas, New Mexico, when it was founded in 1835. For those traveling eastward from New Mexico, the area near La Junta (now Watrous), where the Cimarron and Mountain Routes separated, was the major point of rendezvous to organize for the trip to Missouri.

By the early 1840s, Mexican merchants may have dominated the trade moving in both directions along the route of commerce. Merchants such as Don Antonio José Chávez, his brother Don José Chávez y Castillo, and the Chávez in-laws, Juan Perea and Juan Otero, provided keen competition for American traders like William and James Glasgow, James and Robert Aull, and J. J. Webb. Some of the New Mexican families, Ortiz, Delgado, Armijo, and Chávez, sent their children over the trail to be educated in the United States. Many of these families maintained their economic and political leadership during New Mexico's U.S. territorial period, joining other New Mexican merchants in fostering the international trading system

These traders began their journey in Santa Fe, many times continuing on from Chihuahua, Mexico, swinging around the Sangre de Cristo Mountains by way of the Glorieta Pass, and entering the Great Plains. They halted near La Junta (Watrous) to organize and to wait until enough wagons were present to continue a safe journey over the plains. Either the Mountain or the Cimarron Route was then followed to the eastern terminus of the trail, or as far east as it took to sell their goods.

American families used the trail as well. Mary Dodson Donoho was the first Anglo-American woman in Santa Fe, arriving in 1833. Other American women who traveled the route and recorded their journeys include Susan Shelby Magoffin in 1846 and Marion Sloan Russell in the 1850s and 1860s. Gradually, multinational partnerships emerged. Yet, despite the cultural exchanges, economic competition developed between Mexican and American merchants and between Mexico and the United States. In 1845, American interests persuaded the U.S. Congress to help offset inherent Mexican advantages by passing the Drawback Act, which allowed Americans to better compete with their Mexican counterparts. It was not long before the trail was used for the war between Mexico and the United States (1846–48).

General Stephen W. Kearny led the Army of the West from Fort Leavenworth to Bent's Fort and over Ratón Pass on the Mountain Route to the town of Las Vegas, where he expected to face a Mexican army. [The Mormon Battalion (see the chapter on the Mormon Pioneer National Historic Trail) and other elements of the army used the Cimarron Route]. Finding no resistance, he proclaimed annexation of New Mexico by the United States and continued on to Santa Fe. A resistance force had been organized by Gov. Manuel Armijo at Canoncito, but it was withdrawn in advance of the approaching U.S. force. Entering Santa Fe, Kearny raised the U.S. flag over the Palace of the Governors.

After Kearny's departure, Lt. Col. Sterling Price remained to provide military support to the Kearny-appointed governor, Charles Bent. But resistance to U.S. occupation assumed the nature of guerrilla warfare. During an uprising at Taos, Bent, the first American governor of New Mexico Territory, was killed. He was succeeded by Donaciano Vigil. The war ended in 1848 with the Treaty of Guadalupe Hidalgo.

The United States gained almost half of Mexico, including present-day New Mexico, Arizona, California, Nevada, Utah, and parts of Colorado, Wyoming, Oklahoma, Kansas, and Texas. After the war, the volume of traffic on the Santa Fe Trail rose considerably, although some aspects changed. More emigrants began to follow the trail to the Southwest. The trail of commerce also accommodated teamsters who began to convey more and

FORT UNION

Adobe ruins, extensive ruts, and remnants of wagons are found at the junction of the Cimarron and Mountain Routes at Fort Union National Monument in Watrous, New Mexico. From 1851 to 1891, the fort served as the foremost military post on the Santa Fe Trail.

more military supplies now that the U.S. Army had the responsibility of protecting the American Southwest. Military posts were established along the route, including Fort Mann (1847), Fort Atkinson (1850), Fort Larned (1859), Fort Union (1859), and Fort Lyon (1860). Each post required supplies and provided protection for caravans on the trail. In 1858 alone over eighteen hundred wagons crossed the plains.

Indian traders were also using the commercial route, and Bent's Fort (1833–49) on the Arkansas River in southeast Colorado symbolized that trade. In 1853 William Bent opened Bent's New Fort, some forty miles downriver near a favorite Indian camping area, Big Timbers. Increasingly, the Jicarillas, Comanches, Kiowas, and other tribes were being threatened by traffic on the trail. Though threats from American Indians were common during the Mexican period (1821–48), the dangers intensified as traffic increased, especially with the beginning of stagecoach and mail service over the trail in 1850.

Troubles along the trail resulted in expanding American pressure on the Indian population in the Southwest, leading to disruption of tribal life and the loss of traditional tribal lands. Negotiated treaties between Americans and American Indians were violated or not fulfilled. In the 1840s the longer Mountain Route was used for wagon traffic to avoid troubles with Indians along the Cimarron Route. Because of the difficulty in taking wagons over Ratón Pass, however, the Mountain Route was not heavily used until improvements were made during and after the Civil War.

Beginning in 1861, the Civil War spread westward, eventually reaching New Mexico. In early 1862 a Confederate force marched up the Rio Grande, intent on capturing Fort Union and ultimately Colorado and California, thereby bringing enormous mineral resources to the Confederate treasury and affording the Confederacy an outlet on the Pacific Ocean. Meanwhile, to the southwest, the Confederates captured Tucson and established the Confederate Territory of Arizona. After the fall of Albuquerque and Santa Fe, only Fort Union blocked a Southern invasion of the Colorado Territory. A combined Union force of regular troops and volunteers from New Mexico and Colorado met the Confederates at Glorieta Pass. Even though Union troops initially lost ground, a separate unit of volunteers slipped behind the Confederate soldiers and destroyed the Confederate supply train at Johnson's Ranch. This forced the Confederates to retreat, and they were soon driven from New Mexico. The Union victory was decisive in protecting the West and the main military supply route, the Santa Fe Trail, from the invading Confederates.

With American Indian resistance growing along the trail during the Civil War, the army was forced to establish Fort Dodge, Camp Nichols, and Fort Aubry in 1865. This situation led to increased traffic on the Mountain

SANTA FE—ALL THE WAY

Amtrak's *Southwest Chief* retraces the old Santa Fe Trail along the Mountain Route. In 1866, just when traffic along the trail peaked at five thousand freight wagons, the Atchison, Topeka and Santa Fe Railroad reached eastern Kansas. Tracks crept westward, and in 1879 when the first locomotive steamed into northeast New Mexico, the Santa Fe Trail passed into history.

Route, which only became more popular when Richens Lacy "Uncle Dick" Wootton opened a toll road over Ratón Pass on the Mountain Route after the end of the Civil War. In 1878, however, he sold out to the Atchison, Topeka and Santa Fe Railway, which won the right-of-way through the pass to build along the route of the Santa Fe Trail.

Railway construction had begun southwest from the Missouri River near the end of the Civil War. As the Union Pacific, Eastern Division (known after 1869 as the Kansas Pacific), worked with the Atchison, Topeka and Santa Fe to build the track westward, the Santa Fe Trail continued to diminish in length —but not importance. Trade items and military freight were simply carried by rail and transferred to wagons for the trail branches. Within a few years a progression of towns—Junction City, Hays, and Sheridan in Kansas; Kit Carson, Granada, Las Animas, and Trinidad in Colorado; and finally Las Vegas, New Mexico—served as the eastern terminal for wagon traffic. In February 1880, the first steam engine entered Santa Fe, ending nearly sixty years of overland use of the Santa Fe Trail. The era of freight wagons, oxen, and mules crossing vast distances over the rutted plains ceased and the Santa Fe Trail passed into history.

THE BENT BROTHERS

Bent's Old Fort on the Arkansas River in southeastern Colorado was once the frontier hub from which American trade and influence radiated south into Mexico, west into the Great Basin (and beyond to the Pacific), and north to southern Wyoming. Completed in 1833–34 by the brothers Charles and William Bent and Cerán St. Vrain, it became the most important port of call and depot between Independence, Missouri, and Santa Fe, New Mexico.

Charles (1799–47) and William (1809–69) Bent were the eldest of four brothers whose activities fill a large space in the history of the Santa Fe Trail. As a result of the father's appointment as principal deputy surveyor of the new Territory of Louisiana, the family moved to St. Louis in 1806. Drawn to the Upper Missouri fur trade, the elder sons were probably employees of the American Fur Company as early as 1823. The following year, they joined Cerán St. Vrain, who would be their associate for many years, on a fur-trapping expedition on the upper Arkansas. It is believed that Charles traveled as a member of St. Vrain's 1826 expedition to trap New Mexico streams. Sensing greater opportunities, the two joined the Santa Fe trade.

In 1829, Charles Bent led a caravan escorted by Maj. Bennet Riley and two hundred U.S. Army troops as far as the Mexican border (the Arkansas River in western Kansas). Soon after entering Mexican territory, the caravan was attacked by Indians. The major, some Mexican buffalo hunters, and trappers from Taos (including St. Vrain and Kit Carson) came to their aid. Heading for Taos and then Santa Fe, Bent and St. Vrain formed a partnership that would dominate commerce and make them the most influential men in New Mexico. An equally strong friendship developed between the younger Bent and the nineteen-year-old Carson. The profits made in Santa Fe that year were extraordinary, and Charles Bent learned some valuable lessons: Oxen could outtravel mules in rough country, and they were safe in Indian raids—and frontiersmen were better guards than infantry (until mounted troops were available).

Charles continued to trade successfully in Santa Fe, while William, Little White Man to the Cheyennes, traded for buffalo robes and beaver skins with the Cheyenne and Arapaho Indians in Colorado, building a stockade on the Arkansas River. Outgrowing the stockade, he asked his brother to join him in building a new trading post along the river on Cheyenne hunting grounds near present-day La Junta, Colorado. They used some of the $190,000 they had made in trade to partner with St. Vrain to form Bent, St. Vrain & Company, which ultimately established the largest trading post in the West. Originally named Fort William, it was built in 1833. William Bent managed it, along with his two younger brothers, George (1814–46) and Robert (1816–41). Charles, the senior partner in the firm, handled much of the business operations between St. Louis and Santa Fe. Spending little time at the fort, St. Vrain was active in trade operations and mercantile outlets.

Together, the Bents and St. Vrain built up a profitable business, which became a center for a huge fur-trade network with the American Indians, Mexicans, and trappers who called it Bent's Fort. Through William's efforts, rival tribes met and traded in a peaceful atmosphere. Everyone who came to the fort was his guest, and to feed these guests, he contracted Kit Carson and his already-famous Carson men to supply him with buffalo meat.

As one historian wrote, the Bents "were truly mighty men whose will was prairie law, who could sway whole tribes, who knew Indians and Mexicans as few others did." But tragedy came as quickly as did fortune. In order to handle the Santa Fe trade, Charles and St. Vrain had located in New Mexico. Charles married into a prominent Taos family, and his wife's sister subsequently married Kit Carson, who also resided in Taos. Soon after Gen. Stephen Watts Kearny's 1846 conquest of New Mexico, he appointed Charles governor of the New Mexico Territory. St. Vrain, who had served as an American consul in Santa Fe in the 1830s, ran the company's stores in Taos and Santa Fe. But during the '40s, three of the Bent brothers lost their lives. Robert was killed by the Comanches, George died of consumption, and soon after Charles's appointment as governor, he was killed in the uprising in Taos, a tragedy felt deeply on the American frontier. The same year that Charles died, William's Cheyenne wife, Owl Woman, the daughter of a powerful Cheyenne priest, died after giving birth to his fourth child.

With the retirement of St. Vrain at the end of 1848, William became the sole owner of Bent's Fort. In these latter years, a military presence had become a fact of life at the fort. The first of several intertribal councils was organized at the fort by Gen. Henry Dodge; it brought the Cheyenne and Arapaho to the table with their enemy, the Pawnee. Explorer John Charles Frémont was greeted there, and General Kearny used the fort as an advance base for his invasion of New Mexico. But as the war progressed, army wagon trains congregated in ever-increasing numbers, and government cattle overgrazed nearby pastures. Military stores piled up in the fort, and soldiers, teamsters, and craftsmen occupied its rooms. The steady flow of soldiers, together with the influx of settlers, gold seekers, and adventurers that came later, fouled the watering places, wantonly used up precious wood, and frightened away the bison. Bent, St. Vrain & Company was caught between the millstones of resentful Indians and invading whites. When Indian warfare commenced seriously in 1847, the days of rich trading were over. The final blow came when cholera, most likely brought by emigrants, spread through the tribes.

The U.S. government wanted to buy the fort to use as a military post in 1849, but their offer was low. Disillusioned and disappointed, William Bent blew up much of the fort, loaded his children, his new wife, Yellow Wo-man, the sister of Owl Woman, and his employees into wagons and left. At Big Timbers, only forty miles downstream from Bent's Old Fort, as it was named by historians, he built Bent's New Fort. He continued to do business there until he rented it to the government, which renamed it Fort Lyon. Moving to a ranch at the mouth of the Purgatoire River (Las Animas), Bent built a stockade and served as an Indian agent. In 1867, after the death of his second wife, he married Adalina, the daughter of Alexander Harvey and a Blackfoot. Other settlers, including Kit Carson, moved into the ranch area and the town of Boggsville, named for Kit Carson's nephew who was born there.

William Bent's life ended shortly after his third marriage. Like his brother Charles and his partner St. Vrain, he was widely known for his fair dealings. A special friend of the trapper and hunter, he also held the confidence of the American Indians with whom he dealt. The first permanent settler in Colorado, he also became its most prominent citizen and perhaps the most well known frontiersman of the West. Bent's Old Fort was an instrument of Manifest Destiny and a catalyst for change. The company's influence with the Plains Indians and its political and social connections in Santa Fe helped pave the way for the occupation of the West and the annexation of Mexico's northern province. Its trade with the In-

dians introduced a level of tech-
nology that, for better and worse,
irrevocably altered their culture.
And the fort's immediate effects
on the land and water were signs
of wider environmental change to
come.

The primary routes of the trail,
the Cimarron and the Mountain Routes, as well as the major
branches have several historic
sites and landmarks, plus segments where wagon ruts more
than a century old are still evident. An auto-tour route parallels
the trail, which crosses public and
private lands. Wagon trail trips
are also available. Other recreational opportunities to retrace
the trail include short- and long-
distance hiking, backpacking, and
horseback riding. Some of the
best potential for future hiking is
found in Mora County, New
Mexico. Near Las Vegas, the hiker
can detour for a pleasant hike
along the Pecos River, which
crosses the trail. The trail also
passes throug the rolling valleys
of eastern Kansas, the grasslands
in the Flint Hills, and the Comanche National Grassland in
Colorado and the Kiowa National
Grasslands in New Mexico.
Twenty miles of hiking trail are
found in the Cimarron National
Grassland in southwestern Kansas. National parks sites associated with the trail include Fort
Larned National Historic Site in
Kansas, Bent's Old Fort National
Historic Site in Colorado, and
Fort Union National Monument
and Pecos National Historical
Park in New Mexico.

In 1974, a museum was dedicated to preserving and interpreting the history of the trail. The
Santa Fe Trail Center offers bi-
annual seminars, exhibits, a research library, archives, and a
broad selection of Santa Fe Trail
books and maps. Locally owned
and privately funded, the center is
situated near Larned, Kansas, just
a few miles east of the fort and
down the trail from Pawnee
Rock, one of the most prominent landmarks on the trail.
Designated a certified site on
the National Historic Trail in
1991, the center serves as headquarters for the Santa Fe Trail
Association.

Of the 1,203 miles of trail
route, more than two hundred
miles of ruts and trace remain
visible, with approximately thirty
of these miles protected on
federal lands. Starting as early
as 1900, the Daughters of the
American Revolution began
marking the trail. A large granite
boulder marks the original eastern terminus of the trail in New
Franklin, Missouri. Trail markers
commemorate the route, marking
most of the Missouri sites, which
include trail-era homes and businesses, museums, and trail ruts.
In Kansas, well-preserved ruts are
found between the towns of
Cimarron and Dodge City. A
short hiking trail and exhibits
mark this site, which is easily

The
Trail
Today

reached along U.S. Highway 56. Near present-day Dodge City, the trail splits into the Cimarron and Mountain Routes.

The Cimarron Route moves southeast to the Cimarron River, with U.S. Highway 56 passing through Elkhart, with its museum exhibits, and then paralleling the route into Oklahoma. As the trail exits Kansas, it crosses Cimarron National Grassland where shortgrass prairie replaces land that was decimated in the dust bowl years of the 1930s. Today's thriving grassland is now home to native antelope and elk, which were reintroduced to the area. A 150-mile strip in the far northwestern corner of Oklahoma, in the tip of the panhandle region known as No Man's Land, also shows clear ruts in several areas near Black Mesa, the highest point in the state. Other interesting sites include Autograph Rock, and Dinosaur quarries where visible tracks are still seen in streambeds of Carizzo Creek and the Cimarron.

The longer, safer route in old trail history was the Mountain Route, which stretches into Colorado where the most renowned landmark was Bent's Fort. Today's reconstruction can be visited near La Junta, where the headquarters of the Comanche National Grassland offers information on hiking, biking, and birding opportunities in the area. More wagon ruts survive along Timpas Creek, and amazing views of the Rockies greet the traveler. Beckoning with its clear skies, abundance of sunshine, and limitless landscapes, New Mexico offers a land of contrasts. The Mountain Route continues through New Mexico's high plains while the Cimarron Route ascends the Dry Cimarron, crossing tributaries to the Canadian River. Uniting again at Watrous, the trail threads Glorieta Pass before reaching its destination in Santa Fe, where a large granite boulder in the plaza marks the end of the trail.

A voluntary certification process through the National Park Service is available to owners and managers of nonfederal historic sites, trail segments, and interpretive facilities who would like their sites to become official components of the Santa Fe National Historic Trail. Standards for resource preservation and public enjoyment must be met and maintained in order to achieve and retain this designation. The list of certified sites grows ever longer and is updated periodically by the National Park Service's Long Distance Trails Group Office in Santa Fe. Certified sites display the official trail logo and are open during the hours noted. Points of interest on private lands not certified may not be accessible by the public. Visitations to private sites should be made only if and when permission is obtained from the landowner.

MISSOURI

1. OLD FRANKLIN. Franklin became the eastern terminus of the international trail after the Becknell party left the area (1821), following parts of the Osage Trace. Floods (1826 and 1828) contributed to the town's demise, but the certified National Historic Trail site can be located north of the Missouri River, about 0.5 mile west of the Booneville bridge on Missouri Highway 87. To the east, St. Louis was the commercial hub where traders purchased and warehoused goods and supplies for westward freighting on the trail. Mexican goods were then sold or shipped east. *St. Louis attractions:* Jefferson National Expansion Memorial with the Gateway Arch with visitor center and Old Courthouse; Laclede's Landing, the site of the city's original settlement; Jefferson Barracks Historical Park (1826), site of a supply post for troops in the West; the Laumeier Sculpture Park; Missouri Botanical Garden; Forest Park with the History Museum and the St. Louis Art Museum.

2. BOONVILLE. Harley Park Overlook (a certified NHT interpretive facility) overlooks the Missouri River where William Becknell began and ended his first trip. Tours of several historic homes and the town's seven historic districts can be arranged through the Boonville Area Chamber of Commerce. *Nearby:* At Boonesboro, Boone's Lick SHS has two saltwater springs, or licks, that were developed by Daniel Boone's sons. Becknell was also associated with salt production and owned some of the area.

3. ARROW ROCK. Arrow Rock, a certified NHT site, preserves the earlier town, founded in 1829 and a major stopping point on the Santa Fe Trail. The town was named after a bluff used as a landmark on the west side of the Missouri River. The old Arrow Rock Tavern still serves meals. Arrow Rock Landing (1811 until 1927) is accessible by foot. A ferry across the river led from the Boonslick Road to what was originally the Osage Trace to Fort Osage (later followed by the Santa Fe Trail). Ruts are visible from the landing to the community (NHL, NRHP). Santa Fe Spring (NHL), also known as Big Spring, is a certified NHT site and was used by early traders, including Becknell, as a point of departure on the trail.

4. LEXINGTON. James and Robert Aull outfitted trading caravans in Lexington, where the trail passed "Old Town" and the first courthouse. Robert Aull is buried in Macahpelah Cemetery; Water Street was the location of warehouses and other businesses that served the trail. *Other attractions:* The Lafayette County Courthouse still has a cannonball lodged in one of the columns of the clock tower from the battle of Lexington (1861); the Battle of Lexington SHS; Lexington Historical Museum with Civil War and Pony Express exhibits; *Madonna of the Trail,* a monument that overlooks the Missouri

Points of Interest

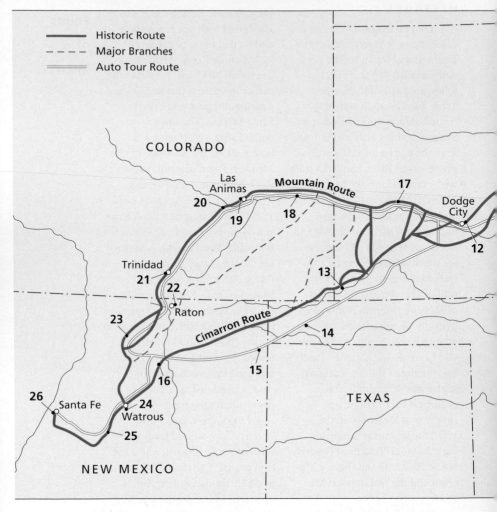

Historic Route
Major Branches
Auto Tour Route

COLORADO

Las Animas
20
19
18
Mountain Route
17
Dodge City
12

Trinidad
21
22
13

23
Raton
Cimarron Route
14

15

16

26
Santa Fe
24
Watrous
25

TEXAS

NEW MEXICO

SANTA FE NATIONAL HISTORIC TRAIL

River; an 1830s log cabin, restored, is open for tours. *Nearby:* At Sibley, Fort Osage (NHL), a certified NHT site, served for a short time as the westernmost outpost and rendezvous point for the SFT caravans. The re-created fort (1808) offers historical reenactment tours and special events.

5. INDEPENDENCE. The town played a major role in outfitting western trail travelers and offers many historical sites. The Lower Independence Landing (1832–90s) served steamboats on the banks of the Missouri River. The landing, since covered over by Santa Fe Railroad tracks, is located about five miles northeast of town. Upper Independence Landing was shorter-lived and not as busy. Although it no longer

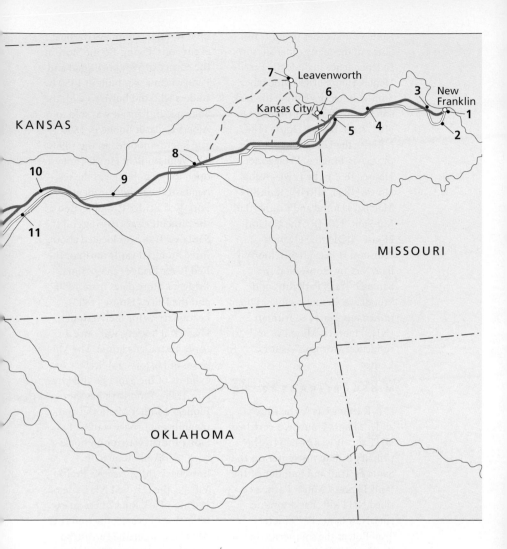

exists, its location is marked by a
sign about three miles north of
town and just north of Cement
City Road. Independence Square
has markers that offer interpretation. Here the trail forked, to
rejoin at the Kansas-Missouri
border. The Jackson County
Courthouse (NRHP), remodeled
in 1933, occupies the center of
the square and still incorporates

parts of the original brick courthouse (1836). Large caravans
nearly encircled the courthouse
on the square's four streets as
they prepared to leave for Santa
Fe. One of the oldest intact buildings on the square is at 205 North
Main. The National Frontier
Trails Center (a certified NHT
interpretive facility) has a museum and research library on the

Santa Fe and other major trails. Some of the many other sites in Independence include the Ferril-Henley House (1830); the Jabez Smith Overseer's House; the Jackson County Log Courthouse (1827); the Kritser House (1847, NRHP); the Lewis Jones House; the Lewis-Bingham-Waggoner House (1855); the Lewis-Webb House (1834, NRHP); the 1859 Marshal's Home and County Jail Museum (NRHP); the Noland House (1831); the Overfelt-Johnston House (1850); the William McCoy House; and the Santa Fe Trails Park Ruts and Woodlawn Cemetery Ruts. *Other attractions:* Harry S. Truman (NHS) Library, Museum, and residence; Mormon Visitors' Center.

MISSOURI/KANSAS

6. KANSAS CITY. The Alexander Majors House is a certified NHT site. It was owned by the primary military freighter on the Santa Fe Trail and founder of the Pony Express. Minor Park, a certified NHT site, has dramatic ruts. New Santa Fe Cemetery Trail Rut, at the southern edge of the Kansas City metropolitan area, marks the location of a small settlement with trading stores (1850s); the certified NHT site, has a small section of ruts. Schumacher Park, also a certified NHT site, has interpretation and commemorative trail markers. Westport Landing was rivaled as a point of organization after 1850 only by Fort Leavenworth. The location where steamboats tied

up now offers summer riverboat excursions. Ewing-Boone Store at the corner of Westport Road and Pennsylvania was built in 1850 by traders who did business with the Shawnee Indians. It was sold to Albert Gallatin Boone in 1854 and later remodeled in the 1890s. The William Bent House (not open to the public) was the residence of the builder of Bent's Fort. Red Bridge Crossing, one of the difficult river crossings on the Santa Fe Trail, was located about three hundred yards north of the Red River Bridge (1859). Jim Bridger's Store dates from 1850, and the Harris House (1855), headquarters for the Westport Historical Society, was once a Santa Fe trader's home. The Museum of History and Science has exhibits of the Santa Fe and Oregon Trails. Penn Park has the Pioneer Mother Memorial and a magnificent bronze statue of a Sioux Indian warrior on horseback. Benjamin Ranch offers horseback rides. *Nearby:* Prairie Village, the certified NHT site of Harmon Park Ruts, offers an exhibit that interprets the trail ruts. At Olathe, Mahaffie Farmstead (NRHP), a certified NHT site, was an active farm and stage stop in the 1850s and 1860s. Lone Elm Campground, located three miles south of Olathe, was a major campground for travelers on the main branch. At Fairway is the Shawnee Mission. An NHL, the museum was relocated to the present site near a branch of the Santa Fe Trail with visible ruts. At Bonner Springs, the Grinter

House and Ferry are located on a branch of the trail where Moses Grinter built the house (NRHP) and operated a ferry. The site of the ferry can be viewed from the house, now a museum.

KANSAS

7. LEAVENWORTH. Fort Leavenworth (NHL) was established (1827) by Col. Henry Leavenworth and served as the shipping point for military freight over the trail. The Fort Leavenworth River Landing (NHL) has the remains of one warehouse and ruts (NHL) that are visible to the west. *Nearby:* The Santa Fe and Oregon Trails junction is marked by a sign located about two miles west of Gardner on U.S. Highway 56. At Edgerton, the Lanesfield School Historic Site is a certified NHT site. The trail may have crossed the school's property, and in the trail's later years the town of Lanesfield provided travelers with supplies and services. Douglas County Prairie Park in Baldwin City has some of the finest ruts along the Santa Fe Trail. The Narrows, west of Black Jack SP, is an area where wagon trains stayed on a ridge to avoid rough terrain. Palmyra (also known as Santa Fe) Well, once used by trail travelers, is marked with a sign. South of Lawrence, the large hill in the area called Blue Mound was a landmark for Santa Fe Trail and other western trail travelers. At Burlingame, the Atchison, Topeka and Santa Fe Railway met the trail in 1869.

8. COUNCIL GROVE. The two small routes converged again at this historically important spot, which the Flint Hills community had the foresight to preserve. It was the first town to complete the certification program under the National Trails System Act. Nine locations are certified NHT sites and twelve are on the National Register of Historic Places. The Hays House restaurant (NHL) is the oldest continuously operated restaurant west of the Mississippi; the Seth Hayes Home (1867) is operated as a museum (NHL). At Council Oak, a treaty was negotiated with the Osage Indians (1825) for safe passage on the trail. Post Office Oak is a tree with a hole at its base that was reportedly used as a cache for mail. The Conn/Stone/Pioneer Store (1858) served as an important trading post; the Neosho River Crossing (located about where U.S. Highway 56 bridges the river) has a riverwalk and exhibits; and Hermit's Cave was a trail landmark. Kaw Mission SHS (1851), a school for American Indian children, displays mission period artifacts. Last Chance Store remains in its nearly original state (1857). Diamond Springs was a popular water source and campsite along the trail; and Six Mile Creek Crossing and Stage Station, named for its location from Diamond Springs, has ruts. *Other attractions: Madonna of the Trail* is a statue erected as a memorial to the courage of pioneer mothers. *Nearby:* West of Lost Springs the water source of the same name

still flows. Ruts can be found in the area near the small creek on the south side of the paved road (NRHP). Cotton Creek Crossing near Durham and Durham Ruts are sites with outstanding ruts; Konza Prairie; Tallgrass Prairie National Preserve (locally referred to as the Z-Bar Ranch).

9. McPherson. A marker commemorates the Mormon Battalion's (MPNHT) march over the SFT during the first year of the Mexican-American War (1846). *Nearby:* Dry Turkey Creek at Elyria is the site where a treaty (1825) with the Kaw tribe was negotiated to grant travelers access to the SFT. The area around Canton offers visitors a glimpse of prairie that looks much as it did in the days of the trail. *Other attractions:* Maxwell Game Preserve has buffalo, antelope, and elk. Guided tours are available upon request at the state-owned site. At Lyons, the Coronado/Quivira Museum is a certified SFT interpretive facility with a research library and information on the trail, Coronado, and the Quivera Indians. Located four miles west of Chase, Ralph's Ruts are some of the finest on the route. A DAR marker points out the location. Plum Buttes, also four miles to the west, were dunes covered by plum bushes that provided a landmark.

10. Great Bend. The DAR has marked the site where the Santa Fe Trail joined the Arkansas River at its great, or north, bend. Some of the most notable landmarks are found along this stretch of the trail to Kinsley. *Nearby:* Pawnee Rock SHS (NRHP) commemorates the site that served as a vital landmark and lookout position for traders and Indians. A drive to the top offers a view of the vast expanse of prairie. Bird-watching is available at Cheyenne Bottoms Wildlife Refuge north of Great Bend and at the Quivira National Waterfowl Refuge to the south.

11. Larned. Fort Larned NHS (1859–78), a certified NHT site, is one of the best preserved prairie forts in the country. This major army post protected Santa Fe Trail travelers and settlers from the Plains Indians. One of the fort's buildings serves as a museum and National Parks interpretive center. A forty-four-acre tract about five miles from the fort preserves ruts. The certified SFT center, devoted to the trail and regional history, is headquarters for the Santa Fe Trail Association. Santa Fe Trail Days, with living-history action, takes place over Memorial Day weekend.

12. Dodge City. Fort Dodge (1865–82), built to protect the trail, has marked buildings located in a state veterans' retirement community open to the public. Dodge City became a boomtown when the railroad replaced the trail, and longhorns driven from Texas met the railroad. *Other attractions:* The Santa Fe Depot; Santa Fe Park; Chifon Park; Kansas Heritage Center; *The Plainswoman* statue at Dodge City Community College; Boothill Museum. To the west (on U.S. Highway 50), Point of Rocks is a

low, rounded hill that served as a major landmark; Ford Mann site (1847); Fort Atkinson site (1851). Boot Hill Museum Ruts, a certified NHT site and on the NHL register, has ruts and exhibits. *Nearby:* The Dodge City, Ford & Bucklin (DCF&B) Train follows the original route of the trail for seventeen miles. To the west, near Ingalls, the trail forks into the Cimarron Route and the Mountain Route.

Cimarron Route

KANSAS

13. ELKHART. The trail leaves Kansas through the shortgrass prairie of Cimarron National Grassland, where native antelope and elk have been reintroduced. Adjacent to the trail ruts of this certified NHT site is a twenty-mile companion trail, with exhibits, that has been developed for hiking, biking, wagons, and horseback riding. Morton County Historical Society Museum, another certified NHT site, offers an exhibit.

OKLAHOMA

14. BOISE CITY. The annual Santa Fe Trail Daze Celebration (June 1–4) allows visitations and tours of historic trail sites on private property. Arrangements to visit the sites can be made with the chamber of commerce. *Nearby:* Autograph Rock, a certified NHT site, has names and dates chiseled into the cliff. A wayside exhibit offers interpretation but visitors must contact the Cimarron County Historical Society in Boise City to obtain permission to visit the site. Willow Bar, located 11 miles north on private property was a campsite, watering spot, and crossing. Wolf Mountain, where branches of the trail passed on both sides of the mountain, is located on private property 9 miles north and then northeast. Upper Spring, also known as Flag Spring (9 miles north and 1.5 miles west), offers a great view of the Cimarron Valley, but is located on private property. Black Mesa, a "geological wonder of the North American continent," was formed when Mount Capulin—now an extinct volcano some 60 miles west—erupted, leaving the hot lava flow that formed the cap of the mesa. *Nearby:* Dinosaur quarries and rock formations such as "Old Maid's Profile" and the "Wedding Party."

NEW MEXICO

15. CLAYTON. The Clayton Complex NHL includes several geographic features and campsites along the trail, starting with McNees Crossing NHL (two miles from the Oklahoma border). Eklund Hotel has been a landmark for travelers since the 1890s. *Nearby:* Clayton Lake SP has eight different kinds of dinosaur footprints. The certified NHT site of Kiowa National Grassland offers a hiking and horseback riding trail. Ruts of the Cimarron Route are visible. The Dry Cimarron River flows through Folsom; the Folsom Museum exhibits artifacts and

fossils of Folsom Man (12,000 B.C.). The certified NHT site of Point of Rocks, between Clayton and Springer, was an important volcanic landmark and campsite on the Cimarron Route; located on private land, it is also the site of ruts and graves. At Capulin Volcano NM, visitors can walk into the 415-foot crater.

16. SPRINGER. Here the Cimarron and Mountain Routes meet for motorists. The Santa Fe Trail Museum is located in the historic Colfax County Courthouse (open summers only). *Nearby:* Wagon Mound NHL, a major landmark, was thought by trail traders to look like a high-top shoe. It later received its name because of its likeness to a covered wagon pulled by oxen. Pilot Knobs, west of Wagon Mound, represents two additional trail guides. A stretch of ruts along I-25 leads to Watrous.

Mountain Route

KANSAS

17. GARDEN CITY. This town on the Arkansas River is a major cattle raising and shipping site. Beef Empire Days (early June) includes cattle shows, cowboy poetry, a rodeo, and a western art show. *Nearby:* Buffalo Game Preserve is a four-thousand-acre preserve with a large herd of bison. Indian Mound is a natural landmark located about five miles southwest of Lakin. Further west, the Aubry Cutoff (1850) became an important route from the Arkansas River to the Oklahoma panhandle.

COLORADO

18. LAMAR. The *Madonna of the Trail* statue is in front of the chamber of commerce. Big Timbers Museum has American Indian and cowboy exhibits. Bent's New Fort was operated by William Bent from 1853 to 1860. Foundation ruins can be found one mile west of the Prowers-Bent county line on U.S. 50, then one mile south on Prowers County Road 35, 0.2 mile east, and 0.5 mile south. Foundation of Old Fort Lyon can be found one mile west of Bent's New Fort.

19. LAS ANIMAS. The area, taking its name from a river that flows into the nearby Arkansas, flourishes as a trading center for stock ranches and irrigated farms. Santa Fe Trail Day is held in April. Boggsville, two miles south, a certified NHT site, is a complex of restored adobe buildings (NRHP), exhibits, and a gift shop. Hiking trails are available at this old trading point. *Nearby:* John Martin Reservoir, a certified NHT site, has views of original ruts. A hiking and biking trail will parallel the original trail here. Toward La Junta, Bent's Old Fort NHS marks the site established as a trading post by Charles and William Bent and Cerán St. Vrain (1833). It was a center of trade on the plains and of national significance in the opening of the American West. Bent's Old Fort (NHL) has been faithfully reconstructed.

20. LA JUNTA. Once the junction of the Santa Fe Trail and the

old Navajo Trails, the town was moved from its original site at Bent's Fort with the arrival of the Atchison, Topeka and Santa Fe Railway, and became a major cattle- and produce-shipping center. The Arkansas River crossing may have been one of several crossings in the area. The northern unit of Comanche National Grassland lies southwest of town and offers exhibits at sites along U.S. Highway 350; there are visible ruts. *Other attractions:* The world-famous Koshare (Boy Scout) Indian dancers perform at Christmas and during the summer; the Koshare Indian Kiva is patterned after kivas of the Southwest. The DAR has marked the Otero County Courthouse and ruts located near Timpas Creek.

21. **TRINIDAD.** Located below Fisher's Peak, a landmark, the town is known for its architecture and brick streets. Hough-Baca (NRHP) and Santa Fe Trail Museum (a certified national historic trail site and interpretive facility) has two restored adobe buildings and exhibits depicting days on the trail. *Other attractions:* The statue of Kit Carson on Kansas Street; the Mitchell Memorial Museum of Western Art; the Trinidad History Museum; the Bloom House (1869); and the old Columbian Hotel. *Nearby:* Spanish Peak, a landmark to the west-northwest.

NEW MEXICO

22. **RATON.** Southwest of Fisher's Peak, Uncle Dick Woot-ton's Toll Road (1866–79) marked the ascent (7,834 feet) of Raton Pass (NHL). The pass is now the route of the railroad and I-25. Ruts are located above the base of the pass about eleven miles north of Raton. The Wootton Ranch (near I-25) is located on private property. The trail came into Raton down Railroad Canyon to the Willow Springs Forage Station site (1868). On First Street, the Victorian architecture preserves the town's mining and railroad heyday, as does the Ratón Museum. Clifton House (1866–79) Ruins, southwest of town, marks the site of the once well-known hostelry. Red River Peak, just past the Clifton House, served as a landmark; ruts are found north of U.S. Highway 64. *Nearby:* Four miles west, the National Rifle Association Whittington Center offers a 33,300-acre shooting facility, with a section of SFT ruts. Sugarite Canyon SP offers recreational activities.

23. **CIMARRON.** Founded (1848) by trail merchant Lucien Maxwell, the town lured gamblers and outlaws (1870s) and lived up to its Spanish name, "wild." Several Santa Fe Trail sites can be seen in town, including the certified NHT site of St. James Hotel (1872–80); the Lucien Maxwell Mansion site; the Old Aztec Mill Museum; the Dahl Brothers Trading Post and Warehouse (1848); the National Hotel (1854); Swink's Gambling Hall (1854); and Meagers Sanderson Stagecoach Line Office (pre-1870).

Rayado and Kit Carson Museum, located at the Philmont Scout Ranch, is a certified NHT site and is open June through August. To the south, ruts ascend a hill near the Waite Phillips mansion; Ocate Crossing was crossed by Kearny's Army of the West (1846). *Nearby:* Maxwell NWR supports eagles, hawks, and falcons; Valle Vidal Park offers backpacking, hunting, and fishing.

24. WATROUS. Called La Junta (The Junction) by the Spaniards for the meeting of the Mora and Sapello Rivers, Watrous is also where the Cimarron and Mountain Routes rejoin. It was the main rendezvous for traders heading east. When the Atchison, Topeka and Santa Fe Railway reached the area (1879), the town changed its name to honor Samuel B. Watrous. Watrous Store NHL and Ranch House (1849) are restored as a private residence; Barclay's Fort Site NHL, located on the south bank of the Mora River, was the site of the trading post (1849); Sapello Stage Station NHL is a private residence with ruts nearby. It is said that the two trails met in the valley behind the station. To the north, there are ruts on both sides of I-25. Ruts also encircle the certified NHT site of Fort Union NM (1851), which became a major supply depot (after 1862). Ruins of the fort, from where soldiers once led campaigns against the southern Plains Indians and defeated Confederate travelers on the trail, still remain. Reenactments of activities at the trail's foremost military

post (1851–91) are presented during the summer months.

25. LAS VEGAS. Originally settled by the Mexicans (1835), the town is part adobe frontier town and part Victorian-era railroad town and shipping point. Once the largest and wealthiest city in the state, it was a silent-film capital. Its nine historic districts boast nine hundred homes and buildings on national and state historic registers. The certified NHT site of Las Vegas Plaza served as a commercial center for Mexican and American traders and housed the one-story building that Gen. Stephen W. Kearny climbed when he proclaimed New Mexico a U.S. Territory (1846). The Las Vegas Museum and the Rough Rider Memorial commemorate Theodore Roosevelt's volunteer cavalry regiment. This certified NHT interpretive facility is located at the former city hall and offers historical displays. *Nearby:* Pecos NHP preserves ruins of an ancient Indian pueblo that was a remnant of the past by the time the Santa Fe Trail was developed. The park has ruins of the pueblo, two Spanish colonial missions (seventeenth and eighteenth centuries), and trail ruts and sites, as well as Civil War sites relating to the battle of Glorieta Pass (1862), which ended the Confederate attempt to carry the war west.

26. SANTA FE. Founded by the Spanish (1610), the City of the Holy Faith is the oldest continuously occupied capital in the United States. It is known for historic preservation, adobe archi-

tecture, and art galleries. Faint traces of the Santa Fe Trail are found at Amelia White Park, a certified NHT site. On the plaza, another certified NHT site, are Soldiers' Monument (1667); the Palace of the Governors, also a certified NHT site (1609–10); and the stone marking the end of the trail. Of interest are the homes of trail merchants Felipe Delgado (1890), Pinckney Tully (1851), Gregorio Crespin (1747), and James Johnson (1849). Remnants of Fort Marcy, a certified NHT site in Prince Park, give evidence of the post established in 1846 to protect the American presence in Santa Fe. The army officer quarters date from 1870. Other nineteenth-century sites include Sena Plaza (1828); St. Francis Cathedral (1869); Loretto Chapel (1874–78); and San Miguel Mission (1610). *Other attractions:* The Institute of American Indian Arts, the Museum of Indian Arts and Culture, the Museum of Fine Arts, and the Cross of Martyrs. *Nearby:* A loop drive takes today's travelers through Taos, Red River, Cimarron, Raton, Rayado, Wagon Mound, Watrous, Fort Union, and Las Vegas before returning to Santa Fe.

SEQUOYAH
This sculpture from a single giant California sequoia honors the inventor of the Cherokee alphabet, Sequoyah, at the Museum of the Cherokee Indian in Cherokee, North Carolina. In 1838–39 the government forced most of the Cherokees to leave the Southeast in a tragic migration called the Trail of Tears.

Trail of Tears National Historic Trail

I wish I could forget it all, but the picture of six hundred and forty-five wagons lumbering over the frozen ground with their Cargo of suffering humanity still lingers in my memory. Let the Historian of a future day tell the sad story with its sighs, its tears and dying groans. Let the great Judge of all the earth weigh our actions and reward us according to our work.

JOHN G. BURNETT, VETERAN OF THE U.S. CAVALRY, ON DECEMBER 11, 1890, HIS EIGHTIETH BIRTHDAY

The Trail of Tears National Historic Trail (TTNHT) commemorates the tragic experience of the Cherokee people, who were forcibly removed by the U.S. government in 1838–39 from their homelands in the southeastern United States to new homes hundreds of miles to the west. To facilitate settlement by whites, the Cherokees were driven from their homes into stockades scattered throughout Alabama, Georgia, Tennessee, and North Carolina and then moved to internment camps in southeastern Tennessee. From that point, detachments of Cherokees were forcibly moved over land and water routes to Indian Territory in what is now Oklahoma. The sorrowful journey, made under adverse conditions and accompanied by a high rate of illness, resulted in the death of nearly one-fourth of the exiled people.

ADMINISTERING AGENCY
National Park Service, Southwest Region
Long Distance Trails Group Office—Santa Fe
P.O. Box 728
Santa Fe, NM 87504-0728
505-988-6888

FURTHER INFORMATION
The Trail of Tears Association
c/o American Indian Center of Arkansas
1100 North University Avenue, Suite 133
Little Rock, AR 72207

ESTABLISHED
1987

APPROXIMATE MILEAGE
2,219 miles (3,573 kilometers)

STATES
Alabama, Arkansas, Georgia, Illinois, Kentucky, Missouri, North Carolina, Oklahoma, Tennesse

The History of the Trail

The arrival of Europeans in the New World created endless problems for American Indians.* Their lands were gradually lost and their cultures altered, or even destroyed. The first contact between southeastern American Indians and Europeans came with the expedition of Hernando de Soto in 1540. De Soto took captives for use as slave labor. Later, others were abused because the Europeans deemed them savages. Epidemic diseases brought by the Europeans spread through the Indian villages, decimating native populations. As more and more white settlers arrived over the next two centuries, native cultures responded to pressures to adopt foreign ways, but this led to the deterioration of their own cultures.

During the colonial period, American Indian tribes often became embroiled in European colonial wars. If they were on the losing side, they frequently had to give up parts of their homelands. Taking protective steps, England placed American Indian lands off limits to further settlement. This political move discouraged expansion, which made land speculators furious. After the American Revolution, the native people faced another set of problems. The insatiable desire of white settlers for lands occupied by American Indians inevitably led to the formulation of a general policy of removing the unwanted inhabitants.

Political leaders, including Pres. Thomas Jefferson, believed that the American Indians should be civilized, which meant converting them to Christianity and turning them into farmers. Many other whites agreed, and missionaries were sent among the tribes. But when the transformation did not happen quickly enough, views changed about the Indian's ability to be assimilated into white culture. National policy to move native inhabitants west of the Mississippi developed after the Louisiana Territory was purchased from the French in 1803. And whites moving into the new land pressed the U.S. government to do something about the Indian presence. The government formally adopted a removal policy in 1825, which was carried out extensively in the 1830s by Pres. Andrew Jackson and Pres. Martin Van Buren.

The result was particularly overwhelming for the American Indians of the southeastern United States—primarily the Cherokees, Chickasaws, Choctaws, Creeks, and Seminoles—who were finally removed to a new home hundreds of miles away. Perhaps the most culturally devastating episode of this era was that concerning the removal of the Cherokee Indians, who called themselves *Ani'-Yun'wiya*, or the Principal People. Traditionally, they had lived in villages in the southern Appalachians—

*Material in this section is taken from the National Park Service's *Trail of Tears National Historic Trail Comprehensive Management and Use Plan*.

present-day Virginia, West Virginia, Kentucky, Tennessee, western North Carolina and South Carolina, northern Georgia, and northeastern Alabama. Here in a land of valleys, ridges, mountains, and streams they developed a culture based on farming, hunting, and fishing and took on some of the ways of white society, including the adoption of slavery. They built European-style homes and farmsteads, laid out European-style fields and farms, developed a written language, established a newspaper, formed the Cherokee National Council, and wrote a constitution. New Echota, Georgia, became the Cherokee capital, and in 1828 John Ross was elected principal chief. Ross, only one-eighth Cherokee, spoke little of the native language. He had served as an adjutant under Gen. Andrew Jackson, married a Cherokee, and owned a plantation. By the time he assumed office, his people were already under pressure to move westward.

As early as 1791, a series of treaties between the United States and the Cherokees living in Georgia had given recognition to the Cherokees as a nation with their own laws and customs. Nevertheless, the treaties and agreements were gradually whittled away. By the late 1700s some Cherokees sought refuge from white interference and moved to northwestern Arkansas, between the White and Arkansas Rivers. As more and more land cessions were forced on the Cherokees during the first

two decades of the 1800s, the numbers moving to Arkansas increased. In 1819 the Cherokee National Council notified the federal government that it would no longer cede land and hardened their resolve to remain on their traditional homelands. The Cherokee situation was complicated, however, by the issue of states' rights and a prolonged dispute between Georgia and the federal government.

In 1802 Georgia was the last of the original colonies to cede its western lands to the federal government. In doing so, the state was responding to a promise that all titles to land held by American Indians be extinguished. This did not happen, but in 1817 Jackson coerced several Cherokee leaders into signing a treaty in which a third of the Cherokees' territory was exchanged for a tract of equal size in the western part of the Arkansas Territory. Emigration to the new land was voluntary, but by 1835 nearly six thousand Cherokees had willingly moved. Many of the Cherokee, however, continued to occupy their ancestral homelands, which had been guaranteed to them by treaty. Their success in holding onto their tribal lands and governing themselves was resented by Georgia residents.

Settlers continued to encroach on Cherokee and neighboring Creek lands. In 1828, forcing the states' rights issue with the federal government, Georgia passed a law pronouncing all laws of the Cherokee Nation to be null and void after June 1, 1830. Because the state no longer recognized the rights of the Cherokees, tribal meetings were held just across the state line at Red Clay, Tennessee. In 1829 gold was discovered in Dahlonega, Georgia, on Cherokee land, and efforts to dislodge the Principal People from their land intensified. President Andrew Jackson began to aggressively implement a broad policy of extinguishing American Indian land titles in affected states and relocating the Indians to the little-known and arid lands west of the Mississippi.

In 1830 Congress passed the Indian Removal Act, which directed the executive branch to negotiate for Indian Lands. This act, in combination with the discovery of gold and an increasingly untenable position with the state of Georgia, prompted the Cherokee Nation to bring suit in the U.S. Supreme Court. In *Cherokee Nation v. Georgia* (1831) Chief Justice John Marshall, writing for the majority, held that the Cherokee Nation was a "domestic dependent nation," and therefore Georgia state law applied to them. In his decision, however, Justice Marshall, an anti-Jacksonian and Federalist, rendered a new definition of the relationship of the tribes to the American government. Henceforth, he wrote, they should be considered "domestic dependent nations" whose relationship to the "United States resembles that of a ward to his guardian." The implication was that the govern-

ment was obliged to protect the Cherokees, but this was ignored by the Jackson administration.

Refusing to give up, the Cherokees hoped for a more conclusive and positive ruling in a case heard the next year. The second case, *Worcester v. Georgia,* was brought forward to the Supreme Court by the Cherokees, their missionary, and other white supporters in 1832. Under an 1830 law, Georgia required all white residents in Cherokee country to secure a license and to take an oath of allegiance to the state. Missionaries Samuel A. Worcester and Elizur Butler had refused and were convicted and imprisoned for living among the Cherokee without securing a state permit or swearing allegiance to Georgia. This time the court found that American Indian nations were capable of making treaties, that under the Constitution treaties are the supreme law of the land, that the federal government had exclusive jurisdiction within the boundaries of the Cherokee Nation, and that state law had no force within Cherokee boundaries. Worcester was ordered released from jail. The Cherokees were elated, but President Jackson refused to enforce the court's decision and advised Georgia to do the same. He is said to have privately remarked, "John Marshall has rendered his decision, now let him enforce it."

After adopting many practices of the white culture and using the court system in two major

Supreme Court cases, the Cherokee were still unable to halt the removal process. The State of Georgia continued to press for American Indian lands and in 1833 held a lottery for Cherokee property. The government buildings in New Echota were given away to the lottery winners. John Ross and John Ridge, the son of Major Ridge who had fought with the United States in the War of 1812, were among those who lost their plantations. Ross and Ridge both moved their families to Tennessee.

As the situation grew desperate, a group of Cherokees known as the Treaty Party began negotiating a treaty with the federal government. Led by Major Ridge, the group, which included Ridge's son, his nephew, Elias Boudinot, the editor of the *Cherokee Phoenix,* and his brother, Stand Watie, signed a treaty in 1835 at New Echota. They were motivated as much by economic and political ambitions as by concern for the Cherokee people who had opposed removal. The once-unified Cherokees were now bitterly divided. Despite the majority opposition to the treaty, which was led by Principal Chief John Ross, the eastern lands were sold for $5 million. It had been further agreed that the Cherokees would move beyond the Mississippi River to Indian Territory. Boudinot said, "I know I take my life in my hand . . . but the great Cherokee nation will be saved."

Fifteen thousand Cherokees, almost the entire population,

signed a petition protesting the treaty made by the unauthorized minority. Nevertheless, the angry protests of Ross did not stop the Senate from ratifying it. Within two years the Cherokee were to move from their ancestral homelands. Ross, certain that justice would prevail, campaigned tirelessly to have the treaty annulled. Under his determined leadership, the Cherokees remained, making no preparations to leave. In 1838, Pres. Martin Van Buren ordered the implementation of the Treaty of New Echota. U.S. Army troops under the command of Gen. Winfield Scott, who did not relish his assignment, began rounding up the Cherokees and moving them into stockades in North Carolina, Georgia, Alabama, and Tennessee. Altogether, thirty-one forts were constructed for this purpose — thirteen in Georgia, five in North Carolina, eight in Tennessee, and five in Alabama. All of the posts were near Cherokee towns, and they served only as temporary housing for the Cherokees. In an address, Scott warned the people not to resist, saying "Unhappily, the two years which were allowed for the purpose, you have suffered to pass away without following, and without making any preparations to follow, and now, or by the time that this solemn *address* shall reach your distant settlement, the emigration must be commenced in haste, but, I hope, without disorder."

As soon as it was practical, the Cherokees were transferred from the removal forts to eleven internment camps that were more centrally located—ten in Tennessee and one in Alabama. In North Carolina, for example, Cherokees at the removal forts were sent to Fort Butler, and by the second week in July on to the principal agency at Fort Cass. By late July 1838, with the exception of fugitives hiding in the mountains, some scattered families, and the Oconaluftee Citizen Indians, virtually all other Cherokees remaining in the East were in the internment camps. A July military report records that the seven camps in and around Charleston, Tennessee, contained more than forty-eight hundred Cherokees. There were another seven hundred at the agency post, six hundred at Rattlesnake Spring, eight hundred seventy at the first encampment of Mouse Creek, sixteen hundred at the second encampment on Mouse Creek, nine hundred at Bedwell Springs, thirteen hundred at Chestooee, seven hundred on the ridge east of the agency, and six hundred on the Upper Chatate. Some two thousand Cherokees were camped at Gunstocker Spring thirteen miles from Calhoun, Tennessee. Many were separated from their children in the process. Their cabins and the crops that they had been encouraged to grow were burned to discourage them from escaping and returning to their homes.

Because the Cherokee had made such strong efforts to comply with the federal government's "civilization" program, their removal has been ranked as one of the greatest American tragedies. Nearly fifty years after the removal, John G. Burnett, who had served as a private in the U.S. Army during the winter of 1838–39, recorded his account.

[I] witnessed the execution of the most brutal order in the history of American warfare. I saw the helpless Cherokees arrested and dragged from their homes, and driven at the bayonet point into the stockades. And in the chill of a drizzling rain on an October morning I saw them loaded like cattle or sheep into six hundred and forty-five wagons and headed for the West.

One band of Cherokees, the Oconaluftee Citizen Cherokees, remained behind in the remote mountains of western North Carolina. When the forced removal came in 1838, they claimed that the 1835 treaty did not apply to them as they no longer lived on Cherokee lands. Their origin, traced to an 1819 treaty, permitted Cherokees living within ceded territory to register for individual allotments of land and become citizens of the state of North Carolina. Many elected to remain on that land rather than move across the Little Tennessee River, which had become the boundary of the Cherokee Nation. Unlike the leaders of the Cherokee, they had been less resistant to changes from their traditional way of life. With Yonaguska, their leader, they settled along the Oconaluftee

River and supported themselves by selling livestock and the medicinal herb ginseng to white traders.

To the Oconaluftee's good fortune, Yonaguska had at one time adopted a young white boy named William Holland Thomas; he now acted as their spokesman. He had helped them consolidate their landholdings by purchasing tracts for them as land became available, and he lobbied for them in Washington, D.C., and pleaded their case before the North Carolina legislature. Winning the right to stay on their land, however, left them in a precarious situation. If they aided those who managed to evade troops by fleeing to the mountains, their own status would be jeopardized. When an elder named Tsali and his sons killed a soldier during the Cherokee roundup, tensions were at their height. General Scott announced that he would abandon the search for other holdouts in the mountains if Tsali would turn himself in. When he and the others responsible came forward, they were ordered executed, and, by command of Scott, a detachment of Cherokee prisoners was compelled to do the shootings. True to his word, Scott ignored the traditional Cherokee in the mountains who were ultimately given permission to stay. These fugitive Cherokees also joined the Oconaluftee, and in time this group became the Eastern Band of Cherokees, who still reside in North Carolina.

During the roundup, intimida-

OZARK BRIDGE AND FORT SMITH MURAL

Motor boats and the Delta Queen Steamboat Company pass Ozark Bridge on the Arkansas River. A mural in downtown Fort Smith, Arkansas, depicts the water route of the Trail of Tears.

tion and acts of cruelty at the hands of the troops, along with the theft and destruction of property by local residents, further alienated the Cherokees. Finally, Chief Ross appealed to President Van Buren to permit the Cherokees to oversee their own removal. Van Buren consented, and Ross and his brother Lewis administered the effort.

The Cherokees were divided into sixteen detachments ranging in size from seven hundred to sixteen hundred people each. Three of these detachments, totaling about twenty-eight hundred persons, traveled ahead by river to Indian Territory. The first of these groups left on June 6, 1838, by steamboat and barge from Ross's Landing on the Tennessee River (present-day Chattanooga). They followed the Tennessee as it wound across northern Alabama, taking a short detour by railcar around the shoals between Decatur and Tuscumbia Landing. Their route then took them north through central Tennessee and Kentucky to the Ohio River. The Ohio took them to the Mississippi River, which they followed to the mouth of the Arkansas. The Arkansas River led northwest to Indian Territory, where they arrived aboard a steamboat at the mouth of Sallisaw Creek near Fort Coffee on June 19. The other two groups did not arrive in Indian Territory until the end of the summer. Low water levels beyond Little Rock, Arkansas, forced overland travel. During the journey, these groups suffered from severe drought and disease that caused the death of over two hundred people, mainly children and the elderly.

Other Cherokees traveled overland on existing roads. Each detachment was headed by a conductor and an assistant conductor appointed by John Ross. A physician, and sometimes a clergyman, usually accompanied each detachment. Supplies of flour and corn, and occasionally salt pork, coffee, and sugar, were obtained in advance but were generally of poor quality. Drought and the number of people being moved reduced forage for draft animals, which often were used to haul possessions, while the people routinely walked.

The most commonly used overland route followed a northern alignment, while some detachments (notably those led by John Benge and John Bell) followed more southerly routes, and some followed slight variations. (Benge's detachment of 1,200 Cherokees took the most southerly route. Bell's detachment consisted of 660 supporters of the Treaty of New Echota who were moved under the charge of U.S. Army Lt. Edward Deas.) The northern route started at Calhoun, Tennessee, and crossed middle Tennessee, southwestern Kentucky, and southern Illinois. After crossing the Mississippi River north of Cape Girardeau, Missouri, these detachments trekked across southern Missouri and the northwest corner of Arkansas into Indian Territory. Road conditions, illness, and the distress of winter, particularly in southern Illinois, where detachments waited to cross the ice-choked Mississippi, made death a daily occurrence. Estimates vary on the number forced to march and the numbers that died. One estimate has it that as many as eighteen thousand Cherokees were rounded up and almost four thousand died in stockades or on the journey. Most estimates hold that one-fourth of the Cherokee people died. It is known that during the winter of 1838–39 an endless line of wagons, horsemen, and people on foot made their exodus to Oklahoma in a twelve-hundred-mile journey that took an average of six months to complete. Because of the hardships and loss of life associated with the march, it became known as the Trail of Tears. John Burnett wrote:

FLAGS FLY IN HOPKINSVILLE

The trail of the exiles was a trail of death. . . . They had to sleep in the wagons and on the ground without fire. I have known as many as 22 of them to die in one night of pneumonia due to ill treatment, cold, and exposure. Among this number was the beautiful Christian wife of Chief John Ross. This noble hearted woman died a martyr to childhood, giving her only blanket for the protection of a sick child. She rode thinly clad through a blinding sleet and snow storm, developed pneumonia and died in the still hours of a bleak winter night.

Located on the land route, Trail of Tears Commemorative Park in Hopkinsville, Kentucky, flies the flags of the nine states whose lands and waterways were traversed during the Cherokee removal. Whitepath and Fly Smith, two notable Cherokees, are buried here.

As the Cherokee removal drew to a close, President Van Buren sent an extraordinary message to both houses of Congress:

Most of the land-route detachments entered present-day Oklahoma near Westville, being met there by a detachment of U.S. troops from Fort Gibson on the Arkansas River. The army officially received the Cherokees, who generally went to live with those who had already arrived or awaited land assignments while camped along the Illinois River and its tributaries east of present-day Tahlequah.

It affords me sincere pleasure to be able to apprise you of the entire removal of the Cherokee Nation of Indians to their new homes west of the Mississippi. The measures authorized by Congress with a view to the long-standing controversy with them have had the happiest effect, and they have emigrated without any apparent resistance.

Once in Indian Territory, problems quickly developed between new arrivals and Cherokees who had already settled in the area. In 1839 Major Ridge, his son, and his nephew were assassinated for

TAHLEQUAH SIGN

Located in Oklahoma's region of lakes within the Ozark Mountains, Tahlequah has been the capital city of the Cherokee Indian Nation since 1839. Every Labor Day, powwows and other festivities commemorate the establishment of the nation.

having signed the Treaty of New Echota. John Ross sought to quell the outbreaks by passing an act of forgiveness to "treaty men," provided that they would appear at the council grounds and confess their sorrow for signing the treaty of 1835. As the problems were resolved, the Western Cherokees proceeded to adapt to their new homeland, establishing their own system of government modeled on that of the United States. Tribal government was headquartered in Tahlequah and adhered to a constitution that divided responsibilities among an elected principal chief, an elected legislature known as the National Council, and a supreme court with lesser courts. Local districts similar to counties, with elected officials, formed the basis of the nation. They maintained a bilin-

gual school system, and missionaries from the American Board of Commissioners for Foreign Missions were active in the nation.

Autonomy remained reasonably strong until the Civil War, when a faction of the Cherokees sided with the Confederacy. During Reconstruction they suffered a loss of self-government and, more importantly, their land base. Government annuities were reduced, and lands were sold to newly arrived tribes. Cessions of land continued during the later nineteenth century, and the federal government emerged as the major force for land cession under the Dawes Act of 1887, which divided up tribal lands. The establishment of the State of Oklahoma in 1907 increased pressure for land cessions, and many people of questionable Cherokee ancestry managed to get on the tribal rolls and participate in the allotment of these lands to individuals. The Western Cherokees eventually lost title to over 19 million acres of land.

The depression years of the 1930s brought difficult times, as did the government's policy of relocating American Indians from tribal areas to urban America. Many Cherokees found themselves in city slums with their basic needs unmet. Differences also emerged between traditionalists and those who adapted to mainstream society. In 1961, the Cherokees won a settlement against the U.S. government and were awarded $15 million for the forced sale of property in 1839. Since the 1970s, the Cherokees' situation has been improved through self-rule and economic programs. By 1987, the Cherokee Nation in Oklahoma had accumulated assets of more than $40 million, and a renewed commitment to traditional communities drew many Cherokees back to Oklahoma.

LACROSSE LESSON

Eager young visitors learn how to play the western version of lacrosse at the Cherokee Heritage Center at Park Hill near Tahlequah. In this version, the target is a single goal-post in the center of the field. A fish symbol typically adorns the top of the goalpost.

The Eastern Cherokee were periodically encouraged by the government to join their brethren in the West. Some, looking for better opportunities, occasionally moved west but most remained in North Carolina. After removal of the other Cherokee, the lives of Eastern Cherokees changed little until the Civil War, when Col. William Holland Thomas convinced some to enlist in the Confederate army in a legion he had organized. In prison camp, many of them learned for the first time that they were defending the right of slavery. Federal pardons were granted to those who joined the Union army. During Reconstruction, the Eastern Cherokee acquired the right to vote, wrote a constitution, elected a chief and council, and were recognized by the federal government as distinct from the Western Cherokees, but not a separate nation. Colonel Thomas, in the meantime, suffered debts after the war. He had not sorted out the land investments he held in trust for the Cherokee, and, as a result, titles to their property were seized by his creditors.

A lawsuit on the Oconaluftee Cherokees' behalf awarded them much of the land, with the federal government accepting the title in trust. This new arrangement created social change, particularly in the area of education, which was directed toward destroying Cherokee culture through assimilation. In time, the Eastern Cherokee established themselves as a corporation, which gave them many more freedoms and protections. To this day, they have continued to govern themselves in this fashion and are successfully engaged in a number of enterprises, including tourism because of their proximity to the Great Smoky Mountains National Park. The Qualla Reservation of the Cherokee in North Carolina is the largest reservation in the eastern United States.

Though living in widely different geographic areas, the Eastern and Western Cherokees today consider themselves one people. In April 1984, they met formally in a joint council held at Red Clay, Tennessee, where they had met many years previously when the State of Georgia outlawed their government. The modern Cherokee look to the future while they seek to maintain much of their cultural identity. To increase public awareness of their heritage, many Cherokee advocated the designation of the Trail of Tears as a national historic trail.

SEQUOYAH

Sequoyah, also known as George Gist, is remembered for giving his people the gift of reading and writing. In 1776 (some records say the 1760s), he was born in Taskigi, near Loudon, Tennessee, to the daughter of a Cherokee chief. His non-Indian father, Col. Nathaniel Gist, served in the American Revolution but deserted the family before Sequoyah's birth. Raised by his Cherokee kin, he had a traditional Cherokee upbringing and learned to be a hunter and trader. At an early age, while on a hunting trip, he injured his leg and arthritis developed, leaving him permanently crippled. As a result, he was nicknamed "the Lame One."

Perhaps out of frustration over his physical condition, he turned to alcohol during his youth. Then, realizing what it was doing to him, he turned away from liquor. From childhood, he had had artistic ability and a creative imagination. He developed these talents and became a skilled blacksmith and craftsman. He was also noted for his drawings and paintings, though none are known to exist today. In time, he emerged as an outstanding silversmith. (Among the Cherokee, only the men wore ornaments, and the wealthier decorated their horses.) To keep his records, Sequoyah drew a picture of each individual who had commissioned him and entered the amount due with his own code. Growing tired of the time-consuming task, he became increasingly fascinated with the ability of the whites to convey messages by writing and began to ponder their "talking leaves." He resolved to master the secret and help his people apply the technique to their own language. By learning to read and write in their own tongue, he believed that the Cherokees could better preserve their own expression.

In 1809 Sequoyah began experimenting with a written alphabet for the Cherokee language, but in October of 1813, with the nation at war, he joined the U.S. Army. He fought under Andrew Jackson at the battle of Horseshoe Bend and was discharged in April 1814. Upon his return, he continued with his experiments. At first, he tried to use a different pictorial symbol for each word, but this proved to be impractical. At last, he came up with the idea of devising a character for each sound. When the sounds were combined, they conveyed words. Deciding eventually that there were eighty-six sounds in the Cherokee language, Sequoyah created a simple symbol for each sound, borrowing from the Bible, the *McGuVey Reader,* and a Greek text. In this manner, he began to produce a syllabary rather than an alphabet.

The process took Sequoyah twelve years to accomplish, and he faced a great deal of ridicule and opposition before completing his table of characters. It is said that so much time was spent on his project in its early stages that he ignored his business, making his family dependent on his sons. His spouse grew increasingly frustrated and, in desperation, destroyed his records in a fire. For a short while he returned to alcohol, but he could not escape the compulsion to complete his work. Leaving his wife, he went back to work in solitary concentration. Many of his friends believed that he was wasting his life and making a fool of himself. But the ridicule did not seem to bother him. He simply replied, "It is not our people that have advised me to do this and it is not therefore our people who can be blamed if I am wrong. What I have done I have done from myself. If our people think I am making a fool of myself, you may tell our people that what I

am doing will not make fools of them."

To escape public scorn and gossip, Sequoyah moved into a small cabin several miles from his village. According to some accounts, his cabin was burned to the ground, including his work on his syllabary, by people who thought he was working with magic and witchcraft. He persevered, though, and taught his six-year-old daughter, Ahyoka, to read the sounds that he had created from the symbols, now reduced to eighty-five in number. Now he was ready to win over the skeptical members of the tribe. The many visitors who came by to examine the mystery found that Sequoyah and Ahyoka could communicate, even when separated. Soon another child learned to read, followed by another, a nephew, and his son.

To demonstrate the practical value of his system, Sequoyah and his daughter presented it to the Cherokee tribal council at the New Echota capital in the Nation East. Inside the council chambers, Ahyoka wrote a message given to her. Sequoyah, who was out of the room, returned and read the secret message. Still there was doubt. John Ross, chairman of the council and educated at Dartmouth, suggested that the two reverse roles. When Ahyoka read the message that Sequoyah had recorded, it was clear that Sequoyah's invention had passed the test. He was asked to teach his system to others.

Attracted to his invention, the

brother of Chief John Watts asked Sequoyah if he could write down some of the speeches he had heard at councils. Sequoyah's first composition was on the subject of the boundary lines between the Cherokee Nation and the States of Georgia and Tennessee. Asked to speak on the matter at a court held at Chatonga, he read his marks. In 1822, he carried letters from the East to Arkansas, and after teaching his system in the West, he returned with letters of response—further proof that the Cherokee Nation could communicate across the miles. Because Sequoyah's syllabary could be learned in a matter of days by anyone who spoke Cherokee fluently, the people quickly became a literate nation, the first tribe north of Mexico to have its own system of writing.

In 1824, Sequoyah moved to Arkansas with other Cherokees who had migrated there. That same year translated portions of the Bible drew missionary support, and a year later the entire New Testament was translated into the Cherokee language. By 1828, the Cherokee had established a bilingual newspaper under the editorship of Elias Boudinot, who had been educated in mission schools in New England and later joined Major Ridge and his Treaty party. The *Cherokee Phoenix* became a weekly newspaper. It carried local and world news, human interest stories, the laws of the nation, Bible passages, editorials, and advertisements. Its first issue appeared on February 21, 1828, and the paper flourished until its suppression by the State of Georgia in 1835. Subscribers included not only the Cherokees but interested whites in the United States and Europe.

Joining a delegation of Arkansas Cherokees, Sequoyah helped design a treaty to exchange their Arkansas lands for lands in the present state of Oklahoma. The owner of a salt production and blacksmith works near present-day Russellville, Arkansas, Sequoyah made the exchange in 1828 and moved to Indian Territory. There, in 1829, he built a one-room log cabin, which is still standing in a place called Skin Bayou north of Sallisaw, married, and continued to make ornamental silver buckles and other adornments. Most of his time was spent teaching his written language, however, and adapting its use for the Choctaws. By stimulating education through his system, he contributed toward the development of the state of Oklahoma. His contributions were not unnoticed by his own people. He became one of the Advisors of the Nation, the Old Beloved Men as they were called, and the Eastern Council presented him with an engraved silver medal for his great contribution. With it came a message from Chief Ross:

The present generation have already experienced the great benefits of your incomparable system. The old and the young find no difficulty in learning to read and write in their native language and to correspond with their distant friends with the same facility as the whites do. Types have been made and a printing press established in this nation. The scriptures have been translated and printed in Cherokee and while posterity continues to be benefitted by the discovery, your name will exist in grateful remembrance. It will also serve as an index for other aboriginal tribes, or nations, similarly to advance in science and respectability: in short, the great good designed by the author of human existence in directing your genius in this happy discovery, cannot be fully estimated — it is incalculable. Wishing your health and happiness I am your Friend

—John Ross

Cherokee Alphabet.

(Cherokee syllabary chart)

Sounds Represented by Vowels

a, as a in father, or short as a in rival | o, as o in note, approaching aw in law
e, as a in hate, or short as e in met | u, as oo in fool, or short as u in pull
i, as i in pique, or short as i in pit | v, as u in but, nasalized

Consonant Sounds

g nearly as in English, but approaching to k. d nearly as in English but approaching to t. h k l m n q s t w y as in English. Syllables beginning with g except Ꮝ (ga) have sometimes the power of k. Ꭺ (go), Ꮝ (du), Ꮙ (dv) are sometimes sounded to, tu, tv and syllables written with tl except Ꮈ (tla) sometimes vary to dl.

Cherokee Alphabet, from Ruth Bradley Holmes and Betty Sharp Smith, *Beginning Cherokee,* Second Edition (University of Oklahoma Press, 1977).

In 1841, the Cherokee National Council voted Sequoyah an allowance for his invention; the allowance was soon altered to an annuity of $300, which would be transferred to his wife in the event of his death.

Though feeble and arthritic now, he, like many other Cherokees who had voluntarily moved west, enjoyed his surroundings. In 1842, he decided to form an expedition to look for a portion of the Cherokees who had moved into an area of Mexico that is now part of Texas. It was his final hope that he could persuade them to join the main body of his people in what was to become eastern Oklahoma and to adapt his system for their dialect. The next year, he, his son, and a few of his son's friends set off for Mexico. His age made the journey especially difficult, and his health began to fail. At one point during the trip, he complained of a pain in his chest but still refused to return home.

In Shawnee country, Sequoyah was received by those people, who knew of him and respected him as a chief. They offered help and gave Sequoyah's group directions. Later, a band of Tewockenee Indians stole the Cherokee horses. Still, Sequoyah traveled on, aided by the Comanches, until, too weary to move on, he was left in a cave while his companions searched for help. While they were gone, the waters of the river rose into the cave, forcing Sequoyah to escape without his food and supplies. By the time his friends found him, he was near death. Sending the expedition on, he asked them to tell the Cherokees in Mexico that Sequoyah wished them to know that a great nation was emerging and that they were not only welcomed but were needed.

Sequoyah never returned to his home, dying that summer near the Mexican village of San Fernando. His exact burial site is unknown. Yet, this remarkable man is remembered worldwide as the inventor of a nation's written language. When the Five Tribes —the Cherokee, Chickasaw, Choctaw, Creek, and Seminole— called a convention for the pur-

pose of securing statehood in 1905, they proposed that the name of the new Indian state be Sequoyah. When, instead, Oklahoma became a state in 1907, the county area of his residence was given his name. His log home in Oklahoma and the lands that surround it have been named a National Historic Landmark and are protected by the Oklahoma Historical Society. He was selected as one of Oklahoma's two greatest men and as such is honored in the National Statuary Hall in Washington, D.C. California's giant redwoods were named in his honor by scientist Stephen L. Endlicher as tribute to his genius, and today Sequoia National Park protects these magnificent trees.

The Trail Today

The Trail of Tears National Historic Trail (TTNHT) encompasses both water and land routes crossing 2,219 miles.* The water route to Indian Territory was taken by the three detachments. The land route was taken by eleven detachments who traveled along existing roads. Two other major routes were also followed; they are marked on the map, though they are not congressionally designated as part of the historic trail. These include the more central route used by John Benge's detachment, known

*Material in this section is taken from the National Park Service's *Trail of Tears National Historic Trail Comprehensive Management and Use Plan.*

as Benge's Route, and the southern route taken by John Bell's Treaty Party detachment.

Today the rivers the Cherokees traveled are considerably different from what they were 150 years ago. The Tennessee River has been changed by the dams of the Tennessee Valley Authority, which has made use of the river for power generation and industry as well as navigation. Even along the free-flowing portions of the Tennessee, the development of chemical, paper, and petroleum plants, as well as of urban areas, has dramatically changed the character of the landscape. Commercial water traffic is considerable, and recreational boating facilities are scattered throughout the corridor.

Towns and industrial plants have also changed the character of the Ohio and Mississippi River corridors. Both rivers have heavy, but interesting, barge traffic and related development to maintain that traffic. The Arkansas, perhaps the most dramatically changed of the rivers because of the McClellan-Kerr navigation system, stretches from the mouth of the river all the way to Catoosa (outside Tulsa), Oklahoma. A series of dams, locks, and impoundments make the river navigational far into the interior of Oklahoma. As with the other rivers, there is a considerable amount of development along the banks of the Arkansas. Vistas along a few less-developed and less-populated areas of the water route give an indication of how the river corridors looked at the time of removal.

The nineteenth-century road system that was used during the removal is overlaid by present-day roads. A complex network of county, state, and federal roads stretches from the mouth of the Hiwassee River all the way to Westville, Oklahoma. These roads wind through large areas of countryside and a few major urban areas, notably Nashville, Tennessee, and Springfield, Missouri. Scattered along the roads are numerous communities, agricultural areas, and rural landscapes that have grown up since the removal. A few segments of the route remain basically undeveloped and provide a feeling of the countryside through which the detachments passed. The land route totals 993 miles, including the routes of Taylor's Detachment (45 miles) and Hildebrand's Detachment (122 miles).

The eastern sections of the Trail of Tears—in the Blue Ridge province and the Ridge and Valley province in North Carolina, Tennessee, and Georgia—showcase a rugged terrain, with steep ridges, narrow hollows, and peaks over six thousand feet. The southern Appalachians also contain the headwaters for many rivers, including the Tennessee, Little Tennessee, and Hiwassee. Adding to the region's attractiveness are the clear, cool streams that rush through deep, rugged valleys. From the Appalachians in east Tennessee and northeastern Alabama, the land begins to drop away. The three groups who made the journey by water floated down the Tennessee River from Ross's Landing near Chattanooga to its confluence with the Ohio River. The entire river has been dammed many times since and now consists of a series of reservoirs, but in some areas, like at Shiloh below Pickwick Dam, the river is probably still reminiscent of what the Cherokees saw.

The northern land route crossed the Nashville Basin of Tennessee, going through the areas now occupied by Murfreesboro and Nashville. The route entered Kentucky near the headwaters of the Pond River, an area of gentle slopes created by stream erosion of the Mississippi River and its tributaries. Here and there bluffs are encountered, remnants of former valleys cut by the river. The landscape flattens as the trail descends into swampy bottomlands and crosses the Ohio River near Golconda, Illinois. Southern Illinois offers a hilly, rolling landscape south of the Saline and Big Muddy Rivers. Much of the bottomland has been reclaimed for agricultural and industrial uses. The groups traveling the land route passed from the Interior Low Plateaus into the Central Lowland province in the vicinity of the Cache River, which drains from the Shawnee Hills southward into the Ohio River at Mound City.

One land route passed around the northeastern edge of the Ozark Mountains, while another skirted the southeastern edge before following the White River drainage into the mountains. The northern land route followed the more level areas of the Salem and Springfield plateaus almost entirely across the state before entering Arkansas. The Ozark Mountains have views from elevations up to seventeen hundred feet, views probably similar to what the Cherokees saw. Those taking the water route entered the Coastal Plain at the confluence of the Ohio and Mississippi Rivers. Southeastern Missouri, western Tennessee, eastern Arkansas, and northern Mississippi are all part of this province, which is underlaid with thick deposits of silts

and clays brought down the great river system and deposited in bayous and backwaters during spring floods. Between the Ohio River and the Arkansas River, the Mississippi slowly meanders for some four hundred miles, covering a linear distance of only 270 miles.

Up the Arkansas River, the landscape changes from the Mississippi lowlands to a broad valley in the Ouachita portion of the Interior Highlands, between the Boston Mountains to the north and the Ouachita Mountains to the south. The Arkansas River has been dammed, and part of the valley has been inundated by Lake Dardanelle. Seventeen locks and dams maintain a minimum depth of nine feet for 445 miles between the port of Catoosa, Oklahoma, and the Mississippi River. Farther west, in what is now Sequoyah County, Oklahoma, the Arkansas River has been dammed to form the Robert S. Kerr Lake. North of here, in the Illinois River drainage at the western extent of the Boston Mountains, the Cherokees arrived at their new home. Since the Cherokees made their journey over 150 years ago, much of the landscape between Tennessee and Oklahoma has been altered forever by use and development. However, some areas have escaped a large degree of change, and these fragments still convey to some degree what the Cherokees saw as they made their journey.

The vegetation and wildlife

changes considerably between the southern Appalachian Mountains and eastern Oklahoma. Today the southern Appalachians support a variety of hardwoods, including hickory, birch, maple, and upland conifers such as hemlock and pine. These scenic mountains are highlighted by spring blooms of dogwood, native azaleas, and rhododendron and by spectacular fall colors. Wildlife, including the black bear, white-tailed deer, fox, opossum, ruffed grouse, bobwhite, and mourning dove, can be seen. The Alabama and Tennessee portions of the Trail of Tears were an eastern broadleaf deciduous forest, but much of the land has been converted to agriculture. Wildlife is plentiful along this portion of the trail and includes the black bear, white-tailed deer, bobcat, and gray fox. Wild turkey, ruffed grouse, bobwhite, and mourning dove are common game birds.

In Kentucky and Illinois, vegetation is more representative of northern associations, including hickory, white ash, hackberry, elm, sugar maple, black cherry, and several species of oaks. The floodplains along the Mississippi River and the lower Ohio River are considered a northern extension of the southern floodplain sloughs, with black willow, cottonwood, honey locust, and silver maple. During pioneer times, Kentucky and Illinois were abundant in wildlife, making them a favored hunting region for both American Indians and early settlers. Though most of the area

has been converted to agriculture, white-tailed deer, mink, muskrat, and gray fox are still common. The river and lakes in this region support largemouth and smallmouth bass, catfish, walleye, carp, bluegill, sunfish, and crappie.

Farther west along the trail, vegetation shows adaptations to the drier conditions. Large grassland prairies are interspersed with woodlands. The forests in the Ozark Mountains of Missouri and Arkansas are remnants of vast upland hardwood forests that once covered over half of these two states. Much of the region's oak-hickory forest, along with the bluestem prairies, have been converted to agriculture. Wildlife consists of white-tailed deer, eastern cottontail, fox squirrel, gray squirrel, mink, muskrat, and gray fox. Migratory waterfowl on the Central flyway pass through the region on their annual north-south journeys, and many species of game fish inhabit the Arkansas River along the trail route. In eastern Oklahoma large portions of the oak-hickory forest and tallgrass prairie have been converted to pastureland. When the Cherokees arrived, most of the area was dominated by six species of oak and three species of hickory, considerably different from the broadleaf deciduous forests of Georgia, Tennessee, Alabama, and North Carolina. The prairies were made up of big and little bluestem, Indian ricegrass, switchgrass, and silverbeard grass.

Trail plans include reaching

agreements with private land-owners, organizations, and state and federal agencies to allow opportunities to visit historic sites and to retrace the land trail by foot, horse, bicycle, and/or wagon where appropriate. Nonfederal historic sites, trail segments, and interpretive facilities may become official components of the Trail of Tears National Historic Trail through a voluntary process of certification in which an owner or manager agrees to adhere to National Park Service standards for resource preservation and public enjoyment. A trail marker will be located at certified locations. Updated lists of certified sites and facilities are periodically issued by the National Park Service's Long Distance Trails Group Office in Santa Fe. In the meantime, state, county, and city parks along the trail route that have not yet been certified are open for public use, but permission should be obtained for sites located on private land. Federal lands do not have to be certified; they are included in the Trail of Tears National Historic Trail if they meet the national trail criteria in the National Trails System Act.

Some forty-six sites have historic significance and provide quality experiences. These sites include fords, ferries, structures, natural landmarks, marked gravesites, campsites, and rural landscapes. For example, parts of the Trail of Tears are included within Pea Ridge National Military Park, located northeast of Bentonville, Arkansas. The his-toric significance of the trail's northern route is enhanced because it followed the main road between Fayetteville and St. Louis, which later became known as Telegraph Road, once a telegraph line was strung along it in 1860. Pea Ridge, the site of a Union victory on March 7–8, 1862, was one of the major Civil War engagements west of the Mississippi River. Approximately one thousand Cherokee soldiers from Indian Territory under the command of Stand Watie participated as Confederates in this battle—the only major battle that involved Cherokee troops. Fort Smith National Historic Site, at the Arkansas-Oklahoma border, is located close to both water and land portions of the trail. It was established in 1817 as a U.S. Army base to maintain peace between the Osage and the incoming Cherokees.

Other national park units are located near the trail but are not directly associated with the removal. These include Great Smoky Mountains National Park in North Carolina and Tennessee; Wilson's Creek National Battle-field in Republic, Missouri; Arkansas Post National Memorial on the water route near Gillett; Chickamauga and Chattanooga National Military Parks in Fort Oglethorpe, Georgia, and Chattanooga, Tennessee; Shiloh National Military Park off the water route near Savannah, Tennessee; and Natchez Trace Parkway and Natchez Trace National Scenic Trail from Natchez, Mississippi, to Nashville, Tennessee.

A few trail portions pass through areas administered by the U.S. Forest Service. Nearly seventeen miles of trail pass through sections of the Shawnee National Forest between Golconda and Ware in southern Illinois. Mark Twain National Forest is the site of some sixty miles of trail between Jackson and Farmington and between Caledonia and Steelville, Missouri. Other federal agencies involved include the Tennessee Valley Authority and the U.S. Army Corps of Engineers, which manage rivers that were used during the Cherokee removal. TVA manages approximately 422 miles of the water route along the Tennessee River from Chattanooga, Tennessee, to Paducah, Kentucky. And the Corps of Engineers administers approximately eight hundred miles of the Ohio, Mississippi, and Arkansas Rivers from Paducah, Kentucky, to Fort Gibson, Oklahoma.

Well-developed interpretive centers, found near the eastern and western ends of the Trail of Tears, are operated by the Cherokees. The eastern center, on the Cherokee Indian Reservation in North Carolina, consists of the Museum of the Cherokee Indian, the Oconaluftee Indian Village, and an amphitheater presenting an outdoor drama entitled *Unto These Hills*. The western facility is the Cherokee Heritage Center in Tahlequah, Oklahoma. It consists of the Cherokee National Museum, the Tsa-La-Gi Ancient

Cherokee Village, the Adams Corner Rural Cherokee Village (showing the final period of the old Cherokee Nation), and an amphitheater, currently under reconstruction, to present the outdoor drama, *Trail of Tears*. Other well-developed interpretive programs about trail sites can be found at the New Echota Historic Site in Calhoun, Georgia; the Red Clay state historical area in Cleveland, Tennessee; and the Trail of Tears State Park near Jackson, Missouri.

To make it easier for visitors to follow the trail, an auto-tour route has been established, with plans to include interpretive facilities and wayside exhibits. The auto route will occasionally cross the historic route, but generally identifying the original route will require the use of detailed maps. Future plans call for a recreation trail paralleling the roads. This will require funding and volunteerism. Since approximately 98 percent of the land corridor on either side of the national historic trail is privately owned, this work will also call for agreements with landowners. Nonetheless, a few scattered areas along the land route pass through national forest areas or state parks—such as the Trail of Tears State Park in Missouri—that can provide a sense of the nineteenth-century passage of the Cherokee people. Along the water route, there are many publicly owned lands and some state recreation areas that resemble the nineteenth-century landscape. The

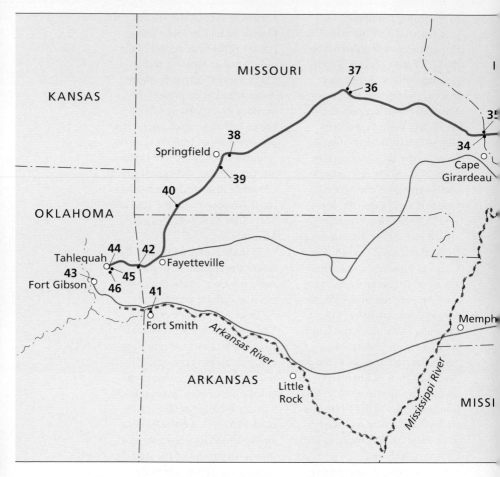

KANSAS

MISSOURI 37
36
3!
38 34
Springfield O Cape
39 Girardeau
40
OKLAHOMA

44 42
Tahlequah OFayetteville
43 45
Fort Gibson 46 41
Fort Smith Arkansas River Memph
ARKANSAS Little
Rock Mississippi River MISSI

TRAIL OF TEARS NATIONAL HISTORIC TRAIL

Delta Queen Steamboat Company offers cruises along the Arkansas, Tennessee, Mississippi, and Missouri Rivers, including portions that were part of the trail. Many of these stretches will be marked for recreational boaters.

Traveling along the Trail of Tears National Historic Trail brings with it a sensitivity to the Cherokee experience and to the experiences of other American Indian tribes of the nineteenth century who faced removal. Though it can be argued that proponents of the removal policy may have believed they were sending the American Indians to a land that would be theirs, and away from conflict and potential wars, the trail cannot help but arouse a sense of the need for cultural awareness, empathy, and control over greed and political advantage.

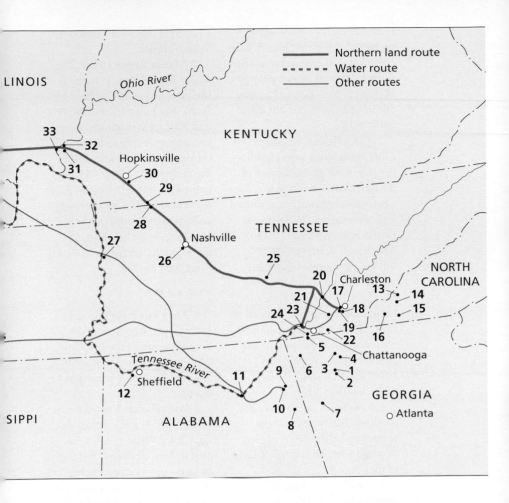

Legend:
- Northern land route
- Water route
- Other routes

LINOIS — Ohio River

KENTUCKY

33
32
31
Hopkinsville
30
29
28
27
26
Nashville
TENNESSEE
25
20
Charleston
17
21
24 23
5
19
22
16
Chattanooga
Tennessee River
Sheffield
11
9
6 3 1
2
12
10
7
8

NORTH CAROLINA
13
14
15
18

GEORGIA
Atlanta

SIPPI — ALABAMA

GEORGIA

1. NEW ECHOTA STATE HIS-
TORIC SITE. The last capital of the
Cherokee Nation from 1825 to
1838 is now managed by the
Georgia State Parks System. The
site (NHL) in Calhoun contains
several reconstructed buildings,
including a typical Cherokee
house, a printing office for the

Some of the material in this section
comes from the *Trail of Tears National
Historic Trail Comprehensive Management and Use Plan*.

Cherokee Phoenix, the supreme
court building, the Vann tavern,
and the home (1828) of New
England missionary Samuel Worcester, who was forced to leave
(1834). *Nearby:* Chattahoochee
NF.

2. FORT WOOL. Fort Wool was
one of the thirteen removal forts
in Ursula, Georgia. All thirty-one
removal forts were near Cherokee
towns and were used only temporarily until the population could
be moved to centralized intern-

Points of Interest

ment camps. Fort Wool was probably behind the Samuel Worcester house at New Echota. The site is located on private property adjacent to New Echota Historic Site in Calhoun and is not open to the public.

3. VANN HOUSE. Cherokee Chief James Vann, who played a key role in the establishment of the Moravian mission to the Cherokees at Spring Place, moved into the mansion (NRHP) near Chatsworth on March 24, 1805. After Vann's death (1809), his son Joseph occupied the home until his forced removal during the 1830s. In 1952 the State of Georgia purchased the three-acre tract on which the house stands, restored it, and opened it to the public in 1958. *Nearby:* Fort Mountain SP, Carters Lake, Chattahoochee NF.

4. FORT GILMER. The fort site, south of Chatsworth, was the temporary headquarters of Gen. Winfield Scott, who was in charge of the removal.

5. JOHN ROSS HOUSE. The two-story log house (1797; NRHP and NHL) in Rossville was built by John McDonald. Ross, who became the principal chief (1828) after serving as president of the National Council of the Cherokees, moved into the house after being forced from his home in Rome (1830).

6. FORT CUMMING. This removal fort (1836) was commanded by Capt. Samuel Farris of the Georgia volunteers. In Big Spring at the northwest edge of La Fayette, it was a stockaded fort

of upright logs with rifle towers at each corner.

7. MAJOR RIDGE HOME. The Major Ridge Home in Rome is the location of the Chieftain Museum. The house (1794; NRHP and NHL) was originally a log cabin that was expanded into a frame plantation house during the early 1800s. Major Ridge occupied the house before his move to Oklahoma. It is now owned and managed by the Junior Service League and has dioramas, photographs, and artifacts dating from 8000 B.C.

ALABAMA

8. FORT LOVELL. Previously named Fort Armstrong, Fort Lovell was one of the five Alabama removal forts. It is south of Cedar Bluff on Williamson Island.

9. FORT PAYNE. Named for its builder (1838) and commander, Capt. John Payne, the fort was used as both a removal fort and an internment camp (the ten other internment camps were in Tennessee). It was the camp for 900 Cherokees in July of 1838. The group eventually numbered 1,103 in the muster roll of Detachment 4, which was conducted to Indian Territory by John Benge. An original building stood until 1946, and a chimney from the original fort still stands on the site in Fort Payne. *Other attractions:* The Depot Museum with American Indian artifacts. *Nearby:* DeSoto SP.

10. ANDREW ROSS HOME. Constructed by Daniel and Molly

Ross (1790), the house (NRHP) became the home of their son Andrew until his removal to Oklahoma. In Fort Payne, it is now privately owned.

11. GUNTER'S LANDING. Steamboats with Cherokees on board stopped here at Guntersville (where the Black Warrior River flows into the Tennessee) for fuel and supplies, and the John Benge detachment crossed the river here after leaving Fort Payne.

12. TUSCUMBIA LANDING. Located in City Park West at the terminus of the Tuscumbia, Courtland, and Decatur Railroad in Sheffield, this Tennessee River landing became a departure point for many groups of Indians from southeastern states. A detachment of Cherokees following the water route traveled by railroad from Decatur, Alabama, around the shoals of the river and reboarded boats at Tuscumbia Landing en route to Indian Territory (1838). *Nearby:* The birthplace of Helen Keller; the Muscle Shoals Area, with twelve hundred miles of scenic lakeshore; the Natchez Trace Parkway and NTNST, connecting Natchez, Mississippi, and Nashville, Tennessee.

NORTH CAROLINA

13. FORT MONTGOMERY. This was one of the five removal forts established in North Carolina to hold the Cherokees prior to moving them to internment camps, and ultimately to Indian Territory. It is located in Robbinsville near Fort Hill and is privately

owned. *Nearby:* The area in the Smokies around Cherokee has been the home of the Eastern Band of Cherokees for centuries. The area offers the Museum of the Cherokee Indian; the Oconaluftee Indian Village; *Unto These Hills,* a drama about the Cherokees from the arrival of Hernando de Soto (1540) through the Trail of Tears; the Cherokee Indian Cyclorama Wax Museum with dioramas presenting three hundred years of Cherokee history; the southern gateway to the Great Smoky Mountains NP at the Oconaluftee Visitor Center; the Blue Ridge Parkway, connecting the Great Smoky Mountains NP to Shenandoah NP; Nantahala NF; Qualla Boundary Cherokee Indian Reservation; ANST.

14. FORT DELANEY. This removal fort in Andrews is privately owned. *Nearby:* Nantahala NF.

15. FORT HEMBREE. This removal fort in Hayesville is also privately owned.

16. FORT BUTLER. The most important fort in the state, above the left bank of the Hiwassee, was built by Gen. Winfield Scott during the roundup. Cherokees from the other removal forts were brought here before being taken to the main agency at Calhoun, Tennessee. The site, in Murphy, is privately owned. *Nearby:* Hiwassee Dam and Lake; Fields of the Wood biblical theme park.

TENNESSEE

17. FORT CASS. One of the eight removal forts in Tennessee,

Fort Cass was the principal Cherokee agency on the Hiwassee (a State Scenic River) and served as the primary emigration depot for removal. The site is on private property in Charleston. *Nearby:* Cherokee NF; to the northeast, in Vonore, the Sequoyah Birthplace Museum; reconstruction of Fort Loudoun, which was originally built by the British during the French and Indian War and burned by the Cherokees in 1760, includes a rebuilt powder magazine, blacksmith shop, gun platform, and visitor center; Tellico Blockhouse, built as an American military post on the border of the Cherokee Nation and the site of several important treaty negotiations, was converted to a trading post and stage stop and is now open for visitation.

18. **LEWIS ROSS HOME.** Lewis Ross lived in this house during the removal period. Like his brother John, Lewis played a key role in the Cherokee removal. The large, two-story home in Charleston is privately owned.

19. **RATTLESNAKE SPRING.** The area around the spring (NRHP) was the site of one of the agency camps. Captain Page reported (July 25, 1838) that the camp at Rattlesnake Spring, north of Cleveland in Dry Valley, had six hundred Cherokees awaiting orders to begin the journey to Indian Territory. *Nearby:* Cherokee NF.

20. **BLYTHE FERRY SITE.** Groups of Cherokees traveling on the forced removal from Camp Ross and the agency area crossed the Tennessee River here (1838) north of Georgetown. The ferry was built by John Blythe (1809) and later operated by his son John. The gravesite of Col. Return J. (White Eagle) Meigs, a Cherokee agent, is nearby. *Nearby:* Dayton boasts the Rhea County Courthouse and Museum and reenactment of the "Scopes monkey trial" (1925) in which a science teacher was accused of teaching the theory of evolution as a fact.

21. **HAIR CONRAD CABIN.** Conrad served as a conductor for the first detachment of Cherokees to leave Rattlesnake Spring (in August 1838). His duties were later assigned to Daniel Colston. According to local tradition, Conrad lived in a single-pen log cabin built (about 1804) near the confluence of Candies Creek and Hair's (now Harris) Creek. The cabin (NRHP) is on Blythe Wood Road west of Cleveland.

22. **RED CLAY.** South of Cleveland, the Red Clay SHP (NRHP) is managed by the Tennessee Department of Conservation. The Cherokee tribal government met here between 1832 and 1838, holding eleven general councils with as many as five thousand Cherokees attending. The James F. Corn Interpretive Center contains exhibits, a theater, and a resource reading room and sponsors Cherokee Days of Recognition each August.

23. **ROSS'S LANDING.** Altogether, some 2,000 Cherokees were held at this internment camp, 970 of whom made up the

eleventh detachment, which was conducted overland by Richard Taylor. Three large groups departed by water from this point. The site is near the Market Street bridge over the Tennessee River in Chattanooga. *Other attractions:* The Aquarium; the Chattanooga Regional History Museum; Chattanooga Riverboat Company cruises sailing from Ross's Landing; the TVA Energy Center; the Tennessee Valley Railroad. *Nearby:* Lookout Mountain, Incline Railway, hang-gliding flights; Lookout Mountain Scenic Highway; Signal Mountain; Chattanooga Nature Center drive-through park; Chickamauga and Chattanooga National Military Park; Cherokee NF; Chickamauga Dam and Lake with visitor center; Nickajack Dam and Reservoir with visitor center.

24. **SPRING FROG CABIN.** The cabin (late 1770s) was home of the Cherokee leader-athlete, Spring Frog, who made the journey to Indian Territory as part of the forced removal. Robert Sparks Walker, a well-known naturalist, was born here, and the house (NRHP) is now owned and administered by the Chattanooga chapter of the Audubon Society.

25. **SHELLSFORD BAPTIST CHURCH SITE.** In late October 1838 Jesse Bushyhead, conductor of one Cherokee detachment, preached here. A namesake Baptist church stands near the site, east of McMinnville. *Nearby:* American Indian mounds; Cumberland Caverns; Fall Creek Falls

State Resort Park; Rock Island State Rustic Park.

26. **NASHVILLE TOLL BRIDGE (DEDRICK STREET) SITE.** This bridge in Nashville spanned the Cumberland River, and groups of Cherokees used it during the removal. *Other attractions:* The *Belle Carol* riverboat and the *General Jackson* paddleboat tours of the Cumberland River; Fort Nashborough reproduction on the banks of the Cumberland, built to withstand American Indian attacks; state capitol with equestrian statue of Andrew Jackson; Tennessee State Museum; NTNST and Natchez Trace Parkway; Grand Ole Opry; Ryman Auditorium; Country Music Hall of Fame and Museum; Cheekwood-Tennessee Botanical Gardens and Museum of Art. *Nearby:* Andrew Jackson's Mansion, The Hermitage (1821); Grassmere Wildlife Park; Percy and Edwin Warner Parks.

27. **REYNOLDSBURG FERRY SITE.** On the Tennessee River, this was the site of the ferry crossing used by the John Benge detachment (November 1838). The ferry and a general store were operated by Thomas K. Wyly, who sold the Cherokees $400 worth of supplies. Now inundated by a TVA impoundment, the general location can be seen from Nathan Bedford Forrest SP.

28. **HALFWAY HOUSE.** The structure was reportedly a stop for the Cherokees, between Turnersville and Port Royal on Brush Creek, near the Kentucky state line. *Nearby:* Port Royal SP.

29. GRAY'S INN. Oral tradition has it that Whitepath, a Cherokee chief, drank from a well at this location west of Guthrie before he died in nearby Hopkinsville. In its later years the inn housed a restaurant and is now known as the Stagecoach Inn.

30. WHITEPATH AND FLY SMITH GRAVES. Whitepath, assistant conductor for the Elijah Hicks detachment, was the first to reach Hopkinsville (1838). According to a letter written to John Ross, Whitepath was already seriously ill by the time the detachment had reached Port Royal, Tennessee. Chief Fly Smith also died near Hopkinsville and is buried at the same location. The site is located at the Trail of Tears Commemorative Park, which has sculptures of the chiefs, flags representing the nine states involved in the removal, a bronze plaque of the route, and a log-cabin heritage center. An intertribal powwow is held the weekend after Labor Day in Hopkinsville. The Pennyroyal Area Museum has exhibits pertaining to the Trail of Tears. *Nearby:* Land between the Lakes with TVA visitor center, welcome station, and campgrounds.

31. MANTLE ROCK. The Nature Conservancy owns the camping spot near the Ohio River crossing, near Joy. *Nearby:* In Wickliffe, the Wickliffe Mounds, a Mississippian site with several mounds built about nine hundred years ago.

32. BERRY FERRY SITE. A ferry across the Ohio River at this site was operated by John Berry. All detachments of Cherokees that crossed the Ohio River used this ferry to Golconda.

33. BUEL HOUSE. The two-story log structure (NRHP) was built in Golconda by Alexander Hall Buel, Jr. (1836 or 1837). During the forced removal, two Cherokees came to the door, drawn by the smell of cooked pumpkin, which Buel's wife gave them. *Nearby:* Trail of Tears State Forest; Shawnee NF.

MISSOURI

34. GREEN'S FERRY (WILLARD'S LANDING) SITE. A ferry was operated across the Mississippi River here. The Missouri side of the landing was near the southern end of what is now the Trail of Tears SP; the trail followed Green's Ferry Road out of the park toward Jackson. The ferry site and a portion of the road (NRHP) are included in the Trail of Tears SP archeological site outside Cape Girardeau.

35. OTAHKI BUSHYHEAD HILDEBRAND'S GRAVE. The daughter of Jesse Bushyhead, Otahki Hildebrand, was buried on the west bank of the Mississippi River near Green's Ferry outside Cape Girardeau. A marker within Trail of Tears SP commemorates her legendary gravesite. There are scenic views of the Mississippi River from Court House Park and Cape Rock.

36. Snelson-Brinker House. This restored log house (1834), as well as the county courthouse (1835), near the Massey Ironworks, was noted as a stop in the diary of W. I. I. Morrow, a physician who accompanied the Richard Taylor detachment. The Cherokees camped and bought corn here at St. James. *Nearby:* In Rolla, the Ed Clark Museum of Missouri Geology; to the south, Ozark National Scenic Riverways.

37. Massey (Maramec) Ironworks. The oldest ironworks in the state (1829, NRHP) was also noted by Morrow. South of St. James, it is now a public use area managed by the James Foundation in Maramec Spring Park, along with the Ozark Agriculture Museum, the Maramec Museum, and the Maramec Nature Center.

38. Danforth Farm. Morrow reported in his diary (March 12, 1839) that the detachment "started before day, traveled 12 miles to Danforths." The farm is still in the Danforth family. The original settler, Josiah Danforth, came to Greene County by way of Tennessee and St. Louis in the early 1830s. He bought the Walnut Forest area land (1834), northeast of Springfield. *Nearby:* Gateway to the Ozarks; Fantastic Caverns; Springfield Nature Center with visitor center; Wilson's Creek NB.

39. Bell Tavern (Dyer) Site. This site is located between the James River and Wilson's Creek south of Springfield in an area

long known as the Delaware Villages near the site of the Gilliss (Delaware) Trading Post. Here the White River trace forked to the southeast, while the Cherokees followed the Indian trace southwest through Stone and Barry Counties.

40. McMurtry Spring. This spring served as a source of water for groups traveling along Flat Creek near Cassville. *Nearby:* Mark Twain NF; Roaring River SP.

ARKANSAS / OKLAHOMA

41 Fort Smith National Historic Site. Administered by the NPS, this frontier military post was established at the junction of the Arkansas and Poteau Rivers (1817). Its purpose was to maintain peaceable relations between the Osage and Cherokee Indians. The U.S. Army began building a permanent fort here (1838) on the border of Indian Territory. Cherokees traveling up the Arkansas Valley via the water route passed the fort (NRHP, NHL). The Fort Smith Cemetery has the graves of Maj. William C. Bradford, who established the first fort, and Judge Isaac C. Parker, who held court at Fort Smith during Indian Territory years. *Nearby:* Ozark NF. To the southeast, Little Rock (water route) Riverfront Park; the Old Statehouse (begun 1833); at Scott, the Toltec Mounds Archeological SP (on bayou of water route), occupied (A.D. 600–950) by the Plum Bayou culture. To the west, in Spiro, Oklahoma, the

Spiro Mounds (water route) Archeological Site with twelve mounds built by American Indians A.D. 600–1450; in Sallisaw, Oklahoma, Sequoyah's Home Site includes his one-room cabin (1829), a statue, park grounds, and small interpretive center; in Gore, Oklahoma, the Cherokee Courthouse, about one mile from Tahlonteeskee, the original capital (before 1830) of the Cherokees who had moved to the area.

OKLAHOMA

42. WOODHALL HOMEPLACE. At this site in Westville most groups traveling by land disbanded.

43. FORT GIBSON. Operated as Fort Gibson Military Park by the Oklahoma Historical Society, this military post (1824, NHL) along the Grand River was initially built by troops moved from Fort Smith to establish a presence in Indian Territory. Several groups of Cherokees completed their removal here, and troops from the post often formally received the new arrivals. Among the graves of officers at Fort Gibson National Cemetery (1868) is that of Sam Houston's Cherokee wife, Talihina. *Nearby:* Sequoyah Bay RA.

44. TAHLEQUAH. Named for Talikwa or Tellico, an early Cherokee town in Tennessee, Tahlequah is the county seat of Cherokee County and serves as the center of the Cherokee Nation. Cherokee commissioners determined the location (1839), and the Cherokee National

Council incorporated the town and platted it (1843). Several historic structures in the community are on the NRHP, and there are also several designated NHLs, including the Cherokee National Capitol, the Cherokee Supreme Court Building, and the Cherokee Female Seminary (second site), which is now used by Northeastern State University, which sponsors the excellent River City Players; the Cherokee National Holiday is observed on Labor Day weekend.

45. PARK HILL. Immediately south of Tahlequah is an area where several Cherokees settled, including John Ross. The Reverend Thomas Bertholf, a Methodist minister, was the first settler to arrive (1821); the Reverend Samuel A. Worcester, an influential Cherokee missionary, established Park Hill Mission (December 1836). Also at Park Hill is the Cherokee Heritage Center with Adams Corner Rural Village, representative of many small communities in Indian Territory; the Trail of Tears outdoor drama; the first Cherokee Female Seminary (NRHP); the Cherokee National Museum, presenting the Cherokee story, with exhibits from prehistoric and recent times; Tsa-La-Gi Ancient Village, which re-creates a sixteenth-century Cherokee settlement, with tours and living history (May–August). About a mile east on Willis Road is the first cabin site of John Ross. Just 1.75 miles north along the Illinois River is the site of a campground

used by several thousand Cherokees during the summer of 1839, while awaiting land assignments in the Indian Territory. Several other historic sites, dating after the forced removal, are in this same area, including the Murrell House (1845), home of George Murrell, son-in-law of Lewis Ross, which stands alone as a tribute to the antebellum era of the Cherokee Nation.

46. ROSS CEMETERY. The Ross Cemetery is one mile southeast of the Cherokee National Museum outside Tahlequah. Key figures involved with the Trail of Tears are buried here, including John Ross and Lewis Ross. *Nearby:* Lake Tenkiller; Sequoyah SP.

WAGON WITH LUPINE

Purple lupine greet vacationers on the Trails West wagon excursion on BLM land along the Oregon, California, and Mormon Pioneer National Historic Trails. The three-day wagon route even crosses the Continental Divide National Scenic Trail near the Sweetwater River just outside of South Pass, Wyoming.

Oregon National Historic Trail

*An April restlessness, a stirring of the blood,
a wind from beyond the oaks' openings, spoke
of the prairies, the great desert, and the
Western Sea.*

BERNARD DEVOTO IN *MARK TWAIN'S AMERICA*

During the mid-nineteenth century the magnetic pull of land, freedom, adventure, and riches drew thousands west along the transportation corridor that connected the United States with the vast expanse of land reaching to the Pacific Ocean. The travels of early-nineteenth-century fur traders and mountain men along ancient American Indian trails showed the rest of the country that it was possible to traverse this territory overland. Later, a succession of missionaries, soldiers, emigrants, religious refugees, goldseekers, stagecoach lines, and lightning-fast Pony Express riders followed roughly the same route. Eventually even the telegraph, the railroad, and highways would retrace these arteries that made it possible to transform the nineteenth-century concept of Manifest Destiny into a reality. For three decades—from 1840 to 1870—this corridor would accommodate the migration of nearly one-half million people to the fertile lands of Oregon, the goldfields of California, and the refuge of the Great Salt Lake Valley.

ADMINISTERING AGENCY
National Park Service
Long Distance Trails Office
324 South State Street, Suite 250
P.O. Box 45155
Salt Lake City, UT 84145-0155
801-539-4095

FURTHER INFORMATION
Oregon-California Trails Association
P.O. Box 1019
Independence, MO 64051

ESTABLISHED
1978

APPROXIMATE MILEAGE
2,170 miles (3,495 kilometers)
[Includes the 1,930-mile route from Independence, Missouri, to Oregon City as well as the alternate southern route of 126 miles and the Columbia River route of 114 miles.]

STATES
Missouri, Kansas, Nebraska, Wyoming, Idaho, Oregon, Washington

The first Europeans to see the trans-Mississippi West were the mountain men, trappers, and the maritime explorers along the west coast.* In Canada, the Hudson's Bay Company fur frontier was approaching the Columbia River basin. Inspired by the Lewis and Clark journey, a New York fur dealer, John Jacob Astor, in a countermove, had posts built along the Columbia River, but during the War of 1812 British traders from Canada took possession of these depots. That same year Astorian Robert Stuart and a company of men traveled overland to carry dispatches to Astor in the East on what became known as the Oregon Trail. By following a Crow Indian trail, the Stuart party found the geographically attractive South Pass. Only 7,550 feet above sea level, with easy gradients, the pass was within the proximity of the upper reaches of the Platte River. "By information received from these men," the *Missouri Gazette* reported, "it appears that a journey across the continent of North America might be performed with a waggon." Wagon transport was essential to mass emigration. A nation grew curious.

Two major circumstances combined to spur Americans to settle in the Oregon country. In the late 1830s, Great Britain was making rumblings about its ownership of the Pacific Northwest. An influx

*Material in this section is taken from *The Oregon Trail,* a publication of the National Park Service, Bureau of Land Management, and U.S. Forest Service.

of settlers in the area, American leaders believed, would cement the United States's claim to the area, preventing further conflict with England. The United States was also rocked by depressions in 1837 and 1841. Money was tight and unemployment high, especially for the lower and middle classes. At the same time, eastern churches saw the American Indians of the Oregon country as ready candidates for European ideas of civilization. Ardent missionary societies were formed. Methodist missionary Jason Lee, writing from Willamette Valley in 1835, noted, "White females would be of the greatest importance to the mission and would have far more influence among Indians than males." In 1836 Marcus Whitman and his new wife, Narcissa, messengers of Calvinist spirituality, along with Presbyterians Henry and Eliza Spalding, headed for Oregon as missionaries. From their trip, the country learned that women could not only go up the trail, but could do so while pregnant! Narcissa Whitman became a heroine to women, and the letters she and her husband sent home publicized the opportunities and advantages of Oregon. In 1838, Jason Lee himself toured the eastern states, extolling the virtues of the West, Oregon in particular. To a struggling people, these words held promise.

Settlers thus began to set out for Oregon. By 1840 there were about five hundred Americans in the Willamette area. Emigration societies formed, exchanged information, and enrolled numbers who were interested in going west. Independence, Missouri, was the gathering site for nearly five hundred hopeful emigrants in the spring of 1841. Facing the long western trek from this settlement on the edge of the frontier, they were not well organized. No guides had been engaged, and a mixture of oxcarts and mule- and horse-drawn wagons composed the ranks. Still others went on foot. Upon departure, most were quickly discouraged and did not continue. Only about thirty of the original number reached Oregon—through the help of trappers and Jesuit missionaries.

But more emigrant societies were soon forming, pushing the federal government toward more active assertion of American rights in the Oregon country. Senator Lewis Linn of Missouri became the great expansionist advocate. He advocated land giveaways to induce families to take the risky journey to Oregon, and he sought to extend the reach of U.S. laws to the U.S. citizens who emigrated to Oregon. Although this legislation was thought to disregard the rights of Great Britain and consequently was not passed by Congress, the momentum began to shift in this direction.

In 1842 news reports of the expedition to Oregon of Lt. John Charles Frémont and his column of army explorers from South Pass (in present-day Wyoming) seized the imagination of the

NATIONAL FRONTIER TRAILS CENTER

The Oregon, California, and Santa Fe Trails all started near Missouri's National Frontier Trails Center in Independence. Quotes from diaries kept along the trail are featured in the museum exhibits, and information on the Lewis and Clark expedition is also available.

country. In the spring of that same year, Elijah White gathered a group in Independence to form the first organized civilian trek to Oregon. A former missionary, White was heading to Oregon to be the subagent to the American Indians there. Equipped with a professional guide hailing from Fort Hall (in present-day Idaho), White's group set out for Oregon's Willamette Valley on the same route taken by traders of Astor's Pacific Fur Company. This group of one hundred blazed the trail for thousands to follow; more importantly, they kindled the hopes and dreams of a nation. Traveling over two thousand miles across the great prairies, mountains, and desert, half the members of White's party would

STEAMBOAT WHEEL

Although fewer in number than at the time of the great western migration, steamboats still ply the waters of the Mississippi and Missouri Rivers. Every summer steamboat excursions leave Westport Landing in Kansas City.

actually settle in Oregon, half would continue on to California a year later.

Independence and Westport, the jumping-off places for fur traders and Santa Fe wagons, became the natural locations to search for traveling companions. Other than those local Missourians who reached the rendezvous point in wagons, most emigrants reached Independence or Westport by traveling up the Missouri in steamboats, since spring snowmelt and rains made the ground too boggy for extended wagon travel and swollen rivers were impossible to ford. Thus, St. Louis, with its convenient location near the confluence of the Missouri and the Mississippi, became the place to board a boat, and that rivertown quickly became known

as "the Gateway to the West." After locating a boat in St. Louis, pioneers headed off to Independence Landing or onward to Westport Landing, long since engulfed by Kansas City.

The streets of Independence, jammed with Mexicans, American Indians, blacks, hunters, townspeople, chicken coops, draft animals, farm equipment, and cattle, were a sight to behold. After setting up camp, the emigrants would return to town to get the provisions they needed. Military-style maneuvers of the fur traders and Santa Fe caravans were led by captains and sergeants, but those taking the Oregon Trail settled into family units, which, once out on the trail, democratically elected officers whom they felt free to disobey. Describing his election as captain of an 1843 train, Peter Burnett observed, "The candidates stood up in a row before the constituents, and at a given signal, they wheeled about and marched off, while the general mass broke after them 'lickety split,' each man forming behind his favorite, so that every candidate flourished a sort of tail of his own, and the longest tail was elected." Citing "10,000 little vexations," Burnett quit the job after one week, but it was his destiny to become California's first governor.

In 1843, over 900 people—240 men, 120 women, and more than 600 children—gathered for the beginning of what history would call "the Great Migration." Partially because of its numbers, and largely because of its success in moving wagons and dragging livestock all the way to the Willamette Valley in Oregon, this group officially opened the trail that thousands more would follow. Their arrival doubled Oregon's American population. Survival in their new home was achieved with the help of Dr. John McLoughlin, chief factor of the Hudson's Bay Company at Fort Vancouver, the main depot of the company west of the Rockies. When rains engulfed the pioneers, he provided credit for supplies, saving lives in the process. Largely because of his friendly policy toward Americans, he was demoted and finally forced to resign his post in 1846. He eventually took U.S. citizenship, but he was never totally trusted by fellow Americans because of his British ancestry. Even so, he came to be called "the father of Oregon."

Following on the heels of that first famous party came the hunting party of Sir William Drummond Stewart, guided by fur trader William Sublette, with Baptiste Charbonneau, son of Sacagawea, as driver. Eighteen forty-four saw nearly four hundred people depart along the trail, and over the next two years over five thousand actually reached Oregon. All the while, expansionists back east were "thundering on" about America's right to the territory, rejecting the old boundary line established with Great Britain at the forty-

ninth parallel. Referring to the desired parallel, the 1844 Democratic campaign slogan became "Fifty-four Forty or Fight!" And when Democrat James K. Polk, who endorsed the occupation of Oregon and the annexation of Texas, won the election, it was widely interpreted as a mandate for expansion. John L. O'Sullivan captured the country's mood in 1845 with a sentence, "Nothing must interfere with the fulfillment of our *manifest destiny* to overspread the continent allotted by Providence for the free development of our yearly multiplying millions" (emphasis added).

But war with Mexico over Texas was threatening. Polk, wishing to avoid war with Great Britain, fell back to the forty-ninth parallel. By treaty in 1846, an agreement was reached to extend the old line of 1818 along the forty-ninth parallel westward to Puget Sound and from there to the Pacific through the Strait of Juan de Fuca. According to the agreement, some territory that was clearly British became American, while the Brits retained Vancouver Island and navigation rights to the Columbia. The British, knowing that they could not compete with American colonization and that the fur trade was nearly defunct, agreed. American lands had been extended without war. A young nation anxiously read every printed word about the mysterious West, but few guidebooks provided solid, reliable information on the trail. Many writers contributed to the "Oregon fever" that swept the country by describing the land in almost biblical terms.

Three significant events occurred in the Far West in 1846. At the outbreak of war with Mexico, Anglo-Californians raised a standard for a Bear Flag Republic in hopes of annexation to the United States. The Donner party took a "shortcut" to California that stranded them for five torturous months in one of the harshest winters on record in the California mountains. The outcome—starvation, cannibalism, and death for half of the party—rendered the Donner experience one of the worst tragedies in the westward movement. And finally, the first of the Mormon pioneers left Nauvoo, Illinois, that year and crossed Iowa, poised to undertake their journey a year later along the northern branch of the Oregon Trail to the Valley of the Great Salt Lake. The company was handpicked according to skill, organized into two large divisions, further split into companies of fifty and ten, and given details on camp behavior and devotional practices.

The contrasting independence of other groups traveling west was noted in James Bennett's account, "A difference of opinion with regard to this day's travel arose this morning, which led to a division of the company. There being but little or no grass for twenty-eight miles to come, Messrs. Dexter, Wilsey and Pullyband were for starting at 3 o'clock p.m. and traveling all night; while Mr. Sweasy preferred making it in two days. They could not agree and separated." In general, independent overlanders democratically agreed to follow certain rules. For instance, they spread out in several columns to raise less dust and rotated positions in the line in a spirit of fairness. No individual, they agreed, should be choked by the dust all day, each day. All had to keep up the pace or risk being left behind. The mountains had to be crossed before winter snows fell.

Attracting much attention was the Cayuse uprising at the Whitman mission in Walla Walla in 1847. Cultural differences were causing antagonism, and friendly Indians warned the Whitmans of danger. The Cayuse, hunters and horse breeders, had not taken to horticulture and, to the dismay of the Whitmans, continued to see all creation, not simply God alone, as sacred. The Whitmans grew impatient "in the darkness of Heathenism." When a measles epidemic hit the mission that year, it was the last straw. Whitman, who medically treated whites and Indians alike, lost only one white child, but two hundred Indians died. On November 29, concluding that the Reverend Whitman was a witch doctor, the Cayuse killed the Whitmans and others and burned the mission. A few survivors escaped but fifty, mostly women and children, were taken captive. A volunteer army was called to seek revenge. Afraid that all Cayuse would be hunted to extinction for the actions of one small party, five individual Indians agreed to turn themselves in. They were hanged. Most of the captives were ransomed, but an era of mistrust and sporadic violence spread throughout the Northwest.

The Oregon killings convinced Congress to grant territorial status in 1848, which entitled the settlers to the protection of federal troops. But there was still one problem. The settlers who had arrived in advance of government control did not have title to their

WHITMAN RUTS

Actual ruts still remain along the trail. These are located at Whitman Mission National Historic Site near Walla Walla, Washington. Marcus and Narcissa Whitman, who helped to blaze the Oregon Trail, later ministered to the sick and destitute pioneers who turned to their mission for comfort.

farms and homes. Repeatedly, they petitioned the government for assistance. That same year, gold was discovered in California, and with that discovery, an explosion of fortune seekers headed west. In April 1849, more than twenty thousand emigrants left the East for Oregon and California. James Pritchard observed, "By noon today we came to where the St. Joseph and Independence roads came together. I counted 90 ox teams in one string . . . the road was just lined with them. It would appear from the sight before us that the nation was disgorging itself and sending off its whole inhabitance." Though travel to Oregon peaked in the late 1840s, California's non-Indian population expanded from 14,000 to nearly 250,000 in the years between 1848 and 1852.

Attention was drawn west, and the Oregonians were heard. In 1850, Congress passed the Oregon Donation Land Act. Any settler who lived on and improved the land for four years was given 320 acres. The occupant's wife was also given 320 acres. This was the first time that the government gave land away, but U.S. law and U.S. Indian policy were clear: Land could not be opened until there was a treaty opening it for settlement. Because so few tribal people were left in the Willamette Valley, few problems arose there. Nonetheless, as settlers moved east of the valley into well-established tribal lands, hostility became inevitable. To rectify the problem, a treaty council was held with the tribes of the interior Northwest in 1848. The intense pressure caused even Looking Glass, a Nez Perce, and one of the most outspoken against the treaty, to sign. Others soon followed, thereby allowing forty-five thousand square miles of land to fall to the hand of the United States. Hostilities did not end, however, until the end of the nineteenth century, when all tribes were moved to reservations.

Contrary to popular belief, early emigrants generally found American Indians along the trail, if they saw any at all, to be congenial and helpful. Numerous times, Indians showed their compassion by offering medical assistance, food, and valuable guidance. But some haunted camps for handouts, and others took livestock as river-crossing tolls, especially if they had experienced careless actions by previous groups of whites. And it was never wise to travel alone or in small parties, since that almost invited attack—and for those who showed too much fear or too much resistance, there could sometimes be death and scalping. Tales of such incidents spread. Nervous overlanders circled their wagons or formed a hollow square around their livestock, but American Indians were generally not foolish enough to attack. The truth is, members of both groups were mostly successful at avoiding trouble. As the influx of emigrants mushroomed, however, the lives of the native inhabitants changed drastically. For example, wagons brought sickness and whiskey, buffalo were killed for sport, the land was stripped, and the cornfields were destroyed, and the wild game vanished. Friendly relationships became strained. Forts were established along the trail in the late 1840s and early 1850s, and by 1860 there had been sufficient hostility and casualties that both sides kept serious guard.

Although the trail continued to be used to some extent into the early 1900s, its importance declined with the completion of the transcontinental railroad in 1869. In all, it was the greatest peacetime migration in the history of the world. Never again would the lives of the individuals who had participated in the four-to-six-month journey be the same, nor would the lives of those who lost control of their lands and were moved to reservations. For the overlanders, the trip brought more than inconveniences. If migration brought disappointment, it was noted as "seeing the elephant," a catchphrase that appeared in many diaries to indicate the difficult and dangerous. First, there was the plodding pace of travel in covered wagons, and the labor of traveling two thousand miles. In summer, water sources dried up, oxen perished, and emigrants who had not brought enough water barrels died of thirst. Some of the misinformed faced starvation when they found it impossible to live off the land. Family furniture was a fatal luxury if it replaced the recommended thousand pounds of flour. In the end, the extra weight caused the trail to become littered with cast-off family belongings. Thunder of stampeding buffalo produced untold fear, and rainstorms made trail life miserable. After a violent storm, journalist James Abbey admitted he had "felt the brush of the elephant's tail."

At least twenty thousand peopled died along the Oregon Trail, or about ten deaths for each mile of the route. Many accidents occurred from the misuse of firearms, but one of the most dreaded dangers first appeared on the trail in 1849. Cholera, later traced to drinking contaminated water, was an infectious disease that killed more travelers on the trail than did anything else. More than five thousand died from the disease in St. Louis in 1849 alone, and it quickly spread to the trail. Its mysterious nature made it especially frightening. A strong, healthy person could develop a slight fever in the morning and be dead by evening. Cholera and other diseases spread rapidly among wagons. In 1852 John Clark noted:

> One woman and two men lay dead on the grass and some more ready to die of cholera, measles and small pocks. A few men were digging graves, others tending the side. Women and children crying, some hunting medicine and none to be found scarcely; those that had were

loathe to spare. With heartfelt sorrow we looked around for some time until I felt unwell myself. Ordered the teams got up and moved forward one mile as so to be out of the hearing of crying and suffering.

Still, there were others who left home looking for health and found it, which encouraged continued emigration. In 1847, Andred Goodyear wrote, "I have now been out 47 days and nites, sleeping with no covering but blankets, and the sky above me for shelter, living mostly on buffalo meat. I have never enjoyed better health than I do now."

During the first third of the trip, the landscape was relatively gentle as the emigrants traveled along tributaries of the Missouri River to the Platte River Valley and headed for the high plains. Campsites and waterholes would not be overgrazed or fouled if the travelers set out early enough in the season. After covering about fifteen to twenty miles in any one day, camp would be formed about 5 in the afternoon. The campfire supplied light and warmth and weary travelers gathered to cook, mend clothes, write letters, make journal entries, play cards, repair wagons, or listen to the music of a fiddle or jew's harp. "Before a tent near the river a violin makes a lively music, and some youths and maidens have improvised a dance upon the green; in another quarter a flute gives its mellow and melancholy notes to the still

cal landmarks of Chimney Rock and Scotts Bluff, about one-third of the way on the trail. Now it was clear that they were making progress. By this time, too, they would have an idea if their money would hold out. As travel on the trail developed, there were tolls at ferries and bridges to be paid. A few days' journey beyond Scotts Bluff brought the emigrants to Fort Laramie, the great supply depot and resting place where they could replenish dwindling stocks of food and other staples — for a price. Here, wheels could be repaired and wagon boxes tightened before setting out on the increasingly difficult terrain of the Rocky Mountains and the ascent to the Continental Divide, where water and grass for livestock would become more scarce. Soon trouble would mount as drier air caused wooden wheels to shrink and the iron tires that held the wheels together loosened or rolled off. Buffalo herds were increasingly hard to find. Surviving the trip was now of paramount importance.

Just west of South Pass, at Fort Bridger, the emigrants parted ways. The Sublette Cutoff was cut through in 1844 to create an alternate route to the north. The cutoff brought a grueling fifty miles of barren, arid countryside, but if survived, it saved the traveler eighty-five miles and about a week's time. Other emigrants ignored the Sublette Cutoff and took the original route to Fort Bridger before heading on to their destination.

INDEPENDENCE ROCK AND CARVED NAMES

Children love to climb Independence Rock to look for names of emigrants carved in this granite boulder known as the Great Register of the Desert. Pioneers tried to reach the popular site near Alcova, Wyoming, by the Fourth of July.

night air . . . it has been a prosperous day; more than twenty miles," wrote Jesse Applegate as he made camp along the Platte River in 1843.

Excitement abounded when the emigrants passed the geologi-

The final third of the journey over the mountains and down the Columbia River was by far the most challenging. If approached too late in the season, the already weary travelers would be trapped by winter storms as they crossed over the Blue Mountains in eastern Oregon and the Cascades further west. And until Sam Barlow opened the Mount Hood Toll Road (more popularly known as the Barlow Road) to Oregon City in 1846, emigrants were forced to raft down the fierce rapids of the Columbia River once they reached The Dalles. Others simply abandoned their wagons at this point and built boats. Either way, it was a risky undertaking to face after having come so far. But those who survived the passage spread out into the Willamette Valley to establish farms and small towns. By obtaining their own personal goal, they welded the upper one-third of the nation to the rest of the United States. James Nesmith, who is known as the father of Polk County, Oregon, captured their "spirit" in his diary:

> Friday, October 27.—Arrived at Oregon City at the falls of the Willamette.
> Saturday, October 28—Went to work.

It was the determination, courage, and sense of adventure of these early arrivals that promoted the West and encouraged further expansion. Their numbers alone caused Britain to eagerly compromise at the forty-ninth parallel,

thereby avoiding war. It was not long before Americans began to settle present-day Washington as well. The economy took off as settlers in the lush, peaceful valleys supplied produce and other goods to the burgeoning gold-rush population in California. Small towns began to grow, and the population that had numbered a mere two hundred a decade earlier now stood at thirteen thousand. Mail arrived regularly by ship via Cape Horn and was distributed to the territory's forty post offices.

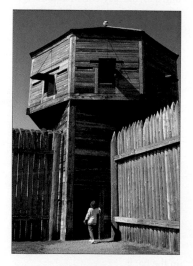

FORT VANCOUVER

Fort Vancouver was the western headquarters of the Hudson's Bay Company fur-trading operations from 1825 to 1849. When American pioneers arrived, they came to the fort for supplies. Today, a trail leads from the Fort Vancouver National Historic Site's visitor center to the fort site. The stockade and five buildings have been restored.

THE WAGON AND TEAM

Emigrant wagons were lighter than the freighters used on the Santa Fe Trail.* The Conestoga, as seen in the movies, was too large and heavy for the Oregon Trail, and the easterners who started off with Conestogas soon traded them for lighter farm wagons. The covered wagon, made of a box, an undercarriage with running gear, and top, was easily dismantled. Yet it could travel two thousand miles across rivers and sand, taking wind, rain, snow, and sun. Simply constructed, it was well ironed and made of a variety of seasoned woods at a cost of approximately $85. The box, four feet wide, ten to twelve feet long, and two feet deep, was usually built by the emigrant. An optional false bottom could be divided into foot-deep storage compartments. Spare parts, carved from available timber or salvaged from abandoned wagons found en route, were lashed on. A cage of chickens might also be tied on. Because the wheels required daily lubrication, a grease bucket was carried in the back.

The ensemble was carried on sturdy wheels made of osage, orangewood, or white oak; the wheels were bolted on for easy removal. (The springless undercarriage made wagon travel un-

comfortable enough that most emigrants preferred to walk.) Smaller wheels in the front aided turns, and earlier wagons did not have brakes. The wagon's cover consisted of a double thickness of cotton canvas or similar material that stretched over five or six hickory bows high enough to allow a person to stand upright in the center of the arch. The cover could be waterproofed with a coat of paint or linseed oil, and handy storage pockets were often sewn inside. If they could afford it, a large family would take along two or three wagons. The rule of thumb was to carry one hundred feet of one-inch rope for every five wagons so that they could be lowered down steep slopes.

No one ever settled the perennial argument about the best kind of draft stock. Oxen were often selected because they were cheaper, less prone to stampeding, covered long distances better, and were more useful to the farmer upon arrival. The ox was more edible in hard times, but the American Indian knew that too! Even so, oxen were less likely to be stolen since they could not be coaxed to move fast enough for a clean get-a-way. Oxen were better suited to eat prairie grass but worse off if they drank alkali water. No one cared to shoe the animal, which had to be turned upside down to be shod. Slower than mule or horse, oxen were stronger and mild-tempered.

*Material in this section is taken in part from the Bureau of Land Management's *A Step at a Time: The Oregon Trail.*

They required that someone walk beside them, cracking a long bull whip, mostly for the noise it made.

Mules called for the use of reins, which meant a jolting wagon ride for passengers who did not sit on the driver's seat which had the benefit of a metal spring to cushion the ride. Faster mules could cause mayhem, particularly at river crossings. And one never knew when a mule might get the notion to dash back to Missouri. A mule that stuck around, however, could always be counted on as a pack animal if anything happened to the wagon. The horse provided the most expensive mode of transportation, not only in its original price, but in terms of the costly grain it required. Bad water would cause distemper, and the animal was very attractive to Indians. Though faster than the ox and mule, the horse was definitely weaker in terms of endurance.

Going prices generally helped finalize the decision. Cheaper oxen sold for $50 to $65 per yoke (two), whereas mules ran about $50 to $90 a head, while horses were $200 in 1849 Independence. (These gold-rush era prices apparently inflated from the 1846 prices quoted by George McKinstry, "I find that the best place to fit out is Independence. Oxen can be had at $25 per yoke, mules or horses from $30 to $40 per head, flour this year $4 per barrel." Another consideration was the fact that it took four to eight oxen to pull a wagon versus a standard six-mule team to do the job.

A wagon outfit hauled about a ton. Goods were packed about four feet high on either side. The narrow passage down the middle allowed room to get at the goods or to carry a sick or injured person. The load was primarily composed of tools, food, and supplies, although most travelers managed some room for a few family treasures. Using the wagon as shelter was almost an afterthought. For the most part, sleeping was done in outside tents. *The Emigrant's Guide to California,* published in St. Louis in 1849, listed the following supplies for three people headed west on the Oregon Trail:

Three rifles at $20	$60.00
Three pairs of pistols at $15	45.00
Five barrels of flour (1,080 pounds)	20.00
Bacon, 600 pounds	30.00
Coffee, 100 pounds	8.00
Saleratus, 10 pounds	1.00
Lard, 50 pounds	2.50
Tea, five pounds	2.75
Sugar, 150 pounds	7.00
Rice, 75 pounds	3.75
Dried fruit, 50 pounds	3.00
Salt and pepper, 50 pounds	3.00
Lead, 30 pounds	1.20
Tent, 30 pounds	5.00
Bedding, 45 pounds	22.50
Cooking utensils, 30 pounds	4.00
Matches	1.00
Candles, soap, 50 pounds	5.30
Personal baggage, 150 pounds	
TOTAL: 2,505 pounds	$225.00

Bacon was stored in sacks, each containing one hundred pounds. In case of high heat, it was recommended that the sacks be placed in boxes surrounded by bran to prevent the fat from

melting. Flour was placed in double canvas sacks, one hundred pounds per sack.

The Trail Today

Today, the Oregon National Historic Trail (ONHT) evokes an instant image of the settlement of the continent, of the differences between American Indians and white settlers, and of new horizons, but by the end of the nineteenth century, successive waves of emigrants had completely eliminated any sense of frontier. Plows and barbed wire subdued the prairies, and the transcontinental railroads knitted the great distances together. As the early pioneers reached the end of their lives, fellow Oregonians began to realize that the state's history was being lost. Starting in 1873, efforts were made to preserve the pioneer experience, and the Oregon Pioneer Association was formed. Every year, pioneers met at the state fairgrounds and related their experiences. These were written down for the association, and though some were romanticized and others exaggerated, the memory was renewed—while the actual trail was forgotten.

Since wagons passed in columns that might be hundreds of yards apart, portions of the trail were never clearly defined. Fainter traces began to shift with the effects of nature and use. Deeper, more permanent traces that marked the best routes were followed by road builders. Interest in the actual trail did not

emerge until seventy-six-year-old Ezra Meeker, who had traversed the trail in 1852, set out in a covered wagon in 1906 to retrace the route from west to east. By making the trip, the tireless champion accomplished a task no one thought he could do. He created a general interest in marking the trail and rejuvenated interest in the old trail's history. The attendant publicity pointed up the loss and damage resulting from careless disregard. In the 1920s, the Oregon Trails Memorial Association, which Meeker founded, began to mark the trail and to preserve written accounts. Meeker met with Presidents Theodore Roosevelt and Calvin Coolidge, testified before Congress, and made publicity trips over the trail before his death at age ninety-seven in 1928. As a result of his efforts, monuments were erected, local histories were written, and national interest revived.

In 1978 the Oregon National Historic Trail was authorized by Congress. It is administered by the National Park Service in partnership with the Bureau of Land Management, the Forest Service, state and local governmental units, citizen organizations, and numerous private individuals whose property the trail crosses. The Oregon-California Trails Association, founded by eleven trail enthusiasts in 1982, has over three thousand members who work toward trail preservation through education and by providing alternatives to destruction. Their efforts have paid off for the thousands who tour the trail today. Additionally, the trail's sesquicentennial celebration in 1993 honored the memory of those who took part in the Great Migration, which left Independence in 1843. Each state sponsored special events, and many people participated in a reenactment by traveling the trail in wagons. Coordination between independent groups was boosted even further, and state brochures continue to increase the traveler's awareness, pointing the way to various sites.

Though twentieth-century developments and modern improved highways along or near emigrant roads have transformed many miles of the original routes, other developments and railroad construction have shifted transportation and settlement patterns away from many of the old grades. As a result, some of the trail's segments were abandoned and remain as they were when the pioneers passed through. These spots provide opportunities for scenic hiking, backpacking, camping, horseback riding, and wagon excursions to historic sites.

Three particularly scenic areas along the trail include the South Pass Segment, the Blue Mountain Crossing, and the Barlow Road. The 125-mile South Pass Segment, running from Independence Rock to Farson, Wyoming, still looks much the same, with most of the route on public land. The Bureau of Land Management offices in Lander and Rock Springs, Wyoming, provide maps and information, and Trails West offers scenic wagon trips departing from South Pass. In Oregon, the Blue Mountain Crossing parallels trail ruts and offers three trails for day hikers. Forest roads provided by the Wallowa-Whitman National Forest District allow use by snowmobiles, four-wheelers, and dirt bikes. Other areas provide opportunities for white-water activities, berry picking during season, and camping. The Barlow Road, also in Oregon, crosses over the Pacific Crest Trail along a scenic stretch through Mount Hood National Forest. Primitive camping sites are found along the route.

The trail corridor contains some three hundred miles of discernible ruts and approximately 125 historic sites. An auto-tour route can be followed from Independence, Missouri, to Oregon City, Oregon. The strands that formed a fanlike beginning of the trail from Independence, Westport (now part of Kansas City), Fort Leavenworth, St. Joseph, and Council Bluffs have now been taken over by farms, highways, and urban areas. The Independence and Westport strands parallel the Santa Fe Trail to present-day Gardner, Kansas. West of the Big Blue River, near Marysville, Kansas, the strands from Fort Leavenworth and St. Joseph join the other two onward up the Little Blue River to the Platte Valley, which is no longer treeless. Along the north bank of the Platte, the Mormon Pioneer Trail, which was also used by some pioneers traveling to Oregon and California, enters from Council Bluffs.

Level highway takes the traveler west into Nebraska along the nation's greatest corridor of westward expansion to reconstructed Fort Kearny and "the gateway to the Great Plains." Almost any exit leads to evidence of fur trappers, mountain men, pioneers, gold diggers, outlaws, Pony Express riders, and cowboys. Lush prairie unfurls from the banks of the river's channels toward the distant sweep of high plains on the horizon. Ash Hollow, one of the great landmarks, leads to the North Platte River Valley and to a series of distinctive formations such as Chimney Rock National Historic Site and Scotts Bluff National Monument and on to Wyoming's Fort Laramie National Historic Site, now restored.

All of the major trails joined at Fort Laramie to follow the same route traveling past landmarks such as Register Cliff, Independence Rock, and Devil's Gate to South Pass, the halfway mark and point where the Continental Divide is crossed. The many miles of well-preserved trail and historic sites make this corridor an excellent destination for those wanting to view the trail in a setting much as it looked more

than 150 years ago. An interesting trip to "Parting of the Ways" can be taken in a four-wheel-drive vehicle. A detour south off I-80 leads to Fort Bridger State Historic Site, where the trail split in two to form the Utah and California-Oregon routes. The trail soon thereafter leaves Wyoming, which contains 90 percent of the physical remains of the entire Oregon Trail.

Although major highways bisect Idaho's Oregon Trail country, much of the land looks as it did during the great expansion. More than 1,700 miles of emigrant trails, including all cutoffs and alternate routes, stretch across the southern portion of the state, with over 580 miles of remnants still in existence. Soda Springs is a major attraction in the Bear River country, and visitors still taste the water of another notable landmark, Hooper Spring, before traveling on to Pocatello. At Raft River, some emigrants took the trail's left fork for California. Several miles of wagon ruts are marked at Milner Ruts Interpretive Site, north of Twin Falls on U.S. Highway 93. Near Hagerman is Malad Gorge State Park, which offers sightseeing information on the nearby North Alternate Oregon Trail and Kelton Road. The roads unite again to enter eastern Oregon. Baker City boasts the Bureau of Land Management's Oregon Trail Center on Flagstaff Hill, where trail ruts are seen in the great sagebrush setting between the Rockies and the Cascades. The trail soon enters the contrasting landscape of fertile grasslands, ascending into the Blue Mountains. At The Dalles in the Columbia Gorge, today's explorer can travel with ease along the Columbia or take the Barlow Road around Mount Hood to Oregon City, home of the End of the Oregon Trail Interpretive Center.

MISSOURI/KANSAS

1. INDEPENDENCE. This town played a major role in outfitting emigrants for the Oregon-California and Santa Fe Trails and is Missouri's fourth-largest city. The National Frontier Trails Center researches, interprets, and preserves the history of the pioneers; the Independence Landing site is located north of the Independence Square. *Other attractions:* Bingham-Waggoner Estate (1855); 1859 Marshal's Home and Jail Museum; Harry S. Truman NHS; Mormon Visitors' Center. *Nearby:* Restoration and living-history museum of Fort Osage, which was America's first outpost in the Louisiana Territory; and Leavenworth (Fort Leavenworth) is the oldest city in Kansas (1854). The fort itself is the oldest continuously garrisoned military installation west of the Mississippi (1827) and offers Oregon and Santa Fe Trail markers, National Cemetery, Buffalo Soldier Monument and Frontier Army Museum. The Leavenworth County Museum occupies the Carroll Mansion (1867).

2. KANSAS CITY (WESTPORT). The trading post became known as Westport Landing during the migrations. It served as a terminus and outfitting point for the Oregon-California and Santa Fe Trails. Today the city of Kansas City, known as the Heart of America, is first in farm distribution. The city is divided by the Missouri River, with State Line Road separating the Missouri and Kansas sides. In historic Westport district, the Kansas City Museum has artifacts and exhibits on the city's role in westward expansion. *Other attractions:* In the Westport area, the Arabia Steamboat Museum; Westport Landing with summer steamboat excursions. Schumacher, Minor, and New Santa Fe Parks contain significant trail resources. In Kansas City proper, the Kansas City Art Institute; Nelson-Atkins Museum of Art; Toy and Miniature Museum of Kansas City; NCAA Visitor Center, and the Hallmark Visitors Center. There are twenty-five lakes in the area for picnicking and water activities.

KANSAS

3. LONE ELM. No elm is any longer found at this emigrant campsite, near Olathe, which was cleared for wood to make campfires. To the west, the Oregon Trail and the California Trail join the Santa Fe Trail near a small roadside park near Gardner.

4. PAPIN'S FERRY. A ferry, started by the Papin brothers (1842), was located on the Kan-

Points of Interest

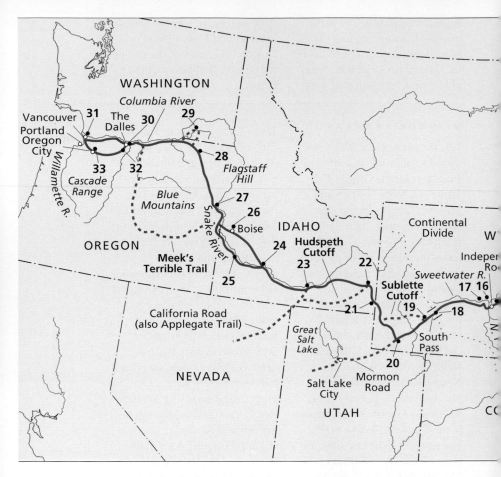

sas (Kaw) River in downtown Topeka where U.S. Highway 75 spans the river. Antislavery settlers (1854) met at the banks of the Kansas River, where the Oregon-California Trail crossed the Santa Fe Trail, to found the Topeka Association, which was responsible for Topeka's early growth. In 1861, it became the state capital. *Other attractions:* Murals and paintings, including the *Pioneer Mother,* at the statehouse; the Kansas Center for

Historical Research; the Kansas Museum of History; the Pottawatomie Baptist Indian Mission (1848 restored); Gage Park, with Reinisch Memorial Rose and Rock Garden. *Nearby:* Lake Shawnee, with picnicking and water activities; Big Springs' Oregon Trails Adventure Company at Serenata Farms offers escorted tours with emigrant reenactors on the Oregon and California Trails.

5. ALCOVE SPRINGS. Near the spring where thousands of over-

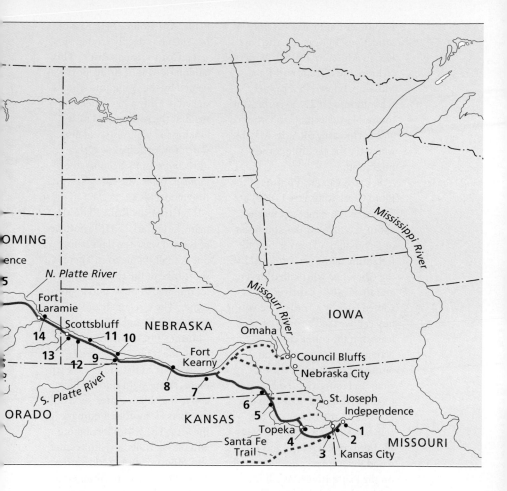

landers drew water, the Sarah
Keys Monument in Blue Rapids
commemorates the lost grave of
a seventy-year-old pioneer
woman who was traveling with
the Donner-Reed party. She
hoped to reach Fort Hall to meet
her son in 1846.

NEBRASKA

6. ROCK CREEK STATION. An
important road ranch on the
Oregon and California Trails, this
site near Fairbury later served as a

Pony Express station associated
with a legendary gunfight after
which James Butler "Wild Bill"
Hickok (1861) was charged with
murder and acquitted. The Rock
Creek Station SHP has a visitor
center, wagon ruts, and seasonal
covered wagon rides.

7. FORT KEARNY. The fort,
named for Gen. Stephen Watts
Kearny, was established in 1848 to
protect the emigrants. An earlier
Fort Kearny once stood near
Nebraska City. Fort Kearny SHP

is southeast of Kearney. *Other attractions:* In Kearney, the Fort Kearny Museum; the Museum of Nebraska Art, Trails and Rails Museum, housed in a pioneer schoolhouse (1871). *Nearby:* Cottonmill Lake Recreation Grounds and Fort Kearny SRA. In March, watch for the sandhill crane migration.

8. PLUM CREEK. Victims of the Plum Creek Massacre (1864) are buried in the cemetery, located about seventeen miles southeast of Lexington. A Denver-bound freighting outfit was attacked by the Cheyenne who killed eleven and took two as captives. Ransomed later by a trader, the young boy captive died soon after release, but the other captive, Nancy Jane Fletcher Moron, wrote her story. *Other attractions:* In Lexington, the Dawson County Historical Museum offers exhibits on the history of the central Platte River Valley. *Nearby:* Johnson Lake SRA and Elwood Reservoir; canoeing rentals on the Platte River. Watch for bald eagles and the sandhill crane migration in March.

9. LOWER CALIFORNIA CROSSING. This river crossing is located approximately 440 miles from Independence. The shrinking South Platte at Brule was about a mile wide during emigration. *Nearby:* California Hill, nine miles west of Brule, has deeply etched trail ruts along which one can hike.

10. ASH HOLLOW. Seen from a landmark hill, Ash Hollow's level plain extended to the North Platte. Ash Hollow SHP east of Lewellen has deeply eroded ruts.

11. COURTHOUSE ROCK. This landmark west of Bridgeport was named by the emigrants who signed it. Only a few names remain in the soft stone. Those looking for names should also watch for rattlesnakes. *Other attractions:* In Bridgeport, the Pioneer Trails Museum. *Nearby:* Bridgeport SRA.

12. CHIMNEY ROCK. This dramatic landmark (NHS) southwest of Bayard was seen days before one actually came to it. There is a short hike to the rock, which is illuminated at dusk, and a visitor center. The Oregon Trail Wagon Train offers 4 and 6 day trips to Chimney Rock and short tours along the trail.

13. SCOTTS BLUFF. The escarpment, rising eight hundred feet above the North Platte, served the pioneers as another landmark in the area. The NM offers hiking and biking trails, a visitor center, and interpretation. *Other attractions:* The Rebecca Winter Grave is three miles east of town on U.S. Highway 26; in Gering, the North Platte Valley Museum; to the north, North Platte NWR.

WYOMING

14. FORT LARAMIE NATIONAL HISTORIC SITE. Southwest of the town of Fort Laramie, this was once the site of a fur-trading post. In 1849, the popular resting place for emigrants was purchased by the U.S. government to aid migrations west. Now restored, Fort Laramie NHS offers a visitor cen-

ter, museum, and living-history demonstrations. A park headquarters' map shows the location of the Old Bedlam ruts, on private land, that extend to Guernsey near Register Cliff, where they grow deeper.

15. **INDEPENDENCE ROCK.** William Sublette named this site on July 4, 1830. If emigrants reached it by July 4, they were on schedule. The large granite dome (SHS) rises 193 feet and bears the names of those who passed. The Jesuit missionary, Jean Pierre De Smet, labeled it "the Great Register of the Desert." Visitors are allowed to climb the rock to view some of the better-preserved names on top. Together with the Mormon Trail, the Oregon-California route is visible here, fifty-five miles southwest of Casper, which offers the Fort Caspar Museum and the Tate Mineralogical and Warner Wildlife Museum. Also in Casper, Historic Trails Expeditions offer wagon trips on the trail. *Nearby:* Pathfinder Bird Refuge.

16. **DEVIL'S GATE.** Visible from Independence Rock, seven miles northeast, this landmark site is a cleft formed in the Rattlesnake Mountains where the Sweetwater gradually sliced through. BLM maintains the historic site located along State Highway 220, with interpretation and a short loop trail (PENHT). At least twenty emigrant graves have been found in the area. *Nearby:* Sun Ranch headquarters (owned by the LDS Church) interprets the trails and provides access to

Martin's Cove which memorializes more than one hundred and fifty Mormons who perished in the deep snow in 1856 near this location.

17. **SPLIT ROCK.** A cleft in the solid granite mountain was visible for two days as the emigrants approached. A Pony Express station was located in the vicinity. BLM interprets the site, a geological landmark in Natrona County.

18. **SOUTH PASS.** Pioneers crossed the Continental Divide (CDNST) through South Pass (NHL), one of the highest points (7,550 feet) along the trail, called "the Cumberland Gap of the Far West." BLM interprets the site at the pass and on Route 28. South Pass City SHS has a visitor center that includes interpretive displays and restored mining era buildings; Trails West in South Pass City offers excellent wagon excursions on the Oregon-California and Mormon Pioneer NHTs. The Pony Express Station in the area was referred to as both the Upper Sweetwater and the South Pass Station. *Nearby:* Atlantic City (1868) was founded when gold mines attracted thousands of miners to the Sweetwater Mining District in South Pass. Its main attractions include mining buildings that date from the turn of the century.

19. **SUBLETTE CUTOFF (ALSO KNOWN AS GREENWOOD'S).** Close to Big Sandy, the fork, later called the Parting of the Ways, was taken by about a third of the Oregon-bound emigrants, who ventured into the desert to save

time. Later it became more important to anxious forty-niners. Emigrants usually reached the cutoff in mid-August when temperatures soared to 90-plus degrees. *Nearby:* Big Sandy RA; Eden Valley and Big Sandy Reservoirs.

20. **Fort Bridger.** Now a state historic site, the trading post was built by Jim Bridger and his partner, Louis Vasquez. Located on the Oregon-California and Mormon Trails, it was a vital stopping point. The Mormons purchased the fort in 1855 and built Fort Supply, twelve miles south. They burned both when frictions developed with the U.S. government two years later. The U.S. Army rebuilt Fort Bridger in 1858 and used it until 1890. Fort Bridger Rendezvous is held on Labor Day weekend, and Bridger Valley Pioneer Days is held in nearby Lyman in July. *Nearby:* Fossil Butte NM, with a thousand-foot escarpment rising above the arid plains and holding the largest deposit of freshwater fish fossils in the Western Hemisphere. The monument offers interpretation at the visitor center, Quarry Trail for hiking, Fossil Discovery Day in mid-July, and Ulrich's Fossil Gallery.

IDAHO

21. **Smith's Trading Post (also known as Big Timbers).** South of Montpelier, the fort, composed of four log cabins, was operated by Thomas "Peg-Leg" Smith. It served emigrants through the 1840s, with the owner making $100 a day from gold seekers in '49. It was gone by 1850. Peg-Leg received his nickname after he was forced to amputate his own leg. According to legend, the wooden prosthesis was used as a weapon to kill at least one man. The Oregon Rendezvous Pageant is held on the trail near Big Hill. *Nearby:* Bear Lake SP; Minnetonka Cave with fossils of tropical plants and marine life; Bear Lake NWR; and Caribou NF.

22. **Soda Springs.** Pioneers marveled at the springs and geysers, including one that regularly gave off a sound like a steamboat. Visitors can still taste the water of another notable landmark, Hooper Spring (aka Beer Spring). *Other attractions:* Pioneer Museum; wagon ruts at local golf course; Camp Connor (1863); Wagonbox Grave (1861); Sheep Rock where some left the Oregon Trail for California on the Hudspeth Cutoff. *Nearby:* Soda Point Reservoir; Lava Hot Springs with Mountain Man Rendezvous–Pioneer Days at the end of July.

23. **Fort Hall.** The fur-trading post (1834) north of Pocatello became an important pioneer resting spot. The replica gives a glimpse into frontier life and what the bustling trade center was like. Goodale's Cutoff (used when gold was discovered in Idaho in 1862) leaves the fort, winding past Craters of the Moon NM. *Other attractions:* Pocatello offers the Bannock County Historical Museum and the Idaho Museum of Natural History with

fossils and dinosaur bones. *Nearby:* Fort Hall Indian Reservation offers tours of the historic trail arranged through the tribal office; the Shoshone-Bannock Indian Festival is held at Fort Hall early in August; west of Burley, Milner Ruts Interpretive Site south of Milner Reservoir; Caribou NF; Bonneville Park; Indian Rocks SP.

24. THREE ISLAND CROSSING. West of present-day Glenns Ferry, emigrants faced the difficult choice of attempting a treacherous crossing to reach a shorter, easier route north of the Snake or to stay with the dry, rough southern route. Many diaries mention the crossing, now part of Three Island Crossing SP, which holds a crossing reenactment each August. Those remaining on the south side saw outstanding natural features, which are still visible and include Bruneau Sand Dunes, the highest in North America. *Nearby:* Outside Twin Falls Shoshone Falls, higher than Niagara, could be heard by pioneers five miles away; in Twin Falls, the Perrine Memorial Bridge spans the Snake; river-rafting excursions along the Snake; the Herrett Museum with Indian artifacts. Near Hagerman, Hagerman Fossil Beds NM with visitor center; Malad Gorge SP.

25. UTTER DISASTER SITE. Twenty-nine emigrants died as a result of the Utter and Van Ornum disaster near Murphy by the Snake on the Meek Trail. American Indians, who may have been led by white renegades, at-tacked circled wagons here. Eventually twelve emigrants were found alive along the Owyhee River; they had resorted to cannibalism to stay alive. After a two-year search, ten-year-old Reuben Van Ornum was rescued north of Salt Lake City.

26. FORT BOISE. Established as an army cavalry post (1863) to protect wagon trains and gold miners, the fort encouraged the growth of a town that became an important stop during later trail use. Deactivated in 1913, the fort became a city park. The Hudson's Bay Company had established an earlier Fort Boise (1834) near what is now Parma, where the Old Fort Boise Replica is located. Early visitors included the Whitmans (1836). That fort closed in 1854 when eighteen emigrants were killed in the Ward Massacre near present-day Middleton, where a commemorative marker designates the spot. Travel along the Oregon Trail continued to be extremely hazardous for the next decade. *Other attractions:* In Boise, O'Farrel Cabin (1863); Old Boise Historic District; World Center for Birds of Prey; Idaho Botanical Garden; Morrison Knudson Nature Center; state capitol. *Nearby:* Snake River Birds of Prey Natural Area, home to one of the largest concentrations of birds of prey in the world; Boise NF.

OREGON

27. FAREWELL BEND. At this campsite near Huntington, emigrants bid farewell to the Snake

after it had guided them nearly 320 miles. *Nearby:* At Birch Creek, wagon ruts are interpreted; Wallowa-Whitman NF: Hells Canyon National Recreation Area (NPNHT). To the northwest, at Baker City, BLM's National Historic Oregon Trail Interpretive Center of Flagstaff Hill features exhibits, living-history presentations, and trail ruts; Sumpter Valley Railroad offers a short trip through the historic gold-mining district.

28. **GRANDE RONDE.** The fertile grasslands and abundant water of the Grande Ronde Valley contrasted sharply with the sagebrush plains of the previous six hundred miles. Nez Perce, Cayuse, Walla Walla, and Umatilla Indians traded with the emigrants who were in need of food and other supplies. South of La Grande there is interpretation at the Charles Reynold Rest Area. *Other attractions:* Birnie Park was the site of wagon encampments as emigrants prepared for their ascent into the Blue Mountains; Hilgard Junction SP, where thousands camped on the forested slopes of the Blues. *Nearby:* Red Bridge SP; Umatilla NF; Wallowa-Whitman NF.

WASHINGTON/OREGON

29. **WHITMAN MISSION NATIONAL HISTORIC SITE.** Here, west of Walla Walla, missionaries Marcus and Narcissa Whitman founded their mission (1836, NHS) and provided religious instruction to Cayuse Indians for ten years. The Whitmans also provided supplies to travelers on the Oregon Trail. *Nearby:* Pendleton, Oregon, where the emigrants saw the rich Umatilla Valley; McKay Creek NWR. *Other attractions:* In Pendleton, Pendleton Underground, tunnels built by Chinese immigrants in late 1800s; Pendleton Woolen Mills; Pendleton Round-Up, since 1910 one of the West's prominent rodeos.

30. **THE DALLES.** At the great bend of the Columbia River, the emigrants had to float their wagons down the river, once dangerous but now subdued by The Dalles Dam. When the Barlow Road opened (1846), the emigrants had an alternative route to the Willamette Valley. *Other attractions:* The Columbia Gorge NSA encompasses a gorge formed by an ancient river of lava that also created nearby Multnomah Falls (620 feet); The Dalles Dam with tours. *Nearby:* Deschutes River SP offers white-water rafting and fishing; Cascade Locks, where many emigrants portaged the cascades of the Columbia; the Port of Cascade Locks Marine Park (NRHP); Troutdale, Oregon, where emigrants resumed their travel by water (by the late 1840s, some were electing to leave the Columbia at the mouth of the Sandy River, continuing overland or claiming land in the valleys); Hood River, now a popular sailboarding and windsurfing area, has a scenic rail tour to the beautiful Hood River Valley.

31. **FORT VANCOUVER.** At the Columbia Department Headquarters for the Hudson's Bay

Company, Dr. John McLoughlin provided the emigrants with advice, medical care, and supplies. Fort Vancouver NHS in the city of Vancouver, Washington, has a reconstructed stockade and buildings, visitor center, and museum. *Other attractions:* The Covington House (1846) is a log cabin that became the first schoolhouse north of the Columbia River; Clark County Historical Museum with displays of pioneer life. *Nearby:* Portland, Oregon, originally named Stumptown (1844) after the tree stumps found in the area, but renamed within a year. The Oregon History Center in Portland houses journals, artifacts, photographs, and exhibits pertaining to the migration, including the Trails to Oregon exhibit; the James F. Bybee House (1858, restored); at Waterfront Park, the America West Steamboat Company's *Queen of the West* offers overnight cruises on the Columbia River, covering portions of three national historic trails. Other day and evening boat excursions are also available. Other interesting points include the World Forestry Center; Audubon Society sanctuary; the Cowboys Then and Now Museum; the Portland Art Museum; the Oregon Museum of Science and Industry; the Peninsula Rose Garden; Washington Park, with its International Rose Test Gardens and Japanese Gardens; the Hoyt Arboretum.

OREGON

32. **BARLOW ROAD.** Samuel Barlow, along with Joel Palmer, headed southwest from The Dalles, skirting Mount Hood's south shoulder by cutting a path to Oregon City. The road was made available to others for a toll, though many called it the worst part of the trail. In time it became the main route of the Oregon Trail and later part of a state highway. *Nearby:* Mount Hood (11,235 feet) is the highest point in the state; Mount Hood NF; Timberline Lodge NHL; activities include hiking, skiing, cross-country skiing, and snowshoeing. The Pacific Crest National Scenic Trail offers excellent hiking in the area.

33. **OREGON CITY.** After two thousand miles and five months, the emigrants came to the end of the trail at Abernethy Green, where an interpretive display and exhibits commemorate the site. *Other attractions:* The Oregon Trail Interpretive Center; McLoughlin House NHS; Willamette Falls; and the John Inskeep Environmental Learning Center.

TULIPS

Each spring
a profusion
of color
lures visi-
tors to the
Applegate
Trail in the
Willamette
Valley of
Oregon.

California National Historic Trail

Never take no cut ofs and hury along as fast as you can.

VIRGINIA REED OF THE DONNER PARTY, 1846

Before the Great Divide was crossed by the first eager gold rusher, John Augustus Sutter had been drawn to California's attractive ranchero life, Oregon had become a territory, the Mormon pioneer movement west was well underway, and Gen. John C. Frémont had proclaimed the annexation of California. Then in January 1848, a mechanic employed by Sutter in the building of a sawmill on the American River in the Sacramento Valley noticed a few flakes of yellow that tested to be pure gold. This and other California strikes teased Americans of every class and occupation—and people from all over the world—to head to the Pacific Coast. In 1849 twenty-five thousand emigrants took the overland route to California; in 1850 that figure was almost doubled. By 1860, over two hundred thousand emigrants had traveled the California Trail. But had it not been for the three thousand land seekers who had blazed the way before them, the rush of 1849 and the 1850s might never have been possible.

ADMINISTERING AGENCY
National Park Service
Long Distance Trails Office
P.O. Box 45155
324 South State Street, Room 250
Salt Lake City, UT 84145-0155
801-539-4095

FURTHER INFORMATION
Oregon-California Trail Association
P.O. Box 1019
Independence, MO 84051

ESTABLISHED
1992

APPROXIMATE MILEAGE
5,665 miles (9,064 km)

STATES
Missouri, Iowa, Kansas, Nebraska, Colorado, Wyoming, Idaho, Utah, Nevada, Oregon, California

The History of the Trail

Although the California Trail shared the same corridor with the Oregon, the Mormon Pioneer, and the Pony Express Trails, it evolved as a collection of competing routes during the late 1840s.* It has been aptly described as a great rope stretching from the Missouri River to the California goldfields. But it is a rope that was considerably frayed at both ends—and in the middle. The eastern end of the rope was frayed by the diversity of the "jumping-off" points—first the Independence Road, then the Council Bluffs Road and the St. Joe Road, among others. In the middle, the rope was frayed at the various cutoffs available to the emigrants after they had crossed South Pass. And by the early 1850s, the maze of trails that led from the Sierra into the California goldfields created a frayed western end of the rope. The specific route that emigrants and forty-niners used depended on their starting point in Missouri, their final destination in California, the condition of their livestock and wagons, and yearly changes in water and forage along the different routes.

The California Trail, including those portions that were pioneered and developed before the 1849 California gold rush, has substantial national significance. For one, it was the route of the greatest mass migration in

*Material in this section is taken from the National Park Service's *California and Pony Express Trails Eligibility/Feasibility Study*.

American history. During the 1840s and '50s, the trail carried over two hundred thousand farmers and gold rushers to the rich farmlands and goldfields of California. Trail remnants are reminders of the sacrifices, struggles, and triumphs of these early American settlers, travelers, and stampeders. Their emigration to California contributed directly to the occupation, settlement, and development of the western part of the United States, from the Missouri River to the Pacific coast. The following sections briefly summarize how the California Trail was gradually developed, making it possible for new residents to settle the country's farthest western frontier.

The Early Routes: 1841–44

The first pioneers were the members of the Bidwell-Bartleson party, a group of thirty-five men, women, and children who left Independence, Missouri, in spring 1841, planning to travel by wagon to California. While in Independence they accidentally met and joined a party of Jesuit priests who were heading toward the Hudson's Bay Company trading post at Fort Hall in present-day Idaho. The route to Fort Hall had already been fairly well established by fur trappers and traders, but it was not known whether families and wagons could make it through.

The Bidwell-Bartleson party was guided by the experienced mountain man Thomas Fitzpatrick, who took them by way of the American Fur Company trading post known commonly as "the fort on the Laramie." They arrived in Soda Springs (Idaho), twelve hundred miles from Independence, on August 3, 1841. Along the way, the party had actually grown, as a few other late-starting emigrants caught up with them. At Soda Springs the party split. Fitzpatrick, the missionaries, and some of the emigrants headed northwest toward Fort Hall. Those who continued on to Oregon arrived in 1841, marking the way for the opening of the Oregon Trail.

The other party, consisting of thirty-one men, one woman, and a baby girl, headed toward California. Without a guide, and with only the western lore they had gained from Fitzpatrick, they had little idea of how to proceed except to keep moving west. After wandering through present-day northwest Utah and northeast Nevada, they finally managed to find the Humboldt River, which they followed to its sink, where it disappeared into the desert floor. From there they headed southwest, found a crossing of the Sierra Nevada near Sonora Pass, and finally stumbled to safety in early October. The trip had been a disaster. All the wagons and goods had long been abandoned, and most of the horses and mules had either been slaughtered for food or had died from starvation and thirst. The emigrants arrived in California with nothing but what they carried on their backs.

The following year, only in-

COWBOY AT FIRE

Seeking their fortune in gold, forty-niners on the California Trail contrasted starkly with families seeking the promise of good land on the Oregon Trail. Today, outfitters take care of all the "fixins" on pack trips along the trail.

direct progress was made in opening the California Trail, but 125 emigrants made their way into Oregon by following the route opened in 1841. Their wagons helped to mark the trail for future California-bound emigrants at least as far as Fort Hall. In addition, Joseph Chiles, a member of the 1841 Bidwell-Bartleson party, returned east in 1842, searching for a better route. Chiles wandered for much of his journey, but he did follow the

Mary's River (later renamed the Humboldt) from its sink up toward Fort Hall, verifying the validity of that portion of the trail. Chiles arrived in Missouri in September, convinced that wagons could be taken all the way into California.

So it was that in the spring of 1843, Chiles left Independence with approximately thirty California-bound emigrants in eight wagons, trailing a party of a hundred-plus wagons bound for Oregon, some of whom eventually switched over to the Chiles train. At Fort Laramie, Chiles met Joe Walker, another of the famed mountain men, who agreed to guide the emigrants to California for $300. Pushing west by way of the newly established trading post of Fort Bridger, the train reached Fort Hall in early September. Then, because of the lateness of the season, the party split.

Chiles and a group of men on horseback began to explore for a northern pass over the Sierra Nevada into California, where they arrived in November 1843. This route across the Sierra south of Mount Shasta, however, proved to be too circuitous for later emigrant travel. In the meantime, Walker led the rest of the train southwest, following the Humboldt River to its sink, and then turned south, finally crossing the south end of the Sierra in early December 1843 by way of Walker Pass. Again wagons had to be abandoned east of the mountains, food supplies were ex-

hausted, and starvation threatened the group. By the end of the year, a stretch of 500 miles of the primary route had been defined from Fort Hall to the Humboldt Sink. This, together with the established wagon route from Independence to Fort Hall, left only a 250-mile stretch to be opened between the sink and Sutter's Fort.

In 1844, the final piece was put in place. The Stevens party, as it became known, started from Miller's Hollow in Iowa (renamed Kanesville in 1848, and, later, Council Bluffs), another jumping-off spot upriver from Independence. A group of forty-six emigrants headed for Oregon, with a few planning to split off the Oregon Trail at Fort Hall for California. From Council Bluffs to Fort Laramie, they stayed on the north side of the Platte River, along what was later to be known as the Council Bluffs Road, and still later as the Mormon Trail. West of South Pass in southwestern Wyoming the party tried a new cutoff that eliminated the dip down toward Fort Bridger. This was the first of many such variations later collectively called the Sublette Cutoff. Just west of Fort Hall, the train swung off the Oregon Trail in the vicinity of the Raft River and headed toward the Humboldt. The trail of Walker's party, broken the year before, was easy to follow.

At the Humboldt Sink, the Stevens party met an Indian named Truckee, who told them through sign language of a river that flowed easterly out of the Sierra. This river was only fifty to sixty miles straight west, and along its banks were good grass and trees. In between there was desert. Provided with cooked rations and filled water casks, the emigrants made a forced march for two days and one night to become the first to cross the dreaded Forty Mile Desert. In later years the stretch would be littered with dead stock and abandoned wagons. After reaching the river, which they named the Truckee, the emigrants followed it straight west through present-day Reno and upwards into Truckee Canyon through the foothills of the Sierra. But as the canyon narrowed, progress became increasingly difficult. Finally, the party reached a beautiful lake, later to be named Donner, beyond which rose nearly vertical mountain walls. After several days of exploring, the group decided to forge straight ahead. Leaving half their wagons, they worked the remaining wagons around the north shore of the lake and then almost literally carried them up a thousand feet of steep granite slope. Once the crest was reached, it was relatively easy to work out their descent down the gentler westside canyons toward Sutter's Fort, where the first group of wagons arrived in mid-December 1844. With the limited success of this Truckee route, the California Trail could be declared open.

Trail Development: 1844–49

Nicknamed "the pathfinder," John Charles Frémont had been exploring the West since 1838, when he was assigned to the newly formed Army Corps of Topographical Engineers under the command of Joseph Nicollet. As leader of the corps on an expedition to the Rocky Mountains in 1842, Frémont developed the eastern half of the Oregon Trail with the help of his guide, Kit Carson, and his cartographer, Charles Preuss. Still accompanied by Carson and Preuss in his 1843–44 expedition west, Frémont reached Oregon to complete the mapping of the Oregon Trail, but he returned to the United States by heading south to California. He arrived at Sutter's Fort in February 1844 and from there mapped the route back to the United States, noting the "Great Basin" formed between the Rocky and Sierra Nevada ranges. Later, in his 1844–46 expedition, he gave names to several locations. He also named the Carson River after his scout and changed the name of the Mary's River to the Humboldt River. Though his small party of 1844 left no real trace of the route, their excellent maps and reports were widely read by later trailblazers, including Jesse and Lindsay Applegate. The brothers used Frémont's reports as a guide in 1846 when they opened the Applegate Trail, which left the "great bend" of the Humboldt River (near present-day Imlay, Nevada), thereby influencing the later development of the Lassen Trail and Nobles Road to California.

As more and more emigrants headed toward California, certain portions of the early routes were improved over several years of trial and error. Other portions, like the Platte River Valley, were such natural corridors that they were never really changed. Major improvements to the basic route were made each year from 1845 to 1848, leaving the California Trail system fairly well established before the start of the great gold-rush years. These improvements are best discussed in geographical order, east to west, rather than chronological order.

EASTERN FEEDER ROUTES

In the East, the new Missouri River towns continued to rival Independence as the favored starting points. Primary among these was St. Joseph, beginning with the opening of the St. Joe Road in 1845. Connecting with the main Oregon-California Trail in northeast Kansas, this road eliminated ninety miles of travel. Both prior to and during the gold-rush years, the three river towns of Independence, St. Joseph, and Council Bluffs competed bitterly for the lucrative outfitting trade. Regardless of their starting point, once the emigrants reached the Platte River in the vicinity of Fort Kearny, established by the U.S. Army in 1848, they were on a stretch of trail that remained essentially unchanged

throughout its use. This part of the trail, on both the north and south banks of the river, was aptly called the Great Platte River Road. Likewise, the route from Fort Laramie to South Pass was never significantly improved. The route was the gentlest possible crossing of the Continental Divide, making wagon travel to the West feasible.

CENTRAL CUTOFFS

The Sublette Cutoff. On the other side of South Pass, numerous cutoffs and alternatives were developed during the late 1840s. The Sublette Cutoff was first used by fur trader William Sublette in 1826. The route became known among the mountain men, who later became guides for parties headed west. Tom Fitzpatrick led the De Smet party across the cutoff in 1841. First used for wagons in 1844, it gradually gained favor over the older Fort Bridger route because it saved emigrants the long loop down to Fort Bridger and then back up toward Fort Hall, saving miles and days.

Traveling the Sublette Cutoff was not without its trade-offs. Its major drawback was lack of good water, including over one fifty-mile stretch of dry desert known as Sublette Flats. Following the cutoff also gave emigrants some of the roughest country they had faced so far. After crossing the Green River, the trail began a steep ascent west. On the plus side, many travelers found the higher elevations with trees and more abundant grass to be a refreshing change. Emigrants continued to use both the Sublette and the Fort Bridger routes, depending on the time of year, reported water and grass conditions along the two routes, and their need for rest and refitting at Fort Bridger. Later, the forty-niners, who generally traveled faster than emigrants, showed a preference for the Sublette Cutoff.

The Hastings Cutoff. In 1846 the ill-fated Hastings Cutoff was opened by Lansford W. Hastings, an adventurer who, on the basis of his travels to Oregon and California and back between 1842 and 1846, became convinced that the best route to California lay directly through the Great Salt Desert. He hoped to open that route and lead emigrants to California, apparently believing he would then be able to lead a California rebellion against the Mexican government, thereby finding fame and fortune. As it turned out, John C. Frémont did exactly that while Hastings was on the trail.

In 1846 Hastings began meeting emigrants along the trail between Independence Rock and Fort Bridger, trying to recruit some followers. Most of the early emigrants in the 1846 migration rejected the alternative, since they were making good time and had no reason to risk an unknown route. As the summer wore on, however, late-starting emigrants began to consider a route that was promised to save 150 to 500 miles of travel. Finally, about eighty wagons decided to try

Hastings's new route. The last of them was the Donner-Reed party. On July 20, Hastings led the first group of forty wagons southwest out of Fort Bridger along a nonexistent trail that he had never traveled. With untold labor and much wandering, a trail was cut over the Wasatch Mountains, finally breaking out through the Weber River Canyon into the Salt Lake Valley. Hastings then led the group around the south shore of the lake and headed west across the salt flats. Instead of the forty miles of desert predicted by Hastings, the waterless crossing turned out to be eighty-three miles, inflicting horrible casualties on both emigrants and stock.

Pushing farther west, Hastings hit the Ruby Mountains. At this point, he was only one good day's journey from the Humboldt River and the main trail to the northwest. Ignorant of the geography though, he turned south, skirting the foot of the mountains, searching for a pass. Finally finding one, now named Overland Pass, Hastings crossed and headed north, desperately seeking the California Trail. When he finally reached it, just west of present-day Elko, Nevada, he discovered wagon trains that had been far behind him at South Pass were now a week ahead. The Hastings Cutoff, which had actually added miles to the journey, was a failure. Unfortunately, the story did not end there. The failure turned into disaster, resulting in the most famous tragedy

RAFTING

While shooting the rapids of the Columbia River on their way to Oregon in 1843, Jesse and Lindsay Applegate each lost a son in a violent whirlpool. To spare others their grief, they blazed the Applegate Trail through California to the Willamette Valley. Safer trips attract adventurers to Grants Pass, Oregon, where Morrison's on the Rogue River offers spectacular rafting trips near the Applegate Trail.

of the entire California Trail history.

The Donner-Reed party, already lagging far behind the majority of the 1846 emigration, and already plagued by illness, death, and bad luck, followed the Hastings Cutoff in a desperate attempt to make up for lost time. The party left Fort Bridger on July 31, but they were delayed by the necessity of cutting yet another trail through the Wasatch Mountains, since the Weber River Canyon route pioneered by Hastings

was unusable. They were further delayed by dying oxen and broken wagons on the salt flats, and they were in serious trouble before they even reached the junction with the main trail. By this time the vanguard of the 1846 emigration had already crossed the Sierra. Subsequently caught by early October blizzards below the crest of the mountains, the remnants of the Donner-Reed party slowly succumbed to starvation and cannibalism throughout the winter of 1846–47. Forty of the eighty-seven members of the party died that winter in the vicinity of Donner Pass. As news of the disaster spread, the Hastings Cutoff was thoroughly discredited. Except for a few foolhardy gold rushers in 1849, whose lust for gold outweighed their common sense, the Hastings Cutoff was never used again.

The Salt Lake Cutoff. The only positive outcome of the Donner disaster was the forty-mile stretch the party had cut across the Wasatch Mountains. Once opened, this proved to be the best route to the Salt Lake Valley. In 1847 it was used by the vanguard of the Mormon pioneers heading toward their new home, and it subsequently became an integral portion of the Mormon Trail.

In 1848, the Wasatch Mountains Cutoff became even more important when a chance meeting between some mountain men and a group of Mormons traveling east from California to Salt Lake resulted in the blazing of a trail from the Raft River route of the California Trail down to Salt Lake City. The completion of this loop, from Fort Bridger to Salt Lake and back up to the main trail, soon known as the Salt Lake Cutoff, made it feasible for emigrants in need of assistance or supplies to stop at that fast-growing Mormon community after 1848. In later years, particularly during the height of the gold rush, the Salt Lake Cutoff was increasingly used, and some gold rushers who jumped off too late in the season even wintered in the Salt Lake Valley.

WESTERN ROUTES

The Humboldt River valley, like the Platte River valley, was a safe and natural travel corridor. Emigrants could use either the north or south bank of the river, but essentially the route was never improved. West of Humboldt Sink, however, several alternative routes were developed in order to avoid the Truckee

Route, with its exhausting climb over the Sierra, and to provide for a wider choice of settlement areas in central and northern California as well as in southern Oregon.

The Carson Route. The most significant of new routes was the Carson Route between Humboldt Sink and Sutter's Fort. It was opened in the summer of 1848 by a group of Mormons who were returning from California to the Salt Lake Valley. Having heard of the difficulties of the Truckee Route, they decided to try a different way back over the mountains. Building a road as they went and sending scouts out ahead, they discovered an easier pass south of the Truckee Route and reached the summit of the Sierra Nevada at West Pass. From this point, they moved down to a valley they named Hope, found the west fork of the Carson River, followed it down out of the mountains south of Lake Tahoe, and then turned northeast, hitting the Truckee Route along the Truckee River. They had accomplished one of the most significant feats of trail opening in the history of the West. Although still not avoiding a crossing of the Forty Mile Desert, the Carson Route offered a considerably easier ascent of the eastern side of the Sierra and a much better descent on the western side. Once the Carson Route was opened, it quickly eclipsed the rougher Truckee Route as the main gateway to California.

The Applegate Trail. Among the

thousands who had traveled the Oregon Trail to Oregon were three brothers—Lindsay, Jesse, and Charles Applegate—and their extended families. At the Columbia River, tragedy struck when two of the Applegate children were lost in a violent whirlpool. Their fathers, Lindsay and Jesse, vowed to seek a safer route into Oregon, sparing other families their grief. In 1846 they joined the famous explorer of the Northwest, Levi Scott, and a dozen other settlers, to form the South Road Expedition. Under the captaincy of Jesse Applegate, a professional engineer, they set out in an attempt to work out a southern wagon route into Oregon—a route very much needed if war over the Northwest began with Britain. The route could provide a means of escape if necessary.

Like the Carson Route, the Applegate Trail was opened from west to east. Working carefully, the group slowly marked a trail through the forests and then across the northwest (Nevada) desert, locating water holes and leaving behind notices to future emigrants describing directions and distances. A daring expedition, it resulted in success when they struck the main California Trail just below the big bend of the Humboldt River. Some of the party then followed the trail east to Fort Hall to publicize the new route and the settlement potential of southern Oregon. Promoting his southern route in 1846, Jesse Applegate stated, "The

new route follows the California Road about 350 miles from here . . . it shortens the road—avoids the dangers of the Snake and Columbia rivers and passes S. of the Cascade Mts—there is almost every place plenty of grass and water."

For the first wagon train leaving the Humboldt River and heading across the Black Rock Desert, the trip was torture. They were attacked by American Indians, and springs were far apart, with some of them scalding hot. There was no feed for the livestock, some stock were stolen, others died, and they ran out of food. Just before winter came, however, relief arrived and the emigrants pressed on. J. Quinn Thornton viciously attacked Jesse Applegate in the press. Although never heavily used as a southern emigration route into Oregon, the Applegate Trail did have a significant impact on California emigration. The carefully marked portion across the Nevada desert was incorporated two years later by Peter Lassen (below) as part of his new trail. The upper portion, intended to feed settlers into southern Oregon from the California Trail, actually worked in reverse. When news of the California gold strikes reached Oregon, a small rush ensued, with eager gold seekers pouring down the Applegate and Lassen Trails into northern California.

The Lassen Trail. Realizing a potential for profit, Peter Lassen decided to capitalize on the growing California emigration by opening a cutoff from the Applegate Trail. Extending south from Goose Lake in northeast California, the so-called shortcut conveniently passed Lassen's trading post near present-day Chico before leading the emigrants into the goldfields. To entice the overlanders to use his trail, Lassen rode east to Fort Hall, where he recruited ten wagons to follow him back to his ranch. As an inducement, he promised to show them a more northerly route into California that would avoid the troublesome ascent of the Sierra necessitated by both the Truckee and Carson Routes. He did not tell his recruits that his route was largely imaginary.

About September 1, 1848, Lassen's party came to the junction of the main California route and the new Applegate Trail, at a location now known as Lassen's Meadows. Since the Applegate Trail was already broken and well marked, Lassen followed it northwest across the desert to Black Rock. At this point, he was directly east of his ranch and could have easily headed straight for it. But because of his ignorance of the geography, and the fact that he had never seriously explored his new route, he knew nothing better than to continue to follow the Applegate Trail to the northwest through High Rock Canyon and then to a lake Lassen thought was the headwaters of the Sacramento River.

Here Lassen left the Applegate Trail and turned south, through rough, forested, and untracked terrain. At this point the journey turned into a nightmare; the emigrants, with exhausted animals and broken-down wagons, attempted to take advantage of an unknown shortcut. Dead-end canyons seemed to constantly block the way, requiring miles of backtracking and days of scouting, while food supplies grew shorter. Wagons were cut down to two-wheel carts, and starving cattle slaughtered for meat. By October, with no visible progress being made, the emigrants threatened to hang Lassen. Finally, at the end of October, they reached his ranch. His trail was not a shortcut. Instead it had taken an extra month of travel to cover the additional 135 miles of the long northern swing. Nonetheless, Lassen had opened a third route into California, which would be heavily used by some fifteen thousand to twenty thousand stampeders in 1849.

The Gold-Rush Years

On January 24, 1848, "some kind of metal that looks like gold" was discovered in the tailrace at Sutter's mill. The discovery was kept secret for a short time. And even when the news was out, it still took several months for the East to learn of the strike. In the meantime, an internal California gold rush ensued in 1848, and many Oregon settlers used the northern end of the Applegate Trail and the western portion of the Lassen Trail to rush to the goldfields.

But the gold seekers were soon

GOLD PANNING

Gold panning for fun is popular in El Dorado County near Sutter's mill where the California gold rush actually began. Pieces range in size from the almost microscopic to the fever-inspiring, but rarely found, fist-sized nugget.

coming across the plains, and their arrival would bring only misfortune to the discoverer of the gold, James Wilson Marshall, and the estate owner, John Augustus Sutter. Their sawmill venture eventually failed, since almost every laborer was feverishly panning for gold. Later adventurers set aside their claims, squatters settled on Sutter's estate, and his flocks and herd disappeared. Marshall became despondent, bringing misfortune to himself and others, and Sutter, "the father of California" who befriended early settlers, was bankrupt by 1852.

Using the Early Routes

In the spring of 1849, the rush began, as thousands of eager stampeders crammed the river-

banks at the trail's principal starting points. Traffic along the California Trail that year almost doubled the number that had traveled to Oregon and California during the preceding eight years. In striking contrast, only 450 emigrants went to Oregon in 1849.

If the backbone of the California Trail had not already been in place, the rush of thousands of ill-prepared forty-niners attempting to travel overland would have been unimaginable if not a disaster. As it was, spring grass on the prairies came out earlier than usual in 1849, providing good stock forage for the first part of the journey, and summer rains in the West were heavier than normal, again providing better forage along the western trails than had been experienced in previous years. Even so, the suffering was often intense. The worst calamities befell those who had the misfortune to follow the Lassen Trail. Crossing in September 1849, during the height of the emigration, J. Goldsborough Bruff reported seeing 511 dead oxen, 10 dead horses, 9 dead mules, and a dead cow and calf, plus the graves of a three-year-old girl and a fifty-year-old man, in just the fifty-two miles between Lassen's Meadow and Black Rock.

THE HUDSPETH CUTOFF

Another important cutoff was opened along the trail in 1849. On July 19 Benoni Hudspeth, leading a large train of rushers, came to Soda Springs along the main trail. Like many other travelers, he was annoyed at the repeated meandering of the trail, and decided to cut out the northern swing up to Fort Hall by striking out directly west, aiming for the main trail as it came back down the Raft River. Unlike most others who tried uncharted shortcuts, he was lucky. On July 24, his party intersected the main trail near City of Rocks. Although the Hudspeth Cutoff saved only a few miles, and at best two days, it became the preferred route almost immediately. Emigrants and gold rushers heading for California in subsequent years used the new cutoff almost exclusively, leaving the road to Fort Hall for use by Oregon-bound emigrants.

Trail Modifications after the Gold Rush

Refinements to the California Trail system continued throughout the 1850s, as thousands of overland emigrants made their way to the goldfields. More and more alternative routes and cutoffs were developed by emigrants and commercial promoters. As before, the new routes were developed at all three areas where cutoffs had previously been developed.

EASTERN FEEDER ROUTES

In the East, the old Fort Kearny Road, sometimes called the Nebraska City Road, was first used in 1850 by emigrants too impatient to wait in line to jump off at Independence, St. Joseph, or Council Bluffs. Opened in 1847 by the U.S. Army as a supply road to the new Fort Kearny, this road left the Missouri River at Nebraska City, about halfway between St. Joseph and Council Bluffs, and ran almost directly northwest to meet the Platte River just east of Fort Kearny.

CENTRAL CUTOFFS

The Childs Cutoff. At Fort Laramie, where the Council Bluffs Road crossed the North Platte River to join the main trail on the south bank, Andrew Childs pioneered a new route in 1850 by staying on the north bank between Fort Laramie and Fort Caspar. It was tougher going than the main route, but it did attract some use by those in later years who wished to avoid the crush of wagon trains on the south bank, two river crossings, and/or contamination from the diseases being spread along the main trail during peak travel years.

The Seminoe Cutoff. A fur trapper named Seminoe pioneered an alternative route in central Wyoming between Ice Slough and Burnt Ranch in 1850. This route stayed on the south side of the Sweetwater, thereby avoiding three crossings of the river. The Seminoe Cutoff, as it became known, was never much of a favorite with emigrants or gold rushers, who liked to stay near water, but it was used by freighters and others wishing to bypass the slower-moving emigrant wagons.

LASSEN

Traces of the Nobles Emigrant Trail that linked the California Trail in Nevada to the Sacramento Valley are still visible in Lassen Volcanic National Park in California. The trail meets the Pacific Coast National Scenic Trail and crosses the Lassen Trail.

Other Cutoffs. In 1852, emigrants and gold rushers who sought to take advantage of the shortcut, yet avoid the fifty-mile crossing of the waterless Sublette Flats, blazed numerous alternatives to the Sublette Cutoff. Two of these were the Slate Creek Cutoff between the Green River and Rocky Gap and the Kinney Cutoff east of the Green River. These cutoffs were heavily used as soon as they were opened, as was the Baker-Davis Road, a later alternative to the Kinney Cutoff. In 1856 the Dempsey-Hockaday Cutoff was opened just west of Rocky Gap, which saved several miles of travel on the western end of the Sublette. Most of the trail alternatives in this maze between

South Pass and the Bear River divide could be used interchangeably.

Finally, with the discovery of gold in Colorado in 1858, the South Platte Trail was quickly developed between the new goldfields and the California Trail in western Nebraska. When Julesburg (Colorado) was established as a major stage station in 1859, most emigrant and freight traffic on the California Trail shifted down through there. Although this added a few miles to the route, it enabled travelers to take advantage of the station's amenities—and to avoid the hard ascent of California Hill and the precipitous descent to the North Platte through Ash Hollow.

WESTERN ROUTES

The California Trail was never improved along the Humboldt River basin, but additional routes were developed from where the trail passed the Humboldt Sink. In 1851 and 1852 alone, no fewer than seven new routes were opened into California. These competed with the pre-gold-rush choices of the Truckee, Carson, and Lassen Cutoffs. Most of these were opened from the California side of the mountains to the East, and all as commercial ventures by either towns or private businesspeople eager to attract settlers, laborers, and consumers. None were very good, but they were all passable.

The Beckwourth Trail. The first of the alternative routes, this trail was opened in 1851 by trapper Jim Beckwourth, who found an easier pass through the Sierra in the spring of that year. With the backing of mining operators at Bidwell Bar and merchants from Marysville, he intercepted trains headed down the Truckee Route and guided them into Marysville. His route left the Truckee near present-day downtown Reno, angled northwest and over Beckwourth Pass, and then back down to the southwest through Bidwell Bar to Marysville. It was a shorter route for gold rushers headed to Bidwell Bar, but a somewhat longer route for those going to Marysville. Although no statistics are readily available to substantiate the use of the Beckwourth Trail in succeeding years, it is safe to say that, if never a favorite, it was at least occasionally used.

The Nobles Road. While searching for gold in the Black Rock Desert, William H. Nobles found a shortcut to California in 1851. Returning to Shasta City, near present-day Redding, he told others about his find, which even boasted a better supply of water. Residents eagerly tested his cutoff from the Applegate-Lassen Route, and town merchants soon offered him $2,000 to divert travel through their city. His first converts came through town in 1852.

The route quickly became a favorite of the gold rushers headed for the Shasta mines, but its popularity did not end there. In 1854, Nobles recommended that the route be improved, and in 1857 Congress approved a $300,000 grant for that purpose. In 1859 and 1860, Frederick W. Lander and his crew mapped the route, developed the road, expanded springs, and established a reservoir at Tugo Hot Springs. When opened to travel in 1859, the Lander Road saved travelers five days between Burnt Ranch, where it left the main trail, and Fort Hall, where it rejoined. Lander estimated that thirteen thousand emigrants used the road in 1859, which may be questionable, since only nineteen thousand emigrants traveled to Oregon and California that year. The road eventually became a segment of the Fort Kearny–South Pass–Honey Lake Wagon Road that superseded the old California and Oregon Trails in the 1860s. As mining activity continued, portions of the Nobles-Lander Route were used to create additional routes. The Chico (California) to Silver City (Idaho) Wagon Route, developed in 1862, used a portion of the road to lead Californians to Idaho mines. Portions were also used to connect boomtowns in the Humboldt Range during their period of greatest activity.

The Sonora Road. The Sonora Road was backed by the merchants and promoters of Sonora, who subscribed funds in July 1852 for a relief expedition for the benefit of stranded and starving gold rushers. Anyone taking advantage of the relief was expected to head toward Sonora in gratitude. The Sonora Road left the Carson Route in the vicinity of Fort Churchill, headed south

and southwest through Antelope Valley, and then west across the mountains, crossing the summit just south of present-day Sonora Pass in the vicinity of Granite Dome. In places, it closely paralleled the route of the Bidwell-Bartleson party. Unfortunately, the high, rough road of the pass —at an elevation of ten thousand feet—and the unbroken trail caused more hardships and suffering for those induced to try it than if they had been left alone. As a result, it never became very popular.

Other Routes. Three other route variations opened in 1852; they were actually improvements of the Truckee and Carson Routes rather than new routes. Henness Pass was developed as a more direct route from the Truckee to Marysville. The Placerville County emigrant road opened off the Truckee Route, using Squaw Pass as an alternative crossing of the summit, and ended in Auburn. Johnson's Cutoff from the Carson Route skirted the southern shore of Lake Tahoe and then headed down into Placerville. Use of these new routes varied from year to year, according to destination or the salesmanship of the various promoters sent east to intercept the wagon trains.

Though Lander's cutoff, starting east of South Pass at Burnt Ranch, came to mark an end of an era, it led to the development of a new age in transportation. The gold rush helped to make Sacramento the headquarters for some of the Old West's most influential men—Collis P. Huntington, Charles Crocker, Leland Stanford, and Mark Hopkins, in particular. These four men met with Theodore Judah and planned the first transcontinental railroad. With its completion in 1869, thousands upon thousands more emigrants came west. Still using portions of the California Trail, the "iron horse" would not allow a busy nation to forget the imprint made by the explorers, emigrants, stampeders, and developers who had so boldly come before them. Meanwhile, gold seekers and farmers learned to live together in a new land, leaving a proud heritage as rich as the gold claims and land they worked.

A TRAIL TO TRAGEDY

To many historians, the sufferings of the Donner party were the culmination of small isolated mistakes.* Others say that the Donners were doomed when they purchased Lansford W. Hastings's *Emigrants Guide to Oregon and California.* At the time of writing, Hastings, a propagandist and land promoter, had not actually traveled the route across the Utah desert, yet, in a brief aside in his guidebook, he stated, "The most direct route, for the California emigrants, would be to leave the Oregon route, about two hundred miles east from Fort Hall; thence bearing west southwest, to the Salt Lake; and thence continuing down to the bay of San Francisco, by the route just described."

In any event, the Donner disaster was based on a combination of uneasy feelings, chance meetings, bad decisions, coincidence, bad luck, and perhaps fate—all of which led the party to the Hastings Cutoff in 1846 and to what would become known as Donner Pass. The group, eventually to be known as the Donner party, included the families of two brothers, George and Jacob Donner, and of James Reed. Each of these men was wealthy, lived in Illinois, and had a large family; and each started out with three wagons. One of Reed's wagons was said to have been a palace on wheels that slowed the group's travel and was a constant reminder of the family's wealth to the poorer members of the group.

During the second week of May 1846, the party joined a large group of emigrants and left Independence, Missouri, on their way west. Although wealthy and influential, the Donners and Reeds were just part of another party under the leadership of Lillburn Boggs, ex-governor of Missouri. On May 29, Reed's mother-in-law, Sarah Keys, died at Alcove Spring and was buried along the trail near present-day Blue

*Material in this section is taken from the Bureau of Land Management's *On the Trail to Tragedy . . . the Donner Party in Wyoming.*

Rapids, Kansas.* Continuing across the plains without incident, the travelers had crossed into Wyoming, when, on the night of June 27, a chance meeting—the kind of meeting that makes a person later ask, "What if?"—took place.

While the party was camped at Fort Bernard, a few miles from Fort Laramie, James Clyman, a mountain man and legend in the history of fur trade, walked up to the campfire. He knew the country as well as any man and had served with Reed in the same regiment in the Black Hawk War. As it turned out, he had just come across the route with Hastings, heading east. Not thinking much of the new cutoff, he warned Reed and the Donner brothers to "stick to the main road" and not take the cutoff described in Hastings's *Guide*. Reed was not persuaded. After all, he was holding the recently published book in his hands. Could a dirty old mountain man know better? One member of the party, journalist Edwin Bryant, decided he would take the route advised by Hastings. But, heeding one part of Clyman's advice, he decided to leave his wagons behind. He sold and traded his outfit for a string of pack animals and pressed ahead.

Compounding the dilemma of Clyman's warning, a few weeks later, on July 17, Reed and the Donners were shown a letter from Hastings at South Pass,

*See Point of Interest 5 in the chapter on the ONHT, pages 180–81.

offering to personally guide emigrants across his new route to California. With their minds made up to take the Hastings route, the group continued west. On July 18, they crossed South Pass and, like so many emigrants before and since, camped at Pacific Springs. Meanwhile, Hastings had met another group, the Harlan-Young party, and was at Fort Bridger preparing to guide them across the Utah desert. On July 19, the Reeds, Donners, and their fellow travelers camped at the Little Sandy crossing, where the group decided to split off. The next morning, most of the families headed over the Sublette Cutoff on their way to Oregon and California. The remainder of the group headed to Fort Bridger after electing George Donner their captain. In hindsight, the election of this friendly father figure may have been pivotal in the final outcome of the Donner experience. Between Little Sandy and the Sierra Nevada, they would camp too long; miss the trail and lose more time; and experience delays caused by one barrier after another. Some believe the younger Reed may have been better suited as the leader in facing these challenges.

While still camped at the Little Sandy, George Donner's wife, Tamsen, cared for Luke Halloran, an emigrant who had been abandoned and left to die by his fellow travelers. When he finally succumbed to consumption in the Utah desert, this "penniless Waif" willed the $1,500 in gold he had concealed in his belongings to the charitable Donners. Because the Donners were already wealthy, this caused quite a bit of dissension among the poorer members of the party.

By the time the Donner party arrived at Fort Bridger on July 28, Hastings, who was leading the Harlan-Young group across his cutoff through the Wasatch Mountains, was already several days ahead of the Donners. With the going next to impossible, Edwin Bryant sent a letter back to Fort Bridger to be delivered to his friends, the Donners. The letter warned them *not* to take Hastings's route. But conjecture has it that Louis Vasquez and/or his partner, Jim Bridger, never delivered the letter (though there is no proof of this, Reed believed for the rest of his life that he had been deceived). It seemed the duo stood to gain financially if the Hastings Cutoff was used by emigrants who would thus pass by the fort. Worse yet, it appears that the Hastings Cutoff may have even been endorsed by Vasquez and Bridger. James Reed wrote on July 13, 1846, "Mr Bridger informs me that the route we design to take, is a fine level road, with plenty of water and grass."

Compounding their problems, the Donners did not depart Fort Bridger until July 31. The time they lost resting at the fort would haunt them later. After leaving Fort Bridger, the Donners followed the tracks left by Hastings as far as they could but were soon lost. Forging ahead, they hoped to find signs that would tell them they had reached the fabulous shortcut. Days became weeks as they crossed mountains and desert. Dissension arose, and Reed accidentally killed another emigrant in a fight. When another member of the party died under suspicious circumstances, the group sent Reed on his way. Some of the emigrants lost their minds under the strain, and heartache became a traveling companion. Three months after leaving Fort Bridger, the party found themselves trapped in Donner Pass in the high Sierra. The rest of the story is one of the most famous tragedies in American trail history.

Thousands of miles of trail and hundreds of historic sites are found in the eleven states along the trail.* Approximately 20 percent of the complete California Trail system, or about eleven

*Some of the material in this section is taken from the National Park Service's *California and Pony Express Trails Eligibility/Feasibility Study.*

hundred miles of trail, can still be seen in the form of ruts and traces. Most of these are west of Casper, Wyoming, with new discoveries constantly being announced. The estimated 320 historic sites along the entire California Trail include forts, trading posts, natural landmarks, river crossings, campsites, trail

The Trail Today

junctions, and gravesites. Of these sites, 100 are also associated with the Oregon and Mormon Pioneer National Historic Trails. Of the 320 sites, 74 (23 percent) are in federal ownership, 70 (22 percent) are owned by states, 48 (15 percent) are under the jurisdiction of cities or counties, and 128 (40 percent) are privately owned.

Some visitors stop only at major historic sites. This is seen in the large visitation figures at major sites such as Fort Laramie National Historic Site and Sutter's Fort State Park, as opposed to the smaller samples at lesser-known sites such as Lassen Meadows and the Susan Hail grave near Kenesaw, Nebraska.* At the major sites, activities include visiting museums, looking at interpretive exhibits, and walking along short, self-guided trails.

Cross-country trail users constitute a special category of visitors who are willing to take the time and effort to retrace the actual wagon routes. Whether as individuals or as groups, these visitors are the most consistent users of the cross-country portions of the trail system, returning year after year to hike or ride along various portions of the trail, many of which have been marked by members of Trails West, Incorporated, in some of the most isolated and treacherous

*Hail died suddenly, probably of cholera. Her grief-stricken husband went back to St. Joseph to purchase an engraved marker which he brought back in a wheelbarrow.

areas in the United States as far as vehicular travel is concerned. A large number of these visitors have the ultimate goal of retracing the entire Oregon-California trail systems from one end to the other. The majority use four-wheel-drive vehicles; a smaller percentage hike, ride horses, or use mountain bikes. Other popular activities along the trail include panning for gold, rock hounding, photography, rafting, kayaking, camping, and backpacking.

A great deal of caution should be taken when planning backcountry trips in remote, isolated regions. Dry season in the Far West generally extends from June to early October, but this season can be considerably shorter or longer, depending upon the particular year, and it may vary from one area to another. Rain and snow may make some areas impassable during some months. Local inquiry is necessary, and even then one should proceed with caution. Weather can range from icy, cold, and windy to hot, dry, and windy, all in the same day. Vehicles with high clearance and four-wheel drive are necessary in some areas. They should be in excellent operating condition and filled with gas at every opportunity. It is important to bring plenty of food, water, extra clothes, sleeping bags, a shovel, a tow chain or strap, an inflated spare tire, a CB radio, the best maps, and a compass. Being prepared is critical, even when planning a day trip. Traveling with others is highly recommended, and someone should be told where you are going and when you are returning. Help is not always available the day it is needed. All decisions should be made with intelligence and common sense. To visit sites on private land, the landown-er's permission is needed.

Points on major cutoffs are listed in the section below. The locations shown do not include the sites along the main branch, or overland route, which are included in the coverage of the Oregon and Mormon Pioneer National Historic Trails.

WYOMING

1. **FORT LARAMIE NATIONAL HISTORIC SITE.** The Childs Cutoff left Fort Laramie to travel the north bank of the Platte River. Fort Laramie NHS, southwest of the town of Fort Laramie, has a visitor center, museum, and living-history demonstration at the restored fort, once the site of a fur-trading post. During the beginning of the gold rush (1849), the military took over Fort Laramie and expanded it. It continued to serve emigrants as a major resting and refitting place. A park headquarters' map shows the location of the Old Bedlam ruts on private land that can be traced northwest to Guernsey. *Nearby:* Outside Douglas, Fort Fetterman SHS offers the fort's (1867) restored officers' quarters.

2. **FORT CASPAR.** The Childs Cutoff joined the main trail again at Fort Caspar, which was established at the site of Louis Guinard's trading post and bridge (1858). First called the Platte Bridge Station, it was renamed (1866) after Lt. Caspar Collins was killed in an American Indian engagement (1865). The post was never rebuilt after being burned by the Indians (1867). In Casper, the Caspar Museum has a reconstruction of the fort. *Nearby:* Edness Kimball Wilkins SP. To the northwest, the unusual topography in Hell's Half Acre, west of Powder River.

3. **SOUTH PASS.** The Lander Road provided an alternate route, saving five days, after Congress appropriated funds (1857) to improve emigrant trails. The route started in the South Pass area at Burnt Ranch and ended at Fort Hall. *Other attractions:* South Pass City State Historical Site has a visitor center, interpretive displays, and restored mining-era building. Trails West, headquartered at South Pass City, offers excellent wagon excursions on the Oregon-California-Mormon Trails. *Nearby:* Atlantic City (1868) was founded when gold mines attracted thousands of miners to the Sweetwater Mining District in South Pass. Its main attractions include mining buildings that date from the turn of the century.

4. **SUBLETTE CUTOFF.** Southwest of South Pass, a fork marks

Points of Interest

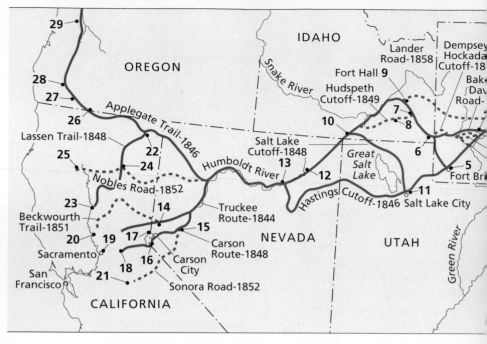

CALIFORNIA NATIONAL HISTORIC TRAIL

the point where emigrants could take a shortcut across the Little Colorado Desert to the junction with the main trail on the Bear River or continue on the main route to Fort Bridger. The shorter route, the Sublette Cutoff, was a waterless track of fifty miles that did not become popular until the gold-rush days when California-bound travelers were eager to reach the goldfields. Part of the savings came when ferries were established to speed up crossings. Often reaching the cutoff in mid-August, emigrants endured temperatures that reached 90-plus degrees. The many related sites found in the area include the Green River ford upstream of the ferry crossings; the Old Mormon Ferry; the Mountain Man Ferry,

run at least in part by Jim Bridger; numerous unmarked emigrant graves; burned wagon sites, near the Big Sandy at the Sublette County line; Names Hill (NRHP) which registers over two thousand inscriptions, beginning with petroglyphs, near La Barge. *Nearby:* Big Sandy RA; Fossil Butte NM.

5. **FORT BRIDGER.** In 1846, journalist Edwin Bryant described this stopping point as "two or three miserable log cabins, rudely constructed and bearing but a faint resemblance to habitable houses." The small trading post built by Jim Bridger and Louis Vasquez was a vital stopping point on the Oregon, California, and Mormon Pioneer Trails to Fort Hall, the Hudspeth

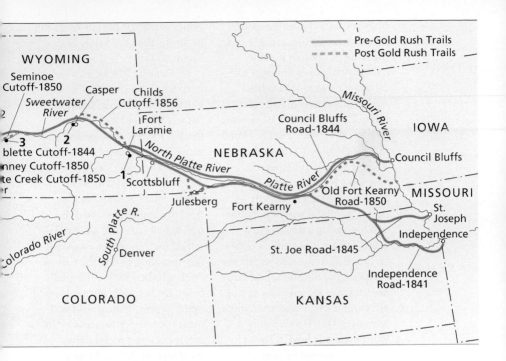

Map labels:

WYOMING

Seminoe
Cutoff-1850   Casper   Childs
Sweetwater   Cutoff-1856
River
                 Fort
                 Laramie
3   2
blette Cutoff-1844
nney Cutoff-1850
te Creek Cutoff-1850 — 1 Scottsbluff
r
North Platte River   NEBRASKA
Julesberg
South Platte R.
Colorado River
Denver

Pre-Gold Rush Trails
Post Gold Rush Trails

Missouri River

Council Bluffs
Road-1844   IOWA

Council Bluffs

Platte River
Old Fort Kearny   MISSOURI
Road-1850   St.
Fort Kearny   Joseph
                         Independence

St. Joe Road-1845

Independence
Road-1841

COLORADO   KANSAS

Cutoff, and the Hastings Cutoff. The Mormons purchased the fort (1855) and later built Fort Supply to the south. The Fort Bridger site was taken over by the U.S. Army, which rebuilt and enlarged it. Outside the town of Fort Bridger, it is now a state historical site. The Fort Bridger Rendezvous is held on Labor Day weekend, and Bridger Valley Pioneer Days is observed in July in nearby Lyman. *Nearby:* Seedskadee NWR is passed en route to Fort Bridger.

IDAHO

6. SMITH'S TRADING POST. From Fort Bridger or the Sublette Cutoff, the emigrants pushed on, heading north by northwest over Oyster Ridge, across Muddy Creek, then Thomas Fork, and

into the Bear River Valley southeast of Montpelier, to Smith's Trading Post. The fort, composed of four log cabins, served emigrants until 1850. The owner, Thomas "Peg-Leg" Smith, made $100 a day from gold seekers (1849). *Other attractions:* The Oregon Trail Rendezvous Pageant is held on the trail near "the Big Hill." *Nearby:* Bear Lake SP; Minnetonka Cave; Bear Lake NWR; Caribou NF.

7. SODA SPRINGS. The Hudspeth Cutoff, an old American Indian route, was designed to cut out travel to Fort Hall. It left the main trail four miles west of Soda Springs and came out on the California Trail near City of Rocks. Hordes of gold seekers followed the cutoff. At Soda Springs, the

pioneers marveled at the springs and geysers. Visitors can still taste the water of another notable landmark, Hooper Spring. *Other attractions:* Pioneer Museum; wagon ruts at a local golf course; Camp Connor (1863); Wagonbox Grave (1861); Sheep Rock, a landmark also known as Soda Point. *Nearby:* Soda Point Reservoir.

8. **LAVA HOT SPRINGS.** West of Soda Springs, the Hudspeth passed through Dempsey's Bath Tub hot springs, now Idaho's world-famous hot pools, a popular health and pleasure resort. For centuries, the Shoshone and Bannock Indians regarded the springs as a neutral site. *Other attractions:* Mountain Man Rendezvous–Pioneer Days is held in Lava Hot Springs at the end of July.

9. **FORT HALL.** The Oregon-California Trail and the Lander Road both came into Fort Hall. From there, the traveler followed the Snake downstream for forty miles, then along the Raft River to the major landmark on the trail, the City of Rocks. Fort Hall, built by Nathaniel Wyeth (1834) as a fur-trading post, became an important pioneer resting spot, though abandoned in 1856. The replica, north of Pocatello, gives a glimpse into frontier life and what the bustling trade center was like. *Other attractions:* In Pocatello, the Bannock County Historical Museum; the Idaho Museum of Natural History. *Nearby:* Fort Hall Indian Reservation, with the Shoshone-Bannock Indian Festival held the second week in August; Caribou NF;

Bonneville Park; Indian Rocks SP; to the northwest, Craters of the Moon NM.

10. **CITY OF ROCKS.** Not far from where Hudspeth's Cutoff joined the California Trail, gold rushers followed it to the landmark, City of Rocks, west of Almo. From the Salt Lake Cutoff, near the City of Rocks, it was 784 miles, or sixty days, to Sacramento. Some gold rushers, in need of supplies, followed the trail to Salt Lake and wintered or settled there. Another estimated fifty thousand passed the City of Rocks on their way to the goldfields. Dr. Joseph S. Sheperd (1850) wrote, "a most wild and romantic scenery presents to the eye, rocks upon rocks, named and piled high in the most fantastic shapes." The pioneers scratched their names into the rocks or signed them with axle grease. The fascinating monoliths, spires, domes, and walls, some 2.5 billion years old, were caused by erosion. City of Rocks National Reserve is located on the northern edge of the Great Basin and is popular for picnicking, camping, rock climbing, and hiking.

UTAH

11. **SALT LAKE CITY.** Gold rushers in gravest need of new equipment followed the Mormon Road to Salt Lake. They rested and traded for supplies at a stiff price then headed out again around the north side of the Great Salt Lake toward the City of Rocks by following the Salt Lake Alternate — part of the Kelton

Road, a major stage line from Kelton, Utah, to Boise, Idaho. *Other attractions:* Temple Square; This Is The Place SP. *Nearby:* Great Salt Lake; Donner Hill, the location of the Donner party's time-consuming climb out of Emigration Canyon (1846) on their way to California; Bonneville Salt Flats. The Donner party failed to take enough water and lost a critical number of oxen and had to abandon four wagons just northeast of the flats.

NEVADA

12. **WELLS.** Here the Fort Hall, or California, route reached the Humboldt River. The site provided the emigrants with welcome springs in addition to the river, which they followed for three hundred miles across Nevada to a point where it dwindles into a marshy sink. Travel along I-80 takes in much of the same scenery. Wells was named for the number of springs found there. Ruts left can still be seen. *Nearby:* Angel Lake.

13. **ELKO.** When Hastings finally reached the end of his cutoff, just west of present-day Elko, he discovered that the wagon trains that had been far behind him at South Pass were now a week ahead. The cutoff that actually added miles to the journey was considered a failure. Further trail divisions occurred as the Sierra drew near. *Other attractions:* In Elko, the Northeastern Nevada Museum exhibits American Indian and mining artifacts and a Pony Express cabin; a Basque

Festival is held the first weekend in July. *Nearby:* Humboldt NF.

14. **RENO.** The Beckwourth Trail left the Truckee near Reno, leading into Marysville, California. Reno, the city of diversity, offers downhill and cross-country skiing, snowmobiling, hiking, white-water rafting, and boating opportunities. Other activities vary from gambling and stage shows to the scenic rose garden of Idlewild Park, along the Truckee River. *Nearby:* Pyramid Lake, Nevada's largest natural lake; Pyramid Lake Indian Reservation; Toiyabe NF.

15. **FORT CHURCHILL HISTORICAL STATE MONUMENT.** The fort was established (1860–69) on the Carson Branch of the California Trail, south of Silver Springs. Like other military forts, it had no stockade surrounding it, and it became the most expensive fort in its time. Though the fort is now in ruins, a visitor center reconstructs its history with interpretive exhibits. The Sonora Road left the Carson at Fort Churchill. *Nearby:* Lahontan SRA; Yerington Indian Reservation; Dayton SP; Carson City.

16. **MORMON STATION HISTORIC STATE PARK.** The Carson Branch went south of Lake Tahoe. The restored log stockade and trading post (1851) has a museum. Emigrants were drawn to the area to rest before continuing over the Sierra Nevada to California. Johnson's Cutoff soon became the main gateway. U.S. Highway 50 traces the route into Placerville and Sacramento.

17. TRUCKEE. The Truckee Route fell out of favor after the Donner disaster. Forty-five members of the Donner Party were rescued here at their campsite in early 1847. Many of them had resorted to cannibalism to avoid the starvation that, along with the freezing cold, claimed the lives of thirty-six fellow emigrants. Six others in the party had died earlier along the trail. Banished member James Reed arrived in California ahead of the Donners, and he returned with a rescue party to bring the survivors to safety. The Donner Memorial SP has several sites, a pioneer monument, a visitor center with a slide show of the Donner experience, and the Emigrant Trail Museum. *Nearby:* Reno, Tahoe SRA; Lake Tahoe. *Other attractions:* The Yuba-Donner Scenic Byway (Routes I-80, 49, 20, and old 40) is a 175-mile drive through the historic towns of Nevada City, Sierraville, Downieville, and Truckee. The Tahoe-Pacific Heritage Corridor (Routes 20, 101, I-80, and 89) from the coast of Mendocino to the western shore of Lake Tahoe presents California's cultural and climatic diversity while cutting through the north-central valley and historic gold country for some 292 miles.

18. MARSHALL GOLD DISCOVERY STATE HISTORIC PARK. This is the site of the discovery that started the great gold rush. The park at Coloma has a replica of Sutter's sawmill, the discovery site, a mining exhibit, Chinese stores, and a visitor center with museum and artifacts. *Nearby:* Placerville, the heart of the mother lode region, connects many of the gold-rush communities of the Sierra foothills and several boomtowns. Johnson's Cutoff headed down from Carson into Placerville, first known as Dry Diggins and later Hangtown. *Other attractions:* El Dorado County Historical Museum; Gold Bug Mine, on the east side of the mother lode vein, where an estimated 60 to 90 percent of the lode still lies in the ground. The Golden Chain Corridor (State Highway 49) links mining towns and historic attractions for some 321 miles.

19. SUTTER'S FORT. The first European outpost in California, New Helvetia on the American River (1839) served as a temporary refuge for new emigrants (1841–49). As a result of troubles arising from the gold rush, Sutter was forced to sell his fort (1849) and most of it was destroyed by the late 1850s. The restored adobe fort in Sacramento has relics of the gold rush, a diorama depicting life in the fort, living history, and the state Indian museum. It was Sutter who organized the four relief parties that came to the aid of the Donner party. *Other attractions:* Old Sacramento (NL) has fifty-three historic buildings; the B. F. Hastings Museum (PENHT) is the site of the Pony Express office; the California State Railroad Museum is

the world's largest railroad museum. Also, the California State Parks Store; *Spirit of Sacramento* sight-seeing cruises; Dixieland Jazz Festival, the largest in the world (last week of May); American River Parkway for bicycling, walking, horseback riding, rafting, fishing, and picnicking. The Mariposa to Yosemite Highway (Route 140) climbs through the scenic and historic Merced River canyon; the Pioneer and Gold Rush Heritage Corridor (I-80 and old Route 40) follows the major trail of early California pioneers and gold seekers for 197 miles, from San Francisco through Sacramento, Auburn, and Truckee to the Nevada state line; the River Road (Route 160) follows the Sacramento River through historic agricultural areas of the delta for 44 miles. *Nearby:* Yosemite NP.

20. **MARYSVILLE/YUBA CITY.** Ellis Lake is central to Marysville, the destination of the Beckwourth Trail. A boulevard along the shore allows walking and jogging. Riverfront Park links Marysville and Yuba City, founded (1849) as a gold-rush development. *Other attractions:* Community Memorial Museum, containing American Indian and pioneer artifacts. *Nearby:* Gray Lodge Refuge, a Pacific flyway stopover for waterfowl and a nesting ground; Sutter Buttes, referred to as the world's smallest mountain range; Sutter NWR.

21. **SONORA.** First settled by miners from Sonora, Mexico, Sonora became one of the largest and wealthiest towns in the Mother Lode country. *Other attractions:* Tuolumne County Museum, housed in the old county jail (1857) has gold-rush era displays and pioneer trails exhibit; Bradford Street Park has exhibits of mining equipment and a stamp mill. *Nearby:* Stanislaus NF; Yosemite NP.

22. **GOOSE LAKE.** The Lassen Trail cut off the Applegate at the southeast corner of Goose Lake. A marker is located at Davis Creek near Highway 395 and Modoc County Road 11. It was here that the Applegate Trail headed toward Oregon and the Lassen Trail to California. *Nearby:* Modoc NF; to the west, Clear Lake Reservoir NWR and Lava Beds NM.

23. **VINA.** North of Chico, the Lassen Trail ended at Peter Lassen's ranch. Today the site is near the entrance to the Trappist monastery of Our Lady of New Clairveaux. (Women are not allowed to enter the monastery grounds, and men must ask for permission at the gate.) There is nothing left of the original buildings and the entire area is under cultivation. *Nearby:* Woodson Bridge SRA; Red Bluff, the gateway to Lassen Volcanic NP; the William Ide Adobe (1850) SHP serves as a memorial to the founder and president of the short-lived California Republic; a diversion dam on the Sacramento River offers the Salmon Viewing Plaza.

24. **LASSEN VOLCANIC NATIONAL PARK.** Though Lassen,

for whom the park is named, guided emigrants near the park, it is the Nobles Emigrant Trail that is still visible in the park. The park's high elevations can leave the hiker short of breath. Time should be taken to acclimatize, and exposed terrain should be avoided during lightning storms. A ranger should be told of extended trip plans and the expected time of return. Lassen Peak is one of the volcanoes (active, dormant, or extinct) that extend around the Pacific Ocean in a great "ring of fire." The park has a visitor center, an information center, hiking, canoeing, fishing, picnicking, and camping. The Pacific Crest National Scenic Trail offers excellent long-distance hiking opportunities. *Nearby:* Lassen NF.

25. **Shasta.** The Nobles Trail ended at Shasta, where a marker is located on the right of Highway 299 at the southeast corner of the post office. Once known as "the Queen City of the North," Shasta is noted for its gold-mining history. In 1872, with the construction of the railroad through the Sacramento River canyon, its boom days ended. Some of the old buildings have been restored. *Nearby:* West of Redding, Shasta SHP, a former mining town, offers an old courthouse that serves as a museum, a restored barn, and a stagecoach; Shasta-Trinity NF; Yolla Bolly–Middle Eel Wilderness Area and the Trinity Alps Wilderness; Mount Shasta; Whiskeytown, Shasta, and Clair Eagle Lakes; Shasta Dam;

Whiskeytown-Shasta-Trinity NRA. The Pacific Crest National Scenic Trail passes through the area.

OREGON

26. **Malin.** After initially cutting off the overland route at Humboldt, Nevada, the Applegate Trail moved from Goose Lake into Oregon at this small town on the California border. First used to bring emigrants to Oregon, the trail was later used by gold rushers headed to California. I-5 closely parallels the Applegate, linking major cities to the Willamette Valley, and Highway 97 travels the eastern length, from Klamath Falls up to the Washington border. *Nearby:* In California, Tule Lake; Lava Bed NM. In Oregon, Klamath NWR, one of the nation's oldest; Klamath Lake; to the north, Crater Lake NP features the deepest lake in the United States. Klamath Falls, Klamath County's largest city, provides a vast array of outdoor activities, including birdwatching, fishing, canoeing, snow skiing, sailing, mountaineering, trail riding, windsurfing, and hiking. *Other attractions:* Favell Museum of Western Art and Indian Artifacts; Klamath County Museum.

27. **Ashland.** Known as a crossroads for culture and outdoor activity, Ashland, home to the Oregon Shakespeare Festival, was developed by early settlers (1852) with ties to Ashland County, Ohio, and Ashland, Kentucky, thus its name. *Other attrac-*

tions: Pacific Northwest Museum of Natural History. *Nearby:* Jacksonville, one of the few towns in the nation recognized as a NHL in its entirety, was a gold-mining town (1852); Siskiyou NF.

28. **GRANTS PASS.** The town is now a central point on the Rogue River and the departure point for many downriver rafting trips such as Morrison's Rogue River Rafting. There are also kayaking and jetboat excursions. The Rogue River National Recreation Trail follows the river. *Nearby:* Siskiyou and Rogue River NFs. To the south, Oregon Caves NM.

29. **DALLAS.** Tentative but unsuccessful probes into the Cascades were made in search of a new, safer route into the Willamette Valley. On June 20, 1846, Jesse and Lindsay Applegate joined others in the search, establishing the Applegate Trail. Dallas was first settled in the 1840s. *Nearby:* Baskett Slough NWR; Independence, featuring a historic district and Heritage Museum with artifacts from the Oregon-California Trail era.

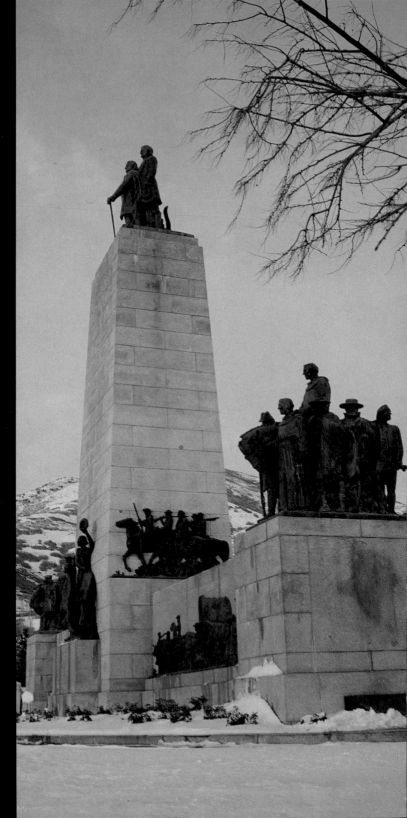

Mormon Pioneer National Historic Trail

It is enough! This is the right place.

BRIGHAM YOUNG, JULY 24, 1847

The Mormon pioneer migration was one of the most dramatic events in the history of American westward expansion. It was unique, when compared with other migrations, in purpose, organization, and cultural impact. Not entirely voluntary, the Mormons, members of the Church of Jesus Christ of Latter-day Saints, journeyed west for a chance to build a new "Zion," free from religious persecution. In a migration they called "the gathering," nearly seventy thousand church members and converts from the British Isles and Scandinavia followed the trail of the faithful between 1847 and 1869. This monumental move required of church leaders detailed planning, organization, and supervision, all of which came to distinguish this emigration to a barren promised land.

ADMINISTERING AGENCY
National Park Service
Long Distance Trails Office
P.O. Box 45155
South State Street, Suite 250
Salt Lake City, UT 84145-0155
801-539-4095

FURTHER INFORMATION
Mormon Trail Association
300 Rio Grande
Salt Lake City, UT 84101

ESTABLISHED
1978

APPROXIMATE MILEAGE
1,300 miles (2,095 kilometers)

STATES
Illinois, Iowa, Nebraska, Wyoming, Utah

Unlike the sometimes loose discipline of other wagon trains, the Mormon pioneer company was organized in semi-military fashion into divisions of ten, fifty, and a hundred emigrants.* Led by their general, Brigham Young, followers served as company captains, hunters, and scouts. Unlike many other emigrant companies, the first thoughts of Young's pioneers were to improve the route for the Mormons who followed. Distances were measured, mileposts set up, and good locations for camping, wood, water, and forage were noted. In general, Young's first pioneer company of 148 (143 men, three women, and two young boys) became the guide for the thousands of hopeful emigrants destined to follow.

En route, the Mormons established semi-permanent communities and ferry crossings of major importance. They graded down steep approaches to fords, cleared boulders out of the trail, and made the route generally easier for those who would follow. These efforts identified a two-way wagon road as a continuous route eastward to pick up supplies and new converts at the Missouri River or to meet faltering companies and help them on to Salt Lake City. In southern Iowa, particularly, Mormons established some of the first com-

munities, roads, and bridges. Winter Quarters, near present-day Omaha, Nebraska, and Kanesville, present-day Council Bluffs, Iowa, became outfitting points that rivaled the Missouri towns of Independence, Westport, and St. Louis. The path followed became a major transportation route culminating in the centralization of a religious community as well as the settlement and industrial development of Utah. Another unique aspect of "the gathering" was the use of handcarts instead of wagons to carry the belongings of nearly three thousand poorer "saints" in the 1850s.

Mormon history began with their prophet, Joseph Smith (1805–44), who compiled a detailed history recounting some of the important events that led to the establishment of the church. In the early spring of 1820, while living in Palmyra, New York, Smith retreated to the woods to pray for direction. There, according to the account, he had his first vision, being informed that "the fullness of the gospel, should, at some future time, be made known to him." On September 21–22, 1823, similar experiences occurred, and the angel Moroni, son of the prophet Mormon, told him of an ancient record hidden in a nearby hill. Finally, on September 22, 1827, Smith was allowed to take gold plates inscribed with symbols, which he translated into *The Book of Mormon*. The Church of Jesus Christ of the Latter-day Saints

*Material in this section is taken from the National Park Service's *Comprehensive Plan, Mormon Pioneer National Historic Trail.*

(LDS) was formally organized on April 6, 1830, in Fayette, New York.

In January 1831, the church moved to the area of Kirtland, Ohio, where a temple was built and extensive missionary work began. One of the missions that had been opened in Jackson County, Missouri, later became the new headquarters. But religious intolerance and antagonism caused Smith's followers to move

NAUVOO

Tour guides greet visitors at the Seventies Hall in Old Nauvoo. This missionary training center and chapel is one of twenty-five restored historic homes and shops along the Mississippi River. Winter visitors see eagles nesting in trees, and summer visitors can take a carriage ride around the town. Artisans and crafters are always happy to demonstrate their skills. The Mormons were forced to leave their Illinois home in 1846–47.

again, leaving behind their homes and farms. By November 1833, the Mormons had been driven from Jackson County into adjacent Clay County, where they stayed until the summer of 1836. Then, pressured again, they moved northeast into the sparsely populated upper part of Ray County. Trouble broke out once more in August 1838. By November of that year, general expulsion was well under way, and by spring 1839, nearly all Mormons had fled Missouri. They purchased a desolate tract of swampland on the Mississippi and, after draining the land, built what was to become one of the larger cities on the river in Illinois. Smith named the place Nauvoo, which he said meant "beautiful place" in ancient Hebrew.

Once again, peace was short-lived. Smith, a prophet, church president, author, and mayor of his flourishing community, was also a lieutenant general of the authorized Nauvoo Legion, a paramilitary organization, and a candidate for the presidency of the United States. As his importance grew, so did the unpopularity of his sect. Rumors spread about polygamy, and scandal about Smith's business affairs even produced a schism within the church. His destruction of a local newspaper, published by dissenters, caused an uprising among the community's neighbors and prompted warrants for his arrest. While he and his brother were awaiting trial, they were shot and killed by an armed

HANDCART

A unique feature of the Mormon migration was their use of handcarts, two-wheeled carts pulled by European converts. This one is on display near the Mormon Trail Center at Winter Quarters in the Omaha, Nebraska, area.

mob in Carthage, Illinois, on June 27, 1844.

After the prophet's assassination, conditions in Nauvoo became increasingly unsettled. The state legislature revoked the Nauvoo charter, and persecution was renewed, resulting in expulsion of the Mormons from Illinois. Plans were formulated to leave the United States and settle in Mexican territory, somewhere in the Rocky Mountain area. Familiar with the journal kept by John C. Frémont on his 1842 expedition west and with Lansford W. Hastings's guide to Oregon and California, Brigham Young did not take long to decide where the spot must be. Proving

to be a practical leader, he rallied the church and, in February of 1846, led the exodus from Nauvoo, crossing the Mississippi River by ferry to Iowa's shore. From there, the Mormons improved an overland route, establishing way stations across the state before settling in Winter Quarters (near present-day Omaha, Nebraska). Thirty-seven hundred Mormons settled at Winter Quarters and Kanesville (Council Bluffs, Iowa), and thousands of others were strung out in different camps across the state in what was actually the first 265-mile leg of their journey. Harsh winter weather in 1846–47 and inexperience brought the deaths of hundreds of pilgrims—and the question of how the church leaders would ever successfully transport the multitude westward.

The answer came when war erupted with Mexico. This enabled 526 men to enlist as the Mormon Battalion in the Army of the West. The battalion was ordered to drive through New Mexico to California (see SFNHT). Their pay and clothing allowances, roughly $50,000, were donated to the church to help finance the "journey of faith." It became clear that a lead party must hurry west to plant crops that would be ready for harvest by the time the main body of the migration arrived. A call for volunteers was made, and members of that first westward company were selected according to skill and talent. Roads had to be made, bridges built, and temporary quarters erected. On April 19, 1847, the first 148 pioneers continued west with scientific instruments to aid them in mapping the road that would be used by others. En route, a "roadometer" was invented to measure mileage, which was then recorded on posts for future companies. Another significant innovation included taking a wagon along to carry a large leather boat to be used for ferrying. Everything, including rests, were carefully prescribed.

Upon reaching the site of present-day Kearney, Nebraska, the party remained on the north bank of the Platte, on what was sometimes called the Great Platte River Road. In this way, the Mormons would not have to compete for campsites with Oregon and California emigrants. Here roughness of the country led them to the south side of the Platte where they met a group who had been discharged from the Mormon Battalion and another party of Mormons who had come from Mississippi. From this point, they generally followed the path of the Oregon and California Trails to Fort Bridger. From Bridger, the Mormon pioneers diverged from the trail leading west, and veered southerly, following the Hastings Cutoff route into Utah and the valley of the Great Salt Lake.

Some of the men stayed behind at Fort Caspar to earn the money that was sorely needed. The first Mormon ferry was established for trains crowding along behind them on their way to Oregon and California. This was the beginning of what became an extensive system of ferries. Most of those

MOUNTAIN RENDEZVOUS

Donning deerskin clothing, three mountain men join in the fun at the three-day Rendezvous held each year on Labor Day weekend at Fort Bridger State Historic Site in Wyoming. In 1855, enterprising Mormons bought Fort Bridger to supply emigrant parties.

operated by Mormons for the benefit of their own people were made available to others at a stiff price. It was also at Fort Caspar that the Mormons enjoyed and drank so much of an herbal brew that to this day it is known as Mormon tea.

After crossing South Pass, the main body of Mormons met more members of the battalion. Some of these men continued on their way eastward to Winter Quarters to meet their families, while others stayed to help the larger group through the Wasatch Mountains that had so fatally delayed the Donner party the year before. Company scouts reached the Valley of the Great Salt Lake on July 21, 1847, followed by the main body on July 22, and at last, two days later, by their leader, who had been suffering from a common illness known to pioneers as "mountain fever" and most likely caused by ticks. Upon seeing the valley, Young is reported to have said, "It is enough! This is the right place."

Shortly after the arrival of the first wagons, crops were planted, a system of irrigation was put in place, and adobe homes and a log fort were constructed. On July 27, the leaders located a site for the temple around which the city was planned, and on August 2, Young and a small company returned to organize the next season's migration.

In many ways the Mormons who followed shared a trail experience much like that of their contemporaries on the Oregon and California Trails. They shared campgrounds and ferries, triumphs and tragedies. They differed mainly in their organization and in the extent to which they used handcarts. Almost three thousand Mormons pulled these two-wheeled carts, loaded with belongings and goods, along the trail during the handcart emigrations of 1856 to 1860. Though most completed the journey with few problems, the handcart tragedy of 1856 claimed more lives than any other disaster in Oregon-California-Mormon Trail history.

That year, the late arrival of a ship from England gave the James G. Willie Handcart Company a late start. Caught in an October blizzard, the company was severely weakened and suffered at least twenty-one deaths at the base of Rocky Ridge. It is not known exactly how many others died when they attempted the two-mile ascent up the ridge. Rescuers from Salt Lake arrived in early November and moved the survivors two miles further along the trail to an area near Rock Creek. There the company suffered more losses as they waited while their rescuers continued on to help the next handcart company. Thirteen graves are marked at Rock Creek; two others are nearby. In total, nearly seventy of the 404 members of the Willie Company perished and many more suffered crippling frostbite. Robert Reeder later told of losing his father and his sister. Each night, he said, his father

would drop after pulling his cart all day. One morning Reeder found him dead. Reeder's sister's death followed. On October 15, in preparing the evening camp, she went out to collect sagebrush. Weary, she lay down on her bundle and fell asleep, never to regain consciousness. Others simply sat by the roadside and died.

The storm that decimated the Willie Handcart Company claimed more than 150 lives in the Edward Martin Company that was trailing them. Rescuers finally found that company in dire straits and trapped by the blizzard approximately sixty-five miles east of Devil's Gate at Red Bluffs. Leaders of the party and rescuers together decided to push on to Devil's Gate, but 65 members of the party died between the crossings of the North Platte and the first crossing of the Sweetwater. When they finally reached Devil's Gate, they took cover in a sheltered cove, known today as Martin's Cove. There, more members of the company died. It is estimated that in all one in four members of the Martin Company perished.

Though many died, hundreds more found their way, making the Mormons a major factor in westward expansion. After founding Salt Lake City, they settled over 350 communities in the West. Most were in Utah, but others ranged from Canada to Mexico. Vital to the western economy, they provided food and supplies to mining and industrial towns.

ROCKY RIDGE INTERPRETATION AND ROCKY MOUNTAIN WILDFLOWERS

At seventy-three hundred feet above sea level, Rocky Ridge near South Pass, Wyoming, is one of the higher points on the Mormon and Oregon Trails. Here, a descendant of the Mormon pioneers tells members of a modern Trails West wagon train of the seventy members of the James G. Willie Handcart Company who perished after crossing during an early blizzard in October of 1856. Pioneers, generally crossing during the summer, were met with white saxifrage and yellowstone crop instead of deadly snow.

Forbidding as the Valley of the Great Salt Lake may have seemed, it was occasionally proclaimed the most promising area of the intermountain region. Nonetheless, its barrenness did not attract others until the rush to California in 1849 and the completion of the Union Pacific Railroad twenty years later, which would bring the days of the Mormon Pioneer Trail to en end.

During this time, irrigation made the desert flourish, and the community grew and thrived. With the signing of the Treaty of Guadalupe Hidalgo in 1848, the region that had been part of Mexico was ceded to the United States and became the Utah Territory. Trade with the stampeders and soldiers who were stationed in the area during the Civil War brought a certain amount of prosperity to the Mormons, and with it the addition of new converts. Tenacity and resourcefulness resulted in the design and construction of historic Temple Square. Mammoth blocks of granite were hauled by oxen for miles down a canyon and across the valley to the temple building site. Construction on the Mormon Temple began in 1853, but it was not until forty years later that the magnificent structure was completed. The 1890s brought the official end to the practice of polygamy, and in 1896, Utah became the nation's forty-fifth state.

Today Mormonism has become a worldwide religion, one of the few religious denominations with exclusively American roots. With a membership of nearly 10 million, the church has more believers who live outside the United States than within. Had it not been for the sacrifices of the Mormon pioneers who established a new land for the sake of their faith, the Church of Latter-day Saints might never have grown to its present stature.

THE MORMON TABERNACLE CHOIR

Upon founding his church, Joseph Smith completed his declaration of faith by saying, "If there is anything virtuous, lovely, or of good report or praiseworthy, we seek after these things." Being both "lovely" and "of good report," the cultural arts were sought after by his early followers. Settlers in Iowa were often amazed to see these Mormon pioneers clear land around their campfires so that they could dance and sing sometimes until the early morning hours. When food was scarce, to add to their commissary they gave brass band concerts for others.

As the Mormons journeyed westward, singing hymns around the campfire became standard practice. "As I write I hear the sound of music and dancing on the other side of the circle," noted Erastus Snow, who traveled with the second company to arrive in the wide valley of the Great Salt Lake. For many, singing the songs of Zion gave them the strength to endure.

Within a month of the first group's July 22–24, 1847, arrival, the Mormon Tabernacle Choir had been established. Without a tabernacle, an organ, or even yet a formal name, the choir sang on August 22, 1847, at the first general conference held in Utah. At this conference the community, then smaller than today's choir, established its original name, the City of the Great Salt Lake.

But not all of the settlers remained in Salt Lake City. It was not long before Brigham Young directed the establishment of other colonies. Individuals with differing skills were selected to accompany various groups sent out to colonize. Important to each group were musicians who could help build morale by providing entertainment and who would serve the Lord through song. These communities developed their own choirs; some even delayed their departure from Salt Lake as they awaited the arrival of a baritone or soprano. One bishop offered ten acres of his town's best land to a good tenor who would agree to sing in the choir in his ward. Choirs also participated in concerts, public celebrations, and funerals. Some organized music schools, and in one town everyone participated in singing classes. When President Young visited Provo, the town's band greeted him and the choir serenaded him in the town square.

In the meantime, the choral tradition continued in Salt Lake City. At age sixteen, John Parry became the choir's first conductor, serving from 1849 to 1854. By 1850, the city's population had swelled to 11,380, and in 1851 the first tabernacle was erected. Its adobe walls held a congregation of 2,500 and housed the first pipe organ, which arrived from Australia and was assembled by 1857. In 1852, theatrical events, dances, concerts, and choir rehearsals were scheduled in the social hall near Temple Square. Ten years later, the Salt Lake Theatre, the best facility of its kind between Chicago and San Francisco, provided a new home for the concert and theatre arts. Young, who acted in the theatre, appointed Charles John Thomas as musical director. Thomas composed many of his own scores and later became the Tabernacle Choir's fourth conductor.

A new area for the choir opened when their fifth director moved them from the old building to the new tabernacle. Located immediately west of the Mormon Temple, the auditorium was first used in 1867 and dedicated in 1875. The building became the first in the country to be selected as a National Civil Engineering Landmark by the American Society of Engineers. Legend has it that Brigham Young originated its unusual design after contemplating a hollowed-out eggshell, cracked lengthwise. Because he wanted the roof to be self-supporting, without pillars or posts to obstruct the audience's view, he employed the bridge-building techniques of the day. The building's domed roof was created by using steam to bend the massive beams and weighting them at the ends. Red sandstone for the tabernacle's forty-six supporting pillars was quarried from Red Butte Canyon east of Salt Lake City, and lumber was brought in from the Wasatch Mountains.

The splendid auditorium houses one of the world's finest musical instruments. The eleven-thousand pipe tabernacle organ features prominent golden pipes made of round wood staves, hand-carved from Utah timber. Ten pipes from the original organ still work. The remarkable acoustics of the auditorium are responsible for the distinctive sound of the organ and are the reason the Grammy-winning Mormon Tabernacle Choir makes it home. The acoustics are so sensitive that a pin dropped on the floor will ring clearly throughout the hall.

In existence now for over a century and a half, the impressive Mormon Tabernacle Choir is one of the most respected organizations in music. To keep that place, it is constantly challenged to present a broad arrangement of high-quality yet spiritually motivating music to the general public. First transmitted on July 15, 1929, the choir's weekly radio show is the oldest continuous nationwide network broadcast in America. "Music and the Spoken Word" is now released worldwide to over fifteen hundred radio, television, and cable stations. Additionally, the choir has toured internationally, performed at presidential inaugurations, created award-winning recordings, and been involved in major motion pictures, television specials, and satellite broadcasts.

Members, including some husband-and-wife combinations and some families who have participated for two or more generations, represent a large cross section of occupations. These dedicated individuals follow the legacy of music that the early settlers brought with them. Holding an exalted place in their repertoire is William Clayton's "Come, Come, Ye Saints," written at Locust Creek, Iowa, on April 13, 1846, as the pioneers made their way westward. The hymn includes the lines:

And should we die before our
    journey's through,
Happy day? All is well!

**The
Trail
Today**

The Mormon Pioneer National Historic Trail (MPNHT) covers 1,300 miles, including 1 mile in Illinois, 268 miles in Iowa, 494 miles in Nebraska, 466 miles in Wyoming, and 71 miles in Utah. The cross-country route begins in west-central Illinois at the Nauvoo National Historic District, where the Mormon pioneers launched their original exodus from the east bank of the Mississippi. In Iowa, the trail leaves Montrose Landing, crossing a terrain that includes rolling hills, river bottoms such as those of the Des Moines and Missouri Rivers, wooded areas, and level lands. Memorial markers commemorate the emigration, although croplands and highways have removed all but a few traces of the original Mormon Trail. Council Bluffs later became the Mormon departure point.

In Nebraska, Mormon influence is still seen in Winter Quarters, now Florence, a suburb of Omaha. Throughout the state, the route traverses the river valleys and adjacent lands of the Loup, Platte, and North Platte Rivers. Much of the eastern segment includes urban development, farmlands, and highway and railroad systems that have destroyed the original trail. These level lands, often monotonous to the pioneers, received considerable comment in their diaries. The eroded range of the sand hills in the west and the impressive landmarks of Indian Lookout Point and Ancient Bluff Ruins offered relief from the level landscape. Other noted landmarks, more closely related to the Oregon Trail, include Courthouse Rock, Chimney Rock, and Scotts Bluff. In western Nebraska, there are places where the route traverses rolling rangeland that appears much as it did in pioneer times.

The trail crosses to the south side of the North Platte River in Wyoming and almost immediately passes a corner of Fort Laramie National Historic Site. From there to Fort Bridger, it follows the same route as the Oregon National Historic Trail. The topography is rough and broken uplands. Wagon ruts etched several feet in sandstone are found near Guernsey. In the eastern section, the vegetation is principally sagebrush and juniper, and the area is largely roadless. The trail recrosses the North Platte River near Casper and traverses a cross-country route over hilly rangeland to Independence Rock. This landscape is largely what it was during emigrant travel. The trail then funnels westward along the Sweetwater River, where rolling hills and grasslands with distant mountain vistas provide interest and variety. At South Pass, the trail crosses the Continental Divide, entering the Pacific slope region where it follows broken sagebrush to Fort Bridger. The route continues westerly over the Bear River divide and exits Wyoming southwest of Evanston.

The Utah portion follows beside I-80 down Echo Canyon, then crosses the Weber River and runs westerly through the various hollows, canyons, and summits of the Wasatch Mountains. From the mouth of Emigration Canyon, a bike trail leads to the first campsite. The MPNHT terminates at the This is the Place Park on the eastern edge of Salt Lake City. Each of the pioneer campsites through the Wasatch Range is marked by the state or by private interests.

Sixty-four percent (822 miles) of land ownership along the trail is in private hands, 20 percent (264 miles) is under federal management, and 16 percent (214 miles) is held by state and local agencies. Though much of the trail is no longer visible, there are trail segments that can be visited, and long stretches in Nebraska and Wyoming offer excellent recreation opportunities—wagon trains, horseback rides, or hikes beside the trail. An auto route is clearly marked, but sites on private land should not be visited without the owner's permission.

Mormons and others gathered in Nauvoo in June 1996 for the sesquicentennial commemoration of the Mormon exodus. In the same manner as their pioneers, they walked, rode wagons and horses, and pulled handcarts to their destination just outside of Omaha. The event continued the next year as nearly seven thousand people took turns retracing portions of the second part of the journey. Starting on April 17, the group arrived at This Is the Place Park, the official end of the Mormon Pioneer National Historic Trail in Salt Lake City on June 22, 1997, 150 years after the first Mormons had arrived. For many Mormons the event expressed the continuance of their faith. Speaking so well for so many, Mike Otterson, director of public relations for the Church of Jesus Christ of Latter-day Saints, said, "That experience—when people are in the same location and going through the experience [of their ancestors]—is something they will never forget. This will be a life-changing experience." And so it is as well for many who enjoy our national historic trails.

Points of Interest

ILLINOIS

1. **NAUVOO.** Nauvoo Landing, adjacent to the Nauvoo NH District, was the original jumping-off point. The ferry landing is marked by a monument and plaque, and the Mississippi River provides a major natural feature. Many of the Mormon dwellings in Nauvoo have been restored, including the homes of Joseph Smith and Brigham Young. Carriage rides are provided through Old Nauvoo, where skilled artisans give demonstrations. Two visitor centers offer interpretation. *City of Joseph,* an outdoor musical, is presented in early August, and a grape festival is held on Labor Day weekend.

IOWA

2. **MONTROSE LANDING.** The landing point on the western shore of the Mississippi is commemorated with a bronze marker and a wayside exhibit. This was also the site of Fort Des Moines (1834–37). After their 1838–39 expulsion from Missouri, some Mormons temporarily lived in

the abandoned fort. The first camp, Sugar Creek, now farmland, was located five miles west of Montrose. *Nearby:* Burlington was selected by Zebulon Pike for a government fort (1805), and later a fur-trading post was established. The area was first known as the Flint Hills community (LCNHT). The Heritage Hill Historic District displays a variety of architecture, and Snake Alley is called the crookedest street in the world.

3. DES MOINES RIVER CROSSING. This is the site of the pioneers' first major river crossing west of the Mississippi (March 5, 1846). The area has other historical interests, including ruins of an old mill and river locks. *Nearby:* In Bonaparte, the Van Buren County Historical Museum.

4. LACEY-KEOSAUQUA STATE PARK. The park south of Keosauqua contains the site of a Mormon river crossing at Ely's Ford, and portions of the park are set aside as a wildlife refuge. *Nearby:* Milton, the approximate location of the first blessing of a sick animal to restore its health.

5. CHARITON RIVER CROSSING. Near Centerville, the Mormon pioneers were reorganized into companies of one hundred families, which were then subdivided into groups of fifty and ten. *Nearby:* William Clayton wrote the now-famous Mormon hymn "Come, Come, Ye Saints" (April 13, 1846), on Locust Creek near Seymour.

6. WAYNE COUNTY PIONEER TRAILS MUSEUM. Exhibits of

MPNHT and an authentic oxen-drawn wagon are found at the museum in Corydon. *Nearby:* To the southwest, near Allerton, the original Mormon Trail runs through Bob White SP.

7. GARDEN GROVE. The grove is historically known as the first place of permanent habitation in Pottawattamie Indian lands. The Mormons and the Pottawattamie formed a friendship, as both groups had been driven from their homelands. The park to the west of town interprets the way station's development and use to 1852.

8. MOUNT PISGAH. A way station (until 1852) is interpreted at a county park northeast of Talmage, between the towns of Thayer and Afton. *Nearby:* Creston SP; Green Valley SP.

9. MORMON TRAIL PARK. This park commemorating the trail lies east of Bridgewater.

10. COLD SPRINGS STATE PARK. South of Lewis, traces of the Mormon Trail are seen at the state park, which offers camping, picnicking, hiking, water and winter activities.

11. COUNCIL BLUFFS (KANESVILLE). The staging point for Mormon pioneers en route to the Rocky Mountains was Kanesville (LCNHT). Sites include the Grand Encampment, Mormon Battalion Mustering Grounds, Middle Mormon Ferry, Council Point, Emigrants Landing, and the Reconstructed Kanesville Tabernacle. Kanesville was renamed Council Bluffs after the Mormon departure. *Other attrac-*

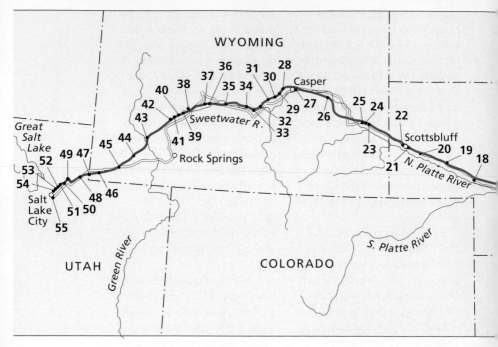

tions: The Historic General Dodge House; the Historic Pottawattamie County Jail; the Railroad Museum with an HO-scale model railroad; the Wabash Trace Nature Trail (LCNHT). *Nearby:* Lake Manawa SP.

NEBRASKA

12. **WINTER QUARTERS.** At this Mormon community, today a part of Omaha, the Mormon pioneers prepared for travel (1847). Huddled in drafty cabins and tents, they seldom had enough fuel or food. Over six hundred died before spring. Winter Quarters Historic Mormon Pioneers Monument and Cemetery contains a monument, the Mormon Trail Center, and a replica of a log cabin, handcart, and covered

wagon. The Mormon Mill is one of the oldest structures in the area. The MPNHT joins with the LCNHT at Florence, the oldest city in Nebraska. *Other attractions:* In Omaha, the Heartland of America Fountain and Park; the Joslyn Art Museum; the General Crook House Museum; the Union Pacific Museum; the Henry Doorly Zoo. Other interesting sites include Boys Town; the USS *Hazard* and USS *Marlin* at Freedom Park; the Omaha Playhouse; St. Cecilia's Cathedral; President Ford's Birthsite and Gardens; the Old Market Area. *Nearby:* Standing Bear and Glenn Cunningham Lakes; Trailwood Ski Area for downhill and horseback riding.

13. **CROSSING OF THE ELK-**

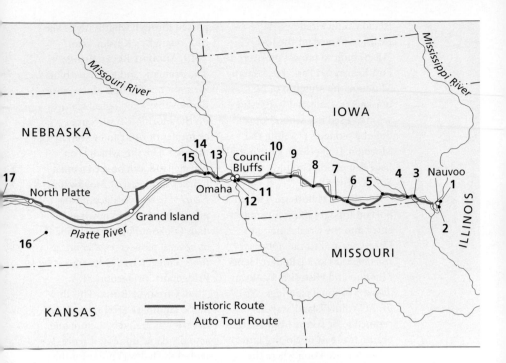

Historic Route
Auto Tour Route

HORN RIVER. The first major crossing west of the Missouri River is thought to be just south of Highway 36, west of Winter Quarters.

14. **LIBERTY POLE CAMP.** A monument in Barnard Park recognizes the camp where the Mormon pioneers organized in semi-military manner (April 17, 1847) in the pattern of Moses and the children of Israel. The actual crossing site and a reproduction pole are located at a former bend in the river near State Lakes Avenue, just west of Fremont (named for Gen. John C. Frémont) on the road to Fremont Lakes SRA. A new wayside exhibit is planned for the site. *Other attractions:* The Fremont & Elkhorn Valley Railroad crosses

the Mormon Trail at Fremont.

15. **FREMONT LAKES STATE RECREATION AREA.** Located along the MPNHT west of Fremont, the SRA offers camping, picnicking, hiking, water and winter activities. *Nearby:* Lake Babcock Reservoir outside Columbus; the Fullerton area, where a way station was burned by the Sioux (1846) and the Loup River was forded (April 24, 1847); northeast of Palmer, the Upper Loup was forded (April 24, 1847); northeast of Palmer, the Upper Loup was forded by later Mormon pioneers trains, but this crossing was avoided by other pioneers because of a Pawnee village in the area. At Grand Island, the Stuhr Museum of the Prairie Pioneer and Mormon

Island Crane Meadows. At Kearney, named for the fort (1848) built to protect pioneers, Fort Kearny SH Park, Fort Kearny Museum, the Museum of Nebraska Art, Trails and Rails Museum housed in a schoolhouse built by pioneers traveling the Mormon Trail (1871), Cottonmill Lake Recreation Grounds and Fort Kearny SRA.

16. **100TH MERIDIAN.** The important topographic point marks entry into the Great American Desert, west of Cozad. *Other attractions:* At Cozad, Robert Henri Museum and Historical Walkway displays original paintings. *Nearby:* At Willow Island, wagons camped to be secure from a large prairie fire; east of North Platte is Confluence Point where the north and south forks of the river join; Johnson and Midway Lakes; Elwood and Jeffrey Reservoirs.

17. **FAMOUS ODOMETER START.** At Paxton, the "roadometer," to be attached to a wagon wheel and used to accurately measure and mark the trail, was completed. *Nearby:* Good examples of ruts are found northeast of Sutherland, one of few points the Mormon pioneers had to leave the river to go around hills; Maloney and Sutherland Reservoirs.

18. **ASH HOLLOW STATE HISTORIC PARK.** The hollow, on the south side of the North Platte River, east of Lewellen, where the Oregon Trail struck the river, was a landmark and a source of wood. The Mormon pioneers used the location to determine their position. *Nearby:* The Mormon Trail

passed through what is now Lake McConaughy's Kinsley Dam.

19. **ANCIENT BLUFF RUINS.** The dramatic and extensive bluff formation is the first of the North Platte Valley's geological features on the Mormon Trail. Some examples of ruts can be seen in the area. The site, which is on private land, can be seen from a marker southeast of Broadwater. *Nearby:* East of Bridgeport, the prominent feature known as Indian Lookout Point was climbed by several pioneers. *Other attractions:* Pioneer Trails Museum at Bridgeport; Bridgeport SRA.

20. **CHIMNEY ROCK.** This dramatic landmark (NHS) south of Bayard was seen days before one actually came upon it; it represented the halfway point for the Mormons. From the visitor center there is a short hike to the rock, which is illuminated at dusk. Courthouse and Jailhouse Rocks could be seen from here by the Mormons. *Other attractions:* Oregon Trail Wagon Train offers trips from Bayard to Chimney Rock and a short tour of the trail.

21. **REBECCA WINTERS GRAVE.** One of the few known graves of the nearly six thousand Mormon pioneers who died crossing the plains, this one marks the final resting place of Rebecca Winters who died of cholera in 1852. The grave is located along U.S. Highway 26 at a pullout with a state historic marker three miles east of Scottsbluff.

22. **SCOTTS BLUFF NATIONAL MONUMENT.** This NPS site southwest of Scottsbluff served as a

landmark for all western travelers. Today it offers hiking and bicycle trails, an auto road to the summit, a visitor center, a museum, and interpretation. *Nearby:* To the south, in Gering, the North Platte Valley Museum; to the north, the North Platte NWR. On a ridge two miles east of Henry is the Prayer Circle, thought to be the site of a special service called by Brigham Young for his followers to rededicate themselves to their faith.

WYOMING

23. FORT LARAMIE NATIONAL HISTORIC SITE. The fur-trading post, the second trading post in the Rocky Mountain area built by the American Fur Company (1841), was purchased by the U.S. government (1849) to aid migrations. Called "The Fort on the Laramie," it was a popular resting place for all emigrants. The NPS offers interpretation, a museum, and living-history demonstrations at the restored site. The center also offers a map to the Old Bedlam ruts, where wagons bound for Utah, California, and Oregon converged. The ruts are on private land.

24. MEXICAN HILL. This steep, dramatic cut through the river bluff still shows signs of trail ruts.

25. REGISTER CLIFF STATE HISTORIC SITE. Southeast of Guernsey is a prominent limestone cliff that still bears the marks of emigrants who carved their names and dates. The site offers interpretation. *Other attractions:* In Guernsey, a visitor cen-

ter, the Guernsey SP Museum; Oregon Trail Ruts SHS. *Nearby:* Guernsey Reservoir offers camping, picnicking, hiking, horseback riding, boating, and a museum; Glendo Reservoir and SP.

26. AYRES NATURAL BRIDGE. In 1847, some Mormon pioneers visited and described this famous stone arch west of Douglas, formed as the river cut through a high rocky bluff. *Other attractions:* In Douglas, the Wyoming Pioneer Memorial Museum and to the northwest, the restored Fort Fetterman SHS (1867). *Nearby:* La Prele Reservoir.

27. FORT CASPAR MUSEUM / MORMON FERRY. The Mormon pioneers built (1847) and operated a ferry across the Platte River for money and provisions. The Fort Caspar Museum has a replica of the original Mormon Ferry at Mills. *Nearby:* Casper began as a ferry site instigated by the Mormon pioneers. In the 1850s a toll bridge, which required military protection, was built. *Other attractions:* In Casper, Historic Trails Expeditions follow the Mormon Trail in wagons; Tate Mineralogical and Werner Wildlife Museums. West of Powder River, examples of unusual topography are found in Hell's Half Acre.

28. EMIGRANT GAP. West of Casper emigrants passed through this shallow gap in the hills as they left the North Platte River Valley to begin their ascent into the Rocky Mountains.

29. AVENUE OF ROCKS (ALSO KNOWN AS THE DEVIL'S BACKBONE). Also west of Casper is the

prominent feature mentioned by the Mormon pioneers as the place where the trail passed between high rocks that formed a gateway or avenue. Construction of the Oregon Trail Road has impacted the site.

30. **WILLOW SPRINGS.** North of Alcova, the emigrants found the first good, clear, cool water they had encountered since leaving the North Platte River. The popular camping spot can be seen from the Oregon Trail Road.

31. **PROSPECT (RYAN) HILL.** Visible ruts run up the east slope here. From the top of the hill the view that greeted the Mormon pioneers (June 20, 1847) would have been similar to the view today. *Other attractions:* Pathfinder Reservoir is one of the oldest projects built by the Bureau of Reclamation; the USFWS administers Pathfinder NWR on part of the reservoir; the MPNHT crosses the northwest side of the refuge.

32. **INDEPENDENCE ROCK STATE HISTORICAL SITE.** West of Alcova is the major landmark on the Sweetwater River called, "the Great Register of the Desert." An estimated five thousand names were carved on the granite boulder by explorers, trappers, missionaries, soldiers, and emigrants.

33. **DEVIL'S GATE/MARTIN'S COVE.** The landmark was the site often used as an emigrant campground and later as a mail relay, transcontinental telegraph, and mule pack-train station. Martin's Cove is the rescue site of the Martin Handcart Company. Per-

mission is needed to cross private land to reach the site on the BLM land, and four-wheel drive vehicles are recommended. The Mormons maintain a visitor center that serves as a major interpretive site.

34. **SPLIT ROCK.** The cleft in the top of Sweetwater Rocks became a landmark used by Indians, trappers, and emigrants. Trail ruts are still evident. A BLM exhibit interprets the site.

35. **ICE SLOUGH.** West of Three Forks, pure ice could be obtained by digging below the spring.

36. **ROCKY RIDGE.** Here the trail left the gentle landscape of the Sweetwater River floodplain to move up into a rocky area that was difficult to cross.

37. **WILLIE'S HANDCART DISASTER SITE.** The rescue site at the base of Rocky Ridge is on BLM land. High-clearance vehicles are recommended. A stone marker with bronze plaque (dated June 23, 1933) was installed by the Utah Pioneer Trails and Landmark Association to mark the site of the disaster.

38. **SOUTH PASS.** Near South Pass City pioneers crossed the Continental Divide through South Pass (NHL), the second-highest point (7,550 feet) along the trail, called "the Cumberland Gap of the Far West." *Other attractions:* South Pass City SHS has a visitor center, interpretive displays, and restored mining-era buildings; Trails West offers excellent wagon excursions to many of the Mormon pioneer trail sites in

the area. *Nearby:* At Burnt Ranch, the Mormon Mail Station became an important place for communicating with the Mormon community at Salt Lake City.

39. **PACIFIC SPRINGS.** This was the first water the pioneers encountered upon arriving on the Pacific slope. An important stopping place for later emigrant trains, it served as a Mormon station. A visit to the site requires the private owner's written permission in advance.

40. **PARTING OF THE WAYS/ SUBLETTE CUTOFF.** This marks the fork in the route where emigrants continuing to Oregon could take the Sublette Cutoff, a shortcut across the Little Colorado Desert to Bear River, or continue on the main route of the Oregon-California-Mormon Trails. The Sublette Cutoff (aka the Greenwood Cutoff) was a waterless track of fifty miles that did not become popular until the gold-rush days.

41. **DRY SANDY.** Water pits, where pioneers had to dig deep holes for potable water, are still visible at the site where the river flowed belowground. The wet, boggy sands of the area were difficult to cross in wagons, which often got stuck.

42. **LITTLE SANDY STATION.** The Mormon pioneers camped on the banks of Little Sandy Creek where they met Jim Bridger (June 28, 1847), who gave them advice on the route ahead and his opinions concerning lands suitable for settlement. He warned them that the valley of

the Great Salt Lake was an arid desert, and reportedly said, "I would give a thousand dollars to know if corn could be grown in that valley." *Nearby:* Big Sandy RA: Eden Valley and Big Sandy Reservoirs.

43. **LOMBARD FERRY.** Mormon pioneers built rafts and floated wagons across the Green River, where they later built a ferry (1847) and provided a commercial service, adjacent now to the U.S. Highway 28 bridge. *Nearby:* Seedskadee NWR; Rock Springs, the point of departure for viewing many of the region's geological wonders.

44. **CHURCH BUTTE (SOLOMON TEMPLE).** Northeast of Lyman, this large sandy butte was a prominent landmark (ONHT, CNHT) because of its shape. It is possible that services were held here. *Other attractions:* Lyman hosts Bridger Valley Pioneer Days in July.

45. **FORT BRIDGER/BRIDGER TRADING POST.** One of three settlements on the Mormon Trail at the time of their journey, the trading post later served as a military post. The Mormons bought it (1855) to supply emigrants. Before they bought Fort Bridger, they built Fort Supply twelve miles south of the trading post. They burned both forts after friction developed with the U.S. government two years later. Only a portion of a wall built by the Mormons remains, but some of the buildings constructed during army occupation (1858–90) still stand. The SHS offers a museum

with exhibits about the trail. Fort Bridger hosts Fort Bridger Rendezvous on Labor Day weekend.

46. BEAR RIVER CROSSING. This was the last major river crossing in Wyoming and the highest point (7,756 feet) on the trail. An oil spring in the area was used to lubricate the wagons. The site can be seen from the U.S. Highway 89 bridge northwest of Evanston.

47. THE NEEDLES. Southwest of Evanston on Coyote Creek is the formation (7,600 feet) and landmark on the Wyoming-Utah border where Young came down with a violent attack of what was suspected to be mountain fever. *Nearby:* Woodruff Narrows Reservoir.

UTAH

48. ECHO CANYON. The pioneers passed through the sixteen-mile-long narrow gorge, possibly named by Jim Bridger for its peculiar echo.

49. WEBER RIVER CROSSING. This site, seen from I-80, represents the only major river crossing in Utah. Trail ruts are found in the vicinity, south of Henefer. *Nearby:* East Canyon SP.

50. HOGSBACK SUMMIT. From this summit, the emigrants saw the mountains that they still had to cross; some faint ruts are seen in the area.

51. LITTLE EMIGRATION CANYON. The canyon, connecting Mormon Flats with Big Mountain Pass, offers 4½ miles of hiking in a pristine portion of the MPHNT.

52. BIG MOUNTAIN PASS. Northeast of Salt Lake City, the third-highest point (7,420 feet) on the trail gave the Mormon pioneers their first look at the valley of the Great Salt Lake. The Donner party blazed the original trail through this area (1846), taking fifteen days. A year later, the Mormons passed through in only six days. *Nearby:* Wasatch NF.

53. LITTLE MOUNTAIN SUMMIT/EMIGRATION CANYON/LAST CAMP. The last summit (6,227 feet) served as an entry point to Emigration Canyon and provided some of the most difficult terrain of the entire journey. A final camp was generally made here.

54. DONNER HILL. Here the Donner-Reed party (1846) faced the time-consuming climb out of Emigration Canyon. The 1847 Mormon party found an easier route to the valley, chipping away at the rock and clearing brush and willows until they could get through the canyon bottom without climbing the hill northeast of Salt Lake.

55. THIS IS THE PLACE STATE PARK. Located at the mouth of Emigration Canyon, the park has a large monument honoring the Mormon pioneers and other historic figures from Utah's past. The SP at the end of the Mormon Trail has a visitor center and Old Desert Village, a living-history museum. *Other attractions:* In Salt Lake City, Temple Square with visitor centers; Salt Lake Temple (1853–93); Joseph Smith Memorial Building with a film about the early church and Mormon pioneers; Assembly Hall; the Tabernacle with choir rehearsals and broadcasts open to the public; Pioneer Log Cabin; Museum of Church History and Art; Family History Library; Social Hall Heritage Museum; Brigham Young Monument; Beehive House (NHL), the official residence of Young when he was president of the church and governor of the territory; Lion House, living quarters for Young's many wives; Brigham Young Cemetery and Memorial; Church Administration Building; Church Office Building; Pioneer Memorial Museum; Promised Valley Playhouse; Salt Palace Civic Auditorium; Fort Douglas (1862) with a museum; International Peace Gardens; Hansen Planetarium. *Nearby:* At the Great Salt Lake, a bird-watcher's paradise; in Brigham City, the Golden Spike NHS with trail, auto tour, and visitor center interpreting the completion of the transcontinental railroad.

PONY EXPRESS– OREGON POST

Vast expanses of open land met the pioneers near this intersection of the Pony Express and the Oregon Trails. Today BLM land offers countless recreational opportunities along the trails.

Pony Express

National

Historic Trail

Few enterprises have captured the imagination of the country as has the Overland Pony Express. With the railroad and the telegraph reaching no farther west than St. Joseph, Missouri, the extension of communications to the west coast by the Pony Express became a communications revolution. Initiated by the freighting firm of Russell, Majors & Waddell, the Pony Express made its debut on April 3, 1860. While carrying a twenty-pound mail pouch, lightning-fast riders crossed the Great Plains, the Rocky Mountains, the Great Basin, and the Sierra Nevada to provide ten-day mail service between St. Joseph and Sacramento. Relay stations with stationmasters and attendants afforded riders the opportunity to change mounts every ten to fifteen miles along the way. After every seventy-five to one hundred miles, the rider exchanged his mail pouch in two minutes or less with a fresh new rider, who thundered away to the next station and into American legend.

ADMINISTERING AGENCY
National Park Service
Long Distance Trails Office
P.O. Box 45155
324 South State Street, Suite 250
Salt Lake City, UT 84145-0155
801-539-4095

FURTHER INFORMATION
National Pony Express Association
P.O. Box 236
Pollock Pines, CA 95726

ESTABLISHED
1992

APPROXIMATE MILEAGE
1,966 miles (3,145 kilometers)

STATES
Missouri, Kansas, Nebraska, Colorado, Wyoming, Utah, Nevada, California

The Pony Express emerged at a time when the populations of the country in the East and the West clamored for a closer connection.* Events in the West during the prior decade had ushered in major changes, which brought significant population growth. With the signing of the Treaty of Guadalupe Hidalgo on February 2, 1848, the land in California became part of the territory of the United States. Two years later, with an estimated population of 92,500, California became the nation's thirty-first state. In the meantime, in Oregon the settlers had secured ownership rights, and after negotiations with Great Britain, a territorial government was created in 1849. Then, in 1852, Oregon became the country's thirty-third state. By 1860, the year the Pony Express began, California's population had burgeoned to an estimated 380,000, and over a half million individuals populated the vast wilderness west of the Rockies.

As the gold strikes played out, the nation's attention returned to politics and the issue of slavery. Experiencing booms and busts, California was left to deal with its own problems, and some politicians grew concerned that isolation could foster separatist tendencies in the state. Yet all the while California's citizens were clamoring for news and letters that would connect them to the

*Material in this section is taken from the National Park Service's *California and Pony Express Trails Eligibility/ Feasibility Study.*

land of their origin and demanding eastern merchandise and transportation to the East. The answer seemed to lie in government-subsidized mail contracts for stagecoach operators to supply western settlers and military contracts for freighters to supply the western army posts.

Earlier, in 1848, a contract had been offered to James Brown of Independence to deliver goods on the Santa Fe Trail. A partnership between Brown and a risk-taker, William H. Russell, eventually came to have a profound effect on the nation's history. Brown's sudden death on the trail in 1850 brought about a new partnership between Russell and the conservative William B. Waddell. In 1854 Russell and Waddell teamed with the intensely moral plainsman Alexander Majors to form the prosperous freighting firm of Russell, Majors & Waddell. Eventually this firm would monopolize overland freighting.

It is said that that same year, Benjamin F. Ficklin, later to become the firm's general superintendent, proposed the idea of a pony express mail service to a senator from California, William M. Gwin. Enthusiastic about the idea, Gwin introduced it as a bill in the U.S. Senate the next year, but to his disappointment, the bill was tabled and died. The next year, Californians sent a petition to Congress to strengthen their case for faster mail service. Though mail delivery to California had been government-subsidized since 1849, it traveled from

New York by ocean via Panama, and from Panama up the coast by steamship. Save for periodic desertions by crew members who caught the gold fever, the service was regular but slow. Letters were dated and news was old by the time the mail reached its destination. In the meantime, overland service by pack animal had proved irregular as well as slow.

Congress was willing to subsidize a stagecoach service that would build stations along the route to California so that the mail could be relayed by fresh drivers and teams of horses. Northerners backed a central route through South Pass, while southerners supported a southern route through El Paso and Fort Yuma. Finding no compromise, Congress fashioned a bill that authorized the postmaster general, Aaron V. Brown, to accept bids and make decisions. Brown, a southerner from Tennessee, liked John Butterfield's proposal. The founder of the American Express Company and one of the East's leading stagecoachers, Butterfield suggested a route through Albuquerque, but he also indicated his readiness to accept modifications. In 1857 the route was arranged to start from St. Louis, Missouri, as well as from Memphis, Tennessee, converging in Little Rock, before moving west near Preston, Texas, across the Rio Grande near El Paso, on to Fort Yuma, and then to Los Angeles and San Francisco. Brown defended his "oxbow route" (as it was derogatorily

called by outraged northerners) as the only all-year route. (The weather along the alternative central route continued to be a major deterrent in the minds of those who recalled the well-known experience of the Donner party.) With Brown's reference to the weather advantages of the southern trail, outrage over the oxbow route turned to a disgruntled grumble. Thus, on September 16, 1858, the Butterfield Overland Mail was launched with Butterfield's command, "Remember, boys, nothing on God's earth must stop the United States mail!"

Northerners, however, still had the faster central route in mind. With the possibility of a civil war looming, a quicker mail service west was needed. The death of Postmaster Brown in 1859 served as a catalyst for change. The enterprising Russell, despite warnings from his partners, tried to fill the void without a government subsidy. With John S. Jones, he established the Leavenworth and Pike's Peak Express Company and borrowed money to build stations and to buy coaches and mules. To build his business further, he bought the John M. Hockaday stage line that controlled the route to Salt Lake City. Without a subsidy, however, Russell soon faced bankruptcy. Knowing his fall would mean an end of their freighting firm, Waddell and Majors were forced to step in. Taking over the stagecoach company, they entered competition for a government

PATEE HOUSE

The Patee House, one of the finest hotels west of the Mississippi, served as headquarters for the Pony Express in St. Joseph, Missouri. Today, the Patee House Museum contains a re-created Pony Express office and numerous Pony Express items, including a saddle and a mochila.

subsidy. Reorganized as the Central Overland, California & Pike's Peak Express (COC&PPE) Company, they secured a contract from the government to carry mail between Salt Lake City and Placerville, California. The partners soon found themselves responding to Russell's promise to Senator Gwin that they would establish a Pony Express all the way from Missouri to California. Senator Gwin, in the meantime, promised to use his influence with Congress to get a subsidy to help pay the expenses of such a line. But this was all to no avail.

From the announcement of the formation of the COC&PPE Company on January 27, 1860, Russell, Majors, and Waddell had approximately sixty days to organize riders along the route from both California and Missouri. To set the project in motion, they had to select a logical and viable route. The company moved its headquarters from Leavenworth, Kansas, to the Patee House in St. Joseph, Missouri. This became the eastern terminus of the Pony Express, and the B. F. Hastings Building in Sacramento, California was designated as the western terminus. From there, the mail would be carried by boat down the Sacramento River to San Francisco. The mail would be carried around the clock in both directions, with departures once each week from each end. The line was organized into five divisions, each with its own superintendent; a general superintendent oversaw the whole operation. Each station agent was to supply efficient local operations. For this to happen, the agents had to depend heavily on their superintendents to maintain and supply the line.

Few records of the Pony Express survive, and those that remain are short on details. Accounts differ with regard to the actual number of stations built or used, but it seems safe to assume that over 150 were connected with the Pony Express. It has been suggested that station keepers and stock tenders were employed at all stations, with two at those used exclusively by the Pony Express while four to six others were employed at the stations also used by stagecoaches.

Beyond Salt Lake City, where the route departed from the existing stage and freight lines, new stations had to be constructed. A shortage of timber in parts of the Great Basin, particularly in western Utah and Nevada, demanded that stations be made of adobe brick or stone. In some instances, dugouts and tents served as temporary shelters. On the eastern segment of the trail, many of the stations, originally part of the company's overland stage stops, were spaced twenty to twenty-five miles apart. Later, additional stations were built in between at ten- to fifteen-mile intervals. The distance between the stations was based on how far a horse could travel at the fastest sustainable speed over a given terrain before a change was needed. For the entire distance, the average speed was 250 miles in a twenty-four-hour period, or 10.4 miles per hour. Each rider changed horses at relay or remount stations and covered from seventy-five to one hundred miles before reaching a home station, where he was relieved by another rider. At the home station, a rider could rest before returning in the other direction.

Crossing the country by stagecoach in 1860, Sir Richard Burton, an English writer and explorer, commented on the countryside and the stations, which varied greatly. The Three Crossings Station on the Sweetwater, for example, was known for its service. The clean, well-decorated station, Burton said, had the best-tasting coffee outside New Orleans. The Rocky Ridge Station, on the other hand, was described as especially unclean. The bunks swarmed with bedbugs, and the food was so atrocious as to cause a stomachache.

Proper care of the ponies and stagecoach mules was a must, however. This made the station keepers just as important as the riders, but attention to them never really developed. Joseph Alfred ("Jack") Slade, who kept stations at Sand Hill and Big Muddy and was boss to William "Buffalo Bill" Cody, did gain a respectable amount of attention. Reputed to have killed twenty-six people, Slade, as division chief, was called upon to evict station keeper Jules Reni, who refused to vacate after being fired. Reni had been accused of consorting with renegades who seemed to know

SPLIT ROCK

BLM signs at this interpretive site in Wyoming point out the famous natural cleft at the top of the Rattlesnake Range that was used as a guide by American Indians, trappers, pioneers, and Pony Express riders. William C. "Buffalo Bill" Cody exchanged horses at the Split Rock Station during his record 322-mile ride.

Horses were used according to the region of the country and the terrain. The route from St. Joseph, Missouri, to Fort Kearny, Nebraska, was considered relatively easy, but from there to Salt Lake City the route became increasingly more difficult. Also difficult was the route between Salt Lake and Sacramento, which the company was forced to blaze almost from scratch. Gray mares were used along the eastern division, western or Indian ponies were distributed across most of the central route from Fort Laramie to Carson City, and half-breed California mustangs were used in the West.

The riders used a unique jockey-type saddle, weighing less than thirteen pounds. The leather seat with saddle horn and cantle provided a soft cushion for comfort while riding long distances. Thrown over the saddle, with openings for the horn and cantle, was a rectangular leather blanket called a "mochila," or mail pouch. Four locking cantinas, hard leather pockets, were sewn to the mochila and lined with oilskin to protect the mail from the sweat of the horse and rain or snow. Only the rider's weight held the mochila on the horse, so it could be whisked off in seconds when he changed ponies. Three of the cantina pockets contained "through mail" and were locked during the entire trip. "Local mail" was placed in the fourth packet and deliveries were made en route. Upon arrival at the relay stations, Pony Express riders were

when to hold up a stagecoach. When Slade came to call on him, Reni made the mistake of shooting at him from behind a door. An aggravated Slade filled Reni full of lead from the extremities inward. Finally, as a warning to others who might be thinking about misbehaving, he cut off Reni's ears, nailing one to a corral post. Mark Twain gives Slade several pages in his book *Roughing It,* and Julesburg, Colorado, was named for Jules Reni.

The Pony Express Company bought over five hundred of the best horses available. They were selected for speed and endurance at a cost of $150 to $200 each. For a one-way trip, approximately seventy-five mounts were needed.

allowed two minutes to switch the mochila and themselves from one horse to another. But the exchange was often made in an unbroken stride, without the rider's feet ever touching the ground, and hence in far less time than the required minimum.

The riders were the heroes. Originally forty riders were needed to cover each direction. Young and fearless, they were accustomed to outdoor life and able to endure hardships. Orphans were said to be preferred because the venture was so risky. There is, however, some question about this preference, which may have developed later—possibly as late as the 1940s—for publicity purposes. Riders included men and boys of several ethnic backgrounds, and Mormons composed the majority of the riders who handled the runs between Horseshoe Creek near Fort Laramie and Roberts Creek west of Salt Lake City. In the interest of speed, it was imperative that each rider weigh no more than 120 pounds. Upon qualifying, every rider took an oath not to use profane language, drink intoxicating liquors, or fight with other employees. After being sworn and signed, the rider was issued a small Bible to sustain his courage during rides through potentially dangerous country.

In addition to receiving a monthly salary of $50 to $150 (rates varied according to the number of rides and dangers encountered) plus bonuses, each rider was housed and fed at company expense. Wearing a bright red shirt and blue pants, he rode ten to twelve miles before changing horses. He could carry a light rifle and Colt revolver for protection and a small brass horn to signal his coming—until it was discovered that hoofbeats did the same thing. With a fanatical devotion to duty, riders rode through snowdrifts in below-zero blizzard, icy floods, murderous heat, bandits, and hostile Indians. Their adventures, magnified to extraordinary proportions, are retold today in books, movies, and television dramas.

The operation was ready to begin in record time; administrative offices were established in New York, Washington, Chicago, and St. Louis to forward mail to St. Joseph. The letters, generally written on thin tissue paper, were carried at $5 a half ounce (later reduced $1 an ounce), with an additional charge of 10¢ for U.S. postage. Telegraph messages arriving at each terminus were forwarded at a cost of $2.45 per communique. Total weight of the dispatches, both letters and telegraph messages, was not to exceed twenty pounds. Because the paper was so thin, hundreds of letters could by carried "by pony," as it was called. Generally, magazines and newspapers were shipped by stagecoach, although some special editions were printed on tissue paper for delivery by pony.

With offices and rates established, the only thing left was to advertise the route. On March 17,

1860, the first advertisement appeared in the *San Francisco Bulletin*: Pony Express—Nine Days from San Francisco to New York. On March 26, advertisements followed in the *New York Herald* and *Missouri Republican*: To San Francisco in eight Days by the Central Overland California and Pike's Peak Express Co.

On April 3, 1860, the inaugural run began. Crowds gathered to see the riders off with a great deal of fanfare, including cheering, speeches, and ceremony. Slight delays were caused by outside circumstances in both Missouri and California. In the East, letters from Washington, D.C., and New York missed their connection in Detroit, which caused a late start. In the West, a celebratory start in San Francisco sent the first rider off on the steamer *Antelope,* which experienced delays as it carried the mail upriver to Sacramento. Hard rains resulted in a ten-hour delay and thus a night start for the rider waiting in Sacramento.

The first riders from the West raced across a grueling route, facing disagreeable weather, roads that were virtually nonexistent in many places, and some trails that were nearly impassable. Because the ride out of California was delayed three days by blizzards in the Sierra Nevada Mountains, the riders passed each other somewhere outside of Salt Lake City on April 8, rather than near South Pass in Wyoming, as anticipated. Yet the chain of young riders and their hard-pressed

mounts moved ever forward, making up for lost time along the way. The first westbound rider rode into Sacramento after nine days and twenty-three hours, one hour ahead of schedule. The eastbound rider arrived in St. Joseph just minutes short of exactly ten days.

In May and June 1860, just a month after the historic first run, the Pony Express bore the brunt of the Pyramid Lake Indian War. This Paiute uprising was costly in both lives and money. Among the casualties were dozens of station keepers, their assistants, and one express rider. In an attempt to stop the Indian raids, several military-civilian expeditions were launched. One, led by Maj. William Ormsby of Carson City, resulted in the loss of 76 of the 105 volunteers because of an ambush

RIDER STATUE

A monument commemorating the 1,966-mile mail run is found in Old Sacramento, California, just across the street from the B. F. Hastings Building, the western terminus of the Pony Express.

on the morning of May 12. During these two months, and intermittently for weeks to come, two hundred fifty miles of the Pony Express Trail lay in a virtual state of siege as bands of aggressive warriors burned and destroyed numerous stations.

The resulting loss of revenue, and the subsequent expense of resupplying stations and equipments, cost the company an estimated $75,000. By July service resumed, but conditions remained tense. To appease public demand, the Pony Express extended its service to a twice-weekly schedule, leaving Sacramento every Wednesday and Saturday. In deep financial trouble, the company hoped to impress Washington officials with the need to grant a contract subsidy. The strain upon the riders as well as the field staff under this new schedule increased greatly. Despite the strain, records for speed and endurance of the express carriers mounted. Mark Twain observed, "[M]an and horse burst past our excited faces, and go winging away like a belated fragment of a storm."

Even though the Pony Express proved the practicability of the central route, monetary assistance was never provided, and every effort to secure financial support through a government subsidy failed. Unfortunately, the COC&PPE became known as "Clean Out of Cash & Poor Pay Express." To further complicate matters, in December 1860 Russell became involved in an

TWO BOYS ON HORSEBACK

Re-creating the Pony Express experience each June, the National Pony Express Association organizes a ten-day "Re-Run" for a new generation of riders. Carrying express mail, the riders retrace the original trail.

$870,000 bond scandal that sealed the company's doom. Although no one is sure how or why, the Pony Express continued to run on schedule. Only some crucial missing records of the company and its co-owner, Alexander Majors, who ran the operations, could ever answer that question. By late spring and early summer of 1861, telegraph lines were being built from the east and west, coming together at a rate of six miles a day. All the while, the Pony Express continued to carry mail over its full route, while telegrams were carried between the narrowing gap of telegraph termini. On October 26, 1861, coinciding with the completion of the telegraph link, the Pony Express officially terminated. Messages that took eight weeks by ship or eight days by the

Pony Express now took four hours by wire. Swift as the ponies and riders had been, they were not fast enough to keep up with the changing times.

Before its demise, the Pony Express had achieved national prominence, carrying some of the century's most urgent news. President Buchanan's message to Congress in December of 1860 reached the West in eight days; in March 1861 President Lincoln's inaugural address was carried in a record seven days and seventeen hours; and a month later the West Coast learned of the attack on Fort Sumter and kept abreast of the imminent outbreak of the Civil War through the efforts of the Pony Express riders and their support groups. Overseas, French and German publications produced articles and pictures showing Pony Express riders being chased by warriors; London sent a representative from *Illustrated News* to write a cover story on the fascinating couriers; and while England and China were at war, the Pony Express carried official war documents.

In the eighteen months that the Pony Express was in operation, its riders made more than 150 round trips, covering over six hundred thousand miles and transporting nearly thirty-five thousand pieces of mail. With unprecedented speed, they successfully crossed the Great Plains, the Rocky Mountains, the Great Basin, and the Sierra Nevada to provide regular year-round mail service from the Atlantic to the Pacific. Not only had the Central Overland California and Pike's Peak Express Company accomplished its objective of rapidly delivering mail, it had also set a precedent for transportation and communication in the developing West. Following its example, the central overland trail became the route used by the telegraph lines and nine years later by the transcontinental railroad. By fulfilling demands for rapid communication to the West Coast, the Pony Express gave residents a sense of contact with the events and governmental activities in the East, and California stayed firmly with the Union during the Civil War. In the end, the Pony Express became one of the enduring symbols of the American frontier, and the trail became a dramatic page in transportation and communication history.

WILLIAM F. "BUFFALO BILL" CODY

One of the most colorful figures of the Old West was Buffalo Bill Cody, Pony Express rider, Colorado "fifty-niner," Civil War soldier, scout, trapper, bullwhacker, stagecoach driver, guide, wagonmaster, hotel manager, showman, rancher, and promoter. Cody was born to an Iowa farm family on February 26, 1846, but his father soon abandoned the farm to become a stagecoach driver. After moving the family to Salt Creek Valley near Fort Leavenworth, Kansas, the elder Cody, an abolitionist, was forced to flee for his life after being stabbed in the back by a slaveholder. Eight-year-old Cody went on his first adventure, galloping thirty-five miles to warn his father that a mob had heard of his hiding place. His father was saved, though he died a few years later of complications from the wound.

At age eleven, Cody became the family breadwinner. Joining the company of Alexander Majors, he ran dispatches between army supply wagons. On his first long wagon trek west, the wagons were attacked by Mormon zealots who took the horses, forcing young Cody to walk much of the thousand miles back to Kansas, where he apparently met Wild Bill Hickok. At Wyoming's Fort Laramie, he also met famed scouts Jim Bridger and Kit Carson and vowed that he too would become a scout.

Gold fever drew Cody to Denver in 1859, but a year later the penniless boy returned to Kansas and secured a job as a Pony Express rider. Initially, he rode a short route of thirty-five miles, since he was only fourteen years old. When a desperado tried to hold him up, he claimed that he caused his pony to rear so that his front foot struck the man in the head. Then, strapping the would-be thief to his horse, Cody turned him in at the next station. Later, on a run outside of Fort Laramie, Bill Cody made one of the longest recorded Pony Express rides.

Covering for a relief rider who had died, he rode 322 miles in twenty-one hours and forty minutes, using twenty-one horses. (Later accounts claim a shorter distance, though still credit it as quite a feat.) During the record ride, according to his own account, Cody noticed "a little speck of color" on some rocks; it turned out to be the headdress of an Indian. Anticipating an ambush, he ducked behind his pony and swerved off the path. The sudden move may have saved his life, for just at that moment, a shot was fired. When other Indians approached from the front, he pulled his revolver, shot his attackers and scampered off to the next station.

During the Civil War Cody enlisted with the Union Army. He was assigned as bearer of military dispatches at Fort Larned, where one of his first adventures included avoiding an ambush by some Confederates who bore a grudge against him dating back to the time he had saved his father's life. As Cody told it, upon discovering fresh horse tracks he became suspicious but rode quietly on. Suddenly aware of attackers, he turned and shot before any of the Confederates could pull a trigger. Spurring his horse, he got off one more shot before riding on. On his return with answers to the dispatches, there were no signs of the attacking party, but pulling up to an old shanty, Cody found one of the men left alone to die. The man turned out to be someone he had

known in his early years, someone who was supposed to have
been his father's friend. Cody
stayed with him until he died,
whereupon he returned to Fort
Larned.

On March 6, 1866, Cody married Louisa Frederici in St. Louis.
From 1867 to 1868 he worked for
Goddard Brothers, food contractors, as a buffalo hunter. Supply-
ing fresh meat for the railroad
construction camps, he is said to
have killed 4,280 bison, and was
thereafter known as Buffalo Bill.
From 1868 to 1872, he served the
army as a scout, becoming chief
of scouts for the Fifth Cavalry
and winning the Congressional
Medal of Honor. The Fifth's
favorite scout, he was considered
good luck. In 1868 Gen. Philip
Sheridan complimented Cody
for his endurance and courage
after he had carried dispatches
through three hundred miles of
enemy territory in fifty-eight
hours. Cody knew the territory so
well that once, during a blinding
blizzard in southeastern Colorado, he successfully led a relief
column to the starving infantry
under the command of Gen. William Penrose. In a letter of July 3,
1878, Gen. Eugene A. Carr, one-
time field commander of the
Fifth, wrote that Cody's eyesight
was better than a good fieldglass
and that he was the best trailer
Carr had ever known. He was a
perfect judge of distance and of
the lay of the land, the general
said. He never tired and was
always ready to go.

In 1872, Cody was elected to
the lower house of the Nebraska
legislature but declined to serve.
Already popularized by his friend
Colonel Judson ("Ned Buntline"),
who had written—loosely—of
his exploits, he attracted eastern
and European gentry who asked
him to guide them on buffalo
hunts. Cody referred to them as
dudes and to his camps as dude
ranches. When he guided the
Grand Duke Alexis of Russia, it
made national headlines and
brought him even more fame.
Meeting Buntline in New York, he
watched a distorted production
about his life called Buffalo Bill.
Adapting readily to the fame, he
entered the world of high society
dressed in his finest silk clothes
and Western hat. He appeared on
stage playing himself in *Scouts of
the Prairie* (or *Plains,* as it was
sometimes billed) with another
scout, "Texas Jack" Omohundro.
He also played with Wild Bill
Hickok. Their acting was apparently so bad as to almost be good!
At any rate, the theatre was
packed, and Cody continued to
act and to scout.

In 1876 the Sioux War brought
Cody back to the frontier. His
daring exploits were the basis of
countless dimestore novels. So
embellished were his deeds that
his real activities during this time
in his life will never be fully
known. Returning to the stage, he
continued to play to larger and
larger audiences. At the same
time, he formed a partnership
with Maj. Frank North, establishing a large ranch and entering the
cattle business. In 1883, his Wild

West Show was inaugurated in Omaha, with authentic cowboys and Indians portraying the "real West." Annie Oakley was one of his stars, and through the show he became friends with Sitting Bull. Re-creations of Pony Express rides were on the program, which no doubt preserved much of the short-lived operation's glamour. Ten of the show's thirty years of existence were given to tours in Europe; in 1887 Buffalo Bill was the featured attraction at Queen Victoria's Golden Jubilee. At its peak in the late 1890s, the show brought Cody more than a million dollars in profit each year, and one newspaper reported that the show had "out-Barnumed Barnum."

The Wild West Show's phenomenal success was, undoubtedly, founded on the nostalgia for the passing frontier that swept the nation in the late nineteenth century. By the turn of the century, Cody was arguably the most famous man in the world. He used his fame to draw attention to causes that he supported—the rights of American Indians, the rights of women, and conservation of natural resources. As early as 1879, he called for the government to keep its promises to the Indians, saying, "Every Indian outbreak I have ever known has resulted from broken promises and broken treaties by the government." In 1894, when asked if he thought that the majority of women were qualified to vote, he answered that they were "as well qualified as the majority of men."

He also believed that women in the Wild West Show were as skilled and courageous as the men and should be paid equally. He spoke against hidehunters of the 1870s and '80s for slaughtering the buffalo cruelly and recklessly and worked to establish game preserves and limited hunting seasons. Gifford Pinchot, conservationist and head of the U.S. Forest Service under Theodore Roosevelt, applauded him as "not only a fighter, but a seer."

In 1894, Cody acted as guide for the Prof. O. C. Marsh's fossil-hunting expedition to the Big Horn Basin in Wyoming, where he determined he would settle. He bought and developed his famous forty-thousand-acre TE Ranch near Yellowstone National Park. The town he helped to establish and promote was named Cody in his honor.

William Cody died on January 10, 1917, while visiting his sister in Denver. At the time of death, he was almost penniless because of bad investments, loans to friends, and dealings with the crooked owner of the Denver Post, H. H. Tammen, who used him in his later years to attract people to his own show, forcing Cody's Wild West Show into bankruptcy in 1913. Nonetheless, Cody's fame remained, and his body was carried to the Wyoming state capitol for viewing by an immense crowd. Eventually he was buried on the top of Lookout Mountain, near Golden, Colorado. His wife was buried beside him in 1921.

Cody is remembered not only for his adventure-filled life, but also for helping the "wild west" move into the future. The Buffalo Bill Historical Center in Cody, Wyoming, started by the Buffalo Bill Memorial Association from a humble log structure erected in 1927, gives tribute to his name. This celebrated historical center features four museums, including the world-renowned Buffalo Bill Museum, which provides an unforgettable look at Cody's life and times. In North Platte, Nebraska, the Buffalo Bill State Historical Park preserves Cody's home and mementos from his personal life and his Wild West Show. Only fifty yards away from his final resting place atop Lookout Mountain in Colorado is the Buffalo Bill Memorial Museum where special events, such as the commemoration of his birthday and the annual Buffalo Bill Days Celebration in July, highlight his history.

The Trail Today

The Oregon Memorial Association commemorated the Pony Express in 1938 by placing a fourteen-inch metal disk with a silhouetted rider at various points along the trail.* Then, during the one-hundredth anniversary of the Pony Express, a renewed interest led to extensive research in order to locate the station sites that had been lost in the interceding years.

At the time of the American bicentennial, a Pony Express '76 group formed to organize a nonstop horseback ride through the states of Washington, Oregon, Idaho, Wyoming, Nebraska, Iowa, Illinois, Indiana, Ohio, West Virginia, and Pennsylvania. Over five hundred individuals participated in the elaborate twelve-day event, traversing 3,022 miles. Though the actual route was not used—

*Material in this section is taken from the National Park Service's *California and Pony Express Trails Eligibility/ Feasibility Study.*

even in passing through Wyoming and Nebraska—the event emphasized the importance of the Pony Express in the annals of our country's history. Also as part of the bicentennial, the Bureau of Land Management marked the Pony Express Trail and developed permanent interpretive roadside facilities in Wyoming, Utah, and Nevada. By 1978 the National Pony Express Association (NPEA), an all-volunteer organization, was founded to "reestablish, identify and re-ride the Historical Pony Express Trail." And in 1984 Congress directed the National Park Service to study the desirability and feasibility of establishing a Pony Express National Trail. Legislation creating the trail was passed in 1992.

The National Pony Express Association, with its headquarters located in Pollock Pines, California, is composed of members from state divisions in the eight states on the trail. These members participate in local commemorative events, trail work, parades, and trail rides. Each June, a commemorative "re-run" is made over a ten-day period. Over 550 riders, all members of NPEA divisions in the eight states on the trail, participate. Letters carried over the trail in a mochila give a new generation the opportunity to ride the trail or to receive mail "by pony." All riders are required to take an oath of conduct similar to the one required by Alexander Majors. After being sworn in, each is presented with a small Bible, as were the riders of history. Each envelope is hand-stamped with a special U.S. post office cancellation. Envelopes also bear two oval Pony Express stamps showing the date and place of departure and arrival. And, like the original mail of 1860, letters at $5 each, paid in advance, are carried by horseback in one of the four cantinas on the leather mochila. The eight-state event continues twenty-four hours a day until the mail is delivered to its destination.

The Pony Express National Historic Trail (PENHT) may actually be considered a route rather than a continuous trail. It can be followed by horse, foot, or auto for most of its length from St. Joseph, Missouri, to Sacramento, California. Along many trail segments, the actual route and exact length are a matter of conjecture because the solitary riders left little physical trace of their passage. Also, the trail often changed from week to week because of weather, passability of

streams, and danger of attack. Even so, short, pristine segments believed to be traces of the original trail can be seen in Utah and California, and tangible evidence of original Pony Express stations and related features are still possible to identify in each of the states. Museums and associated forts, trading posts, river crossings, and natural landmarks offer interpretation and preservation.

Large expanses of the territory traversed are still very scenic. For the most part, the eastern segment of the route follows the Oregon, California, and Mormon Pioneer Trails through Kansas, Nebraska, and Wyoming. It then follows the Mormon Pioneer Trail and the Salt Lake Cutoff of the California Trail from Fort Bridger to Salt Lake City. One privately owned stretch from Needle Rock to Cache Cave, north of Castle Rock, Utah, contains original trails. The western segment, starting west from Salt Lake City, departs from the California Trail and more well-known routes and cuts across central Utah through some of the most barren and desolate desert in the state until it reaches the Nevada border on the present-day Goshute Indian Reservation. Entering Nevada (then a part of Utah Territory), the trail began its most dangerous stretch across mostly high desert, traversing several mountain ranges to reach Carson City and then scale the Sierra Nevada at Echo Summit. Approximately 80 percent of the trail in Nevada lies on public lands. The many remote jeep trails can be followed by horse or four-wheel drive.

From Echo Summit, the trail enters California, there to generally follow what is now old U.S. Highway 50 through Placerville to Sacramento. It is not coincidental that the route has become a major interstate transportation corridor. In more remote sections, such as through Eldorado National Forest, a ten-mile section is believed to be the original single track. The route also passes through several rustic mining towns and historic communities that predate the Pony Express. Most of the California sites were marked and interpreted by active public and private organizations in the state years ago.

After only a few months in existence, the trail underwent a permanent route change near Carson City. No longer dropping south to Genoa, the trail went over Dagget Pass and the Johnson Pass to cut off twelve miles. The route in California, which had first crossed Echo Summit to descend the South Fork of the American River to Placerville, later used the Kingsbury-McDonald route over Johnson Pass to reach the South Fork before descending into Placerville. Eventually, as the trail terminus moved to Folsom and then to Placerville, other minor route variations were made.

Vegetation along the route is as varied as the topography, from woodlands, prairies, and farmlands on the eastern flatlands to the high sagebrush plains of Wyoming and the eastern Great Basin. Although the valley bottomlands of the Great Basin are dotted with deciduous trees, the deserts are dominated by creosote bush and other drought-tolerant species. Coniferous trees (pinyon, juniper, and various pines) are common at higher elevations around the rim of the Great Basin and where the trails cross the Sierra.

As suggested by the diverse topography and vegetation, this broad section of the western United States also exhibits climatic extremes. On the eastern plains the relatively long summers are hot and dry; winters can be severe, with substantial snows and occasional blizzards. The Rocky Mountains, the edges of the Great Basin, and the Sierra Nevada all have relatively cooler and shorter summer seasons, a mild spring and fall, and winters with zero and subzero temperatures. Within the Great Basin itself, summers are long, hot, and very dry, and winters are relatively mild. In general, recreational activity along the trail routes occurs in the spring, early summer, and fall. Winter weather may, with extreme caution and preparation, be suitable for limited activities such as retracing sections of the trail by car or making longer cross-country hikes or rides. Where permitted, one can travel segments of the trail by four-wheel-drive vehicle or snowmobile.

Discrepancies exist regarding several station names, locations, and functions. These will only be resolved with additional intensive archival research and fieldwork. Approximately fifty markers depict sites relating to the Pony Express from St. Joseph to San Francisco. Sites in California are marked with California Registered Historical Landmark plaques. At least twelve stations along the Pony Express National Historic Trail are listed on the National Register of Historic Places (NRHP).

MISSOURI

1. ST. JOSEPH. As the eastern terminus and headquarters of the Pony Express, St. Joseph has long been known as the "home of the Pony Express."* The mass migration following the discovery of gold in California (1848) and Colorado (1858) transformed the frontier town into a major wagon-train staging area and supply depot. When Joseph Robidoux, St. Joe's founder (1826), drove the last spike on the Hannibal and St. Joseph Railroad (1859), it made the town the westernmost railroad terminal. The Pony Express National Memorial, where the PENHT begins, features stables (NRHP) and a museum with exhibits. The Patee House Museum (NRHP), the Pony Express headquarters, has reconstructed offices of Russell, Majors & Waddell; Pony Express items; and an antique transportation and communications collection. There is a Pony Express monument in Patee Park and a Pony Express statue at Frederick and Ninth. Other attractions: St.

*Some material in this section is taken from the National Park Service's Historic Resource Study Pony Express National Historic Trail by Anthony Godfrey.

Joseph Ferry Site and monument in Hustan Wyeth Park; Pony Express Saddle and Mochila Monument, where the first west-bound rider was said to have departed on April 3, 1860; the St. Joseph Museum, which focuses on American Indians, westward expansion, and the Civil War; the Jesse James Home; the Albrecht-Kemper Museum of Art. Nearby: Mound City and Squaw Creek NWR.

KANSAS

2. MARYSVILLE STATION. Once known as Palmetto City, Marysville, which thrived by selling whiskey, was settled by travelers along the Oregon Trail. The original Pony Express Home Station No. 1 Museum with post office boxes from the state's first civilian post office is housed in a Pony Express horse barn (1859). The barn (NRHP) is the oldest building in Marshall County and the only original home station along the Pony Express route that is still at its original site. In 1876, a hip-style roof replaced the board roof that was lost in a fire. A small research library specializes in Pony Express history. A bronze statue of horse and rider commemorate the heroic enterprise.

3. COTTONWOOD/HOLLEN-

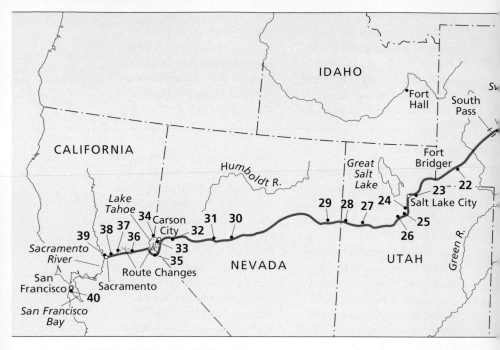

BERG STATION. The last Pony Express relay station in Kansas also served as a stagecoach stop on the COC&PPE Co. stage line. The Hollenberg Station (1857) east of Hanover is a state historic site with a museum and is the only remaining original, unaltered Pony Express station (NRHP) in Kansas. It was built at the crossroads of the Pony Express route and the Oregon Trail.

NEBRASKA

4. ROCK CREEK STATION STATE HISTORIC PARK. A stage and Pony Express stop that served a feeder trail to the Oregon Trail (ONHT), the park, east of Fairbury, has a visitor center. Stablehand James Butler "Wild Bill" Hickok is said to have begun his bloody career as a gunfighter here (July 12, 1861), when he shot down David McCanles, who had built and owned the log-structured station, when McCanles came to collect a mortgage payment. Two others were killed as well. McCanles's twelve-year-old son witnessed the event. Hickok was tried and acquitted and went on to gun down at least three dozen more men on his escapades throughout the Old West. The serenity of the 392-acre state historic site visitor center affords a panoramic view of the Rock Creek Valley, where ranch houses, bunkhouse, post office, and Pony Express barn can be explored. *Other attractions:* Oregon Trail ruts.

5. THIRTY-TWO MILE CREEK

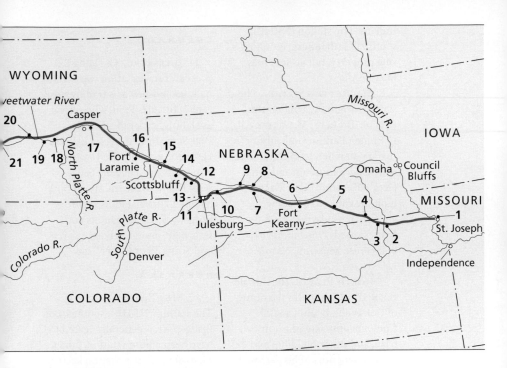

STATION. The long, one-story building was named after the distance between it and Fort Kearny. In August 1864, George A. Comstock, station keeper, abandoned the station, which was later burned to the ground by Indians. The station's location, southeast of Hastings, has been designated as an NRHP.

6. FORT KEARNY STATE HISTORIC PARK. Named for Stephen Watts Kearny, the fort (NRHP), south of Kearney, was established (1848) to protect the emigrants (CNHT, ONHT, MPNHT). An earlier Fort Kearny had stood near Nebraska City. Pony Express riders possibly stopped at the fort to service the mail needs of the military, pulling up at the sod post office. The ground includes a

stockade replica, a reconstructed sod blacksmith shop, and a visitor center with a slide show about the fort and the Pony Express. *Other attractions:* In Kearney, the Kearney Museum offers glass-bottom boat rides on Museum Lake; the Museum of Nebraska Art; Trails and Rails Museum.

7. COLD WATER RANCH/MIDWAY STATION. There is some controversy concerning the exact location of this station, which may have been a log structure. The Oregon Trail Memorial Association recognized this station with a Pony Express bronze plaque, and a second bronze marker noted rider Jim Moore's emergency trip from Midway to Julesburg (June 3, 1860) during a time of unrest with the American

Indians. The station (NRHP), south of Gothenburg, is on private property, but visitors may look inside.

8. MACHETTE'S STATION. The station, originally built on the Oregon Trail (1854), was moved to Ehmen Park in Gothenburg. A marker attached to the building, which has a museum and artifacts, tells visitors that Machette built the cabin as a trading post and ranch house that the Pony Express used. *Other attractions:* Sod House Museum. *Nearby:* Lake Helen RA.

9. NORTH PLATTE. The Buffalo Bill SHP, which marks the home of Col. William "Buffalo Bill" Cody, encompasses the house, barn, and other buildings and exhibits mementos of his personal life and his Wild West show. Buffalo-stew cookouts and trail rides are available. *Other attractions:* The Lincoln County Historical Museum with artifacts of the Sioux and settlers, the fossil of a two-hundred-pound land tortoise, Railroad Town; Buffalo Bill Rodeo (June). *Nearby:* Lake Ma-loney; Jeffrey Reservoir; Sutherland Reservoir; Lake McConaughy.

10. DIAMOND SPRINGS STATION. Glass telegraph insulators found at the site (NRHP) suggest that the Pony Express station later served as a telegraph station as well. A monument identifies the site on the south side of U.S. Highway 30, 0.9 mile west of Brule. *Nearby:* California Hill has deeply etched ruts along which one can hike.

COLORADO

11. JULESBURG. The Pony Express and stage station was originally established as a trading post (1859) by Jules Reni, who served as station keeper for the Pike's Peak stage line and Pony Express. He was eventually fired by the Pony Express. The Fort Sedgewick Depot Museum, site of both a Pony Express station and Fort Sedgewick, offers exhibits and information on the Pony Express and South Platte River Trail.

NEBRASKA

12. MUD SPRINGS STATION. The station (NRHP), southeast of Bridgeport, is generally agreed to have been a home station. James McArdle served as station keeper for the Pony Express stage lines, which probably shared the same sod structures. Later the station served as a telegraph relay office. In 1865, Fort Laramie soldiers clashed (1865) with American Indians returning from the Julesburg siege in the battle of Mud Springs. The station site was donated to the Nebraska State Historical Society, which dedicated a monument with a Pony Express symbol and plaque on the site.

13. COURTHOUSE (ROCK) STATION. From Mud Springs, riders followed a route through Pumpkin Seed Crossing and past the Courthouse Rock formation where the Pony Express station was located, southwest of Bridgeport. *Other attractions:* Bridgeport SRA; Pioneer Trails Mu-

seum. *Nearby:* Chimney Rock NHS.

14. CHIMNEY ROCK STATION. The exact location of the station is unclear. The dramatic landmark, south of Bayard, now Chimney Rock NHS, was also used by the westward emigrants. A short hike can be taken from the visitor center to the rock (NHS), which is illuminated at dusk.

15. SCOTTSBLUFF. The Oregon Trail Memorial Association placed a granite marker with the circular bronze Pony Express motif near the North Platte bridge, which stood as late as 1960, to mark the relay or home station, which probably stood near or at old Fort Mitchell (1864–68). The escarpment rising 800 feet above the North Platte served as another landmark in the area. The Scotts Bluff NM offers hiking and biking trails, a museum, and visitor center. *Nearby:* North Platte NW Refuge.

WYOMING

16. FORT LARAMIE STATION. Sources generally agree on the identity of a station at Fort Laramie (NHS), although its exact location is unclear. Still standing, Fort Laramie's adobe-stone sutler's store housed a post office in the 1850s, '70s, and '80s, although its status during the Pony Express era remains unknown. The restored Fort Laramie NHS outside Fort Laramie offers a visitor center, museum, and living-history demonstrations.

17. FORT CASPAR. Louis Guenot, manager of the Platte Bridge–North Platte Station, is said to have built the station (1859) at a cost of $40,000. The station may have been located in North Platte or Fort Caspar. The Red Butte(s) Station, just west of Casper was the home station of William Cody, known later as Buffalo Bill. *Other attractions:* Fort Caspar Museum. *Nearby:* West of Alcova is Independence Rock SHS. West of Powder River are examples of unusual topography in Hell's Half Acre.

18. DEVIL'S GATE STATION. The Pony Express or stage station appears to have been located just south of the Devil's Gate rock formation. The landmark site is a cleft formed in the Rattlesnake Mountains where the Sweetwater River gradually sliced through. BLM maintains the historic site, located along State Highway 220, with a short loop trial and interpretation. At least twenty emigrant graves have been found in the area.

19. SPLIT ROCK STATION. A French-Canadian named Plante managed the station, known by both his name and the name of the natural formation to the northeast. The cleft in the solid granite mountain also provided a landmark for pioneers. BLM interprets the site.

20. THREE CROSSINGS STATION. Sir Richard Burton enjoyed the home station run by the Moore family. He described it as "neatly swept and garnished, papered and ornamented. The

tablecloth was clean, so was the cooking, so were the children." When William Cody came to the end of his run at this station, he had to extend his ride when he found that rider Charlie Miller had been killed in a brawl, making this the longest ride in Pony Express history.

21. **SOUTH PASS.** Two French-Canadians are said to have managed station operations at South Pass, near the Continental Divide. The actual site of the Upper Sweetwater, or South Pass Station, has not been identified. The Pacific Springs station, approximately two miles west of the Continental Divide, near South Pass, served as a relay station for stage lines and the Pony Express. *Other attractions:* South Pass City SHS has a visitor center, interpretive displays, and restored mining-era buildings. *Nearby:* Atlantic City (1868) was founded when gold mines attracted thousands of miners to the Sweetwater Mining District in South Pass. Its main attraction includes buildings that date from the turn of the century. A trip north will take the traveler to Yellowstone NP and the Buffalo Bill Historical Center in Cody.

22. **FORT BRIDGER.** A station may have existed in the quartermaster building. Its function has never been clearly understood, however, given the fact that the fort had little land for grazing or for a pony station. A logical link may well have been the association between the freighting firm of Russell, Majors & Waddell and

Gen. A. S. Johnston's Army of Utah, which had established winter quarters (1857) at the fort (NRHP). *Other attractions:* Fort Bridger SHS (1843) has a museum housing artifacts of Indian cultures and the periods of military and civilian occupancy. It also has Pony Express stables and living-history demonstrations.

UTAH

23. **SALT LAKE CITY.** The Salt Lake City Station served as a home station for stage lines and Pony Express riders. The wood-frame structure, kept by A. B. Miller, stood on the east side of Main Street, between First and Second South. *Other attractions:* Temple Square with visitor center. *Nearby:* Great Salt Lake SP, which visitors can reach by boat or causeway; west of Brigham City, Golden Spike NHS with trail, auto tour, and visitor center interpreting the joining of the transcontinental railroad.

24. **CAMP FLOYD/FAIRFIELD STATION.** Originally named for the secretary of war, John B. Floyd, the station was renamed Fort Crittenden after Floyd joined the Confederacy. The Pony Express National Back Country Byway begins near Fairfield and ends at Ibapah. Along the route visitors can enjoy history and a variety of recreational activities. Camp Floyd—Stagecoach Inn SP—was the site of the largest army encampment in the United States (1858–61), with more than fifty-six hundred troops gathered to suppress a Mormon rebellion

that never materialized. Today only the Johnston Army Cemetery remains. Located adjacent to the fort, the Fairfield Station, within John Carson's adobe Stagecoach Inn, can be visited by the public. Used for both Pony Express and stage travel, it lodged such personalities as Mark Twain and the English writer and explorer Sir Richard Burton.

25. RUSH VALLEY/FAUST'S STATION. A change of riders took place and the mail stage stopped for rest at this station, named after its keeper, Doc Faust, who purchased the two-story stone structure after it was built (1858). A marker north of the site was constructed by the Civilian Conservation Corps as part of its project to mark the Pony Express Trail in 1939. The site is interpreted by the BLM with visitor information. *Nearby:* Onaqui Mountain Wild Horse Management Area; Wasatch-Cache NF.

26. SIMPSON'S SPRINGS/ EGANS' SPRINGS STATION. This station, which probably served the Pony Express and Overland Express, was rebuilt by the BLM. Explorer and Camp Floyd topographical engineer Capt. J. H. Simpson stopped here (1858) while searching for an overland mail route between Salt Lake City and California, before laying out an acceptable route from Salt Lake City to Carson Valley (1859). George Chorpenning established the mail station (1858), which provided one of the most dependable watering points in this desert region.

Nearby: Simpson's Springs Campground.

27. BOYD'S STATION. One of Utah's best-preserved stations is maintained, protected, and interpreted by the BLM. Located north of Fish Springs, the station gets its name from Bid Boyd, a station keeper who continued to live here into the early years of the twentieth century. In the days of the Pony Express, it was known as Butte or Desert Station. A portion of the rock walls that once provided protection from the elements still remains. The partially dug-out, rock-walled living quarters contained bunks that were built into the walls. Furniture consisted of boxes and benches, and life at the station was lonely. The monotony of caring for the horses was broken only by the arrival and almost immediate departure of two riders each day. *Nearby:* Fish Springs NWR.

28. CANYON/BURNT STATION. East of Ibapah, stone outlines of Round Station (1863) are still seen and the nearby depression —south of the parking lot— attests to the corral and blacksmith shop. The earlier Pony Express station, located northwest of this site in Overland Canyon, consisted of a log house (1861), a stable, and a dugout where meals were cooked and served. After the station was attacked and burned in an American Indian raid, the Canyon Station was called Burnt or Burned Out by locals while the replacement was referred to

locally as Round Station. *Nearby:* Goshute Indian Reservation.

NEVADA

29. **SPRING VALLEY STATION.** The Pony Express probably used the station of the Overland Mail Company during its final months. While stopping for something to eat and to "get the lay of the situation," seasoned Pony Express rider Elijah N. "Uncle Nick" Wilson found two young boys tending the station that had been left abandoned by the keeper. During this visit, Wilson spied Indians attempting to steal the station horses. When he tried to stop them, he was shot with an arrow just above his left eye. A doctor removed the flint-headed arrow but left him to die in the care of the two boys. Instead, Wilson regained consciousness and was soon riding again, although he had episodes of terrible headaches for the rest of his life. The exact location of the station, northeast of the Humboldt Forest in Pine County, is unknown.

30. **COLD SPRINGS/EAST GATE STATION.** The station (March 1860, NRHP) was attacked in May 1860 by warriors who killed the station keeper and took the station's horses. A few weeks later, it was raided again. Much of the station's stone ruins still exist; thick walls, complete with windows, gunholes, and fireplace, identify the site. The walls have been structurally stabilized for preservation purposes and for safety. The remains of a corral stand nearby. This locations was selected so that men could take advantage of the horses' body heat during cold winters. A moderately strenuous 1.5-mile hike leads to the site from the BLM wayside located on U.S. Highway 50, sixty miles east of Fallon.

31. **SAND SPRINGS.** Like the Cold Springs Station, the station at Sand Springs was built by the COC&PPE Company. Sir Richard Burton described it as "roofless and chairless, filthy and squalid, with a smoky fire in one corner, and a table in the center of an impure floor." Travelers found a reliable source of water here, but its poor quality often poisoned animals and probably made people ill as well. In addition to the Pony Express, others used the site until World War II. The telegraph came through the area and the site served as a freight, milling, and ranching center. Structural ruins (NRHP) from many of these activities still exist near Sand Mountain, at one of the best-preserved stations in Nevada. Sand Mountain, twenty miles east of Fallon, is one of the few "singing mountains" in the country—grains of sand create a low moan as they shift. *Other attractions:* The Churchill County Museum and Archives at Fallon has memorabilia connected with the Pony Express and transcontinental telegraph, the emigrant trail, and Nevada Indian tribes. *Nearby:* Walker River Indian Reservation.

32. **FORT CHURCHILL STATION.** The station, located in the head-

quarters building of a historic adobe fort (1860), was given positive reviews by Burton (October 1860). The outpost protected the Pony Express and other mail routes against American Indian attack. Although the fort, southwest of Silver Springs, is now in ruins, a visitor center reconstructs its history with interpretive exhibits at Fort Churchill SP. *Nearby:* Pyramid National Scenic Byway goes for thirty-seven miles along one of the largest desert lakes in the world and is the only byway in the nation entirely within a tribal (Paiute) reservation.

33. **CARSON CITY.** The town named for Kit Carson (1858) lies along U.S. Highway 50, which has been called "the loneliest road in America." Pony Express division superintendents used Carson City as a base (March 1860) to hire riders and station keepers. The old station was located near the original Ormsby House on what is now Carson Street between Fourth and Fifth. *Other attractions:* The Stewart Indian Museum; the chamber of commerce offers a historic sites walking map. *Nearby:* Virginia City and Reno.

NEVADA / CALIFORNIA

34. **LAKE TAHOE.** The portion of U.S. Highway 50 heading west from Carson City to Lake Tahoe and the California border is especially scenic. Lake Tahoe is North America's third-deepest lake. The Eastshore Drive National Scenic Byway provides breathtaking views of the Lake Tahoe basin, and the visitor center offers accounts of pioneer and American Indian history. In Genoa, Nevada, the Genoa Station/Old Mormon Station post office, located just south of the courthouse, served as a station, with the livery stable across the street. *Other attractions:* Mormon Station SHP has a restored log stockade and trading post (1851) where emigrants rested before continuing over the Sierra Nevada to California. The park has a visitor center and museum, with a Bible carried on Pony Express. *Nearby:* At the border: Friday's Lakeside Station conducted a profitable business for several years after the demise of the Pony Express. The original blacksmith shop, still standing, is located on private land.

35. **WOODSFORD'S.** California's first westbound station, Woodsford's Station served originally as an outpost (1847) and later as an unofficial post office and remount station for the Pony Express. The site, now covered by U.S. Highway 88, is identified by a California Registered Historical Landmark marker. *Nearby:* Pyramid Lake, north of Reno; Toiyabe, Eldorado, and Tahoe NFs offer forest activities, including camping, hiking, and cross-country skiing. The Forest Service's visitor center between Camp Richardson and Emerald Bay offers free orientation programs. At South Shore, Heaven Valley Tram offers a panaora view of the lake and hikin at the summit; *MS Dixi*

sightseeing cruises. The North Shore also offers a wide range of activities.

CALIFORNIA

36. **SPORTSMAN'S HALL STATION/TWELVE-MILE HOUSE.** The hotel, twelve miles east of Placerville, was operated in the late 1850s and '60s by John and James Blair. It was a stopping place for stages and teams of the Comstock Company. It became either a relay or home station for the Pony Express and is identified with a California Registered Historical Landmark plaque.

37. **PLACERVILLE STATION.** Louis Lepetit managed the station at Placerville, known earlier as Hangtown, as a roadside stop for travelers. On July 1, 1861, the gold-rush town became the western terminus of the Pony Express and remained so until the company disbanded on October 26. A granite monument with a bronze plaque identifies the station site in this gold-rush town. *Other attractions:* Gold Bug Mine Park; Hangtown Annual Pioneer Days with annual wagon train parade in June; gold-panning trips with Gold Country Prospecting. *Nearby:* Coloma, Marshall Gold Discovery SHP.

38. **FOLSOM STATION.** Folsom was the western terminus for the Pony Express from July 1, 1860, to June 30, 1861 (nearly two-thirds of its existence). From ..., the Sacramento Valley ... carried the mail to .... A California Registrical Landmark plaque

stands at the site. A gold-rush and railroad town dating from the 1860s, Folsom retains much of its historic character with its many restored homes and buildings lining Sutter Street. These include the Wells Fargo Office, the former Pony Express terminus. *Nearby:* Folsom Lake SRA.

39. **SACRAMENTO.** The Sacramento Station is often referred to as the western terminus of the Pony Express, although mail bound for San Francisco was forwarded on the ferry *Antelope.* From 1860 to March 1861, the Hastings Building, on the southwest corner of J and Second Streets, served as the terminal, with the Alta Telegraph Company and the California State Telegraph Company serving as agents. When the terminus moved to the Adams Express Building at 1014 Second Street in March of 1861, Wells Fargo and Company had the responsibility of delivering the letters and putting some on boats to San Francisco. *Other attractions:* Old Sacramento (SHP); B. F. Hastings Building and Wells Fargo Bank Museum, with exhibits on Pony Express and Wells Fargo operations; Pony Express Monument across from the Hastings Building; California State Railroad Museum; Sutter's Fort and State Indian Museum; California State Parks Store; the state capitol (built 1860–74); *Spirit of Sacramento* sight-seeing cruises on the Sacramento River; one-day delta riverboat cruises to San Francisco; Dixieland Jazz Festival, the

largest in the world, the last week of May; American River Parkway (American Discovery Trail) for biking, walking, horseback riding, rafting, fishing, and picnicking.

40. **SAN FRANCISCO.** San Francisco was the final California stop on the Pony Express station list. The office of the Alta Telegraph at 153 Montgomery Street served as the western business headquarters for the COC&PPE. Western representative William W. Finney oversaw all business activities in San Francisco for the owners. *Other attractions:* Wells Fargo History Museum; Golden Gate National RA with Fort Point NHS (1861); bay cruises.

NEZ PERCE (NE-ME-POO) TIPI

When members of Young Chief Joseph's band were forced to move to a small reservation at Lapwai, Idaho, embittered young warriors decided to avenge past murders of tribal members. Their actions resulted in the 1877 flight of the Nez Perce (Ne-Me-Poo) which ended some forty miles from the Canadian border at Bear's Paw battleground in Montana.

Nez Perce (Nee-Me-Poo) National Historic Trail

Hear me, my chiefs. I am tired; my heart is sick and sad. From where the sun now stands, I will fight no more forever.

CHIEF JOSEPH, OCTOBER 5, 1877

The Nez Perce (Nee-Me-Poo) National Historic Trail (NPNHT) honors the heroic attempt by the Nez Perce Indians to escape capture by the U.S. Army in a saga that Gen. William Tecumseh Sherman referred to as "the most extraordinary of Indian wars." Drawn into a fight by the impulsive actions of a few revengeful young warriors, some 750 nontreaty Nez Perce Indians were forced to flee their lands. Of the 750, only 250, at most, were warriors who fought some twenty, generally defensive, battles and skirmishes against a total of more than two thousand soldiers aided by numerous civilian volunteers and Indians of other tribes. Through a combination of skillful strategy and good fortune, the Nez Perce covered over eleven hundred miles before being trapped just short of safety at the Canadian border.

ADMINISTERING AGENCY
U.S. Forest Service, Northern Region
Federal Building
P.O. Box 7669
Missoula, MT 59807
406-329-3510

FURTHER INFORMATION
Nez Perce National Historic Trail Foundation
P.O. Box 20197
Missoula, MT 59807

ESTABLISHED
1986

APPROXIMATE MILEAGE
1,170 miles (1,885 kilometers)

STATES
Oregon, Idaho, Montana, Wyoming

The
History
of the
Trail

Originally composed of a
number of independent villages and bands, the Nez Perce—
who call themselves Nee-Me-Poo,
or The People—were long
known as friends of the whites.
They had welcomed Lewis and
Clark, fur trappers, and missionaries to their homelands in southeastern Washington, northeastern
Oregon, and north-central Idaho.
Increased settlement and mount-
ing public pressure influenced
Washington's territorial governor,
Isaac Stevens, to negotiate an
1855 treaty with the Nez Perce
chiefs. Recognizing their right to
their traditional homeland, the
treaty established a reservation of
some five thousand square miles.
Nevertheless, settlers and miners
unlawfully encroached on reservation land. Then, when gold was
discovered in Orofino, Idaho, in
1861, the ensuing rush of ten
thousand miners, followed by
merchants and settlers, overran
large parts of the reservation.
Even though there were many
incidents of theft and mistreat-
ment, the Nez Perce remained
peaceful.

To cope with the crisis, the U.S.
government engaged the Nez
Perce in new treaty negotiations
in 1862 and 1863 that would
pacify the settlers and give them
unobstructed access to the newly
discovered mines. As a result of
the controversial treaty of 1863,
the Nez Perce Indian Reservation
was reduced to an area 10 percent
original size. During the
tion process, the Nez
said to have come to a

friendly division among themselves. Those who agreed to the
terms of the treaty eventually
became known as the "Christian"
or "treaty" Nez Perce. Those who
did not agree became known as
the "nontreaty" Nez Perce. The
government negotiators had
assumed that Lawyer, leader of
the treaty faction, was the leader
of all Nez Perce because of the
role he had played in negotiating
the treaty of 1855. Acting on this
assumption, Lawyer and his followers signed the treaty of 1863
in the absence of the nontreaty
Nez Perce leaders. Lawyer's authority to sign for all the Nez
Perce was quickly disputed by the
nontreaty leaders, including Old
Joseph, White Bird, and Looking
Glass of the Upper Nez Perce,
who never recognized the treaty
of 1863.

Consequently, the nontreaty
Nez Perce remained on their traditional homeland, ignoring
orders to move to the new reservation. In the meantime, with the
announcement of the new treaty,
white settlement of the Snake and
Clearwater River bottoms and
Wallowa Valley continued.

Foremost among the nontreaty
Indians was Old Joseph, who led
a band that lived in Oregon's
Wallowa Valley, an area totally
excluded from Indian land by the
new treaty. When his son, known
to the whites as Young Joseph,
succeeded his father as chief, the
mantle of authority fell upon
him. He held his young braves in
check in spite of the growing re-
sentment they felt at losing more

land and horses to the encroaching population. Joseph hoped that a peaceful solution could be found, as he did not wish to go to war *or* to leave his home.

During the 1870s, pressure mounted to force all nontreaty Nez Perce onto the reduced reservation. Finally, in May 1877, under threat of force from the U.S. Army, the nontreaty bands decided to move onto the small reservation at Lapwai (Idaho) rather than risk war. General Oliver O. Howard gave them only thirty days to complete the move. Chief Joseph, a nontreaty spokesman, asked for more time, explaining that their stock was scattered and that the Snake was high with spring runoff. When his appeal was refused, his band— consisting of four hundred people, including about sixty-four braves aged sixteen and over — rounded up as much of their far-ranging livestock as possible and collected all the possessions they could pack. Gathering at Dug Bar, a traditional river-crossing area, they crossed the Snake and then the Salmon Rivers with considerable loss of young livestock. All the nontreaty Nez Perce then met at Tepahle-wam, the traditional camping ground on the Camas Prairie at Tolo Lake, before entering the reservation only a few miles away.

The rendezvous was an emotional one. Not all had agreed to the course of peace and compliance. On June 14, a few warriors, led by Wahltitits, crossed the Salmon River to seek revenge against

WALLOWA LAKE

The Nez Perce (Ne-Me-Poo) National Historic Trail begins at Wallowa Lake State Park in northeastern Oregon. Old Chief Joseph's gravesite is nearby, out-side Joseph.

some settlers whom they blamed for the death of Wahltitits's father. The proclaimed success of their mission roused the desire for vengeance among other warriors. More attacks were made on settlers in the area. Seeking refuge, the settlers moved to larger townships that were hastily converted to forts. Messages, demanding military assistance, were sent to Fort Lapwai. Realizing that General Howard would be preparing to send soldiers against them, the Nez Perce moved to the defensible canyons of Lahmotta on June 16. That night, sentinels reported to camp, warning the Nez Perce of approaching soldiers. After a great deal of deliberation, they decided to stay at Lahmotta, make an effort to avoid war, and fight only if forced to do so. At daybreak, warriors were in various stages of preparation for an attack, and a truce party bear-

HELLS CANYON JET BOAT

Jetboaters and whitewater rafters meet the Nez Perce (Ne-Me-Poo) National Historic Trail at Dug Bar, where the Nez Perce crossed the Snake River in Hells Canyon National Recreation Area. Hikers, backpackers, and horseback riders can reach the same site by following the trail through the Wallowa-Whitman National Forest. Dug Bar campground offers primitive campsites. Hells Canyon, North America's deepest canyon, hugs the borders of Oregon and Idaho.

ing a white flag waited. Companies F and H of the First Calvary and volunteers under General Howard's orders arrived at White Bird to quell the raids and escort the Nez Perce onto the reservation. For reasons never fully explained, a shot from a volunteer's rifle began the bloody battle of White Bird Canyon, a war, and the long tortuous journey of the Nez Perce.

Outnumbered two to one and fighting uphill with mostly inferior weapons, the Nez Perce managed to defeat the army. By midmorning, 34 of the 106 sol-

diers had been killed and two wounded. In addition, 2 of the 11 volunteers had been injured within the first moments of the battle. In contrast, only 3 Nez Perce warriors were wounded. The soldiers retreated, but the Nez Perce were aware of the consequences of wars fought against the army. From stories passed from tribe to tribe, they believed that the military would eventually pursue and retaliate. After gathering approximately sixty-three carbines, many pistols, and hundreds of rounds of ammunition left by the soldiers—weapons that would be used against the army in the weeks and months ahead—they prepared to move their families out of the Lahmotta area. With their small arsenal greatly enhanced, they recrossed the Snake River on July 2.

On July 1, a detachment of cavalry and volunteers had made an unprovoked attack on the Looking Glass campsite located on the reservation. A mother and child were shot and 725 horses were taken. Looking Glass, no longer in a neutral position, aligned his band and a neighboring band of Palouse Indians with the nontreaty bands of Joseph, White Bird, and Toohoolhoolzote, who joined the Looking Glass camp on the South Fork of the Clearwater on July 7. On July 11, General Howard and his troops arrived and the battle of the Clearwater began. Within minutes the cavalry was pinned down, eight soldiers were killed and twenty-five wounded; four

Nez Perce were killed. The next day the Nez Perce retreated and the army declared victory. Instead of pressing, however, Howard awaited the arrival of soldiers from Arizona, California, and Georgia. Because of the general's failure to follow up his advantage, the Nez Perce began to refer to him as General Day-after-Tomorrow. But Howard was organizing his command at Fort Lapwai: he telegraphed Capt. Charles Rawn at the three-week-old Fort Missoula to keep the Nez Perce from entering Montana until his forces arrived.

Clearly, the Nez Perce knew that they could not escape from the army in Idaho Territory. In council, the five bands agreed to follow the leadership of Chief Looking Glass, who persuaded them to leave their homeland and head east to Montana, where they would join their allies, the Crow, in buffalo country. They would follow the Lolo (Buffalo) Trail, which Nez Perce hunters had used for centuries. (It was not until the Lewis and Clark expedition that any white men had followed its path.) Heading eastward, they believed that the army and volunteers would be content to chase them out of Idaho, that they would be safe in Montana. They hoped to find a place where the army would leave them alone and where they would be far enough from settlements to avoid further clashes until they could return to their homeland.

As it turned out, reports of unrest in Idaho had already reached

Montana. The stories bred fear in the settlers when they learned that the Nez Perce were headed their way. Panic prevailed, and newspaper editors demanded action by Montana's territorial governor, Benjamin Potts. Telegrams to President Hayes insisted that the army punish "the hostiles." To block Nez Perce entry into Montana, Captain Rawn, with 30 enlisted men, 4 officers, and 150 volunteers, marched to the eastern end of the trail and constructed a log barricade across a narrow section of the valley. When the Nez Perce arrived at the fortification on July 26, Rawn demanded unconditional surrender. The Nez Perce chiefs made it clear that they would not surrender, but that they had no intention of molesting settlers or property. After the meeting, many of the settlers returned home, but Captain Rawn had clear orders. He told the Nez Perce that they could not pass. The barricade failed when the Nez Perce with their horses and possessions climbed a steep ravine to the north and bypassed the soldiers unchallenged. The previously unnamed barricade became known as "Fort Fizzle."

After avoiding conflict, the Nez Perce followed the Lolo Creek to the Bitterroot Valley, which they reached on July 28. Some wanted to go north to Canada, but Looking Glass insisted on traveling south toward the lush grazing grounds of the Big Hole Valley on their way to join their allies farther to the east. Confident that they had left the war behind them, the chiefs made the fateful decision to go south. Traveling slowly through the Bitterroot Valley, they assured settlers along the way that they wished them no harm. But entrance of the Nez Perce into western Montana Territory caused anxiety among local residents and settlers, who had not yet recovered from news of Custer's defeat of 1876. Colonel John Gibbon, stationed at Fort Shaw near Great Falls, responded to the crisis and to the governor's request. On August 4, he and 149 troops and volunteers left Fort Missoula to enter the Bitterroot. He sent word to Howard, now camped at Lolo Hot Springs with six hundred troops, that he expected to be in battle soon. Leaving his infantry behind, Howard dashed off to the Bitterroot Valley with twenty of his best cavalry.

On August 4, the Nez Perce were camped near the confluence of the Bitterroot River's east and west forks. Two young warriors told of dreams warning that death would follow if they did not hurry. Despite the warnings of some of the chiefs and warriors to make haste, Chief Looking Glass was still convinced that the war was left behind. The warnings were disregarded, and by the time the Nez Perce arrived at Big Hole, the majority believed that they could savor their freedom. The few who wished to scout back along the trail were told by Looking Glass that scouting would violate trust in their

peace agreement with the Bitterroot settlers. In the meantime, many of these settlers were joining Gibbon's forces as volunteers.

Camped beside the Big Hole River, the unsuspecting Nez Perce were awakened by the fire of concealed soldiers and volunteers in the predawn of August 9. In the confusion of the faint light, men, women, and children were shot indiscriminately. Urged by Chiefs Looking Glass and White Bird, the warriors quickly took up sniper positions. Their deadly aim forced Gibbon's men to fall back across the river, where they dug in. Some of the warriors returned to help Chief Joseph care for the injured. Others remained to keep the soldiers pinned down while the bands headed south, leaving many of their belongings behind. Finally, on August 10, the remaining warriors left to join their people. The battle was over, but heavy casualties had been suffered by both sides.

When Howard's troops arrived the next day, they found Gibbon wounded and his command out of action. Their losses were high, with twenty-nine dead and forty wounded, but they had severely damaged the Nez Perce fighting force. Subsequently, seven enlisted men were awarded the Congressional Medal of Honor, and those officers who had survived received promotions.

In a military sense, the Nez Perce had won the battle, but the victory was hollow. About thirty warriors had been killed, as were thirty to sixty women, children, and elders. Every family felt loss and bitterness at the wanton killing of nonwarriors. Though Joseph and the other chiefs advised against blind hate, they had trouble controlling the angry younger men, who decided that they would now treat all whites, civilians as well as soldiers, as enemies. Lean Elk, a half-blood Nez Perce who had joined the nontreaty Indians in the lower Bitterroot, where he and his band had intended to stay for the summer, became the new leader. Looking Glass would not regain a position of leadership until after the Cow Island skirmishes in late September.

As the Nez Perce hurried through the upper Big Hole, several of their wounded died. Ignoring the advice of their chiefs, some young warriors raided ranches, drove off horses, and killed a number of whites. Stories of these raids caused panic. In the mining town of Bannack, residents prepared for war. Rifle pits dug by the Nez Perce near their Horse Prairie camp tell of their vigilance and expectations as they moved south over Bannock Pass, reentering Idaho. A chance meeting with supply wagons at Birch Creek on August 15 resulted in bloodshed.

Finding the whole countryside alarmed, Howard increased his pace. Learning that the Nez Perce were headed toward the lush Camas Meadows, he caught up with them on August 20. Taking the offensive, the Indians scattered most of the army's pack

YELLOWSTONE

The Nez Perce (Ne-Me-Poo) National Historic Trail crosses the Continental Divide National Scenic Trail for a third and final time at Targhee Pass before entering Montana. Yellowstone tourists were taken captive by the Nez Perce while vacationing in the newly created Yellowstone National Park in Wyoming.

mules, slowing Howard's advance. Mounted troops were sent in pursuit, but after a sharp fight, the beleaguered group escaped over Targhee Pass and into the Yellowstone country. Though Howard did not immediately follow them through Yellowstone, he ordered Capt. S. G. Fisher and his Bannock Indian scouts to track them. Meanwhile, Howard went to Virginia City to replenish supplies and replace the livestock he had lost. From there, he telegraphed the military in eastern Montana; Col. Samuel Sturgis and Major Hart were to block escape routes onto the plains while Howard's forces pushed into the then-five-year-old Yellowstone Park.

BUFFALO AND SNOWSHOEING

Taking to the trail during the winter offers excellent wildlife viewing and a refreshing change of pace from the summer experience. Whatever the season, always keep a safe distance from wildlife.

Shortly after entering Yellowstone Park, Lean Elk became confused about which route to take through the wilderness to reach the homeland of the Crows east of the Absaroka Mountains. A prospector whom they had captured guided them across the Absaroka divide. En route, they met a party of nine tourists. Fearing that they would tell Howard of their whereabouts, the bands carried the tourists along with them. After several escaped and two were wounded and abandoned, the others were set free near Hayden Valley. Once across the divide, the Indians proceeded along the Clark Fork of the Yellowstone Canyon. As a rearguard, they left behind three small parties of warriors, who ran into more tourists, killed and wounded several of them, burned a ranch, and captured some horses before riding to join the others.

The Seventh Cavalry under Sturgis was anxious to regain its reputation, which had suffered under Lt. Col. George Armstrong Custer's defeat. In his haste, Sturgis misjudged the Nez Perce intention and ordered his troops to leave their position on the Clark Fork and proceed south toward the Shoshone. This decision allowed the Nez Perce time to escape the "Absaroka blockade," only to find that the Crows had no intention of giving them asylum or assistance. Their intentions were more along the line of stealing the Nez Perce horses. On friendly terms with the whites, they did not wish to offend them by helping the Nez Perce. Now it seemed that the only hope for peace was to follow what Sitting Bull and the Hunkpapa Sioux had done the year before and after defeating Custer at the battle of the Little Bighorn—go to Canada. Quickly, the Nez Perce moved to the north.

When Sturgis realized the Indians had started down the Clark Fork, he hurried to join Howard's forces, who had now crossed Yellowstone National Park. Both commanders, now fifty miles behind, marveled at the Nez Perce escape. Howard dispatched couriers to Col. Nelson A. Miles at Fort Keogh, requesting that he move rapidly to the northwest to intercept the Nez Perce before they reached Canada or joined forces with Sitting Bull. Moving ahead of Howard, Sturgis caught their rear guard just north of the Yellowstone River on September 13. In a brief skirmish, the rear guard effectively held off the military force, permitting their main cavalcade to escape through the rimrocks of Canyon Creek to the high plains above the Yellowstone River. The chase through Yellowstone country made sensational headlines throughout the country.

With some Crow warriors occasionally harassing them by trying to steal horses, the trail-weary Nez Perce pushed on as fast as their footsore horses could carry them. Familiar with the buffalo hunting grounds, they widened the gap between themselves and the military. Temporarily abandoning pursuit, Sturgis waited for Howard at the Musselshell River. With the Missouri River ahead, the Nez Perce considered the remaining miles to Canada a small hurdle compared with what they had been through during the past three months. Meanwhile, the plains country between the Judith and Snowy Mountains provided good water, wild game, and forage, which gave the horses a chance to regain their strength. The trails to the Missouri River were across traditional hunting ground and were easily followed. The bands stopped only briefly on September 21 at the Reed and Bowles Stockade near present-day Lewistown to trade before heading north into the Missouri River breaks. Then, in just thirty-six hours, they covered seventy miles through the rough breaks country.

The Cow Island crossing provided easy access to the north bank of the Missouri. It was the last major physical barrier before reaching Canada. They established camp a few miles up Cow Creek, and several Nez Perce rode back to the Cow Island steamboat landing for supplies, which they offered to pay for. The supplies, however, could not be sold because they were government freight. When their request was denied, some of the disgruntled young men ran off the landing attendants, took the supplies that were needed, and burned the rest.

A company of the Seventh Infantry that had set out several days earlier from Fort Benton joined troops brought down the river in boats at Cow Island shortly after the raid. This combined force now proceeded after the Nez Perce. The warriors had surrounded a party of teamsters and their wagon train near the mouth of the Judith Basin. When the braves learned of the approaching soldiers, they set the train on fire, killed two of the teamsters, and attacked the troops, which withdrew to Cow Island. The Nez Perce warriors chose not to pursue them. Feeling secure, they believed they now had an open march across the Canadian border.

For the final leg of their flight, Looking Glass, the ranking chief, again took over the leadership. He complained that Lean Elk had moved too fast and he slowed the pace again, despite Lean Elk's warnings. On September 29, after passing the main range of the Bearpaw Mountains, they reached Snake Creek, which ran north to the Milk River, less than forty miles from the Canadian border. An arctic wind, with a hint of snow, whipped across the barren, almost treeless plains. The weary Nez Perce knew that Howard and Sturgis were already several days behind, but they had no idea that Miles was closing in. Looking Glass persuaded the other chiefs to let the bands rest until the next morning. It would be their last camp. For Miles, who chanced upon a steamboat at Carroll Landing that carried his troops across, even the Missouri proved to be no obstacle.

At six in the morning on September 30, Miles's Cheyenne scouts discovered the Nez Perce camp, and two hours later the cavalry, together with a large contingent of Sioux and Cheyenne, swept down upon the Nez Perce's Snake Creek camp. The frontal attack resulted in heavy hand-to-hand combat. The attackers succeeded in running off most of the Nez Perce horses but suffered over fifty casualties in their initial assault. Seeing that direct assault was too costly, Miles imposed a siege line around the camp. For six days, he negotiated with the Nez Perce daily. On October 4, General Howard's troops arrived with reinforcements. By then, Toohoolhoolzote, Lean Elk, Ollokot, and Looking Glass were dead, while White Bird and about two hundred Nez Perce had managed a night escape to Canada. Chief Joseph represented the Nez Perce throughout the negotiations. When Howard and Miles stated through interpreters that there would be no more war, Joseph believed the Nez Perce could surrender on their own terms. It was agreed that should the Nez Perce give up their arms, they would be returned to the Lapwai Reservation. After many deaths and much suffering among the Nez Perce people and the pursuing troops, the flight ended. On October 5, 1877, Chief Joseph offered his rifle to General Howard, who yielded the honor to Colonel Miles. Chief Joseph reportedly spoke to Colonel Miles:

Tell General Howard I know his heart. What he told me before I have in my heart. I am tired of fighting. Our chiefs are all dead. Looking Glass is dead. Toohoolhoolzote is dead. The old men are all dead. It is the young men who say yes or no. He who led the young men is dead. It is cold and we have no blankets. The little children are freezing to death. My people, some of them, have run away to the hills, and have no blankets, no food; no one knows where they are—perhaps freezing to death. I want to have time to look for my children and see how many I can find. Maybe I shall find them among the dead. Hear me, my chiefs. I am tired; my heart is sick and sad. From where the sun now stands, I will fight no more forever.

The apparent terms of the surrender were never kept. Miles's agreement that the Nez Perce could return to the Idaho reservation was overruled by his superiors. About five hundred Nez Perce were first escorted to the Tongue River cantonment in eastern Montana, then to Fort Abraham Lincoln in North Dakota, to Fort Leavenworth in Kansas, and eventually approximately three hundred of these internees were settled in Indian Territory in Oklahoma. For the next eight years, Chief Joseph and his friend Yellow Bull lobbied for the return of their people to Idaho. Finally, in 1885, with the support of Miles and others, 150, including Joseph, were sent to the Colville Reservation in the state of Washington, where they be-

NEZ PERCE (NE-ME-POO) POWWOW

A powwow is held at Nez Perce National Historical Park in Spalding, Idaho, near the western border of the Nez Perce Reservation. The visitor center offers craft demonstrations and contains exhibits of the Nez Perce culture. The Lewis and Clark National Historic Trail also passes through the area.

came known as the Joseph band. Other Nez Perce were returned to Lapwai or placed on other reservations.

White Bird, who had moved on into Canada with about two hundred fellow refugees, was received by Sitting Bull. The Sioux chief told him he would have helped the Nez Perce at Bear's Paw had he known of the situation. "But now you are here," he proclaimed, "and as long as you are with me I will not allow the Americans to take even a child from you without fighting for it."

Today, descendants of the nontreaty Nez Perce live in many places. The largest groups are at the Nez Perce Reservation in Idaho, the Colville Reservation in eastern Washington, and the Umatilla Reservation in Oregon. Others of Nez Perce descent live in Canada and a remnant in Oklahoma. The dispersed population is a direct outcome of the war of 1877 that lasted four months. After the war, numerous attempts were made to extinguish the traditional culture and to replace Nez Perce ways with Euro-American ways.

As a result, today each Nez Perce band has its own identity and special programs to preserve language and culture. As far as anyone knows, there are only two Nez Perce living in the Wallowa Valley, now a region of cattle ranches, farms, and winding rivers. Each year, however, a growing number of Nez Perce come to Joseph, Idaho, for the annual Chief Joseph Days festival and rodeo. Representatives of reservations work with townspeople to organize a large encampment, and traditional dances are held with the Wallowa Mountains in the background. The local ranching community is raising money to build a $1.2 million interpretive center and powwow grounds for the Nez Perce; and the San Francisco–based Trust for Public Land has arranged with the Bonneville Power Administration for the Nez Perce to take title to 10,300 acres of land above Joseph Creek. This wildlife preserve will be tribe-managed. Such a promising future prompted one women to say, "I think now [our ancestors] are rejoicing with us."

CHIEF JOSEPH

Chief Joseph, the last great chief of the Nez Perce, was probably born in the Wallowa Valley in Oregon. His Nez Perce name was Hin-mah-too-yah-lat-kekht, which translates as Thunder Rolling in the Mountains, but he was better known as Young Joseph. His mother was Nez Perce, and his father, also known as Joseph, was Cayuse. Chief Joseph, his father, and Chief Timothy were among Henry Spalding's first converts. Spalding, who had arrived among the Nez Perce in 1836 after traveling to Oregon with his colleague, Marcus Whitman, and their wives, baptized Young Joseph in April 1840. The future Chief Joseph's early years were spent in a missionary school, where he learned and experienced the ways of the whites until he was eight years old.

Joseph grew up in the cold shadow of broken treaties, and when his father died, leadership became his burden. He had been taught that to honor the treaty of 1863 would be to dishonor the memory of his father, and he vowed to keep the Wallowa for his people. In his later years he granted an interview to a reporter of the *North American Review*. A translation of his story relays his father's dying words:

> When I am gone, think of your country. You are the chief of these people. They look to you to guide them. Always remember that your father never sold his country. You must stop your ears whenever you are asked to sign a treaty selling your home. A few years more, and white men will be all around you. They have their eyes on this land. My son, never forget my dying words. This country holds your father's body. Never sell the bones of your father and your mother.

Chief Joseph became a strong leader, but his strengths as statesman and orator were tested when the first white settlers came to the Valley of the Winding Waters in 1871. Already living in the Grande Ronde Valley, white settlers came searching for more and better rangeland, and homesteads began to dot the land. As tensions mounted, Joseph counseled his people to keep peace. His wisdom held for five years, but in the summer of 1876, the first blood was spilled. A pair of white settlers came upon a Nez Perce camp and searched it, looking for stolen horses. When a scuffle ensued, one of the settlers

shot a brave. Joseph and his band sought justice, but the two men were acquitted. Animosity on both sides grew, and more incidents occurred. Finally, the government took a hand and ordered the Nez Perce removal from the Wallowa. Joseph, forced to do what he vowed he never would, led his people away from his homeland toward Idaho and the Lapwai Reservation.

Soon after, young warriors killed four white settlers, and the storm that had been brewing for so many years broke. Joseph was now forced to lead his band out of Idaho. When the five nontreaty bands joined forces, all of the headmen met. The historical record makes it clear that no single leader dictated actions. Yet, as a primary spokesman for his people, Chief Joseph's name became known to the general public. As a result, he was incorrectly credited by the press with the brilliant strategic maneuvers used by the Nez Perce during their flight. And when it was Joseph who surrendered on October 5, 1877, the false assumption was only confirmed.

Nevertheless, Joseph was not a war leader; that duty was left to his skilled brother, Ollokot. In fact, the Wallowa band had several leaders. Those successful and skilled in warfare would have taken the lead in developing battle strategies. As a civil leader and as one of the few headmen remaining, Joseph fulfilled his duties by remaining with those who could not escape. After drafting the conditions of surrender, he drew even greater public attention with his eloquent speech. Because federal officials and the media never did understand the autonomy of the different bands or the council style of tribal leadership, Chief Joseph became the symbol of Indian suffering.

During the sad years of exile, Joseph never ceased trying to persuade the government to allow the nontreaties to return to their homeland. Immediately after Congress first appropriated money to transfer them to Indian Territory in July of 1878, several Nez Perce sickened and died. Joseph again pleaded for their return to Lapwai as promised. When Joseph told the commissioner of Indian affairs, E. A. Hayt, of the promises of Howard and Miles, both confirmed their promises, although Howard maintained that White Bird's flight to Canada had voided the agreement. Miles disagreed, saying, "From all I can learn, the Nez Perces' trouble was caused by the rascality of their Agent, and the encroachment of the whites, and have regarded their treatment as unusually severe."

In succeeding months, Joseph made similar appeals to every official who visited, finally inducing the Indian Bureau's inspector general to permit him to travel to Washington, D.C., to seek a hearing from Pres. Rutherford B. Hayes in 1879. On January 14 of that year, he addressed a large assemblage of American and foreign dignitaries who came to see him. They were stirred by the eloquence of the peace-seeking, humanitarian statesman. His speech roused widespread sympathy, but his mission failed. Too many whites in Idaho were still filled with the spirit of revenge, and the government decided it was unsafe to send the Nez Perce back to their homeland. They were, however, moved to a healthier location in Oklahoma. Still the people continued to die, some by suicide.

In the early '80s, Joseph's persuasive appeals began to reach people outside of the government. Interviewed by newspaper reporters and others, he never failed to impress those he met with his dignity and personal qualities. By 1883, the Nez Perces' plight was a national issue, and a few were allowed to return to Lapwai. The next year, Congress agreed to return to the Northwest those who remained in Oklahoma. Still Joseph pleaded for those who had been sent to the Colville Reservation in eastern Washington, where they were not welcomed by other tribes.

In 1897, he traveled again to Washington, D.C., to press his appeal. In 1899 and 1900, he made visits to the valley of his youth and received a courteous hearing but was refused his request to return. He is said to have died of a broken heart on the Colville Reservation in Nespelem on September 21, 1904. He had kept his promise never to take up arms again, and he had given his best efforts to fostering education and industry among his people, while discouraging drunkenness and gambling. The legendary status that followed him in life remains intact. Commemorated in dozens of ways, his name will undoubtedly endure as an eloquent

American leader. "Let me be a free man," Joseph said, "free to travel, free to stop, free to work, free to trade where I choose, free to choose my own teachers, free to follow the religion of my fathers, free to think and talk and act for myself—and I will obey every law or submit to the penalty."

The Trail Today

The Nez Perce (Nee-Me-Poo) National Historic Trail (NPNHT) was used in its entirety only once. However, component trails and roads that made up the route bore generations of use prior to and after the 1877 flight of the Nez Perce. Trails and roads perpetuated through continued use often became portions of transportation systems, though some were later abandoned for more direct routes or routes better suited for modern conveniences. Some of the abandoned segments were altered by floods, power lines, and other structures and cross a variety of ownerships. Where the elements have erased all trace of the momentary passing of the Nez Perce, a best guess was made, on the basis of historical research and topography, to fill in missing links. Now, more than a century after the epic event, the path of the Nez Perce remains a scenic adventure filled with historic information and cultural lessons.

From the deeply incised Columbia Plateau, across the Continental Divide and a succession of ranges, canyons, and valleys, through forests and rolling grassland plains, across badlands and mighty rivers, washes, gullies, and creek bottoms, the Nez Perce (Nee-Me-Poo) National Historic Trail winds through some of the most rugged and spectacular scenery in western America. In the backcountry, the trail is largely inaccessible to vehicles, except where existing roads coincide with or intersect the Nez Perce route. Where the trail had been spared pavement and other imprints of modern use, its historic values are enhanced and in no way diminished by a lack of access by automobile. Yet the route was not chosen by the Nez Perce for its scenery. From the Fort Fizzle incident onward, expediency and strategic advantage dictated their course. While modern travelers enjoy the vast scale and scope of the setting of the Nez Perce flight, following the route can also offer opportunities to relate geographic factors to the strategies involved in the retreat and pursuit. In some localities where the precise route is debatable, hikers and historians have the opportunity to explore and consider their own theories.

The combination of scenic and historic factors makes travel over the length of the Nez Perce route a unique and inspirational experience. While only a few travelers might trace its length in one long journey, many follow parallel existing roads to major points of interest. New and improved hiking trails ease travel over many of the hidden or forgotten portions of the historic route. Opportunities for backpacking and camping are almost unlimited. National forests in the four states have many trails and campgrounds. And horses take riders over a variety of terrain, including rolling prairie grasslands, washes, gullies, creek bottoms, forests, badlands, and low mountain foothills and ridges. In fact, as an outcome of one family's yearly trek on the famous trail, an annual ride was formed by the National Appaloosa Horse Club. The connection is natural enough. After the Spanish brought the horse to North America, the Nez Perce began breeding Appaloosas in Washington's Palouse River region. The name is even derived from "Palouse." These annual trips take about a week and involve about three hundred riders.

Started in 1991 as an outgrowth of the advisory council that assisted in the trail's initial development, the Nez Perce National Historic Trail Foundation continues to promote and interpret the trail, and members bring the Nez Perce story to schools and other public functions. In the spirit of sharing, the Nez Perce National Historic Park (NPNHP) and the National Trail share many common sites, such as Old Chief Joseph's Grave, the Camas Meadows Battlefield, Big Hole National Battlefield, and the Bear's Paw Battleground, to name a few. Originally created in 1965, the Nez Perce National Historic Park was composed of twenty-four sites in Idaho. After 1992 legislation, fourteen additional sites in Oregon, Washington, Idaho, and Montana were added. Each park site is significant to the history of the Nez Perce tribe and the United States. Visiting these sites is unlike touring most national parks; it is more like visiting a mosaic of ideas than a physical entity. The park's sites, under federal, local, and private control, relay the history of the Nez Perce as a people and their region through the gradual accumulation of information attained at each site, such as the traditional Nez Perce homesite and Young Chief Joseph's burial site on the Colville Reservation. Park headquarters are located at Spalding, near Lewiston, Idaho. The national historic trail focuses on and commemorates the flight of Nez Perce, while park sites along the route complete the picture of the Nez Perce.

OREGON

1. WALLOWA LAKE. The re-
mains of Old Joseph were moved
(1926) to this site near Joseph
from the campsite where he died
(1871). After the whites who
came to own the property opened
his grave (1886) and shamelessly
removed his skull for a souvenir,
more respectful whites, with the
permission of the Nez Perce,
transferred his remains to the
more appropriate site. Joseph's
father's grave, now the Chief Joseph Monument, was a key ele-
ment in the events of the Nez
Perce story. The Wallowa Lake SP
has a visitor center and opportunities for hiking, boat rental, fishing, swimming, picnicking, and
camping. *Other attractions:* Chief
Joseph Days Rodeo; pack trips to
the High Wallowas; Gateway to
Hells Canyon NRA. *Nearby:* Traditional campsite of the Wallowa
Nez Perce (a unit of the NPNHP)
where Old Chief Joseph died;
Wallowa-Whitman NF.

IDAHO

2. DUG BAR. Located in Hells
Canyon NRA, the site was a
traditional Nez Perce seasonal
migration crossing point and the
probable Snake River crossing
point when Joseph's band was
forced to move to the reservation
at Lapwai. *Other attractions:* The
Nee-Me-Poo National Recreation
Trail is a 3.7-mile section of the
trail that traverses the Wallowa-
Whitman NF, starting at Lone
Pine Saddle and ending at Dug
Bar. The hike is generally too hot

during the summer and the hiker
must watch for rattlesnakes. Dug
Bar can also be reached by jet-
boating upriver from the mouth
of the Grande Ronde River or by
taking a float trip downstream
from Hells Canyon Dam.

3. WHITE BIRD. Seven stops
along the auto loop southwest of
Grangeville interpret events of
the initial encounter between the
Nez Perce and Howard's soldiers
and volunteers. The trailhead of
the walking tour is located at an
old wagon road that connected
the Camas Prairie with the Salmon River canyons (NPHNP).
Lahmotta, or White Bird, Canyon
lies to the south. *Nearby:* Nez
Perce NF; Nez Perce Indian Reservation.

4. CLEARWATER. Roadside interpretive signs mark the Clearwater Battle Site, the Cottonwood
Skirmishes, and Weippe Prairie
(each are units of the NPHNP).
After an unprovoked attack near
Kooskia, Looking Glass and the
Palouse bands moved to the
mouth of the Cottonwood Creek,
where they were soon met by the
main body who had been involved in skirmishes on July 3
and 5. On July 11 Howard's command crossed the Clearwater
near Stites, hoping to take the
Indians by surprise. *Nearby:*
Weippe Prairie, a traditional
root-gathering place where the
Nez Perce first met and helped
Lewis and Clark (LCNHT), became the meeting place of the
Nez Perce after the Clearwater
battle. At Spalding, the Nez Perce
NHP protects the Spalding site

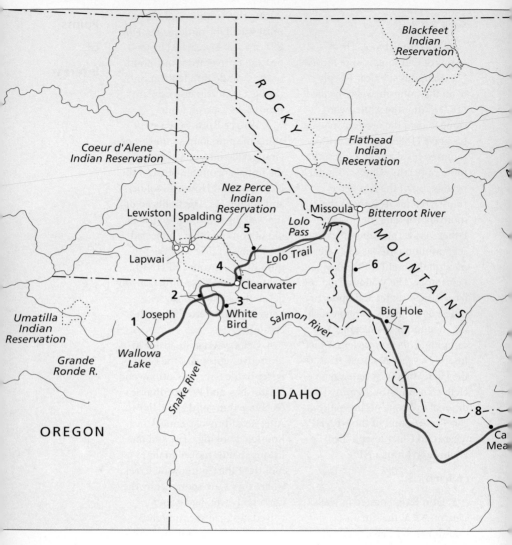

and has a visitor center and museum.

IDAHO/MONTANA

5. LOLO TRAIL NATIONAL HISTORIC LANDMARK. The historic Nez Perce trail extends roughly from Weippe to Lolo Pass. U.S. Highway 12 closely parallels the route. In addition, the rugged one-lane Lolo Motorway can be taken when weather permits. There are no facilities available along the dirt road, which generally takes two days to drive. Before hiking or driving the Lolo Motorway, contact the U.S. Forest Service at Orofino,

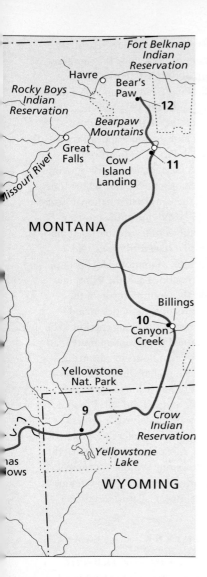

Fort Belknap
Indian
Reservation
Havre
Bear's
Rocky Boys
Paw
Indian
Reservation
12
Bearpaw
Mountains
Great
Falls
Cow
Island
Landing
11
Missouri River

MONTANA

Billings
10
Canyon
Creek
Yellowstone
Nat. Park
9
Crow
Indian
Reservation
Yellowstone
Lake
WYOMING
has
ows

Lolo Pass, or the Powell Ranger
Station for information on current conditions. A seasonal Forest
Service visitor center is available
at Lolo Pass and the Lochsa Historical Ranger Station on U.S. 12.
Lolo NF exhibits at Howard
Creek and Fort Fizzle give details
of NPNHT events. *Other attrac-*

tions: In Missoula, Montana, the
museum at Fort Missoula; the
Missoula Museum of the Arts; the
Rocky Mountain Elk Foundation/
Wildlife Center; the Ninemile
Remount Depot and Ranger
Station, a working ranger station
on a five-thousand-acre ranch;
Smokejumpers Base Aerial Fire
Depot. *Nearby:* Nez Perce,
Clearwater and Lolo NFs; Selway-
Bitterroot Wilderness.

M O N T A N A

6. **BITTERROOT VALLEY.**
Frightened settlers gathered
together in forts along the route
as the Nez Perce passed through.
Other attractions: Chief Looking
Glass RA, south of Lolo; Fort
Owens State Monument and St.
Mary's Mission — the first Ro-
man Catholic mission in the
Northwest — at Stevenson; Medi-
cine Tree, south of Darby; Sula
Peak, north of Sula; Gibbons
Pass, from the Scarred Trees
down Trail Creek to Big Hole.
Nearby: At Hamilton, the Ravalli
County Museum; Bitterroot and
Nez Perce NFs.

M O N T A N A / I D A H O

7. **BIG HOLE.** Big Hole NB
(NPNHP) memorializes the Nez
Perce men, women, and children,
the soldiers, and the Bitterroot
volunteers who clashed at the
battle of the Big Hole (August 9–
10). This battle convinced the
Nez Perce that they could not
expect to be left alone by the
army. The park, west of Wisdom,
Montana, has a visitor center that
overlooks the battlefield, a mu-

seum, trails, and picnicking. En route to Camas Meadows, the Nez Perce had raided some of the neighboring ranches. *Other attractions:* Bannock State Monument, east of Jackson; Pierce Ranch, south of Grant; Brenner Ranch and Donovan Ranch, south of Red Butte; Birch Creek Monument, south of Leadore near Birch Creek; Hole-in-the-Rock State Station, north of Dubois. *Nearby:* Beaverhead, Salmon, and Targhee NFs.

8. CAMAS MEADOWS. General Howard lost the momentum gained at Big Hole when the Nez Perce scattered his livestock at Camas Meadows (NPNHP), west of present-day Island Park Reservoir. Failing to intercept the Indians before they crossed the Continental Divide at Targhee Pass, he returned to Virginia City for supplies. *Nearby:* Henry's Lake SP; Targhee Pass (CDNST); Targhee NF; West Yellowstone, Montana, with its Museum of the Yellowstone, Grizzly Discovery Center, and nearby Big Mountain Ski and Summer Resort.

MONTANA/WYOMING

9. YELLOWSTONE NATIONAL PARK. The Nez Perce route is well documented but not marked. The Nez Perce traveled from West Yellowstone up the Madison, Firehole, and Nez Perce drainages toward Trout Creek and the Yellowstone River, east of Pelican Valley. They may have taken either of two possible routes through the Absaroka Range. From the convergence of these

two routes at Hoodoo Basin, the trail proceeds along the southern rim of the Clark Fork Canyon, climbing Dead Indian Hill, and descending to the plains near the mouth of Clark Fork Canyon. Much of the route appears today as it did in 1877. Interpretive signs mark many historic sites in the Shoshone NF and Yellowstone NP, the world's first national park (1872) and one of the most successful wildlife sanctuaries in the world. *Other attractions:* Old Faithful, Mammoth Hot Springs, Yellowstone Lake, the Paintpots, and the Grand Canyon of the Yellowstone. Activities include hiking, backpacking (permit to be obtained in person, no more than forty-eight hours in advance), horse rental, rowboat and motorboat rental, fishing, snowcoach tours, and self-guided auto tours. Campgrounds, visitor centers, and museums offer interpretation. At Cooke City, Montana, the Yellowstone Wildlife Museum. *Nearby:* Targhee, Bridger-Teton, Shoshone, Gallatin, and Custer NFs.

MONTANA

10. CANYON CREEK BATTLE MONUMENT. After emerging from Yellowstone NP, the Nez Perce headed toward the Canadian border. Just north of the Yellowstone River, near Laurel, they fought a series of successful rearguard actions that impeded the progress of the pursuing troops (NPNHP). A marker seven miles north of Laurel commemorates the Canyon Creek battle,

where the Nez Perce fought troops led by Sturgis. A life-sized metal statue of Joseph stands watch in Laurel's Fireman's Park. *Other attractions:* In Billings, the Western Heritage Center; Black Otter Trail; Billings Night Rodeo. At Ryegate, the Chief Joseph Monument commemorates the passage of the Nez Perce through the area. *Nearby:* Lake Josephine and Lake Elmo SRAs; Petroglyph Cave State Monument; Crow Indian Reservation.

11. Cow Island Landing. From present-day Lewistown, the Nez Perce followed a series of open ridges along Dog Creek. At Cow Island Landing, they took supplies after a brief skirmish with soldiers and civilians guarding a steamboat freight depot. West of Cow Island they followed a long ridge lying immediately south of the Missouri River. Just above the Cow Island crossing, the ridge ends in rough breaks, which provided easy access to the river. The Cow Island crossing had been used for many years by migrating buffalo and Plains Indians. Today the unique site within Cow Island Landing RA has three congressional designations—the NPNHT, LCNHT, and BLM's Upper Missouri National Wild and Scenic River. *Nearby:* In Lewistown, the Central Montana Museum; Judith Landing and James Kipp RAs; Charles M. Russell NWR.

12. Bear's Paw Battlefield. North of the Missouri, the trail up the Cow Creek canyon bottom and the Cow Island wagon road provided direct access to the foothills of the Bearpaw Mountains. To avoid Cheyenne scouts they traveled canyon trails before reaching the glacial plains east of the Bearpaws. Believing the army to be well behind them, they selected their Snake Creek campsite for its merits as a protective site against an oncoming storm rather than for its defensive position. Roads now parallel much of the route north of Judith Gap, but the historic landscape remains unchanged. South of Chinook, Bear's Paw Battlefield (NPNHP), the site of Chief Joseph's surrender and speech that stirred the nation, marks the end of the trail. There is a self-guided walk and picnic tables. In Chinook, the Blaine County Museum has a multimedia presentation about the battle. *Nearby:* Belknap Indian Reservation; Beaver Creek Park; Black Coulee NWR.

TWELVE DOGS

Descending onto Lake Lucille in Wasilla, contenders in the Iditarod Sled Dog Race may begin with as many as sixteen dogs on their team.

Iditarod National Historical Trail

If you love the grandeur of nature—its canyons, its mountains and its mightiness, and love to feel the thrill of their presence—then take the trip by all means; you will not be disappointed. But if you wish to travel on "flowery beds of ease" and wish to snooze and dream that you are a special product of higher civilization too finely adjusted for this more strenuous life, then don't. But may God pity you, for you will lose one thing worth living for if you have the opportunity to make this trip and fail to do so.

C. K. SNOW, 1919

The idea of crossing the great expanse of the Alaskan interior continues to stimulate the adventurer's imagination like few other thoughts. The stark beauty of the land, the bitter cold of the wind, the mystery of the unknown are all to be found on the Iditarod Trail, whether one is snowshoeing, cross-country skiing, snowmobiling, biking, hiking, or, of course, in the grand tradition of the trail, mushing. Originally developed by native Indians and Eskimos for winter travel, the trail was an important lifeline at the turn of the century for Alaskan gold miners. Mushers delivered food, supplies, and even the U.S. mail to towns such as Ruby, Ophir, Nome, and the trail's namesake, Iditarod. Today, when we hear each March that the Iditarod, "the last great race," is underway, we are transported in our imaginations to the far boundaries of our vast country, where a few are called to test their mental and physical stamina over a dogsled course that exceeds a thousand miles. The significance of the history of the trail to the entire country was recognized in 1978 when Congress established a new category under the National Trails System Act, designating the Iditarod among the first National Historical Trails.

ADMINISTERING AGENCY
Bureau of Land Management
6881 Abbott Loop Road
Anchorage, AK 99507
907-267-1246

FURTHER INFORMATION
Iditarod Trail Committee, Inc.
P.O. Box 870800
Wasilla, AK 99687
907-373-5155

ESTABLISHED
1978

APPROXIMATE MILEAGE
2,450 miles (3,945 kilometers)

MAIN ROUTE
938 miles (1,500 kilometers)

STATE
Alaska

The History of the Trail

The Iditarod National Historic Trail (INHT) is composed of the federally administered areas of the Gold Rush Trail network, which connects Seward in southern Alaska with Nome in northwestern Alaska via the Iditarod Mining District.* The 938-mile trail, commonly known as the Iditarod Trail during the Iditarod gold rush, was formally constructed by the Alaska Road Commission during 1910–11. This constitutes the primary route of the historic trail. Yet branching from this primary route are hundreds of miles of land- and water-based routes and trails that were important not only during the 1910s but also during the entire gold-rush period, from the 1880s into the 1920s. Some routes were based on even earlier American Indian trails.

In addition to trails used during this period, other routes used yearly in the Iditarod Trail Sled Dog Race are also part of this trail system. Collectively, these trail segments and associated historic sites make up what is referred to as the Iditarod National Historic Trail System, which includes the federally administered portions of the gold-rush trail system. Remaining portions of the network are to be officially recognized as components of the

*Material in this section is taken from the Bureau of Land Management's *The Iditarod National Historic Trail, Seward to Nome Route: A Comprehensive Management Plan.*

national trails system once cooperative agreements between the secretary of the interior and the nonfederal land managers are executed.

The Iditarod Trail was developed during Alaska's gold-rush era when it served a string of mining camps, trading posts, and other settlements founded between 1880 and 1920. The Alaska gold rush was an extension of the western mining frontier that dates from the California gold discovery in 1848. In each new territory, gold strikes caused a surge in population, the establishment of a territorial government, and the development of a transportation system linking the goldfields with the rest of the nation. Alaska too followed these stages. With the increase in gold production, the nonnative population boomed from a recorded 430 in 1880 to some 36,400 in 1910. In 1912 President Taft signed the act creating the Territory of Alaska. At that time, transportation systems included steamship and steamboat lines, railroads, and four major cross-country dogsled winter trails. Running from Seward to Nome, the Iditarod was the longest of the latter. Its antecedents were the trails of the Tanaina and Ingalik Indians and the Inupiaq and Yupik Eskimos, who knew the route and who had developed winter modes of travel—the dogsled and the snowshoe. A peaceful collaboration with native groups made settlement easier for the newcomers.

The native sled was built to carry all the owner's possessions from camp to camp or camp to village. The owner ran in front, guiding the dog team. One Russian wrote in the 1840s that his countrymen had introduced the method of harnessing the dogs single file or in pairs in front of the sled. The Russians also introduced the concept of a "leader," or lead dog. This well-trained dog could keep the others in line and recognize voice commands for direction. During the Russian era, guide poles, and later handlebars, were attached to the rear of the sled to direct, push, and balance the weight. Russians also developed part of the later Iditarod Trail as a supply route for fur-trading posts. Fur-trading expeditions, sent by the Russian American Company, crossed the Kaltag Portage to Nulato on the Yukon River along a section built later as part of the Iditarod Trail. When the American fur-trading companies took over the Russian posts (after 1867), they continued using the Kaltag Portage and extended it as part of the Yukon River Trail, linking fur-trading posts into Canada. From there came French-Canadian traders and trappers, with their voice commands for dogsledding: Americanized as "gee" for *ye* (go right), "haw" for *cha* (go left), and "mush" for *marché* (go ahead). Dogsledding as a method of transportation was to aid the movement north by the time of the first gold strikes.

Alaska's gold rushes occurred after the other western states had passed beyond their frontier mining eras. As those frontiers closed, parties ventured north to prospect, trap, and trade. They came north from the industrializing mines of Montana and the Black Hills, from the deserts of Arizona and the mountains of Colorado. Each was in search of an El Dorado, or at least enough of a grubstake to continue an itinerant lifestyle. These were miners after the California fashion, who had moved up the

A FRIENDLY GREETING

The Iditarod National Historic Trail leads dog mushers and snowmobilers to villages and towns settled mainly by native inhabitants. Alaska's Eskimos belong to two distinct language groups. The Yupik Eskimos live along the Bering Sea and in milder settings, while the Inupiaq people live above the northern shore of Norton Sound.

Pacific coast with the series of strikes: into the Cassiar, then into Juneau, and, during the 1880s, into the Yukon. The particular conditions of geography and the arctic climate changed familiar patterns of mining. Dogs and sleds replaced the burro, sourdough replaced johnnycakes, and cigars (with their mosquito deterrent) replaced the plug and chew.

The first mining area to develop along the future route of the Iditarod Trail was the Cook Inlet country. The glacial Kenai and Chugach Ranges cut along the inlet's eastern shores, creating numerous bays and arms. In a few of the streams pouring into the ocean, gold had been deposited in rich pockets. Though Russians and early trader-prospectors found traces of gold, the first major find did not occur until the 1890s. In 1891, Al King, a veteran prospector from the interior, working with gold pan and rocker, located gold on Resurrection Creek, a steeply graded stream flowing north into Turnagain Arm. King kept his find quiet until 1893 when prospectors and traders followed the usual practice of establishing a mining district, creating rules for claim ownership, and electing a recorder. From 1895 to 1896 the Turnagain Arm Mining District boomed.

News of rich finds on the tributaries of the Six-Mile, Resurrection, and Glacier Creeks drew a reported three thousand people into Turnagain Arm. Most arrived by steamship or sailing vessel, precariously navigating the treacherous tides of the arm in order to dock at the log-cabin communities of Hope and Sunrise. Several hundred other miners took the Portage Glacier route. Steamers from Juneau and Sitka unloaded their passengers in winter at Portage Bay, where the miners had a fifteen-mile trek across a glacier, the frozen Placer River, and the frozen arm to Sunrise. It did not take long for the miners to be introduced to the hardships of Alaska's winter travel. Some froze on the glacier, others starved while lost in whiteouts, and a few drowned in the arm. During the 1890s, Sunrise, Hope, and scattered trading posts at Resurrection Bay, Knik Arm, and the Susitna River were connected by roughly blazed trails. Miners and merchants combined to build a wagon road from Sunrise up Six-Mile Creek along the mining claims.

Like their counterparts on the Yukon, miners in south-central Alaska began adapting to the northern climate, and prospecting followed the cycle of seasons. In the fall, after freezeup, they hooked up their dogs and pulled their Yukon sleds, loaded with a year or two's worth of supplies, up the Kenai, Susitna, Knik, or other river, then established camp at a promising location and spent the winter thawing ground and digging gravel. At spring breakup, with plenty of water, they sluiced the hoped-for gold from pay dirt. At season's end they built rafts or poling boats and floated back downstream to the trading posts or towns. In this manner, the land was prospected, and as goldfields were found to the north in the Talkeetna Mountains and the Yenta River drainage, the network of trails was extended. The greatest impetus to Alaska mining occurred, however, in the Canadian Klondike goldfields. After gold was discovered there in 1896, the stampede of 1897–98 brought an estimated fifty thousand north. Many of these never reached the Klondike, but instead flowed over into the Cook Inlet country, the American Yukon River country, and elsewhere.

During the summer of 1898, on the shores of the Bering Sea, a handful of inexperienced prospectors happened upon the gold of Anvil Creek. On September 20, 1898, Jafet Lindeberg, Eric Lindblom, and John Byrneson, "the three lucky Swedes," staked the richest creekbeds of the Cape Nome goldfields. The following July, gold was found mixed in the sand along the Bering Sea. Nome became an instant city as wild stories spread that the seafloor was covered with gold. The stampede that followed became one of the West's and Alaska's largest. The summer of 1900, an estimated twenty thousand to thirty thousand people arrived by steamer to dig the golden sands; coastal and inland hydraulic plants were introduced to wash away gravel. Nome gained national notoriety for its violence and corrupt federal officials, who were later exposed and impris-

BOARD OF TRADE SALOON

Gold on beaches lured thousands to Nome in 1900. Bars are still active, especially in March when visitors fill hotels for the finish of the Iditarod Sled Dog Race. During winter months the frozen Bering Sea is transformed into a golf course and during summer, its beaches still yield gold.

oned. These events were immortalized by the novels of Rex Beach. With the Old West below the forty-ninth parallel losing its rambunctious spirit, other restless souls found their way north. In 1899 Wyatt Earp came to Nome and for two years promoted prizefights and ran a saloon—until news of a new gold strike in Nevada enticed him away.

The people of Nome who missed the last boat "Outside" were isolated when the Bering Sea froze from October to June. In order to break down this isolation, the people focused their concern on wintertime ties to the rest of the nation. A telegraph system was constructed from Valdez across Alaska to Nome.

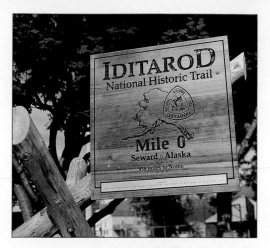

MILE 0 SEWARD

At the turn of the century, mail and supplies brought into the port of Seward were transferred to sled-dog teams for the long trek up the trail. Today, summer cruises take passengers to Seward, where they can catch the beginning of the trail at the Mile 0 marker.

Trails were cleared to bring in needed supplies and the mail. Between 1898 and 1908, four routes were used to connect ice-free ports with Nome. The first ran from Skagway to Dawson, Yukon Territory, then down the Yukon River to the coast of the Bering Sea and Nome. This two-thousand-mile route, though used by express companies and the mail carriers, was considered unsatisfactory because of its great distance and because it crossed Canadian territory. The search for an "all-American route" and the demand for a shorter haul brought about the development of two aborted routes—the Val-

dez to Eagle Trail and the Iliamna Route. Each proved uneconomical. But after the gold rush to Fairbanks in 1903, the Valdez route became feasible through Fairbanks and the Yukon River Trail. By 1904–5, all winter mail bound for Nome went by way of Valdez and Fairbanks.

Nonetheless, wintertime travelers to Nome still believed the shortest route to get there was via the Cook Inlet country. Railroad promoters had already begun construction of the ill-fated Alaska Central Railway north from Seward. Then in 1907, because of the development of Seward on Resurrection Bay and recent gold discoveries in the Innoko District, the army's Alaska Road Commission took action. Major Wilds Richardson ordered Walter Goodwin and a crew of three to blaze a route from Seward through the Cook Inlet country and beyond to Nome. From January to April 1908, Goodwin blazed the Iditarod Trail. In a report to Richardson, he concluded that the eight-hundred-mile proposed trunkline would be feasible only if mines of value were developed, attracting additional traffic. Unknown to Goodwin, two prospectors, John Beaton and William Dikeman, had penetrated the virgin territory and uncovered pay dirt in the area that would soon become the Iditarod Mining District.

The Iditarod became Alaska's last major gold rush and its most productive strike in a vast area known as the Inland Empire, which spread from Ruby on the Yukon River, south along the Kuskokwim Mountains into the drainages of the Innoko and Upper Kuskokwim Rivers. Though prospectors had visited this area since the 1880s, only minor stampedes had occurred before 1907, when strikes were made on Ganes Creek and near Ophir. The rush to Iditarod and Ruby, between 1910 and 1912, set ten thousand stampeders in motion, with each community reaching peak populations of three thousand. Within two decades, $30 million worth of gold was dug from these fields. Unlike Nome and the Cook Inlet country, which were easily accessible by ocean steamers, the interior camps in the Inland Empire (the Iditarod, Innoko, and Ruby Districts) were isolated. The majority of stampeders from May to October took steamships to the tidewater then up the meandering Yukon, Innoko, or Kuskokwim Rivers for as far as a thousand miles. Freezeup then shifted traffic to the trails.

Trails developed in the Inland Empire in direct response to gold discoveries. Prospectors took the natural land routes or native routes to the Innoko mines in 1906 and 1907. The next year William Goodwin and his crew blazed and cleared the Seward-to-Nome winter trail, which became the main winter access route to the Iditarod District. A loop trail left the main trail at Takotna and followed the creeks to the town of

Iditarod, and from there north through to Dikeman to rejoin the trunkline trail at Dishkakat. A trail from Ruby to the Yukon River ran south in response to strikes made on the tributaries of the Nowitna and Upper Innoko Rivers. By 1913, an alternate trail to Nome left the trunkline at Ophir and headed north to Ruby via the gold camps of Cripple, Poorman, and Long. From Ruby the musher followed the Yukon River Trail east to Fairbanks or west to Nome.

These crude trails built by the mining-camp residents were upgraded by the Alaska Road Commission. In 1905 Congress established that commission as part of the army's road and trail building efforts to connect the military posts and the new mining camps with tidewater ports and navigable streams. Major Wilds P. Richardson headed the commission; with his engineers he set the standards for construction and blazed the main trail. The few early wagon roads built by the Alaska Road Commission along the Iditarod Trail ran from communities to mining areas: from Nome to Solomon and Council, from Ruby to Long, from Iditarod to Flat, from Knik to the Willow mines, and from Sunrise to Canyon and Six-Mile Creeks. These roads were improved, enabling their use in the summer as well. Most of the travelers on the Iditarod did not go from trailhead to trailhead or Seward to Nome as they did on the other trails of settlement in the American West, however, Instead, they mushed from the ice-free harbor of Seward to the various mining districts or used trail segments while traveling between mining camps and trade centers.

The majority of the travelers using the trail were prospectors, trappers, or natives who traveled either without dogs or with only one or two to help pull a sledload of supplies to isolated cabins. The dogsled driver who raced along the trail carrying fresh eggs and oranges, mail and express packages, or shipments of gold became the hero of the trail, with noteworthies earning nicknames — Frank Tondreau, known from Belfast to Point Barrow as the Malemute Kid; the famous racer John "Iron Man" Johnson and his indefatigable Siberians; Capt. Ulysses Grant Norton, the tireless Trojan of the trails; the Eskimo, Split the Wind; and the wandering Japanese, Jujira Wada. All were welcomed in the camps. One of these celebrities was sixty-three-year-old Bob Griffis, who drove the annual Iditarod gold train. Griffis, who had driven stages during the Black Hills rush in the Dakotas, ran the mail from Unalakleet to Nome for a decade before the Miners and Merchants Bank of Iditarod acquired his services. In November 1910, he started from Iditarod for Seward with a quarter-million dollars worth of gold lashed to his dogsled. Though the scene was set for a spectacular robbery, he knew that the Alaskan winter was deterrent enough to ward off

robbers. Thirty-seven days later, his three teams and their guards arrived unscathed in Seward. He went on to protect the Iditarod gold trains until World War I. To his credit, the trains, which carried up to $1 million worth of gold on their annual trek to Seward, were never robbed.

The relative ease of travel along the trails during this period was made possible by the maintenance provided by the Alaska Road Commission and by the many roadhouses that once lined the Iditarod Trail and its branches. During stampedes to new gold strikes, numerous impromptu roadhouses vied for traveler patronage. After business settled to a routine, roadhouses were naturally thinned to locations roughly a day's journey apart, or approximately twenty miles. Roadhouse operators might begin business in a tent, then during the first winter build a log cabin, adding another story or wing as business increased. Accommodations varied from filthy to pleasant. Near Iditarod travelers praised the Bonanza Creek Roadhouse as the best on the trail. The fresh meat and roomy bunks were termed luxuries. Henry Cox's Poorman Roadhouse had a lean-to kitchen with running water and a dining room plus an "outside white porcelain bathtub." Patrons were entertained with a pool table, card tables, and a phonograph. The nine single beds had springs and mattresses. Once the stampede days passed and travel on the trails declined, proprietors faced economic problems, and their mainstays became the mail contractors who stopped overnight.

The first mail contract to Iditarod ran from Nulato, on a branch of the Valdez-Fairbanks-Nome route. In 1914, "Colonel" Harry Revell, a stampeder to the Cook Inlet country in 1896, received the first contract to carry the winter mail from Seward to Iditarod. With his father-in-law, he operated a winter mail service connecting Seward, Sunrise, Girdwood, Eklutna, Knik, and Susitna Station and boasted of establishing a mail route between Seward and Nome. Although travel between the two points was common, the mail route actually extended only to Iditarod. Connections with Nome were made via a short spur route from Takotna to Ruby, where the main mail run was joined. After 1918, Revell gave up the mail contract. With the end of the mail runs, the roadhouses began to close. This lack caused residents to demand protection for winter travel.

A strong voice in the territorial legislature during the early 1910s, representatives of the voters along the Iditarod Trail enacted legislation to aid travelers. All roadhouses were required to keep a list of travelers in order to help find the last known location of lost mushers. Funds were also set aside for staking trails and building shelter cabins in order to save the lives of travelers stranded by blizzards.

By World War I, the days of

ROHN CHECKPOINT AND RAINY PASS SIGN

Snow-machine enthusiasts, snowshoers, and cross-country skiers homebase at the Rainy Pass hunting lodge as they enjoy the winter trail in the Alaska Range. Once across Rainy Pass Lake, the trail climbs to the summit, then starts a steep descent along Dalzell Creek to the Tatina River, where it turns sharply to Rohn. There a shelter cabin takes the place of the old Rohn Roadhouse.

TWO DOGS WITH HANDLER

In 1925, the dog team and driver captured the attention of the nation when Nome was threatened by a diphtheria epidemic. Planes were thwarted by weather, but twenty mushers and their dogs carried badly needed serum to Nome. Today veterinarians examine every musher's dogs at the twenty checkpoints along the trail.

isolation were coming to an end. The activities Outside began to have more bearing on local events. Young miners and workers enlisted in the service and left the country, never to return. Money expected to be funneled into trails or mines went Outside instead. The slow construction of the federal government's Alaska Railroad and its anticipated aid to growth did little to stabilize the Inland Empire's economy. Instead, many settlers moved to the railroad town of Anchorage. By the 1920s, dogsled transportation was challenged by airplanes, and on February 21, 1924, the first Alaskan airmail delivery arrived in McGrath. By the end of the decade, airmail had replaced the run to Nome.

The dog team and driver captured the attention of the nation for a final episode known as the "serum run" in 1925. A feared epidemic of diphtheria caught the town of Nome without enough serum to inoculate the community. A wire for help went out, but plans to send an airplane from Fairbanks were thwarted by weather. Instead, a relay of dog teams made the run from Nenana, an Alaska Railroad town, down the Yukon River Trail to the Iditarod Trail and into Nome. Twenty mushers carried the life-saving serum in blizzard conditions for 674 miles in 127½ hours. The mushers became instant heroes, and President Coolidge sent medals. Balto, the mongrel dog leading the last team into Nome, had bravely fought a blizzard and saved his team from open water. Newspapers from all over the world took pictures of him but confused him with his owner's champion racer, Togo, who had also led a team in the relay to Nome. Balto was used as a model for statues of dogs in places as distant as New York City's Central Park. Balto's owner, who thought the statue should have been of Togo, sold his heroic lead dog and team to a movie studio. Years later, when it was discovered that the dogs were traveling with a carnival, the children of Cleveland, Ohio, took up their cause. They worked hard to raise the money to buy them and gave the dogs a new home in the Cleveland Zoo, where Balto was cared for and admired the rest of his life.

With the successful serum run, dogsledding, the Iditarod Trail, and Alaska's gold-rush frontier era went out in a blaze of glory. After that, only the Alaskan natives and others in the backcountry used dogsleds for winter transport. By the 1960s, most of these teams had been replaced with the snowmobile. In time, the Iditarod Trail and the importance of dog teams in Alaska's early settlement were forgotten. Then in 1966, Dorothy Page of Wasilla served as president of a local committee organized to celebrate

JACK, LORI, SUSAN, KATHY

At a stop in McGrath, Iditarod Trail race manager Jack Niggemyer meets with (from left to right) Sky Trekking Alaska's bush pilot Lori Egge, four-time Iditarod winner Susan Butcher, and the author, Kathleen Cordes. In 1997, the Iditarod race celebrated its twenty-fifth anniversary.

the centennial of the Alaska Purchase. She conceived the idea of a modern sled-dog race over the Iditarod Trail. This won the support of Joe Redington, Sr., a musher and kennel operator who had a passion for the dying art of mushing. Together they successfully staged the first Iditarod race, as inspired by Nome's All-Alaska Sweepstakes held from 1908 to World War I.

In 1967 and again in 1969, a sixty-mile race was run over a part of the Iditarod Trail. By 1973, the goal was to have the race go all the way to the ghost town of Iditarod. However, as 1973 came closer, Redington decided the race should go a thousand-plus miles to Nome. Despite comments that it couldn't be done, twenty-two mushers successfully retraced the

The Iditarod Sled Dog Race, known internationally as "the last great race," runs every March, alternating between a southern and a northern route. Both routes take the racers from Anchorage to Nome, but the southern route, which runs during odd-numbered years, generally follows trail segments identified on the Iditarod National Historic Trail system leading from the town of Iditarod to the villages of Shageluk, Anvik, and Grayling and then follows the Yukon River to the village of Kaltag. The northern route heads to Ruby rather than Iditarod before joining the trail to Nome. This route is ten miles shorter, but both are billed as a 1,049-mile race. The distance, Alaskans say, is always over 1,000 miles and 49 signifies Alaska, the forty-ninth state. Without a doubt, the excitement and success of the annual Iditarod Sled Dog Race and the organization behind the race renewed interest in the once-abandoned Iditarod Trail, now recognized as a national trail. The addition of the Junior Iditarod introduces the trail to young mushers, who compete in a 130-mile race, and every February the Gold Rush Classic Iron Dog racers run snowmobiles from Wasilla to Nome and back again along the historic trail for the longest race of its kind. Other competitors participate in Iditasport (cross-country skiing, running, and snowshoeing) and Iditabike.

SKY TREKKING PLANE AND AERIAL VIEW

Bush pilot Lori Egge of Sky Trekking Alaska flies Iditarod fans over the trail to the Finger Lake checkpoint. In roughly nine or ten days' time, the race leaders traverse nearly eleven hundred miles of the Iditarod National Historic Trail from Anchorage to Nome.

steps of the others who had so boldly traveled overland to Nome many years before. It was not long before interest in the event spread to many parts of the world, and mushers from different countries entered the competition.

The Mail

Mush! Husky and malamute!
Keep to the trail! They're
depending on us, for the
government mail!
Council (Alaska) City News
December 17, 1904

The Inupiaq and the Yupik Eskimos used dogsled teams on the native trail of the Tanaina and Ingalik Indians for winter travel. In the nineteenth century, they adapted Russian mushing techniques, including the use of the lead dog. Later, during the gold rush, mushers with their dog teams used the trail to deliver supplies to mining camps and other remote settlements in the interior of Alaska. Early-twentieth-century mushers delivered the U.S. mail along the Iditarod. In 1924, the era of dogsled travel went out in a blaze of glory when fear of a diphtheria epidemic gripped the people of Nome. In a historic relay, twenty mushers transported the lifesaving serum over 674 miles in 127½ hours, using a large portion of the Iditarod Trail. In 1966, as Wasilla resident Dorothy Page prepared to celebrate the centennial of the Alaska Purchase, she conceived of the idea of a dogsled race to commemorate the golden era of the Iditarod. Within a year, the race was on. In 1973, veteran dog musher Joe Redington, Sr., said the race should go all the way to Nome, and twenty-two mushers did just that. Since then, the race has been held each year in March

and is known around the world as "the last great race on earth."

Today, dog mushing is the official sport of Alaska and the top winter draw. From November to March, there is a constant string of sled-dog races. Sled dogs, bred to race, are eager to run and good sled dogs want to work hard. According to Iditarod champion Martin Buser, good sled dogs are the result of 50 percent heredity and 50 percent training. He claims that mushers simply train what is already there, that it is the dog's spirit that creates a good sled dog. In most cases, a musher won't know the true potential of a puppy until it is about a year and a half old. If a musher has dogs that won't quite make the team, he or she can usually find another team where the dogs will fit. If that doesn't work out, mushers can always find good homes for their dogs, and they are quite particular about the homes they allow them to go to. Bob Ernisse of Anchorage expressed the feelings of many racers when he said, "There is a kinship that develops between you and your dogs that is unequaled in any situation."

The Iditarod board of directors, through its race rules and policy, sets very strict standards for dog care during the race. Almost half of the rules deal either directly or indirectly with animal care. To that end, the level of veterinary attention along the trail is high. Approximately thirty veterinarians volunteer their time on the trail to see to the welfare and medical needs of the dogs. Veterinarians are found at every checkpoint, and dogs may receive complete physicals every time they stop. The chief veterinarian has the authority to require a musher to rest or drop a dog if necessary. If a dog is dropped, it is permanently removed from the race. Race rules allow mushers to begin with as many as sixteen dogs and end with as few as five. It takes a very competent musher to handle a large team. Most teams average fifteen dogs, which means over one thousand dogs will leave the starting line.

Rules allow mushers to leave dogs at designated checkpoints along the way. Mushers drop dogs for many reasons. In fact, some actually leave with more dogs than they ever intend to finish with. For example, more power is needed to get through the Alaska Range early in the race. Racers plan to drop some of their dogs after this section, and, in many cases, young dogs start the race only in order to gain experience. Not expected to keep up with the team all the way to Nome, they are dropped en route. Others are dropped because they tire and need a rest. A basic principle of mushing is that a team is only as fast as its slowest dog. Sled dogs may also be dropped because they are in heat or because they become sick. Dogs with flu generally recover in three to four days. Dehydration is a more common problem, so mushers and veteri-narians keep a close watch for that condition. A dog dropped for dehydration can be completely rehydrated and healthy in about forty-eight hours. Few are dropped because of serious illness or injury. Most injuries repair quickly and the dogs race again, many in the same racing season.

At every checkpoint, race personnel care for dropped dogs until they are moved. Veteri-narians examine the dogs and provide medical attention if needed. Excess straw is shipped to major dropped-dog check-points so that they can rest comfortably. As soon as possible, often within twenty-four hours of being dropped, the dogs are flown back to Anchorage, where experienced handlers pick them up and take them to the holding area at Hiland Mountain Correc-tional Center. There the dogs are cared for by responsible inmates until they are picked up by their owners or their owners' handlers. If a dropped dog is critically ill or seriously injured, it is taken im-mediately to Anchorage to a veterinary clinic for treatment.

Penalties are imposed on mushers who do not keep dogs in good condition. Cruel or inhu-mane treatment is not tolerated; it results in disqualification. If abuse is discovered, the guilty musher is banned from future races. A controversial rule, adopted in April 1995, calls for disqualification of any musher whose dog dies from anything other than a cause beyond the musher's control—such as a moose attack. Despite all these precautions, the Humane Society of the United States recommends more checkpoints and a shorter race. Suffice it to say, watchful eyes are always on competitors.

With temperatures ranging between 40 and −60 degrees Fahrenheit, it is the sled dog's dense downlike undercoat that supplies thermal protection. Proper diet is also extremely important to a dog's ability to keep going in extreme conditions. To make certain that dogs have sufficient food for their journey, race rules require mushers to ship at least five pounds of dog food per dog to each of nine checkpoints and two pounds of food per dog to eight others. So that each musher has bedding for the team at checkpoints, the Iditarod committee disperses approximately a thousand bales of straw. Race rules also require that a musher carry, at all times, eight booties for every dog on the team. These booties, usually made of polar fleece, protect the dogs' feet while on the trail. Though the dogs are bred to have good, tough feet, competent mushers keep their dogs bootied from Anchorage to Nome, using

about two thousand booties all together. Booties are typically made of polar fleece and can last up to a hundred miles. Fans collect discarded booties as souvenirs of the race.

Just like mushers, the sled dogs are tired after a race. However, with rest, food, and water, they are refreshed and ready to go again. The level of exhaustion isn't taken to the point where the dogs won't recover. Most dogs are capable of racing for many years, and some go on to compete until they are ten or eleven years old. Once they aren't able to race anymore, they either live out their lives with a place of honor in the kennel or the mushers find good homes to retire them to. DeeDee Jonrowe of Willow, Alaska, who followed her childhood dreams to be able to work with sled dogs for a living and to run in the Iditarod, explains, "My love and affection for dogs started at a very young age when my parents first taught me important values in life through my love and desire to gain the trust of our family pets. This desire has just grown deeper as I have grown older. When I work with my dogs, I see God's neverending grace."

The Iditarod National Historic Trail (INHT) is unique in Alaskan and American history

*Material in this section is taken from the Bureau of Land Management's *The Iditarod National Historic Trail, Seward to Nome Route: A Comprehensive Management Plan.*

because it represents the last vestiges of a truly remote and wild trail, which remains much the same as it was more than seventy-five years ago.* It is made up of a primary route and connecting trails to form a network of more than twenty-three hun-

The

Trail

Today

dred miles of trails now known as the Iditarod National Historic Trail. Although the Iditarod Trail was designated as a National Historic Trail to commemorate Alaska's gold-rush era, it is also a trail system that incorporates many portions of an earlier system of Indian and Eskimo travel routes. It passes prehistoric and contact-period villages, temporary campsites, cemeteries, and traditional gathering places. Many of the historic sites overlie pre-gold-rush-era sites that are important to native Alaskans. Natives served as guides for the early explorers and played a major role in later years in the delivery of mail and freight, a role that is little understood and not well documented.

The trail surveyed by W. L. Goodwin of the Alaska Road Commission in 1908 to connect Seward, Nome, and the town of Iditarod was selected by the Iditarod Trail project team as the *primary route* of the national historic trail because it was the most important travelway of the trail system during the Iditarod gold rush. Branching from the primary route are over a thousand miles of connecting trails that were important components of this gold-rush trail system. Though the terms "primary" and "connecting" tend to indicate a relative level of importance for individual segments of trail, that was not the intent of the project team. In fact, the northern and southern Iditarod Trail race routes use some portions of

Goodwin's route, some connecting trails, and some trails not presently included in the national trails system.

Today only portions of the trail can be hiked. The Iditarod in its entirety is a winter trail, with most of its use occurring when the tundra and rivers are frozen and easier to cross. During the summer months the thick tundra vegetation makes hiking extremely difficult. Much of the trail vanishes in Norton Sound, for example, when the area is alive with wildflowers, birds, and returning salmon. Best places for summer recreation are close to Seward and Anchorage. The twenty-three-mile Johnson Pass Trail is located on the Kenai Peninsula near Seward, and a twenty-mile ski trail over Indian Creek Pass is available for summer use. North of Seward, the U.S. Forest Service and a volunteer group, the Iditarod Trail Blazers, created fourteen miles of hiking trails along the old Iditarod Trail route. The twenty-seven-mile segment of trail east of Anchorage over Crow Pass to Eagle River in Chugach State Park is a popular hike and is the annual site for a marathon run. Other than the road system east of Nome, the rest of the trail is difficult to travel or even impassable during the summer.

During the winter, dog mushers race across frozen rivers and tundra, and visitors can try the trail for an hour or for days. When selecting a tour, a musher would be wise to make sure that he or she has the experience to handle a blizzard, a moose encounter, or a runaway team. The trail has become particularly popular with snowmobilers, and skiers, snowshoers, and even mountain bikers recreate and compete over various sections of the trail in and around Knik, McGrath, Unalakleet, Nome, and other communities. Alaska, known as the state that flies the most, has six times as many pilots per capita as does any other state. Pilots fly passengers over the trail, which is particularly exciting during the Sled Dog Race (SDR). Sky Trekking Alaska of Wasilla has a special bush-plane excursion that follows the race from start to finish, with special outings that include dog sledding and ice fishing.

Many of the sites along the trail are historic remnants of early mining or transportation facilities in use prior to World War I. The BLM and other land managers along the trail are in the process of examining and assessing many of these sites to determine their historical significance. Several sites along the historic trail or in its proximity are listed on the National Register of Historic Places, such as the Hope historic district, Old St. Nicholas Church at Eklutna, the town of Knik, the Iyateyet site at Cape Denbigh, and the Anvil Creek placer mine near Nome. Several other sites are under consideration. Recommendations to rehabilitate many of these sites to their near-original condition have been made or are being made. The many connecting trails also contain historic sites and towns such as Ruby.

As in the gold-rush days, climatic conditions are always a vital consideration when planning travel along many portions of the Iditarod Trail. The major climatic zones—the Maritime, Transition, and Continental—provide varied weather conditions. Extreme temperatures, winds, and heavy snowfall with avalanche conditions will threaten the lives of unwary travelers. Taking an avalanche-awareness class should be considered. Unlike the Appalachian or Pacific Crest National Scenic Trails, which are located near heavily populated areas, most of the Iditarod is in the remote sections of Alaska.

The trail is divided into three major segments according to climatic and other geographic conditions.

Seward to Rainy Pass

The major portion of this trail segment falls in the Transitional Climatic Zone. Near Rainy Pass at the Puntilla Lake Station, precipitation is light—about fourteen inches, including eighty-six inches of snow. Summers are a cool 37 to 63 degrees Fahrenheit, with winters ranging between –7 and 34 degrees. Transition Zone stations at Skwentna, Wasilla, Anchorage, and Seward record similar weather statistics.

Whittier falls into the Maritime Climatic Zone with heavy

precipitation (175 inches, including 140 inches of snow), cool summers (45 to 63 degrees Fahrenheit), and mild winters (26 to 30 degrees). A small cell of the Continental Climatic Zone is situated in the central portion of the Kenai Peninsula and is characterized by light precipitation (30 inches, including 76 inches of snow), cool summers (42 to 65 degrees Fahrenheit), and mild winters (11 to 42 degrees). Needless to say, one must always be prepared for extremes.

Vegetation varies from the coastal western hemlock–Sitka spruce forest communities of the Kenai Peninsula to the alpine-tundra and barren-ground communities of the Chugach Mountains and Alaska Range. From Knik Arm north, the transition from lowland spruce-hardwood forest to bottomland spruce-poplar forests is as subtle as the elevation gain. Wildlife is plentiful in the area south of the Alaska Range; moose, caribou, black bear, wolf, brown-grizzly bear, lynx, beaver, land otter, marten, muskrat, northern bald eagles, and all types of waterfowl abound. Fish species include salmon, steelhead, Dolly Varden trout, arctic grayling, and lake trout.

From sea level at Seward, the trails follow various narrow valleys through the Kenai and Chugach Mountains to Knik Arm. Crow Pass and Indian Pass each reach 3,500 feet. From sea level at Knik, the trail again begins a slow climb across the Susitna River Valley, the Skwentna and Happy Rivers to Rainy Pass (at approximately 3,350 feet) in the Alaska Range, where surrounding peaks are over 5,000 feet. In these mountainous areas, avalanche danger threatens contemporary travelers as it did historic travelers.

South of Rainy Pass the trail receives the heaviest recreational use of any part of the system. Several segments are used year-round for hiking, skiing, and snowshoeing, and some portions are popular routes for sled-dog teams and snowmobiles. No motorized use is allowed within the Chugach National Forest or on the historic trails, which are currently used as hiking trails. The Crow Pass-to-Eagle River traverse is closed to motorized use during the entire year within both the Chugach National Forest and Chugach State Park. Indian Pass, within the state park, is also closed to motorized use year-round. All communities within this region are linked by major transportation systems. Most of the trail between Seward and Rainy Pass is managed as public lands by the State of Alaska, the Matanuska-Susitna Borough, the Municipality of Anchorage, the U.S. Army, and the U.S. Forest Service. Several miles are in private ownership.

Rainy Pass to Kaltag

Branching off the Alaska Road Commission's original Seward-to-Nome Trail, a trail system was developed to connect the villages and mining camps of the Kuskokwim, Innoko, and Yukon Rivers. Remaining today are trails still used each winter, summer roads, and abandoned sections of trail that have probably not been used in over forty years. Along the almost twelve hundred miles of trail system between Rainy Pass and Kaltag, unlike the previous section, no railroads, paved highways, or recreation trails have been constructed.

The Iditarod Trail system between Rainy Pass and Kaltag leaves the thirty-five-hundred-foot level of the Alaska Range and descends for more than three thousand feet into the Kuskokwim River Valley to McGrath, then crosses the Kuskokwim Mountains into the Yukon River drainage to the village of Kaltag at an elevation of two hundred feet. The spruce-hardwood forest of the Kuskokwim and Innoko flats and surrounding mountainous areas predominate in this section of the Iditarod Trail. Bottomland spruce-poplar forest communities are found along the major river valleys of the Yukon, Kuskokwim, Iditarod, and Innoko Rivers. Alpine tundra and barren ground are found throughout this region, especially near the Iditarod loop of the trail and the Alaska Range.

Located in the lowlands between the Kaiyuh Mountains and the Yukon River is the major low-brush bog community. Other smaller, low-brush bog communities are located near the Yukon, Iditarod, and Takotna Rivers. Wildlife is diverse in the interior portion of the Iditarod Trail system and includes caribou, hare, lynx, moose, black bear, wolverine, fox, wolf, brown-grizzly bear, beaver, Dall sheep, marten, land otter, bald eagle, golden eagle, osprey, peregrine falcon, muskrat, weasel, and mink. Waterfowl areas are located in the Innoko and Kuskokwim Valleys, and sport fish species include grayling, northern pike, and several species of salmon.

The entire trail system between Rainy Pass and Kaltag falls into the Continental Climatic Zone. Generally, the weather conditions are characterized by extreme temperatures in the winter and summer. At McGrath, average daily temperatures range from about 45 to 68 degrees Fahrenheit during the summer months and from –1 and –18 degrees in the winter. Precipitation averages eighteen inches, including fifty-six inches of snow. The towns of Flat, Ruby, Galena, and Nulato experience similar conditions. The population of the area is concentrated in the villages along the Yukon River between Ruby and Kaltag, with Galena being the transportation and trade center. McGrath serves as the population-trade center between the Yukon River and Rainy Pass on the Kuskokwim River. Athapaskan Indians make up the majority of the population.

Though active mines can still be found around Ganes Creek, Moore Creek, Flat, Poorman, and Ophir, there are fewer communities along the interior route of the trail today than at the height of the Iditarod and Ruby gold strikes.

Transportation between villages is chiefly by light plane, but riverboats, snow machines, dog teams, and all-terrain vehicles are also used. Extreme weather conditions and lack of support facilities away from communities keep recreational use to a minimum along this portion of the trail. During the fall, some big-game hunting is based out of the Yukon River villages and the McGrath area. Each March, the Iditarod Sled Dog Race attracts mushers, tourists, and support personnel, who utilize portions of the historic route. The State of Alaska is the major landowner of the trail system between Rainy Pass and the Yukon River. Various trail segments are within the Innoko National Wildlife Refuge, which is managed by the U.S. Fish and Wildlife Service, and one frequently used trail segment between Ophir and Iditarod, commonly called the Hunter Trail, crosses designated wilderness. The Bureau of Land Management is responsible for blocks of federal land near the South Fork of the Kuskokwim River and Flat, and other portions of the historic route cross corporation land, native villages, and individual allotment lands.

Kaltag to Nome

Travel routes between the Yukon River and the villages bordering Norton Sound have not changed much since the gold-rush era. Most of the trails follow the beaches and cross Norton Bay. The route leaves the two hundred-foot elevation in the Yukon River basin at Kaltag and follows the low, broad Unalakleet River valley, which reaches an elevation of six hundred feet in the vicinity of Twenty-two Mile Cabin as it passes through the Kaltag Mountains, with peaks averaging two thousand to three thousand feet. From Unalakleet, the trail generally stays at or near sea level as it skirts Norton Sound along the tidewater lagoons and barrier beaches. The normal winter trail actually crosses Norton Bay when sea ice supports such travel. The portion of the trail system that leaves barren beaches reaches a maximum elevation of three hundred feet near the village of White Mountain. Upland spruce-hardwood communities can be found along the Yukon and Unalakleet River valleys, while the various tundra and beach communities border Norton Sound. Wildlife common to the area includes brown-grizzly bear, red fox, moose, arctic fox, land otter, marten, hare, musk ox, caribou, beaver, lynx, walrus, and occasionally polar bear. Important waterfowl nesting areas are located along the shores of Norton Sound. Grayling, arctic char, northern pike, and several species of salmon are found in the Unalakleet River and other creeks and streams along Norton Sound.

Passing from Kaltag to Nome, a traveler will leave the Continental Climatic Zone and enter the Transitional Climatic Zone. In general, coastal summer weather temperatures will be less extreme, but precipitation will be about the same as in the interior region. At Nome precipitation averages nineteen inches, including eighty-two inches of snow. Average daily temperatures range from 38 to 56 degrees Fahrenheit in the summer, and from −6 to −13 degrees in the winter. Other coastal communities experience similar weather patterns. Nome has remained the largest community in this area since the gold-rush boom and serves as the trade, transportation, and service center for the villages of the Norton Sound area. This portion of the Iditarod Trail crosses the boundary between the Indian and Eskimo cultures. Athapaskan Indians inhabit Kaltag, while the people of Eskimo descent make up a majority of the population of the villages along the route between Unalakleet and Nome. People living in Nome and other villages on the route to Kaltag are engaged in seasonal employment such as reindeer herding and commercial fishing. Mining is still the important economic activity of the Seward Peninsula.

Transportation between villages during the winter is by light plane, snow machine, and dog team. Boats or small planes are used during the summer. Only Nome and Unalakleet are connected to Anchorage by commercial airliner. Other villages are connected by regularly scheduled mail planes. A few villages are connected by a state-maintained road system. However, no roads connect the area with Anchorage. Recreation in the region is concentrated around Nome, where a large number of tourists are attracted by the historic townsite, active and historic mining, the annual Iditarod Sled Dog Race, and side trips out of Nome to the land of reindeer, historic sites, monuments, parks, and the Russian Far East. Access to the trail system is by aircraft to the villages along the route. Outside of Nome, recreational use of the trail is limited primarily to local villagers with snow machines and dog teams. Native regional and village corporations hold most of the land along the historic route between the Yukon River and Nome; however, federal easements protect public access to the route. The primary route between Kaltag and Unalakleet crosses the Unalakleet National Wild River, which is managed by the Bureau of Land Management. The trail also crosses U.S. Fish and Wildlife Service withdrawals for the Alaska Maritime National Wildlife Refuge. The State of Alaska manages the historic route between Solomon and Nome along the state-maintained road.

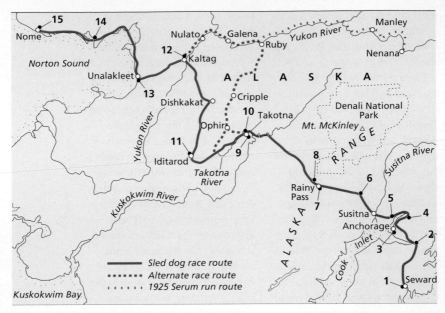

15
14
Nome
Norton Sound
Unalakleet
13
Dishkakat
Ophir
11
Iditarod
Takotna River
Kuskokwim River
Nulato
12
Kaltag
Galena
Ruby
Yukon River
Manley
Nenana
A   L   A   S   K   A
Cripple
10
Takotna
9
8
Rainy Pass
7
Susitna
Anchorage
Cook Inlet
3
Denali National Park
Mt. McKinley
RANGE
Susitna River
6
5
4
2
1   Seward
ALASKA
Yukon River
Kuskokwim Bay

—— Sled dog race route
▪▪▪▪▪▪ Alternate race route
••••• 1925 Serum run route

IDITAROD NATIONAL HISTORIC TRAIL

Points of Interest

1. SEWARD. Seward was named for William Seward, the secretary of state who purchased Alaska. It is a portal for rail and highway travel through Alaska's interior. Historically, mushers began their journey over the Iditarod from Seward or further north from Knik. The activity prompted the Alaska Road Commission in 1908 to survey a trail from Seward to Nome. Today, cruise ships stop at this major ice-free port where a short walk to the corner of Fourth Avenue and Railway Road takes the passenger to the Mile 0 marker of the Iditarod National Historic Trail. A paved bike path along Ballaine Avenue is designated the historic trail in town. Outside of town, the trail continues on the east side of Sawmill Creek to Bear Lake. A twenty-three-mile stretch of the old trail passes Bench and Johnson Lakes; the north trailhead is at Mile 33. *Other attractions:* In Seward, the Ballaine House (1905), which was the home of Frank L. Ballaine, a founder, promoter, and agent of the Alaska Central Railway and founder of the townsite and community; St. Peter's Church (1906), the first Protestant church on the Kenai Peninsula, with its mural *Resurrection* and Resurrection Bay in the background; Seaview Plaza (1904–6), formally known as Brosius Noon Mall, housed the town's first business, a manufacturer of freight sleds for use on the Iditarod; the Swetman House (1916), also known as the Stucco Johnson House, is noted for its sturdy architecture, which survived a slide down the cliff; the Van Guilder Hotel (1916), originally a cable office (1905, NRHP),

is the oldest surviving hotel (1921) in Seward at 219 Sixth Avenue; Resurrection Bay Historical Society Museum; daily cruises to Kenai Fjords NP; saltwater fishing in Resurrection Bay; the Fourth of July Celebration, which brings out residents for a grueling race up and down Seward's 3,022-foot Mount Marathon. *Nearby:* North of Seward, Alaska Nellie's Homestead (1915) marks the townsites of Roosevelt and Lawing and commemorates a widely known Alaskan personality, Alaska Nellie Lawing; Diversion Tunnel was a Corps of Engineers project that eliminated dangers to Seward from spring floods of Lowell Creek. Exit Glacier is found at the edge of Harding Icefield. At Hope, the Hope Historic District (NRHP) was the center of gold-mining activity on the Kenai Peninsula dating back to 1888. The Alaska Central Railroad Tunnel No. 1, near Grandview on the Kenai Peninsula, is an important engineering feature of the first major railroad into Alaska's interior. Cooper Landing Post Office (1921) is the oldest known usable building in Grandview; it served as headquarters for the dog-team mail run. Located on the northern Kenai Peninsula, Lauritsen Cabin (1895) is important for its construction and use in the early period of mining on Canyon Creek, the most lucrative gold claim in the area.

2. **Girdwood.** Crow Creek Mine has authentic mining buildings and offers panning for gold.

Eight of the original buildings and the mine are on the NRHP. Crow Pass Trail, part of the INHT, offers striking views of Turnagain Arm. Sled-dog tours can be arranged in town.

3. **Anchorage.** The Iditarod Trail Sled Dog Race begins here each March and the Fur Rendezvous is held every February. *Other attractions:* The Oscar Anderson House (1915) was among the first wood-frame houses in Anchorage; the Lathrop Building (1915–16) remains as one of the earliest commercial structures in town; and Pioneer School (1915) is the city's first school. Anchorage City Hall (1936) was the architectural predecessor of much of the building that followed; the Federal Building (1939) is a modern concrete structure that has remained a city landmark since its completion. The Fourth Avenue Theater (1941–47), which was completely refurbished in 1992, is noted for its large murals, interior workmanship and art deco style. Spectators from all over the world line Fourth Avenue each March for the start of the Iditarod Trail Sled Dog Race. The Alaska Methodist University Campus Center (1966) is the site of the 1971 ratification by Alaska natives of the Alaska Native Claims Settlement Act, which continues to shape Alaska. Other sites of interest include the Anchorage Museum of History and Art; the Anchorage Aviation Heritage Museum; the Heritage Library and Museum; the Alaska Zoo; Potter's Marsh; the Log Cabin Visitor Center; the Alaska

Public Information Center, and the Anchorage Coastal Wildlife Refuge with scenic boardwalk. *Nearby:* South of Anchorage, Beluga Point Site holds data clarifying boundaries between the Eskimo and Tanaina Athapaskans. Eagle River, the most popular hiking and wildlife viewing area, is located at the Eagle River Visitors Center associated with Chugach SP. Mushers in the Sled Dog Race unharness their teams to truck to Wasilla for a restart when they encounter the traditional lack of snow on the "flats" toward Palmer and open water on Knik River. Denali SP and Denali NP are north of Anchorage.

4. **EKLUTNA.** The village provides a glimpse into native Athapaskan culture and the influences of the Russian Orthodox missionaries. Old St. Nicholas Russian Orthodox Chapel (NRHP), an example of vernacular church architecture, symbolizes Russian missionary activity associated with fur trading in Cook Inlet country dating back to about 1870. The Mike Alex Cabin (1926) was built by the last traditional chief of the village. The sacred burial ground of the Den'ina (Tanaina) Athapaskans has more the eighty "spirit houses." *Nearby:* Eklutna Lake offers hiking, canoeing, birding, picnicking, and camping.

5. **KNIK.** Once the largest community on the Cook Inlet, Knik (NRHP) served as a regional trading and transportation center from about 1898 to 1917. Now it is home to Joe Redington, Sr., the "father of the Iditarod." *Other attractions:* Knik Museum contains materials dating back to Knik's heyday, and the Dog Mushers Hall of Fame commemorates the long history of dug mushing in Alaska. *Nearby:* Wasilla was established around the Wasilla Depot (1917), which served as a transportation and supply point for mining and farming activities in the area, including the famous Matanuska Valley. Its Teeland's Country Store (1917) has operated since the Alaska Railroad established the town. First Wasilla School (1917) served as a center of community, educational, and cultural affairs and is the home of the Iditarod Trail Committee Visitor Center. The Sled Dog Race is restarted here when conditions have necessitated trucking past the flats. The Dorothy Page Museum honors the woman who conceived the idea of the Sled Dog Race. Hatcher Pass SP offers cross-country skiing, panning for gold, and the remains of Independence Mine.

6. **SKWENTANA.** Located near the confluence of the Skwentna and Yentna Rivers, the town has a population of 114. Forty-five miles to the east lies Finger Lake, the heart of snow country and a popular spectator point to view the Sled Dog Race.

7. **RAINY PASS.** This area represents the highest point on the Iditarod Trail as it passes over the majestic Alaska Range with its spectacular scenery. There is a hunting lodge in the area.

8. **Rohn Roadhouse.** The original Rohn Roadhouse used by mushers carrying mail is no longer standing. Instead, a log cabin built in the 1930s is managed by the BLM as a public shelter cabin. During the Sled Dog Race it is known as Rohn Resort. The area, the equal of Rainy Pass for spectacular scenery, marks a transition point into dropping temperatures and is the gateway into the flatlands of the interior. Many mushers take their mandatory twenty-four-hour layover here before heading across the bleak but treacherous Farewell Burn area. *Nearby:* Nikolai, ninety-three miles northeast, is the first of many native villages along the trail. Its Presentation of Our Lord Chapel (1929) was part of the Russian Orthodox Church thematic nomination to the National Register.

9. **McGrath.** Located near the confluence of the Kuskokwim and Takotna Rivers, McGrath, with a population over five hundred, offers limited lodging, which should be booked in advance, especially during the Sled Dog Race when the town's population doubles.

10. **Takotna.** Once a bustling community in the heart of the Iditarod mining district, the town rests on the banks of the Takotna. It is also a dividing point between the historic trail and the race. From here the INHT moves southwest to Moore Creek, but the Sled Dog Race moves thirty-eight miles toward the north to the ghost town of Ophir, where

many items and artifacts remain untouched. The race then moves north and west on a connecting trail to Cripple (the official halfway point in the northern route of the race), Ruby, Galena, and Nulato to Kaltag in even-numbered years. The Ruby Roadhouse is the last remaining evidence of Ruby Camp and incorporates a log cabin built around 1911, a residence built in 1913, and numerous additions made since 1935. The town of Galena was named for the Galena lead sulfate ore found in the area. It is surrounded by the Innoko NWR, Koyukuk NWR, and Nowitna NWR. At Nulato, the Russian trading post built in 1838 at the confluence of the Nulato and Yukon Rivers was burned by the Koyukan Indians. The Russian-American Company rebuilt the trading post in 1841, but it was burned again. In odd-numbered years the race moves south from Takotna to rejoin the INHT to Iditarod and on to Kaltag.

11. **Iditarod.** Gold was discovered here on the Otter Creek by W. A. Dikeman and John Beaton in 1908. Located in the heart of the mining district, it is from this town that the trail received its name. The area offers one of the largest concentrations of intact historic structures along the trail. Dog teams hauled supplies and mail into the area and were laden with gold on their return trip out. Between 1908 and 1925, about $35 million in gold was taken from this area. It is the

official halfway point in the race along the southern route. *Nearby:* Innoko NWR.

12. **KALTAG.** In the rush to Nome, miners came from the Canadian Klondike down the Yukon River to Kaltag. The town signals a brief respite from the driving winds as the trail leads overland from here through Kaltag Portage to the coast of Norton Sound. *Nearby:* Innoko NWR.

13. **UNALAKLEET.** From Kaltag the Klondike miners trekked to Unalakleet before skirting Norton Sound to Nome. Situated on the coast of Norton Sound, just north of the Unalakleet River, the village, with a population of 714, is the largest community between Wasilla and Nome. The trail now enters the gateway to the Bering Sea, where sudden storms and strong winds meet the traveler. Sled-dog racers take a connecting trail to Koyuk after going over the ice of Norton Bay, one of the most treacherous segments of the trail.

14. **GOLOVIN.** From this point the trail moves across Golovin Bay, then overland to White Mountain, located on the banks of the Fish River. Soon the trail begins its coastal route along the Bering Sea to Nome.

15. **NOME.** The end of the trail. Alaska's great gold rush to Nome began when the first large gold placer strike was made at the Anvil Creek District (NRHP, NHL) on September 20, 1898. By June 1899 Nome (Anvil City) had a population of 1,700 and by a

year later the population had swelled to 12,488. The Carrie McLain Home (1900–2) typifies the lifestyle, architecture, and culture of one of the nation's most famous gold camps. Discovery Saloon (1901), Nome's oldest surviving business structure, was originally opened by Max Gordon, who had mining interests in the area; the saloon became one of forty-four drinking establishments in Nome. Front Street, the heart of the business district, burned in the great fire of 1934. The red-light district, between Division Street and Lane's Way, was concealed by the saloons on the north side of Front Street. The A. N. Kittilsen House at 285 First Avenue West was the home of the man who accompanied "the three lucky Swedes" back to Nome to stake their claims after they had discovered gold on Anvil Creek. The A. F. Guinan Home (1906) at 302 First Avenue West belonged to the manager of the Hot Air Mining Company. A visitor center leads the tourist to gold panning on famed black-sand beaches in the summer and walks on the Bering Sea in the winter. Celebrations include the Combined Midnight Sun Festival–4th of July Celebration, the Nome River Raft Race, and the conclusion of the Iditarod Trail Sled Dog Race. *Nearby:* East of Nome, the Cape Nome Roadhouse (1900) is considered the best surviving example of a roadhouse on the Seward Peninsula and is the only roadhouse still standing that was used in the famous "Race to Nome" in 1925 during the diphtheria epidemic. On Cape Denbigh Peninsula on Norton Sound, Iyatayet Site (NHL, NRHP) dates back to 6000 B.C. The Bering Land Bridge National Preserve, a remnant of the land bridge that connected Asia with North America more than thirteen thousand years ago, at the time of the great ice ages, offers rare arctic craters and lava flows, large populations of migratory birds, and paleontological and archeological resources. Cape Krusenstern NM is the site of seasonal marine mammal hunting by Eskimo peoples. Ootukahkutukvik Museum is nearby.

**BROWN
CHAPEL**

Hundreds
of peaceful
demon-
strators
gathered at
Brown
Chapel of
the AME
Church to
join in the
march from
Selma to
Mont-
gomery to
demand full
voting
rights for
blacks in
the South.
The morn-
ing light on
Brown
Chapel
signals a
brighter
future for
all.

Selma to Montgomery National Historic Trail

At times, history and fate meet at a single time, in a single place to shape a turning point in man's unending search for freedom. So it was at Lexington and Concord. So it was a century ago at Appomattox. So it was last week in Selma, Alabama.

PRES. LYNDON B. JOHNSON, MARCH 15, 1965

The Selma to Montgomery National Historic Trail (SMNHT) commemorates the civil rights march of 1965 from Selma, Alabama, to the steps of the state capitol in Montgomery. This protest march served as a catalyst for the Voting Rights Act of 1965. The trail is a reminder of the treasured ideals of a democratic society and of the sad events that can occur when, as a nation, we lose sight of the fundamental civil rights held by each individual. Visiting the trail, one is reminded that the right to vote is a precious one worth exercising.

ADMINISTERING AGENCY
National Park Service, Southeast Support
    Office
Atlanta Federal Center
1924 Building
100 Alabama Street SW
Atlanta, GA 30303
770-760-1668

FURTHER INFORMATION
Selma–Dallas County Chamber of Commerce
Tourism Division
513 Lauderdale Street
P.O. Drawer D
Selma, AL 36702

ESTABLISHED
1996

APPROXIMATE MILEAGE
54 miles (87 kilometers)

STATE
Alabama

On three separate occasions in March of 1965 protesters attempted to march from Selma to Montgomery, Alabama, to highlight discriminatory practices that prevented African Americans from voting in the Deep South.* Color was no longer the obvious criterion for disenfranchisement it had been, but discrimination by race was still rampant, since literacy tests, interpretations tests, and voucher requirements allowed arbitrary decisions by registration officials. In the century since the Civil War, various means had been used to deny full citizenship to African Americans, and by the 1960s the denial of voting rights had become a national issue. As federal judicial proceedings failed to produce changes in the registration process, African-American leaders, including the Student Nonviolent Coordinating Committee (SNCC) and the Southern Christian Leadership Conference (SCLC), united in a direct-action campaign focused at the heart of the Black Belt†—Selma, Alabama.

In striking contradiction to the American Declaration of Independence that affirmed that "all men are created equal," the country's Constitution did not guarantee all Americans the right to vote. Women, Native Americans, freed blacks, and slaves had no voice in government, even though many had risked their lives in service to their country during war and peace. The fact that voting restrictions defied the fundamental principles of democracy was of little concern to most lawmakers, and those who were victimized had little or no political power to change the system. Nevertheless, women and blacks strove for change by creating organizations to educate the public about their plight and by staging nonviolent marches and demonstrations. For women, it was a 132-year struggle, won with the ratification of the Nineteenth Amendment in 1920. For blacks, it was a longer, bloodier battle.

Although a small number of blacks were emancipated during the Revolutionary era, they were not entirely free, since white society refused to recognize them as equal citizens. On the other hand, the newly formed democratic system supposedly guaranteed rights to most citizens. This made voting rights an important issue during the postcolonial era. The reality was that only white male property owners were given the privilege of suffrage. Many northern states rewrote state laws, restricting political rights for black Americans. Depriving them of the ballot reduced them to second-class citizens. In the South, the need for human labor placed free blacks in an awkward predicament. White southerners

*Material in this section is taken from the National Park Service's *Selma to Montgomery National Trail Study.*

†The term "Black Belt" has historically been applied to the area of central Alabama and Mississippi that is characterized by its rich black clayey soil.

viewed the group as a threat to slavery because it gave bondspeople aspirations to become free. As a result, southern society enacted various restrictions on freedmen, including limitations on their right to vote.

Citizenship became a major issue of the civil rights movement during the nineteenth century. Even while protesting slavery, black activists like Frederick Douglass and Martin Delany were also petitioning the federal government for citizenship rights for free blacks. If the nation accepted them as citizens, it was assumed that voting rights would automatically follow. Their pleas came to no avail, however, and many black Americans and white abolitionists saw domestic conflict as the only solution to slavery and citizenship issues.

Contributing to sectional unrest was the country's westward expansion and the designation of slave and nonslave territories. Tensions stretched in 1857 with the *Dred Scott v. Sanford* decision, which not only hindered the antislavery movement but also jeopardized the status of free blacks in American society. Scott, who had accompanied his master to Illinois and Wisconsin Territory, where slavery was barred, brought suit, claiming that his residence in a free state and territory had made him a free man. The real issue, however, was whether Congress or the local legislatures had the power to outlaw slavery in the territories. The highest court in the land avoided the question by simply holding that blacks were not citizens and could not sue in a federal court. The decision, made by a majority of southern justices, ultimately convinced thousands that the South was engaged in an aggressive attempt to extend slavery, and it made it very clear that, regardless of status, black Americans could not enjoy the rights and privileges guaranteed by the Constitution. After Chief Justice Roger B. Taney declared that a Negro "had no rights which the white man was bound to respect," his enemies referred to him as a traitor to the Constitution.

The Civil War gave blacks new hope for complete liberation and citizenship rights. As they had during the American Revolution, many black men volunteered for military service in an effort to gain freedom and citizenship. Even though slaves in the Confederate states were liberated through the Emancipation Proclamation issued by Pres. Abraham Lincoln in 1863, not all bondspeople were recognized as free until the close of the war. With the passage of the Thirteenth Amendment in 1865, slavery was permanently abolished. In 1866 Congress extended citizenship and voting rights to black men through the Civil Rights Act. Their rights were protected in 1867 with the passage of the Reconstruction Act, which required southern states to rewrite their constitutions to include voting rights, and with the adoption of the Fourteenth Amendment. Ratified on July 9, 1868, the Fourteenth Amendment granted citizenship to black Americans (although women's rights advocates argued that the Fourteenth Amendment should have been used to grant *all* citizens suffrage rights, regardless of race or sex).

The hopes of African Americans ran high. During Reconstruction, they were elected to state legislatures, as well as to the U.S. House of Representatives and the U.S. Senate, but the progress proved to be short-lived. In 1870 radical Republicans, who wished to use the black vote to help centralize the nation from a confederation of states, promoted passage of the Fifteenth Amendment. The amendment, which prohibited federal and state governments from denying any male citizen the right to vote because of race or previous condition of servitude, had a weakness. It did not prohibit the use of poll taxes, literacy tests, and property qualifications as a means to deny voting rights. The next year, hoping to prohibit the states from discrimination in voting rights, Congress passed two legislative bills, the Ku Klux Klan and the Enforcement Acts. Despite all of these efforts, white conservatives had begun to regain political control in the state legislatures by the last decade of the nineteenth century. They soon enacted laws that curtailed black suffrage so that their own positions remained secure. These actions were supported in 1876 when the Supreme Court ruled, in *United States v. Cruikshank,* that the Fifteenth Amendment did not prevent individuals from discriminating in granting voting rights, only states. After this ruling, practically every Supreme Court decision made that affected blacks seemed to somehow nullify or restrict their rights. By the late 1890s, blacks had lost virtually all civil liberties accorded by the Constitution and other laws.

As northern support began to wane and federal troops left the South, white conservatives, often known as "redeemers," took total control of the state legislatures and rewrote state constitutions to disfranchise African-American voters. Poll taxes, literacy tests, grandfather clauses, and restrictive primaries were used to deprive thousands of blacks of their voting privileges and to expel blacks from elected positions. By the time the *Plessy v. Ferguson* (1886) decision sanctioned legalized segregation in public places, the status of black Americans had declined drastically.

Many African Americans sought alternatives to remedy their conditions. Black leaders like Booker T. Washington, Dr. William E. B. Du Bois, and Bishop Henry McNeal Turner of the African Methodist Church responded with diverse solutions. Ideas varied from separatism to African emigration, but it was generally agreed that the acquisition and exercise of suffrage rights were the primary concerns of the black community. Clearly, without this essential privilege, African Americans would never be recognized as equal citizens. To combat racial discrimination, black Americans formed civil rights organizations during the early decades of the twentieth century.

The Niagara Movement was organized in 1905 by Du Bois and a team of twenty-nine black intellectuals at a meeting at Niagara Falls. They issued a list of demands, including the unrestricted right to vote. To formally protest segregation and disfranchisement, over thirty branch offices were created in northern cities, and a legal department was formed to fight for civil rights in the courts. Even though a few significant cases were won, because of meager funding the Niagara Movement was unable to survive. After the demise of the organization, its principles and philosophy surfaced in a new organization.

The National Association for the Advancement of Colored People (NAACP) was founded in 1909 by a group of liberals, including Oswald Garrison Villard, Jane Addams, John Dewey, and William Dean Howells. The primary purpose of the interracial organization was to acquire voting rights for black Americans. Since racial discrimination and the lack of political rights had been formalized through the courts, the NAACP developed a legal team, the Legal Defense Fund, to attack discrimination through the judicial system. In an

attempt to secure voting rights, the organization challenged disfranchisement laws by attacking the legality of white primaries created to nominate Democratic Party candidates and to exclude blacks from participating in elections. Although the NAACP won several significant victories on the voting issue, African Americans continued to vote in small numbers.

In addition to demanding political rights for blacks, the NAACP also attempted to eradi-

VOTING RIGHTS MUSEUM AND INSTITUTE

Exhibits at the Voting Rights Institute in Selma, Alabama, include an astounding collection by photographers Mildurn Sneed, Capt. Roy Smith, Tom Posey, and Maj. Emet Dickson of the Alabama Department of Safety, depicting scenes from Bloody Sunday and the march to Montgomery in 1965.

cate social segregation through the landmark case, *Brown v. the Board of Education of Topeka, Kansas.* The Legal Defense Fund, under the leadership of attorneys Charles Hamilton Houston and Thurgood Marshall, argued against the constitutionality of segregation in public education, challenging the *Plessy* decision. After careful consideration, the Supreme Court handed down a unanimous decision on May 17, 1954, declaring that legal segregation was unconstitutional. This monumental victory helped eliminate legal discrimination, but the work of the NAACP did not end with the *Brown* case. The organization continued to be effective even when it did not bring immediate change.

It was the need for immediate change that prompted many black Americans to begin to utilize different methods, including mass demonstrations, sit-ins, and boycotts. Mass demonstrations were essential to the success of the modern civil rights movement because they created crisis situations that required negotiations between white and black leaders. Organizations like the Fellowship of Reconciliation and the Congress of Racial Equality (CORE) had used nonviolent resistance to integrate lunch counters and buses as early as the 1940s. In the 1950s and 1960s, these techniques were adopted by such civil rights organizations as the Southern Christian Leadership Conference (SCLC) and the Student Nonviolent Coordinating Committee (SNCC). Nonviolent protests led to the integration of buses in Montgomery, schools in Little Rock, and public accommodations in Birmingham and to the passage of major national civil rights legislation in 1957, 1960, and 1964. Dr. Martin Luther King, Jr., who led the black boycott of the city buses in Montgomery, told his black colleagues in 1955, "The only weapon that we have is the weapon of protest. . . . The great glory of American democracy is the right to protest for right."

The dynamic young leader knew that securing voting rights was the best method of gaining civil liberties for blacks. In his eloquent speech at the 1957 Prayer Pilgrimage March on Washington, D.C., King, now leader of the SCLC, called for the government to grant voting rights to African Americans, saying, "Give us the Ballot and we will no longer have to worry the Federal government about our basic rights." Civil rights advocates returned to Washington, D.C., on August 28, 1963. Various speakers, such as A. Philip Randoph, John Lewis of SNCC, and Bayard Rustin of CORE, inspired the interracial crowd. King told the world of his dream of racial equality. People listened. As a result of these major marches, the Civil Rights Acts of 1957 and 1964 were passed.

Although the civil rights legislation guaranteed voting rights to African Americans, many were still denied access to the political process. Voting discrimination, for the most part, arose from the government's lack of enforcement of existing laws. In the summer of 1964, civil rights organizations tested federal legislation in the South's Black Belt by conducting mass registration drives, and SCLC, SNCC, and CORE joined forces to form the Council of Federated Organizations (COFO) in Mississippi. The interracial group, primarily northern college students, created freedom schools to educate black Americans as to their citizenship rights and registered them to vote. During this effort, three COFO workers, Andrew Goodman, Michael Schwerner, and James Chaney, were murdered in Philadelphia, Mississippi. Nevertheless, blacks continued to test legislation. SNCC member Robert Moses formed the Mississippi Freedom Democratic Party (MFDP), which challenged the all-white Democratic Party of Mississippi by nominating four candidates, including Fannie Lou Hamer, to the U.S. Congress. Despite its failure to secure elected positions, the MFDP did give black Americans in Mississippi the opportunity to exercise their voting rights and to participate in the political process. The next organized protest would be in Selma, Alabama, where a strong federal voting rights law would be the goal.

Dallas County, Alabama, and its county seat, Selma, had been somewhat more progressive than other areas of the Deep South in that a few African Americans had managed to register by the 1960s. In 1964, 2.2 percent of the county's African Americans over twenty-one were registered. This translated into 335 African American voters versus 9,542 white voters, even though the population of blacks and whites was almost equal. In contrast, neighboring Wilcox and Lowndes Counties had no African-American voters. The Dallas registration was largely attributable to the work of several black citizens organized as the Dallas County Voters League (DCVL), founded in the 1920s. After a short period the organization became inactive but was later revived. C. J. Adams served as president and Samuel W. Boynton, who had been the president of the local chapter of the NAACP, became a key figure in the group.

As the DCVL continued its efforts, forces in Washington, D.C., were moving to assist African Americans in the Deep South. The Civil Rights Acts of 1957 and 1960 authorized the federal government to bring lawsuits against individuals and governments that thwarted African-American voting rights. These laws alone, however, were not enough to guarantee voting rights for African Americans. Delay proved to be the rule as the government was forced to build clear cases documenting discrimination by a particular group of officials.

In February of 1963, the DCVL invited Bernard and Colia La-

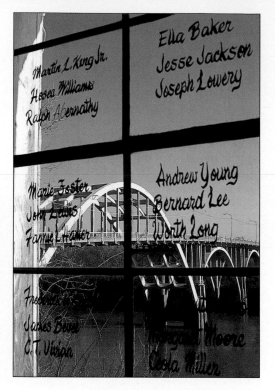

EDMUND PETTUS BRIDGE

Viewed from a window inside
Selma's Voting Rights Museum and
Institute, the Edmund Pettus Bridge
was the site of the Bloody Sunday
encounter. The names on the
window include some of the individuals named in the institute's
Voting Rights Hall of Fame.

fayette of the SNCC to Selma.
SNCC workers had previously
considered Selma a potential
organizing site, but it was not
considered ready for the civil
rights movement. The Lafayettes
soon learned that they faced a
monumental task, given the fear
felt by African Americans in Dallas County. When their initial

efforts in Selma were unsuccessful, they went to the African
Americans who lived in the rural
areas. Many who were outside the
city were property owners, yeo-
man farmers, and small-store
owners. As a result of their economic independence, they were
more immune to the economic
coercion feared by many in the
city. The SNCC workers hoped to
embarrass blacks in the city into
activity, since they often looked
with contempt on the uncultured
rural populace. A dental hygien-
ist, Marie Foster, a member of the
DCVL steering committee, volunteered to teach classes in Selma
on completing the complicated
registration forms required by the
State of Alabama. Other tricks of
the registration process were discussed in these classes. Such
efforts began to catch the attention of national African-
American leaders.

Starting on May 23, mass
meetings were sponsored by the
DCVL and SNCC, and by mid-
June, the Lafayettes had been
successful enough to hold their
own mass meeting in Selma. The
site for the meeting was the Reverend S. S. Anderson's Tabernacle
Baptist Church; the Reverend
James Bevel of the SCLC was the
speaker. The success of the mass
meetings, however, was balanced
by a decline in attendance at the
weekly citizenship classes. U.S.
District Judge Daniel Thomas in
Mobile had denied the Justice
Department's request for an injunction against Dallas County
Sheriff Jim Clark and his efforts

to intimidate potential voters. The movement in Selma also underwent a change when the Lafayettes left the county, and new SNCC workers arrived in August and September. The new workers, including SNCC Chairman John Lewis and Executive Secretary James Forman, intensified SNCC's efforts in voter registration.

October 7, 1963, was designated Freedom Day in Selma, and approximately three hundred people marched to the courthouse to register to vote. The protesters waited all day, but only a small group was registered. The next meeting, on October 15, featured Dr. King, who traveled from Birmingham, where the SCLC was staging a major campaign over public accommodations. The SCLC was hopeful that a new civil rights bill would be enacted by the U.S. Congress. After King's visit, protest activity began to wane until the summer of 1964 when SNCC workers became active in Selma again. In July, SNCC led an attempt to integrate a local theatre, they organized a voting rights rally, and John Lewis led a march to the courthouse to register local residents. On each occasion sheriff's deputies or local whites assaulted the protesters. Rumors soon hit Selma that "outside agitators," including both civil rights and segregationist groups, were targeting Dallas County for further activity. In response, upon the urging of Sheriff Clark, State Circuit Court Judge James

Hare on July 9 enjoined any group of more than three people from meeting in Dallas County. The order was intended to apply equally to civil rights and segregationist groups, but its primary effect was to end the weekly meetings of the DCVL. Efforts to overturn the order were delayed by Judge Thomas.

Meetings and protests came to a virtual halt, which prompted Amelia Boynton, Samuel Boynton's wife and now widow, to meet with the leadership of the SCLC in Birmingham to persuade them to make Selma their next focus. A local black attorney, J. L. Chestnut, made a similar visit to Atlanta. The SCLC had already decided that voting rights would be its next quest after the passage of a public accommodations act, and Selma provided an opportunity, given the strong local leadership of the DCVL and the confrontational style of Sheriff Clark. If left to his own devices, Clark would attract public attention and, perhaps, sympathy for the black cause. The DCVL issued a formal invitation, and in November, the SCLC decided to go to Selma. Local white leaders in Selma were also aware of SCLC's plans since they were described in reports contained in King's briefcase, which had been stolen in Anniston, Alabama.

As the DCVL prepared for the SCLC, so did Selma's new mayor, Joseph T. Smitherman, and his commissioner of public safety, Wilson Baker. Baker even went to Washington to request that Justice Department officials dissuade King from coming to Selma. Unsuccessful, the city leaders decided to adopt a more accommodating position, which they hoped would prompt the SCLC to abandon Selma as they had earlier dropped Albany, Georgia. The leaders proposed to use nonviolence against nonviolence, but one important step would be to control the hotheaded Clark. Clark agreed that he would leave law enforcement within Selma city limits to Baker, but the Dallas County Courthouse and its sidewalks would remain his responsibility.

On January 1, 1965, Reverend Ralph Abernathy, vice president of the SCLC, delivered a kickoff speech for SCLC's involvement in Dallas County. The next day, King defied Judge Hare's injunction, leading a rally at Brown Chapel African Methodist Episcopal (AME) Church and promising demonstrations and even another march on Washington if voting rights were not guaranteed for African Americans in the South. When King left the city, other SCLC staff members organized a series of meetings at various churches for January 7 to inspire the African Americans in Dallas County with ideas of what voting rights could mean in their lives. A series of mass meetings and protest marches began with renewed momentum in Selma and nearby Marion, the seat of Perry County. The ban on mass meetings was successfully broken. The start of activities in Selma

coincided almost exactly with the discussion in Washington over future civil rights legislation. President Lyndon B. Johnson had just won a landslide election, but many in the Johnson administration were reluctant to push for voting rights legislation so soon after the passage of the Civil Rights Act of 1964. Some in the Justice Department were even skeptical whether legislation was sufficient; many officials favored a constitutional amendment instead, like the one ratified in 1964 that prohibited poll taxes in federal elections. Nonetheless, Johnson alluded to the need for a voting rights bill in his State of the Union address that year, and Justice Department officials soon began drafting legislation. Most thought that a voting rights bill would not become a reality until early in 1966.

In the meantime, activities in Selma continued to escalate, as King and Lewis led 400 marchers to the courthouse. On January 19 another march set out for the courthouse, but this time Clark was agitated by Amelia Boynton, whom he assaulted and forced into a police car. Knowing that Sheriff Clark could be provoked, the marchers continued and arrests increased. On January 22, 105 black teachers led by DCVL President F. D. Reese marched to the courthouse from Clark Elementary School near the George Washington Carver Homes. After being threatened at the courthouse, the teachers eventually returned to Brown Chapel. This set off a chain reaction in Selma, resulting in more and more middle-class African Americans becoming involved in the movement.

Armed with a court order from Judge Thomas restraining Sheriff Clark, the SCLC attempted to build on its success by having King arrested to bring national attention to the voting rights campaign. On February 1, more than two hundred marchers followed the familiar path down Sylvan Street to Alabama Avenue. To force their arrest, the group did not separate into small units as previously instructed by Commissioner Baker. Baker arrested the marchers and took them to the city jail in order to avoid a conflict between King and Clark. Baker and city officials feared what might happen if King was arrested by Clark and held in the county's custody. King and Abernathy declined to post bond, hoping that their incarceration would rouse national support. The day after their arrest, U.S. Sen. Jacob Javits of New York became the first member of Congress to publicly react to events in Selma. Marches continued and even schoolchildren began to participate in many of the activities.

On February 4, Malcolm X, responding to an invitation of the SNCC, gave a speech conciliatory to SCLC and SNCC effort, and on the same date Judge Thomas enjoined Dallas County from using the Alabama literacy test. He further required the Dallas County Board of Registrars to allow at least one hundred people per registration day to fill out registration forms until June 1, 1965. It was this dramatic ruling that prompted King and Abernathy to post bond on February 5. On that date, the *New York Times* published an SCLC advertisement titled "A Letter from Martin Luther King from A Selma, Alabama, Jail." The letter clarified the barriers faced by African Americans in attempting to register and explained that there were more African Americans in prison with King in Selma than there were on the voting rolls. That day, fifteen northern congressmen arrived in Selma to investigate King's complaints. SCLC efforts to draw national attention to voting rights and Selma were beginning to prove successful. The SCLC decided they must continue the protest activity.

As protest activities escalated in Selma, voting rights activities in nearby Marion were also beginning to receive media coverage. The SCLC and SNCC sent representatives to Perry County to assist local civil rights leaders who had been working with activists in Perry County for several years to gain voting rights. On the morning of February 18, James Orange of the SCLC was arrested in Marion, and Alabama state troopers began to patrol the community. That evening, a march in Marion ended in violence and death. Alabama state troopers attacked African Americans leaving a mass meeting at Zion Methodist Church. Several, including Viola Jackson and her son Jimmie Lee, sought refuge in a small cafe, but troopers soon found them. When an officer moved to strike his mother, Jimmie Lee Jackson tried to protect her. He was shot at point-blank range, then taken to Good Samaritan Hospital in Selma along with other injured marchers. On February 20, Gov. George Wallace banned night marches, but this did not impede SCLC and SNCC leaders from attempting them. Commissioner Wilson Baker was equally committed to preventing a night march, since he feared that what had happened in Marion might happen in Selma. Meanwhile, Republican political officials in Washington, D.C., began to decry the Johnson administration's delay in proposing voting rights legislation.

Jimmie Lee Jackson died in Selma a week after the shooting from an infection caused by his wounds. His death produced a strong response in Selma as well as in Marion, and a series of memorial services was planned for him in both cities. It appeared that some mass nonviolent action was necessary, not only to win the attention of political leaders, but to vent the anger and frustration of the activists. The idea for a march from Selma to Montgomery, the state capital, was growing. By March 2, plans were confirmed that Dr. King would lead that march beginning on Sunday, March 7. Preparations began

almost immediately, but the danger of such a march was apparent. On March 6, with the support of most white leaders, including Selma's mayor, Governor Wallace prohibited the event. Many whites believed that there was no way to prevent violence along the route, and others did not support blocking traffic on a major highway. That same day, the SNCC executive committee met in Atlanta. They decided not to sanction the march officially but to allow members to participate as individuals. This type of symbolic march was not in keeping with SNCC's emphasis on grassroots organization and indigenous leadership, but SNCC Chairman John Lewis and other SNCC leaders returned to Selma to march the next day. Meanwhile, the SCLC leadership had debated whether to continue with the plans without a court order restraining Wallace and the Alabama troopers. A decision was finally reached that King and Abernathy would return to Atlanta, and a determination would be made Sunday morning. Most expected that the march would proceed only a short distance before all would be arrested.

On Sunday, more than five hundred people, perhaps three hundred or more from Marion, gathered at Brown Chapel AME Church in Selma. SCLC staffers contacted King and Ralph Abernathy in Atlanta. On the basis of a report provided by Hosea Williams, director of voter education, the staff reported that they would authorize the march, and they began to organize the marchers and provide brief training in the principles and techniques of nonviolence. After a rendition of "God Will Take Care of You," Hosea Williams and John Lewis led the marchers from Brown Chapel that afternoon. No logistical preparations had been made; women marchers were even wearing dresses and high-heeled shoes. The march, according to Jamie Wallace, local reporter on the scene, was intended to be only symbolic. Having proceeded down Sylvan Street to Alabama Avenue, the marchers turned south on Broad Street and

CYCLING

Cycling past historic sites along Alabama's new National Historic Trail is a popular activity in Selma. Expanded trails have been proposed along the U.S. Highway 80 corridor.

headed for the Edmund Pettus Bridge. All the while, rumors were circulating that an agreement had been reached with Governor Wallace's legal advisor, Cecil Jackson, Jr., a Selma native and close personal friend of Mayor Smitherman, that the marchers could proceed over the bridge and onto the highway as a symbolic gesture. This was the premise under which Commissioner Baker and city police were reportedly operating as they escorted the marchers to the west end of the bridge, where their jurisdiction ended.

At the top of the bridge, Williams and Lewis could see troopers and members of the sheriff's posse waiting at the opposite side. The marchers, flanked by reporters and photographers, continued across the bridge, east on U.S. Highway 80, to the first traffic light outside Selma city limits. There troopers blocked the road, and the marchers stopped. Major John Cloud, the commander of the troopers, told the marchers their assembly was unlawful and ordered them to disperse. The state's announced position was that, since a portion of the highway was only two lanes through a swamp, the march was not safe and would create traffic problems.

Marchers did not move; some announced that they had the right to continue. Troopers slowly began to move toward Williams and Lewis, pushing marchers back with billy clubs. Pandemonium set in, and troopers, joined by the posse, began to attack, firing tear gas and striking marchers with their clubs. There were screams of terror as bodies fell to the ground. Those who fled were soon surrounded and forced to return over the bridge. Some onlookers cheered officers who continued to pursue marchers all the way back to Brown Chapel. The two hospitals in Selma that admitted blacks—Good Samaritan and the Burwell Infirmary—reported sixty-five injuries from the incident and March 7, 1965, became known as Bloody Sunday.

That night, footage of the attack was broadcast on network television, and Americans watched in horror as the spectacle of law enforcement officers attacking nonviolent citizens unfolded before them. King sent word to SCLC supporters and clergy that a "ministers' march" would be held on Tuesday to continue the voting rights campaign. SNCC also integrated a series of protests across the country. In Washington, congressional leaders across party lines denounced the actions of the law enforcement officers and demanded that President Johnson ensure the protesters' safety and deliver the long-promised voting rights legislation.

On Monday, March 8, SCLC attorneys petitioned U.S. District Judge Frank Johnson in Montgomery to restrain the state and county and permit the march on Tuesday. When Judge Johnson responded by enjoining the SCLC from marching until after a full hearing on Wednesday, March 10, King and the SCLC were left in a quandary. They had never broken a federal court order, but pressure to do so mounted as ministers of all faiths came pouring into Selma in response to King's call. Realizing King's predicament, officials of the Justice Department proposed a compromise: A march could take place, but it would not go all the way to Montgomery. Instead, the march would go as far as Selmont, the unincorporated area just south of Selma where marchers had been attacked on Sunday. From there they were to peacefully return to Brown Chapel. This agreed, the ministers began their march early Tuesday afternoon.

The ministers followed the same route taken by the marchers on Sunday. As they approached the Edmund Pettus Bridge, a federal marshal stood before them and read Judge Johnson's order. The marchers nevertheless proceeded across the bridge toward Selmont, where Alabama troopers were again blocking U.S. Highway 80 near the traffic light. King stopped the marchers yards away from the officers, and several ministers offered prayers before they returned to Brown Chapel. That evening, King explained that the symbolic march demonstrated that law enforcement officers would show restraint in the presence of a white minister. Promising a march to Montgomery after their case was heard by Judge Johnson, he asked for as many ministers as possible to remain in Selma to assist in march preparations. Reverend James Reeb, a Unitarian minister from Boston, agreed to stay. That evening, after eating dinner at Walker's Cafe with two other ministers, Reeb and his companions, having made a wrong turn, passed the Silver Moon Cafe, where a segregationist crowd was gathered. The ministers were attacked by four white men. Reeb was mortally wounded with a blow to the head from a club or pipe. News of his death on March 11 at the University of Alabama Hospital in Birmingham evoked both sorrow and outrage across the country. Though national support for the march to Montgomery was strengthened by Reeb's death, his assailants were eventually acquitted.

On the day Reeb died, SCLC leaders and their attorneys were in Montgomery testifying before Judge Johnson and asking him to permit the march. Officials in Washington were active with the preparation of voting rights legislation and with fielding the continued protests of those who wanted more federal attention directed toward Selma. On March 13, Governor Wallace met with President Johnson in Washington, D.C., and agreed to take a more amicable position on the situation in Selma. At the same time, Johnson learned that the Justice Department had completed a draft of a voting rights bill, and at the request of con-

JEAN JACKSON

Jean Jackson tells of her moving experiences as she hosted Martin Luther King and his advisors in her house while they prepared for the voting rights demonstration marches in Selma.

gressional leaders he planned to introduce the bill before a joint session of the Congress. On March 15, in the first joint session on a domestic issue since 1946, Johnson introduced his voting rights bill. In his speech, he used the words of the civil rights movement, stating "we shall overcome" the heritage of racism and bigotry that haunted America. King and the SCLC leadership, watching on television at Jean Jackson's home in Selma, were emotionally moved by Johnson's identification with the civil rights movement.

The moment was short-lived. Not twenty-four hours after President Johnson's plea, local police attacked a voting rights march led by King and James Forman in Montgomery. This attack also received media attention, but the day's highlight was Judge Johnson's decision to support the SCLC and restrain Sheriff Clark and the State of Alabama from interfering with the SCLC's planned march to Montgomery. Preparations began immediately for the protest, which was scheduled to leave Selma on March 21. King selected Hosea Williams to organize the march. Committees helped plan for anticipated needs; arrangements were made and campsites along the route selected.

Hundreds of people—white and black—from across the country traveled to Selma to join the marchers. Viola Liuzzo, a Detroit housewife, drove south by herself and volunteered to help transport supplies and marchers along the route. In the meantime, Governor Wallace advised President Johnson that the State of Alabama could not afford to protect the marchers. The president responded by federalizing the "Dixie Division" of the Alabama National Guard.

On March 21, 1965, nearly forty thousand people gathered in the area around Brown Chapel. At a little after 1 P.M., Williams and Lewis led three thousand of them on the march toward Montgomery. Before crossing the Edmund Pettus Bridge, the marchers stopped and prayed at the site of the March 7 attack. This time nineteen hundred federalized troops of the Alabama National

Guard, two thousand regular army troops, and two hundred FBI agents and U.S. marshals provided the marchers physical protection, but the bayonet-carrying troops could not protect the marchers from seeing the banners that displayed messages of hate nor from hearing the caustic insults of bystanders. After a seven-mile march, the group reached the farm of David Hall, an African American. There, in Hall's cow pasture, students from a seminary in Berkeley,

DEXTER AVENUE KING MEMORIAL BAPTIST CHURCH

Dexter Avenue King Memorial Baptist Church, founded in 1878, is located just steps from the Alabama state capitol building along the march route. As the first pulpit of Rev. Martin Luther King, Jr., the church was a focal point of the Montgomery bus boycott of 1955 and 1956.

California, had pitched tents for them. Through that cold night, the marchers were warmed by King's words: They were, he told them, a part of "an unstoppable movement."

The march continued on Monday, with the protesters entering Lowndes County before lunch. In his court order, Judge Johnson had stipulated that no more than three hundred marchers could march on the portion of the highway that narrowed to two lanes. A decision had been made to give those present at "Bloody Sunday" priority in crossing that portion, with others adding to the total as needed. As the marchers stepped in unison, they sang civil rights songs, and National Guardsmen were kept busy, watching for snipers hidden in the swamp or for an ambush from behind trees draped in Spanish moss.

It was in Lowndes that Stokely Carmichael, a SNCC worker, first spoke to those African Americans who had come to watch the march. Months later, he returned to Lowndes to help tenant farmers who had been removed from the land for assisting the marchers. He also spoke to them about voter registration and "black power." It was here that the Black Panther Party would be organized.

After walking more than fifteen miles that Monday, the three hundred marchers camped on a field owned by Rosie Steele that was adjacent to the highway. They remained in Lowndes County on Tuesday after marching eleven more miles, camping at Robert and Mary Gardner's farm. It was also on Tuesday that Att. Gen. Nicholas Katzenback testified before the Senate Judiciary Committee on the president's voting rights bill. In his testimony, he specifically cited the situation in Dallas County, Alabama, as a reason for action. The attorney general had also spoken of Dallas County at the House Judiciary Committee hearings a week earlier. A confrontation with congressional members who wanted to include a ban on all poll taxes in the voting rights legislation was building. As the marchers moved across the Black Belt, legislators began to work seriously on the voting rights bill.

On Wednesday, March 24, the marchers traveled twelve miles, entering Montgomery County. They camped at the City of St. Jude, their final campsite before continuing on to the state capitol. Built by Montgomery's black community, the City of Saint Jude represented not only a certain pride of accomplishment but also the goodwill of others. That night more than ten thousand sympathizers arrived at St. Jude's, both to participate in the last leg of the walk and to enjoy the entertainment of Harry Belafonte, Lena Horne, Dick Gregory, Joan Baez, Peter, Paul, and Mary, Sammy Davis, Jr., Johnny Mathis, Alan King, and others. On Thursday, March 25, more than twenty-five thousand marchers converged on Dexter Avenue. From

JAPANESE MAGNOLIA

Flowering Japanese magnolia trees grace the grounds of many of the historic buildings in Selma and Montgomery during spring pilgrimmage time.

a platform at the front of the state capitol, King presented a list of grievances to Governor Wallace, who was watching the spectacle from his office window. King also urged the audience to continue their struggle against racism, violence, poverty, and segregated schools and housing.

Victorious and drained, the marchers dispersed and headed home, undoubtedly reflecting on King's reference to the words of a black woman spoken ten years earlier. In his speech, King told the crowd that during the Montgomery bus boycott of 1955, seventy-year-old Sister Pollard was asked if she wouldn't like a ride. In a poetic, melodic reply, she said, "My feets is tired, but my soul is rested."

For some volunteers, the work was just beginning. Viola Liuzzo worked with Leroy Moton, an African American from Dallas County, to shuttle a group of marchers back to Selma. As they began their trip back to Montgomery to pick up more marchers, a car began to chase them. Near Lowndesboro, the car pulled up beside them and two shots were fired. Liuzzo was killed instantly. Moton managed to stop the car and played dead while the four Ku Klux Klan members pulled around for a second look. After they had driven on, Moton waved down a passing truck for help and told the driver what had happened.

The events were reported that night by one of the Klansmen, who turned out to be an FBI informant. All four men were in custody by the next day, and three were later tried for murder. Despite damaging testimony, the first trial produced a hung jury, the second a not guilty verdict, and finally, after federal charges were brought by the U.S. Department of Justice, a conviction.

Acting on the potent effects of the Selma to Montgomery march, President Johnson signed the Voting Rights Act on August 6, 1965. Immediately afterwards, federal officials arrived in the South to register black Americans and other citizens who had been blocked from casting their ballot. The Selma to Montgomery march is remembered as a symbol of the power of the ballot and its meaning in our democracy, and the Selma to Montgomery National Historic Trail commemorates this historic march.

LEGISLATION	IMPETUS	RESULTS
Civil Rights Act 1866	Civil War	Gave citizenship and voting of rights to all native-born American men except Native Americans
Civil Rights Act of 1875	Reconstruction	Gave African Americans and other citizens equal rights and access to accommodations, places of public amusement, and jury duty
Civil Rights Act of 1957	Prayer Pilgrimmage; Little Rock's attempts to desegregate public schools	Established the Civil Rights Commission and the Civil Rights Division in the Justice Department; gave the Justice Department authority to seek injunctions against voting infractions
Civil Rights Act of 1960	Same as above	Reenforced the Civil Rights Act of 1957
Civil Rights Act of 1964	March on Washington for Freedom and Jobs	Banned discrimination in voting and in public accommodations and required fair employment practices
Voting Rights Act of 1965	Selma to Montgomery march	Allowed African Americans the right to register to vote in many southern counties.

Source: National Park Service's *Selma to Montgomery National Trail Study,* page 9.

The Selma to Montgomery National Historic Trail (SMNHT) is located in the portion of Alabama's coastal plain known as the Black Belt, which stretches across portions of Georgia, Alabama, Mississippi, and Louisiana.* Today it is recognized as one of the great garden spots of the world, but its fertility

*Material in this section is taken from the National Park Service's *Selma to Montgomery National Trail Study.*

was apparent long ago. As early as 1540, Hernando de Soto found great quantities of food stored in Indian villages along the Alabama River, where many crops were grown on the rich river bottoms. It was this fertile soil that attracted farmers to the area. During the antebellum period, diversification gave way to the development of the plantation system of agriculture and the one-crop plan. By the time of the Civil War, about 80 percent of the

The Trail Today

nation's cotton was grown in the Black Belt. Even after the War between the States, the more profitable one-crop plan was not greatly altered, although the whole labor point of view changed, since enslaved African Americans had made up more than three-fourths of the total population in parts of the Black Belt before the war. King Cotton continued to do well until the arrival of the boll weevil. A move toward diversification began then. Today cattle graze on broad pasturelands, horses are raised and ridden recreationally, and the rich soil and temperate climate provide a suitable environment for cotton, grasses, soybeans, corn, and other crops.

The almost level region, ranging in elevation from two hundred to three hundred feet above sea level, is thought to have originally existed as a grassland resembling the western prairie. The rest of the state was covered in hardwood and pine forests. Most of the Selma to Montgomery route still remains unforested, with some pine forest exceptions. Hardwoods of the region include poplar, cypress, gum, hickory, oak, hackberry, ash, holly, persimmon, black locust, beech, sycamore, pawpaw, ironwood, and hornbeam, all native to Alabama.

The Black Belt is considered to be a part of the migratory range of several endangered species: the eastern cougar, Florida panther, red wolf, and gray bat and the Indiana eagle, peregrine falcon, Backman's warbler, and red cockaded woodpecker. Alligators may also be present in the region. At the Selma city limits, the historic route crosses the Alabama River, which parallels it to Montgomery. Several streams are also crossed, and in Lowndes County, near Big Swamp Creek, the route travels through a large wetland area.

Roadways are two lanes with sidewalks in Selma and Montgomery and four lanes in all other areas. The portion of the trail following the highway is actually quite scenic. A wide, grassy median gives the route a "parkway" atmosphere. For its outstanding qualities, the route was designated an All-American Road by the Department of Transportation in 1996. The portion of the route on U.S. Highway 80 has been designated by the State of Alabama as both the Jefferson Davis Highway and the De Soto Trail. The latter extends into other southeastern states, including Tennessee, Georgia, and Florida.

Except for a small section in Montgomery, it is possible to drive the entire fifty-four-mile route. Because Mobile Street between Mildred and Goldwaite Streets is one-way, heading southwest, a detour is required for approximately one-fourth mile. The city may accommodate the route by making Mobile Street one-way in the opposite direction. There is no record of its direction at the time of the march. Today, the character of the corridor followed by the marchers remains essentially unchanged, although road improvements on a portion of the highway in Lowndes County have expanded it from two lanes to four. A new interchange at the intersection of U.S. Highway 80 and U.S. Highway 31 in Montgomery County has altered the traffic pattern in that area, but it has not affected the character of the route or the surrounding landscape. Present use of the route for historical interest has not been fully documented, but plans are being made to mark the trail as soon as possible.

Walking the entire route is possible but not practical, outside of Selma and Montgomery. Recreational alternatives that would parallel the motor route are under study. For example, a twelve-mile trail from the U.S. Army Corps of Engineers Natural Resource and Visitor Center to an area near the Robert and Mary Gardner campsite has been suggested. The trail would provide an excellent opportunity for walking, jogging, bicycling, and horseback riding. A side or connecting trail, following the route traveled by the Marion residents who participated in the Bloody Sunday march, may also be developed. Because the Alabama River parallels the highway, there are tremendous opportunities for boating and other water-based recreational activities. Corps campsites and recreation facilities along the river are easily reached from the highway. The Craig

Airport and Industrial Park, former site of Craig Air Force Base near Selma, is the only public recreation site directly adjacent to the Selma to Montgomery route. The park includes a swimming pool, a nine-hole golf course, athletic fields, and a picnic area.

At selected events, such as reenactments, trail organizers work with state officials to close off the highway to allow trail users access over the entire length of the route. Each year in March, an anniversary celebration, the Bridge Crossing Jubilee, is sponsored by Selma's National Voting Rights Museum. Other special times to visit the trail are during Selma's Spring Historic Pilgrimage in late March, the Battle of Selma Civil War Re-Enactment in late April, and the African Extravaganza in October and during Montgomery's Annual Dixie Jamboree in mid-February and the Jubilee Cityfest on Memorial Day weekend.

As a consequence of the Selma voting rights movement, the 1965 march, and other aspects of the civil rights movement, many of the sites along or near the route have direct historic significance. Two of these sites have National Historic Landmark status, three are listed in the National Register of Historic Places, and others are eligible for consideration. Many sites along the route that have no immediate relation to the march are also listed in the National Register. Selma's historic district is the largest in the state, with over twelve hundred historic structures.

Excellent museums provide information about the march, voting rights, civil rights, plantations, the Civil War, and other regional events. A future visitor center for the Selma to Montgomery National Historic Trail (SMNHT) will have tremendous potential for a variety of cultural and educational programs, including information regarding each citizen's right to vote and the gravity of exercising that right. In Selma, this concept is already developed at the National Voting Rights Museum and Institute, which explores the spirit and struggles of the white women and African Americans who sought to remove barriers to voting. The Martin Luther King Jr. Street Historic Walking Tour pays lasting tribute to the local African-American people who courageously gave of themselves to ensure voting rights for all citizens, regardless of race, creed, or color. In Montgomery, only a few blocks from the state capitol, a Civil Rights Memorial serves as a vehicle for education and reflection. Designed by Vietnam War Memorial artist Maya Lin, the memorial chronicles key events and lists the names of approximately forty people who gave their lives in the struggle for racial equality from 1955 to 1968.

Almost all protest marches in Selma began on Sylvan Street (now Martin Luther King Jr. Street) outside Brown Chapel AME Church. On March 7, 1965, the marchers left the chapel and headed south down Sylvan Street, turning west onto Alabama Avenue. Because Alabama Avenue was a direct path to the Dallas County Courthouse, it had been used by marchers during the previous two months. However, the Bloody Sunday march turned south on Broad Street, since the marchers were, at least in theory, bound for Montgomery. They proceeded down Broad Street and across the Edmund Pettus Bridge. After passing over the Alabama River, they left the city limits of Selma and entered the unincorporated area of Dallas County known as Selmont. The marchers proceeded no farther than Kings Bend Road, the first traffic light after the bridge. The March 9 march, known as Turn-around Tuesday, followed the same route, though it reversed direction near the site of the Sunday confrontation and returned to Brown Chapel.

The march that began on Sunday, March 21, followed a different course. After organizing at Brown Chapel, the marchers proceeded south on Sylvan Street, crossed Alabama Avenue, and went west on Water Avenue. Turning south onto Broad Street, they crossed Edmund Pettus Bridge. From Selmont they followed U.S. Highway 80 to their last campsite at the City of St. Jude. In Montgomery, that section is known as Fairview Avenue. On Thursday, March 25, the marchers left the City of St. Jude, turning north on Oak Street.

They turned east on Jeff Davis Avenue and north on Hold Street to Mobile Road. Mobile Road becomes Montgomery Street farther north and then intersects Dexter Avenue at Court Square. The march proceeded east on Dexter Avenue to the western steps of the Alabama state capitol, once the capitol of the Confederacy.

The marchers followed the same route taken by Jefferson Davis on his inaugural journey from Mississippi to the capitol.

Numerous monuments and markers commemorate the Confederacy along Dexter Avenue and on the capitol grounds. One monument describes the inaugural parade of February 18, 1861, and the playing of "Dixie" for the first time. Ironically, on this same date, 104 years later, Jimmie Lee Jackson was shot in Marion. It was this shot that sparked the march that marked, as author James Baldwin put it, "the beginning of the end to slavery that has endured a hundred years."

1. FIRST BAPTIST CHURCH. Designed by a local African-American architect, the church (1894, NRHP), located on Martin Luther King Jr. Street, gave birth to Selma University (1879), the oldest black junior college in the nation. During the 1960s, the church became the site of voting rights rallies, which helped bring passage of the Voting Rights Act. *Nearby:* Good Samaritan Hospital, on Broad Street, was a black hospital founded by the Baptists (1922) and refounded by the Fathers of St. Edmund (1944). Victims of the Bloody Sunday confrontation came to the hospital for treatment. Tabernacle Baptist Church (1885), also on Broad Street, was the site of the first (1963) mass meeting on voting rights in Dallas County. The Reformed Presbyterian Church, on Jeff Davis Avenue, was the originating point of the Concerned White Citizens March of March 5, 1965. Crossroads Visitor Information Center is also located on Broad Street.

2. BROWN CHAPEL AME CHURCH. The church (1867, NRHP) with the Byzantine-style chapel (1906) served as the headquarters for the Selma voting rights movement and as the starting point for all three marches. The Dr. Martin Luther King Monument is seen in front of the church, and the Martin Luther King Jr. Street Historic Walking Tour begins at the chapel. The state's first AME church created Daniel Payne College (1889). The Methodist school was eventually transferred to Birmingham (1930s). *Nearby:* George Washington Carver Homes, next to Brown Chapel, served as a center of voting rights protests and lodging place for marchers, ministers, and civil rights workers. The Old Depot

Points of Interest

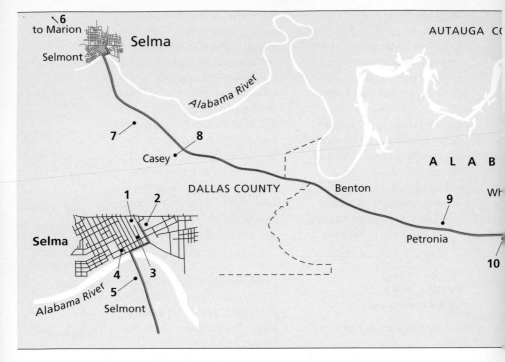

Museum (NRHP), also located on Martin Luther King Jr. Street, is housed in a Romanesque railway depot (1891). Special features include the Keipp Collection of forty-six turn-of-the-century photographs of plantation life and the Black History Wing.

3. **Cecil B. Jackson Public Safety Building (Old City Hall).** Located on Franklin and Alabama Avenue, the current headquarters for the city police and city jail served as Selma City Hall, Selma City Prison, and Dallas County Prison in 1965. King and many protestors were incarcerated there. *Nearby:* The Dallas County Community Center, now the Wilson Building (1939), located adjacent to Old

City Hall, is decorated with murals of black life. The Sullivan Building served as field headquarters of the SNCC and SCLC. Clark Elementary School, on Lawrence Street, was the starting point of the teachers' march of January 22, 1965.

4. **Dallas County Courthouse.** This was the destination of most protest marches in the 1960s; the marches proceeded down Alabama Avenue to the courthouse on Lauderdale. The building housed the Dallas County Board of Registrars and Sheriff James Clark's office. *Nearby:* The Chamber of Commerce, also located on Lauderdale Street, has brochures for the Martin Luther King Jr. Street

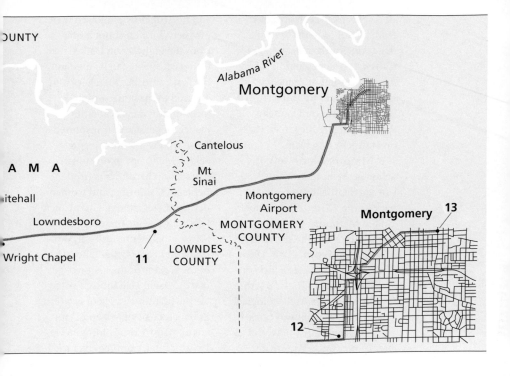

Historic Walking Tour, the Black Heritage Tour, and the Historic Selma Windshield Tour, which includes directions to antebellum structures such as Grace Hall (1857) across from the chamber, Sturdivant Hall (1853) on Mabry Street, and the Smitherman Historic Building (1847) on Union.

5. **BLOODY SUNDAY SITE.** Marchers were confronted by Alabama state troopers and the sheriff's posse on Sunday, March 7, 1965, at or near the Edmund Pettus Bridge (1940), named in honor of the U.S. Senator and Confederate Army brigadier general. The four-lane steel bridge (NRHS) is used as the main access to Selma. *Nearby:* Five blocks of Water Avenue

survived the Civil War and constitute one of the few remaining antebellum riverfront business districts. The National Voting Rights Museum, on Water Street, displays memorabilia honoring the attainment of voting rights. Its staff organizes the annual Bridge Crossing Jubilee. Saint James Hotel (1837) on Water Street, recently renovated, serves as a rare example of an early riverfront hotel. It was once managed by ex-slave Benjamin S. Turner, who in 1870 became the first Selmian elected to the U.S. House of Representatives. Live Oak Cemetery, with monuments to Turner and Vice Pres. William Rufus King (who served briefly under Franklin Pierce), is located on Dallas Avenue. North of Selma: Paul M. Grist SP; Talladega NF; South of Selma: Old Cahawba Archaeological Park, the first capital of Alabama; Roland Cooper SP; Millers Ferry Lock and Dam on Dannelly Reservoir; Six-Mile Creek Park on Dannelly Reservoir.

6. **MARION.** Northwest of Selma is the hometown of Coretta Scott King, which dates back to the 1830s; Zion Chapel United Methodist Church on the town square was the site of mass meetings on February 18, 1965, after which Jimmie Lee Jackson was shot. *Nearby:* To the northwest, Moundville Archaeological Park preserves what was one of the largest and most powerful prehistoric Native American communities in the Southeast during the Mississippian Period, A.D. 1000–1500.

U.S. HIGHWAY 80, THE RURAL SECTION

7. **CRAIG AIRPORT AND INDUSTRIAL PARK.** Located east of Selma on U.S. Highway 80, Craig Air Force Base (1940) was used as a bivouac for federal troops, U.S. marshals, and FBI agents. Originally established for pilot training, the base also provided support for the 720th Military Police Battalion sent to Selma. On March 21, troops separated marchers from several hundred whites who had gathered to oppose the march. Marchers passed the base on Sunday.

8. **CAMPSITE ON MARCH 21, 1965.** Black farmer David Hall and his wife, Rosie, allowed their property, located about a mile from the highway on Dallas County Route 68, to be used as the first campsite. Marchers were reduced to the court-ordered three hundred here, and the Justice Department transported those who were returning to Selma. Men slept in one of two tents set up by students from Berkeley, California, and women in the other. National Guardsmen kept watch while members of the SNCC stood sentry duty at Martin Luther King's trailer. Because of the success of the historic march, David Hall himself voted for the first time in 1966. *Nearby:* Robert F. Henry Lock and Dam has an Army Corps of Engineers visitor center, camping, picnicking, boating, and other recreational opportunities. It has been recommended that a twelve-mile recreation trail, paralleling the highway, begin here.

9. **CAMPSITE ON MARCH 22, 1965.** After traveling seventeen miles, marchers camped at a field owned by seventy-eight-year-old Rosie Steele between Lowndes County Road 23 and Big Swamp Creek. Her store, near the campsite, did a brisk business that night. Residents of the area attended a mass meeting that evening, and the next day marchers trekked through Lowndes County's Big Swamp in rain that turned into a downpour. Steele's store was lost when the highway was later widened.

10. **VIOLA LIUZZO MARKER.** The Detroit volunteer was re-

turning from Selma to Montgomery to pick up a second load of passengers when a car of Ku Klux Klansmen pulled beside hers, firing shots that killed her. In 1991 women of the SCLC placed a historic marker on the spot (NHL) where this third victim associated with the march was killed. The site is located on U.S. Highway 80 just west of Wright Chapel AME Zion Church, south of White Hall. *Nearby:* Mt. Zion Elementary School (1923, Alabama Register of Historic Places) on White Hall Road was once a one-room school. Holy Ground Battle Park, the site of many of the Indian battles during the Creek Indian Wars of 1812 and 1814, is located near five hundred acres of parkland developed by the Army Corps of Engineers.

11. **Campsite on March 23, 1965.** Just before nightfall, marchers made it to a field owned by Robert and Mary Gardner south of Highway 80 on Lake Berry Road. A rally was held, with speeches and singing. The next morning marchers departed Lowndes County and entered Montgomery County, where the highway widened into four lanes once again and the limitation on the number of marchers ended. All afternoon carloads and busloads of new demonstrators arrived. The proposed recreation trail would end at this site.

MONTGOMERY

12. **City of St. Jude.** The last campsite, March 24, 1965, was a social welfare complex. The hospital (1933, NRHP), now apartments, was established by Father Harold Purcell. It provided blacks who otherwise had no adequate access to medical facilities with some of the best care in the South. On March 24, celebrities entertained participants at the site's athletic field, located on the corner of Oak and Fairview. King told the crowd, "I believe this march will go down as one of the greatest struggles for freedom and dignity in the nation's history." *Nearby:* The World Heritage Museum on West Jeff Davis Avenue features photos and displays of the civil rights movement. The Executive Mansion (1907), located on South Perry Street, is the working home of the governor; its architecture is reminiscent of the antebellum Greek Revival homes of the 1850s.

13. **Alabama State Capitol.** On Thursday morning, March 25, more than twenty-five thousand marchers began the last six-mile walk to their final destination, the state capitol (1851), also the first Confederate capitol (NHL). King had selected a twenty-member committee to present a list of grievances to Gov. George Wallace, who said he would not meet with the committee until the marchers dispersed. *Nearby:* Dexter Avenue King Memorial Baptist Church (1878, NHL) was the first pulpit of Reverend King and the focal point of the bus boycott in Montgomery. The Alabama State Supreme Court, on Dexter Avenue, was where

many civil rights cases were tried before being appealed to the federal courts. Court Square, where slaves and cotton were auctioned, is now marked by a fountain that was passed by marchers. The first White House of the Confederacy, home of Pres. Jefferson Davis and his wife, Varina, is located across from the capitol on Washington Avenue. The Civil Rights Memorial, near the capitol on the corner of Washington and Hull, chronicles key events in the struggle for racial equality and includes the names of people who gave their lives for the cause. Old Alabama Town Historic District (NRHP), on North Hull, has restored homes dating back to the 1820s. The Federal Building (NRHP), on Lee and Church, marks where Judge Frank M. Johnson, Jr., issued the injunction that enabled the march to take place. The pastorium (NRHP) of the Dexter Avenue Baptist Church on South Jackson was the home of the Kings during his ministry in Montgomery. Abernathy Home on Hall Street was bombed during the civil rights movement and served as the pastorium for the First Baptist Church when Ralph David Abernathy was pastor. Centennial Hill (1870–90, NRHP), Jackson and High Streets, was the first prominent black residential district to develop after the Civil War. North Lawrence–Monroe Street Historic District (NRHP) served as a major black business district after passage of Jim Crow laws in the late nineteenth century. Oakwood Cemetery (NRHP), on Jefferson and Columbus, is the city's oldest, with a section for slaves' graves. At the Greyhound bus station (NRHP), on Court Street, the Freedom Riders who hoped to end discrimination in the interstate transportation system were met by an angry mob on May 20, 1961. The station is planned to house a civil rights museum. Montgomery Museum of Fine Arts, on Museum Drive, exhibits works of southern artists and features African-American exhibits. Union Station and the Lightning Route Trolley, adjacent to Riverfront Park on Water Street, reveals a Romanesque Revival rail structure and coach that commemorate the nation's first electric streetcar system (1887). The visitor center, on Madison, is located in the historic Thompson Mansion. *Nearby:* R. E. "Bob" Woodruff Lake. Wetumpka, in the foothills of the Appalachian Mountains, is known for its many lakes, older homes, wildlife museum, Jasmine Hill Gardens, and Fort Toulouse/Fort Jackson Park (NHL). South of Alexander City is Wind Creek SP; to the east is Horseshoe Bend National Military Park.

Public Lands Information

Office of Public Inquiries
Room 1013
U.S. Department of the Interior
1849 C Street, NW
P.O. Box 37127
Washington, DC 20013-7127

REGIONAL OFFICES

North Atlantic Region
15 State Street
Boston, MA 02109-3572

Mid-Atlantic Region
143 South Third Street
Philadelphia, PA 19106

National Capital Region
1100 Ohio Drive, SW
Washington, DC 20242

Southeast Region
Richard B. Russell Federal Building
75 Spring Street, SW
Atlanta, GA 30303

Rocky Mountain Region
12795 West Alameda Parkway
P.O. Box 25287
Denver, CO 80225-2500

Southwest Region
1100 Old Santa Fe Trail
P.O. Box 728
Santa Fe, NM 87504-0728

Alaska Region
2525 Gambell Street, Room 107
Anchorage, AK 99503

Pacific Northwest Region
909 First Street, Fifth Floor
Seattle, WA 98104

Midwest Region
1709 Jackson Street
Omaha, NE 68102

Western Region Information
    Office
Golden Gate National Recreation
    Area
Fort Mason, Building 201
San Francisco, CA 94123

National Park Service

347

Forest Service

U.S. Department of Agriculture
Auditors Building
14th and Independence Avenue,
SW
P.O. Box 96090
Washington, DC 20250

REGIONAL OFFICES

Northern Region
Federal Building
P.O. Box 7669
Missoula, MT 59807

Rocky Mountain Region
740 Simms Street
P.O. Box 25127
Lakewood, CO 80401

Southwestern Region
Federal Building
517 Gold Avenue, SW
Albuquerque, NM 87102

Intermountain Region
Federal Building
324 25th Street
Ogden, UT 84401

Pacific Southwest Region
630 Sansome Street
San Francisco, CA 94111

Pacific Northwest Region
333 SW 1st Avenue
P.O. Box 3623
Portland, OR 97208

Southern Region
1720 Peachtree Road, NW
Atlanta, GA 30367

Eastern Region
310 West Wisconsin Avenue
Room 500
Milwaukee, WI 53203

Alaska Region
P.O. Box 21628
Juneau, AK 99802-1628

Fish and Wildlife Service

HEADQUARTERS

Division of Refuges
4401 N. Fairfax Drive, Room 670
Arlington, VA 22203

REGIONAL OFFICES

Region 1
Eastside Federal Complex
911 NE 11th Avenue
Portland, OR 97232-4181

Region 2
P.O. Box 1306
Albuquerque, NM 87103

Region 3
Federal Building
1 Federal Drive
Fort Snelling, MN 55111-4056

Region 4
Richard B. Russell Federal Building
75 Spring Street, SW
Atlanta, GA 30303

Region 5
300 Westgate Center Drive
Hadley, MA 91035-9589

Region 6
Box 25486
Denver Federal Center
Denver, CO 80225

Region 7
1011 East Tudor Road
Anchorage, AK 99503

Office of Public Affairs
1849 C Street, NW, Room 5600
Washington, DC 20240

STATE OFFICES

Alaska State Office
222 West 7th Avenue
P.O. Box 13
Anchorage, AK 99513-7599

Arizona State Office
3707 North 7th Street
P.O. Box 16563
Phoenix, AZ 85011

California State Office
280 Cottage Way, Room E-2841
Sacramento, CA 95825-1889

Colorado State Office
2850 Youngfield Street
Lakewood, CO 80215-7076

Eastern States Office
350 South Pickett Street
Alexandria, VA 22304

Idaho State Office
3380 Americana Terrace
Boise, ID 83706

Montana State Office
222 North 32nd Street
P.O. Box 36800
Billings, MT 59107-6800

Nevada State Office
850 Harvard Way
P.O. Box 12000
Reno, NV 89520-0006

New Mexico State Office
1474 Rodeo Road
P.O. Box 27115
Santa Fe, NM 87502-0115

Oregon State Office
1300 NE 44th Avenue
Portland, OR 97208-2965

Utah State Office
324 South State Street, Suite 301
P.O. Box 45155
Salt Lake City, UT 84145-0155

Wyoming State Office
P.O. Box 1828
Cheyenne, WY 82003

Bureau of Land Management

HEADQUARTERS

HQUSACE (CECW-ON)
20 Massachusetts Avenue, NW
Washington, DC 20314-1000

DIVISION OFFICES

Lower Mississippi Valley Division
(CELMV-CO-R)
P.O. Box 80
Vicksburg, MS 39181-0080

Missouri River Division
(CEMRD-MO-R)
P.O. Box 103
Downtown Station
Omaha, NE 68101-0103

North Atlantic Division
(CENAD-CO-OP)
90 Church Street
New York, NY 10007-9998

North Central Division
(CENAD-CO-OR)
536 South Clark Street
Chicago, IL 60605-1592

New England Division
(CENED-OD-P)
424 Trapelo Road
Waltham, MA 02254-9149

North Pacific Division
(CENPD-CO-R)
P.O. Box 2870
Portland, OR 92708-2870

Corps of Engineers

Ohio River Division
(CEORD-CO-R)
P.O. Box 1159
Cincinnati, OH 45201-1159

South Pacific Division
Attn: CESPD-CO-O
630 Sansome Street, Room 1216
San Francisco, CA 94111-2206

South Atlantic Division
(CESAD-CO-R)
77 Forsyth Street, SW
Room 313
Atlanta, GA 30335-6801

Southwestern Division
Attn: CESWD-CO-R
1114 Commerce Street
Dallas, TX 75242-0216

Bureau of Reclamation

REGIONAL OFFICES

Pacific Northwest Region
1150 North Curtis Road
Boise, ID 83706-1234

Mid Pacific Region
Federal Office Building
2800 Cottage Way
Sacramento, CA 95825-1898

Lower Colorado Region
P.O. Box 61470
Boulder City, NV 89005

North Central California Area
Office
7794 Folsom Dam Road
Folsom, CA 95630

Upper Colorado Region
125 South State Street
Salt Lake City, UT 84138-1102

Great Plains Region
P.O. Box 36900
Billings, MT 59101-6214

PROJECT OFFICES

Grand Coulee Project Office
P.O. Box 620
Grand Coulee, WA 99133-0620

Lower Colorado Dams Project
Office
Hoover Dam Visitor Center
Highway 93
Boulder City, NV 89005

Eastern Colorado Projects Office
11056 West Country Road, 18E
Loveland, CO 80537-4410

Lake Berryessa Recreation Office
5520 Knoxville Road
Napa, CA 94558-9649

New Melones Recreation Office
6850 Studhorse Flat Road
Sonora, CA 95730

Twin Lakes Area
Mt. Elbert Powerplant
Granite Star Route
Granite, CO 81228

APPENDIX B

State Lands
Information

Alabama Bureau of Tourism &
  Travel
P.O. Box 4309, Dept. TIA
Montgomery, AL 36103-4309
205-242-4169
Toll-free: 1-800-ALABAMA

Alaska Division of Tourism
P.O. Box 110801, Dept. TIA
Juneau, AK 99811-0801
907-4655-2010

Arizona Office of Tourism
1100 West Washington
Phoenix, AZ 85007
602-542-8687

Arkansas Tourism Office
1 Capitol Mall, Dept. 7701
Little Rock, AR 72201
501-682-7777
Toll-free: 1-800-Natural

Connecticut Department of Economic Development, Tourism
  Division
865 Brook Street
Rocky Hill, CT 06067
203-258-4355
Toll-free: 1-800-CTBOUND

Delaware Tourism Office
99 Kings Highway
P.O. Box 1401, Dept. TIA
Dover, DE 19903
302-739-4271
Toll-free: 1-800-441-8846

Florida Division of Tourism
126 West Van Buren Street, FLDA
Tallahassee, FL 32301
904-487-1462

Georgia Department of Industry,
  Trade, & Tourism
P.O. Box 1776, Dept. TIA
Atlanta, GA 30301
404-656-3590
Toll-free: 1-800-VISITGA

Hawaii Department of Business,
  Economic Development and
  Tourism
P.O. Box 2359
Honolulu, HI 96804
808-586-2423

Idaho Division of Tourism
  Development
700 West State Street, Dept. C
Boise, ID 83720
208-334-2470
Toll-free: 1-800-645-7820

Illinois Bureau of Tourism
100 West Randolph, Suite 3-400
Chicago, IL 60601
312-814-4732
Toll-free: 1-800-223-0121

Indiana Department of Commerce
Tourism and Film Development
Division
1 North Capitol, Suite 700
Indianapolis, IN 46204-2238
317-232-8860
Toll-free: 1-800-289-6646

Iowa Division of Tourism
200 East Grand, Dept. TIA
Des Moines, IA 50309
515-242-4705
Toll-free: 1-800-345-IOWA

Kansas Travel & Tourism Division
400 West 8th Street
5th Floor, Dept. DIS
Topeka, KS 66603-3957
785-296-3009
Toll-free: 1-800-252-6727

Kentucky Department of Travel
Development
2200 Capitol Plaza Tower,
Dept. DA
Frankfort, KY 40601
502-564-4930
Toll-free: 1-800-225-TRIP

Louisiana Office of Tourism
Attn: Inquiry Department
P.O. Box 94291, LOT
Baton Rouge, LA 70804-9291
504-342-8119
Toll-free: 1-800-33-GUMBO

Maine Office of Tourism
189 State Street
Augusta, ME 04333
207-289-5711
Toll-free: 1-800-533-9595

Maryland Office of Travel &
Tourism
217 East Redwood Street, 9th
Floor
Baltimore, MD 21202
410-333-6611
Toll-free: 1-800-543-1036

Massachusetts Office of Travel
and Tourism
100 Cambridge Street, 13th Floor
Boston, MA 02202
617-727-3201
Toll-free: 1-800-447-MASS

Michigan Travel Bureau
P.O. Box 30226
Lansing, MI 48909
517-373-0670
Toll-free: 1-800-5432YES

Minnesota Office of Tourism
375 Jackson Street
250 Skyway Level
St. Paul, MN 55101
612-296-5029
Toll-free: 1-800-657-3700

Mississippi Division of Tourism
P.O. Box 22825
Jackson, MS 39205
601-359-3297
Toll-free: 1-800-647-2290

Missouri Division of Tourism
P.O. Box 1055, Dept. TIA
Jefferson City, MO 65102
314-751-4133
Toll-free: 1-800-877-1234

Travel Montana
Room 259
Deer Lodge, MT 59722
406-444-2654
Toll-free: 1-800-541-1447

Nebraska Division of Travel
and Tourism
301 Central Mall South, Room
88937
Lincoln, NE 68509
402-471-3796
Toll-free: 1-800-228-4307

Nevada Commission of Tourism
Capitol Complex, Dept. TIA
Carson City, NV 89710
702-687-4322
Toll-free: 1-800-NEVADA8

New Hampshire Office of Travel
and Tourism Development
P.O. Box 856, Dept. TIA
Concord, NH 03302
603-271-2343

New Jersey Division of Travel
and Tourism
20 West State Street
CN 826, Dept. TIA
Trenton, NJ 08625
609-292-2470
Toll-free: 1-800-JERSEY7

New Mexico Department of
Tourism
1100 St. Francis Drive
Joseph Montoya Building
Santa Fe, NM 87503
505-827-0291
Toll-free: 1-800-545-2040

New York State Department of
Economic Development
One Commerce Plaza
Albany, NY 12245
518-474-4116
Toll-free: 1-800-CALLNYS

North Carolina Division of Travel
and Tourism
430 North Salisbury Street
Raleigh, NC 27603
919-733-4171
Toll-free: 1-800-VISITNC

North Dakota Tourism Promotion
Liberty Memorial Building
Capitol Grounds
Bismarck, ND 58505
701-224-2525
Toll-free: 1-800-HELLOND

Ohio Division of Travel and
Tourism
P.O. Box 1001, Dept. TIA
Columbus, OH 43211-0101
614-466-8844
Toll-free: 1-800-BUCKEYE

Oklahoma Tourism and
Recreation Department
Travel and Tourism Division
500 Will Rogers Building, DA92
Oklahoma City, OK 73105-4492
405-521-3981
Toll-free: 1-800-652-6552

Oregon Economic Development
Department
Tourism Division
775 Summer Street NE
Salem, OR 97310
503-373-1270
Toll-free: 1-800-547-7842

Pennsylvania Bureau of Travel
Marketing
130 Commonwealth Drive
Warrendale, PA 15086
717-787-5453
Toll-free: 1-800-VISITPA

Rhode Island Tourism Division
7 Jackson Walkway, Dept. TIA
Providence, RI 02903
401-277-2601
Toll-free: 1-800-566-5404

South Carolina Division of
Tourism
P.O. Box 71, Room 902
Columbia, SC 29202
803-734-0235

South Dakota Department
of Tourism
711 East Wells Avenue
Pierre, SD 57501-3369
605-773-3301
Toll-free: 1-800-843-1930

Tennessee Department of Tourism
Development
P.O. Box 23170, TNDA
Nashville, TN 37202
615-741-2158

Texas Department of Commerce
Tourism Division
P.O. Box 12728
Austin, TX 78711
512-462-9191
Toll-free: 1-800-8888TEX

Utah Travel Council
Council Hall/Capitol Hill
Dept. TIA
300 North State Street
Salt Lake City, UT 84114
801-538-1030

Vermont Travel Division
134 State Street, Dept. TIA
Montpelier, VT 05602
802-828-3236

Virginia Division of Tourism
1021 East Cary Street, Dept. VT
Richmond, VA 23219
804-786-4484
Toll-free: 1-800-VISITVA

Washington, DC, Convention
and Visitors Association
1212 New York Avenue NW
Washington, DC 20005
202-789-7000

Washington State Tourism
Development Division
P.O. Box 42513
Olympia, WA 98504-2513
206-586-2088 or 206-586-2012
Toll-free: 1-800-544-1800

West Virginia Division of Tourism
& Parks
2101 Washington Street East
Charleston, WV 25305
304-348-2286
Toll-free: 1-800-CALLWVA

Wisconsin Division of Tourism
P.O. Box 7606
Madison, WI 53707
608-266-2161
Toll-free in state: 1-800-372-2737
Out of state: 1-800-432-TRIP

Wyoming Division of Tourism
I-25 at College Drive, Dept. WY
Cheyenne, WY 82002
307-777-7777
Toll-free: 1-800-225-5996

Puerto Rico Tourism Company
P.O. Box 5268, Dept. TH
Miami, FL 33102
Toll-free: 1-800-866-STAR, Ext. 17

U.S. Virgin Islands Division of
Tourism
P.O. Box 6400, VITIA
Charlotte Amalie, St. Thomas
USVI 00801
809-774-8784
Toll-free: 1-800-372-8784